The Colonial Present

The Colonial Present

Afghanistan • Palestine • Iraq

Derek Gregory

Blackwell
Publishing

BLACKWELL PUBLISHING
350 Main Street, Malden, MA 02148-5020, USA
9600 Garsington Road, Oxford OX4 2DQ, UK
550 Swanston Street, Carlton, Victoria 3053, Australia

First published 2004 by Blackwell Publishing Ltd

6   2007

Library of Congress Cataloging-in-Publication Data

Gregory, Derek, 1951–
   The colonial present/Derek Gregory.
      p. cm.
   Includes bibliographical references and index.
   ISBN 1-5771-8089-5 (hardcover : alk. paper) – ISBN 1-5771-8090-9 (pbk. : alk. paper)
      1. Middle East—Relations—United States.   2. United States—Relations
   —Middle East.   3. Middle East—Relations—Great Britain.   4. Great
   Britain—Relations—Middle East.   5. Imperialism.   6. War on Terrorism,
   2001– 7. Iraq War, 2003.   8. Arab–Israeli conflict.   I. Title.

   DS63.2.U5G74 2004
   327.73056'09'0511—dc22

                                                       2003026672

   ISBN-13: 978-1-5771-8089-0 (hardcover : alk. paper) – ISBN-13: 978-1-5771-8090-6 (pbk. : alk. paper)

A catalogue record for this title is available from the British Library.

Set in 10.25/13.5pt Sabon
by Graphicraft Ltd, Hong Kong
Printed and bound in India by
Replika Press Pvt. Ltd

The publisher's policy is to use permanent paper from mills that operate a sustainable forestry policy, and which has been manufactured from pulp processed using acid-free and elementary chlorine-free practices. Furthermore, the publisher ensures that the text paper and cover board used have met acceptable environmental accreditation standards.

For further information on
Blackwell Publishing, visit our website:
www.blackwellpublishing.com

To the memory of Edward Said

"I think we agree, the past is over."
George W. Bush

"The past is not dead. It is not even past."
William Faulkner

Contents

Figures

Preface

THIS was not a book I intended to write. I have spent much of the past decade trying to understand how European and American travelers through Egypt in the long nineteenth century came to terms with – found the terms for – cultures and landscapes for which they had no terms, and how this shaped and was in turn shaped by what they did when they went there. I read thousands of letters, diaries, and books, and looked at countless sketches, paintings, and photographs. My purpose was to recover what I would now call the performances that were made possible – authorized, articulated – through these imaginative geographies. This mattered, I realized even then, because representations are never merely mirrors held up to the world; they enter fully into its formation. Two years ago I was about to bring all this together in a book on Orientalism and cultures of travel: *Dancing on the Pyramids*. But until September 11, 2001 I had paid scandalously little attention to the contemporary resonance of these ideas and practices. The attacks on the World Trade Center and the Pentagon, and the fury subsequently unleashed in Afghanistan, Palestine, and Iraq, destroyed much: they also destroyed my privileged – and lazy – immunity. What follows is an attempt to atone for my complacency, and to come to terms with cultures of political violence for which I had no terms.

The result is, I know, both partial and provisional. It is also written in the shadow of two writers whose work I admire enormously. The first is Edward Said, who died while I was completing this book. His luminous critique of Orientalism, and his rare ability to elaborate its implications, not only between the covers of books but also in the pages of newspapers and on radio and television, did much to keep the ideal of a genuinely public intellectual alive. He also continually raised the question of Palestine in ways that never permitted it to be answered on terms dictated by the powerful and the predatory. *Orientalism* was written in the shadow of the civil war in Lebanon in 1975–6, and it opened with the wry lament of a French journalist that, finally, "the Orient of Chateaubriand and Nerval" had been destroyed. To be sure, as Said went on to show, French Orientalism had long been inflected by a sense of belatedness – of loss, even mourning for its own possessive constructions of "the Orient." But whatever the fate of this (and countless other) "Orients," Orientalism itself never loosened its grip on the modern colonial imagination. And so it is not surprising – though it is desperately saddening – that the reissue of *Orientalism* as a Penguin Classic should be framed not only by the untimely death of its author but also by wars in Afghanistan, Palestine, and Iraq that confirm Orientalism is still abroad: emboldened and aggressively exorbitant. Throughout the intervening decades Said's voice provided a passionate and powerful counter-politics that was at once humane and, against all the odds, profoundly hopeful. Like countless thousands of others all over the world, I mourn his loss – and share his hope.

The other writer who has helped me make sense of these turbulent times is Arundhati Roy. In many ways these essays are extended footnotes to just one of hers, "Come September," which travels much of the same ground. In a public lecture she remarked that few of us "can afford the luxury of retreating from the streets for a while in order to return with an exquisite, fully formed political thesis replete with footnotes and references." Mine is neither exquisite nor fully formed, but I hope that my footnotes add something to her footsteps. For I have tried to reclaim the power of words from those who use them too cheaply. I remember as a child thinking that the school-yard chant that was supposed to answer the name-callers and the bullies – "Sticks and stones may break my bones, but words will never hurt me" – was a cruel lie that afforded neither protection nor solace. Words have an extraordinary power to wound and even to kill. My footnotes and references are an attempt to provide evidence against those who have used words to wreak terror in the name of a "war on terror."

In speaking of the colonial present, I don't mean to imply that nothing has changed since the nineteenth century. It may have been long, as historians are always telling us, but not that long. But I do mean to resist those histories punctuated by sharp breaks from one period to another, with their homogenizing sense of Time – always in the singular – and those narratives that celebrate History – always with that imperial capital – as the unambiguous advance of Reason. History is always more complicated than that: always plural, always contested, and shot through with multiple temporalities and spatialities. I speak about the colonial – rather than the imperial – present because I want to retain the active sense of the verb "to colonize": the constellations of power, knowledge, and geography that I describe here continue to colonize lives all over the world. They are not confined to the legatees of empires old or new, formal or informal, so that it is not a matter of colonial guilt – though an Englishman living in a Canada that has treated its First Nations so shamefully is more than usually aware of such considerations – but a matter of recognizing the ways in which so many of us (I include myself) continue to think and to act in ways that are dyed in the colors of colonial power.

What I've tried to do, above all, is to trace the connections between the modalities of political, military, and economic power – the grand strategies of geopolitics – and the spatial stories told by the lives of ordinary people. This is to reaffirm Marx's dictum – "People make history, but not just as they please nor under conditions of their own choosing" – but it is also to insist that people make geographies too: that their actions literally "take place." The essays in this book describe the production of the colonial present in particular places – Afghanistan, Palestine, and Iraq – in which places have been "taken" in the most extraordinarily violent ways. There are, of course, many other places in which colonial cultures of domination, exaction, and violence continue to wreak their havoc (including the United States, Israel, and Great Britain). But the terrifying "war on terror" declared by George W. Bush after September 11 has given my work a particular force and a particular urgency, and I hope that these essays might be read as contributions to a collective project of resistance and as stepping-stones toward a more humane geography.

Derek Gregory

Vancouver
January 2004

Acknowledgments

The reading and research for these essays was made possible in part by a grant from the Social Science and Humanities Research Council of Canada. Successive versions of the arguments were presented to audiences at Durham University, the University of Heidelberg, the University of British Columbia, the University of California at Berkeley, Queen Mary College in London, the National University of Singapore, Panjab University in Chandigarh, the Annual Meeting of the Association of American Geographers at New Orleans, the University of Southern California, the University of Texas at Austin, the Universidad Nacional Autónoma de Mexico and the Universidad Autónoma Metropolitana in Mexico City, and the Aegean Seminars on the island of Naxos in Greece. It has been a long journey, and I am grateful for all the comments I received on those occasions.

I am also grateful for the help and encouragement of John Agnew, James Anderson, Trevor Barnes, Nick Blomley, Mike Bovis, Bruce Braun, Noel Castree, Sharad Chari, Sanjay Chaturvedi, Simon Dalby, Matt Farish, Jim Glassman, Steve Graham, Chris Harker, Marwan Hassan, Dan Hiebert, Jennifer Hyndman, Andrew Jackson, Bonnie Kaserman, Lina Jamoul, Cindi Katz, Satish Kumar, Joanne Long, Kara MacDonald, Colin McFarlane, Donald Moore, David Nally, Tunji Osinubi, Natalie Oswin, David Pinder, Geraldine Pratt, Tanya Reinhart, Edward Said, James Sidaway, Kirsten Simonsen, Adrienne Smith, Neil Smith, Matt Sparke, Erik Swyngedouw, Juanita Sundberg, Nigel Thrift, Alex Vasudevan, Helen Watkins, Michael Watts, and Oren Yiftachel.

I particularly value the advice and friendship of Allan Pred, who read these essays with his usual generosity of spirit and unrivaled critical intelligence, and I am immensely grateful to him for his comments, suggestions, and much more besides.

I also owe (almost everything) to those committed journalists, commentators, and others who have done so much to bridge the gap between my desk and the world I have tried to present in these pages. Part of my purpose has been to try to work out what it is possible to know about "there" from "here." These essays are not front-line reports; I can't claim the privilege of presence. But then few of us can: so how are we to make sense of events that take place around the world in which we are, like it or not, involved and implicated? Part of the answer is to do with critical reading but that, in its turn, is impossible without critical reporting and writing. It is for this reason that I should like to record my particular admiration for the work of Amnesty International, B'Tselem, the Israeli Center for Human Rights in the Occupied Territories, the Electronic Intifada, the Foundation for Middle East Peace, Human Rights Watch, the Israeli Committee Against House Demolitions, and the Middle East Research and Information Project, and – in equal measure – for the principled and courageous reporting and commentary of Patrick Cockburn, Robert Fisk, Suzanne Goldenbeg, Amira Hass, Tanya Reinhart, and Jonathan Steele.

Writing a book is a collaborative project; so too is its production. Eric Leinberger drew the maps, and I have been fortunate to work with a cartographer who could translate my sketches into maps with such grace and professional skill. Thelma Gilbert found many of the images for me, and had a wonderfully sharp eye for what I was trying to convey. Janet Moth copy-edited the text with great sensitivity, and did much to clarify my arguments. The production process was coordinated by Angela Cohen and Brian Johnson, who tolerated my multiple missed deadlines – those plural histories again – with more patience, professionalism, and understanding than I had any right to expect. And Justin Vaughan has been the sort of editor every author dreams of: not only enthusiastic, engaged, and firm in equal measure but also, miraculously, each at exactly the right moment.

None of these individuals or organizations is responsible for the arguments that I set out in these pages: but I hope that they will recognize the part they have played in helping me to formulate them.

Last – but never least – my family had much to put up with while I was preoccupied with this book, and I owe everything else to Angela, Ben, Katie, and Jaimie.

D.G.

* * *

The author and publisher gratefully acknowledge the permission granted to reproduce the copyright material in this book:

Chapter 1. J. M. Coetzee, *Waiting for the Barbarians*. 2003. Secker & Warburg. Used by permission of The Random House Group and Penguin Group (USA), Inc.

Chapter 2. Constantine Cavafy, "Waiting for the Barbarians," 1898 (extract). From C. P. Cavafy, *Collected Poems* (trans. Edmund Keely and Philip Sherrard, edited by George Savidis), Princeton University Press, 1975, p. 15. Copyright © 1975 by Princeton University Press. Reprinted by permission of Princeton University Press.

Chapter 3. Donia Gobar, "The Land Where Red Tulips Grew." From *Home* "The Invisibles: A Collection of Poetry and Artwork" 2003 by iUniverse.Inc at <www.iUniverse.com>. Reprinted by permission of the author.

Chapter 4. Mahmoud Darwish, "Barbed Boundaries" (extract). From *Passport*.

Chapter 5. Harun Hashim Rasheed, "Raise Your Arms," From *Modern Anthology of Palestinian Literature*, edited by S. Jayussi. © 1992 Columbia University Press. Reprinted with permission of the publisher.

Chapter 6. Tom Sleigh, "Lamentation on Ur, 2000 BC" (extract). From *The Chain*, University of Chicago Press, 1996. Reprinted by permission of the author.

Chapter 7. Adonis, "Salute to Baghdad" (trans. Sinan Antoon) (extract). From *Al Ahram Weekly*, London 17–23 April 2003. Reprinted by permission of the translator.

Chapter 8. Thomas Pynchon, *Gravity's Rainbow* (extract). Copyright © 1973 Thomas Pynchon. Reproduced by permission of the author c/o Rogers, Coleridge & White, 20 Powis Mews, London W11 1JN and Penguin Group (USA), Inc.

Chapter 9. Tom Raworth "Listen Up" (extract). Reprinted by permission of the author.

Every effort has been made to trace copyright holders and to obtain their permission for the use of copyright material. The publisher apologizes for any errors or omissions in the above list and would be grateful if notified of any corrections that should be incorporated in future reprints or editions of this book.

1 The Colonial Present

The new men of Empire are the ones who believe in fresh starts, new chapters, new pages; I struggle on with the old story, hoping that before it is finished it will reveal to me why it was that I thought it worth the trouble.

J. M. Coetzee, *Waiting for the Barbarians*

Foucault's Laughter

THE French philosopher Michel Foucault once explained that his interest in what he called "the order of things" had its origins in a passage from an essay by the Argentinian novelist Jorge Luis Borges. There Borges had described "a certain Chinese encyclopaedia," the *Heavenly Emporium of Benevolent Knowledge*, in whose "remote pages" it was recorded that

> [A]nimals are divided into: (a) those that belong to the emperor; (b) embalmed ones; (c) those that are trained; (d) suckling pigs; (e) mermaids; (f) fabulous ones; (g) stray dogs; (h) those that are included in this classification; (i) those that tremble as if they were mad; (j) innumerable ones; (k) those drawn with a very fine camel's-hair brush; (l) *et cetera*; (m) those that have just broken the flower vase; (n) those that at a distance resemble flies.[1]

When he read this, Foucault said that he roared with laughter, a laughter that seemed to shatter all the familiar landmarks of European thought, breaking "all the ordered surfaces and all the planes with which we are accustomed to tame the wild profusion of existing things." In his wonderment at this strange taxonomy, Foucault claimed to recognize the limitation of his own – "our" own – system of thought: "the stark impossibility of thinking *that*."[2]

But what makes it impossible for us to think that – what lets demons and monsters loose in our own imaginary – is not so much the categories themselves. After all, the classification carefully distinguishes the mermaids and fabulous animals from the real creatures that are trained, stray, and tremble. As Foucault realized, our incomprehension arises from the series in which they are all placed together. In short, it is not the spaces but the *spacings* that make this "unthinkable."

Foucault was not in the least surprised that the spacings that produced such a "tableau of queerness" should be found in a Chinese encyclopedia. "In our dreamworld," he demanded, "is not China precisely this privileged *site* of *space*?"

> In our traditional imagery, the Chinese culture is the most meticulous, the most rigidly ordered, the one most deaf to temporal events, most attached to the pure delineation of space; we think of it as a civilization of dikes and dams beneath the eternal face of the sky; we see it, spread and frozen, over the entire surface of a continent surrounded by walls. Even its writing does not reproduce the fugitive flight of the voice in horizontal lines; it erects the motionless and still-recognizable images of things themselves in vertical columns. So much so that the Chinese encyclopaedia quoted by Borges, and the taxonomy it proposes, lead to a kind of thought without space, to words and categories that lack all life and place, but are rooted in a ceremonial space, overburdened with complex figures, with tangled paths, strange places, secret passages, and unexpected communications. *There would appear to be, then, at the other extremity of the earth we inhabit, a culture entirely devoted to the ordering of space, but one that does not distribute the multiplicity of existing things into any of the categories that make it possible for us to name, speak and think.*[3]

Although it would be a mistake to collapse the extraordinary range of Foucault's writings into the arc of a single project, much of his work traced just those orderings of space, at once European and modern, that appear in what he called "the grid created by a glance, an examination, a language" – and in other registers too – which *do* "make it possible for us to name, speak and think." He showed with unsurpassed clarity how

European modernity constructed the self – as the sane, the rational, the normal – through the proliferation of spacings. But these were all spacings *within* Europe. And precisely because Foucault was so preoccupied with these interior grids – the clinic, the asylum, and the prison among them – the production of spacings that set Europe off against its exterior "others," the very distinction between interior and exterior that initiated his journey into the order of things, was lost from view. "The other extremity of the earth," as he called it, was literally that: extreme.[4]

It would be perfectly possible to quarrel with Foucault's stylized characterization of China, whose cultural landscapes can be read in ways that do not confine its spaces to the bizarre and immobile geometries of French Orientalism.[5] But that would be to miss the point. For the strange taxonomy set out in the *Heavenly Emporium of Benevolent Knowledge* was not composed by some anonymous Chinese sage. *It was invented by Borges himself*. In one sense this is unremarkable too. For, as Zhang Longxi remarks with exemplary restraint, "What could be a better sign of the Other than a fictionalized space of China? What [could] furnish the West with a better reservoir for its dreams, fantasies and utopias?" But notice the enormous irony of it all. The nominally "unthinkable space" that made it possible for Foucault to bring into view the modern order of things *turns out to have been thought within from within the modern too*. The joke is on Foucault. For Borges was writing neither from Europe nor from China but from "Latin America," a topos where he was able to inscribe and to unsettle the enclosures of a quintessentially colonial modernity that Foucault was quite unable to see.[6]

I realize that this may not seem ironic at all. Foucault's laughter – and the rhetorical gesture that provoked it – has become so commonplace that it has become axiomatic, so much part of our established order of things that it is easy to forget that this order has *been* established: that it is a fabrication. This does not mean that it is simply false. On the contrary, it is validated by its own regimes of truth and it produces acutely real, visibly material consequences. Its currency – its value, transitivity, and reliability: in a word, its "fact-ness" – is put into circulation through the double-headed coin of colonial modernity. If we remain within the usual transactions of French philosophy then one side of that coin will display the face of modernity as (for example) an optical, geometric, and phallocentric space; a partitioned, hierarchical, and disciplined space; or a measured, standardized, and striated space. And the reverse side will exhibit modernity's other as (for example) primitive, wild, and corporeal; as mysterious, capricious, and excessive; or as irregular, multiple, and labyrinthine. Although the coin is double-sided, however, both its faces milled by the machinations of colonial modernity, the two are not of equal value. For this is an economy of representation in which the modern is prized over – and placed over – the non-modern.

This supplies one reason for speaking of an intrinsically *colonial* modernity. Modernity produces its other, verso to recto, as a way of at once producing and privileging itself. This is not to say that other cultures are the supine creations of the modern, but it is to acknowledge the extraordinary power and performative force of colonial modernity. Its constructions of other cultures – not only the way in which these are understood in an immediate, improvisational sense, but also the way in which more or less enduring codifications of them are produced – shape its own dispositions and deployments. These all take place within a fractured and highly uneven force-field in which other cultures entangle, engage, and exert pressure. But this process of colonial transculturation is inherently asymmetric, and colonial modernity's productions of the other *as* other, however much they are shaped by those various others, shape its constitution of itself in determinate and decisive ways.[7]

In his critique of Orientalism, Edward Said describes this unequal process as the production of *imaginative geographies*, and anthropologist Fernando Coronil connects it umbilically to what he calls Occidentalism. By this he means not the ways in which other cultural formations represent "the West," important though this is, but rather the self-constructions of "the West" that underwrite and animate its constructions of the other.[8] This has two implications that bear directly on the arguments I pursue in the essays that follow. First, the stories the West most often tells itself about itself are indeed stories of self-production, a practice that (in this case) does induce blindness. They are myths of self-sufficiency in which "the West" reaches out only to bring to others the fruits of progress that would otherwise be beyond their grasp. The subtitle of historian Niall Ferguson's exculpatory *Empire* provides a parochial proclamation of such a view: *How Britain Made the Modern World*. "As I travelled around that Empire's remains in the first half of 2002," he enthuses, "I was constantly struck by its ubiquitous creativity":

> To imagine the world without the Empire would be to expunge from the map the elegant boulevards of Williamsburg and old Philadelphia; to sweep into the sea the squat battlements of Port Royal, Jamaica; to return to the

bush the glorious skyline of Sydney; to level the steamy seaside slum that is Freetown, Sierra Leone; to fill in the Big Hole at Kimberley; to demolish the mission at Kuruman; to send the town of Livingstone hurtling over the Victoria Falls – which would of course revert to their original name of Mosioatunya. Without the British Empire, there would be no Calcutta; no Bombay; no Madras. Indians may rename them as many times as they like, but they remain cities founded and built by the British.[9]

Ferguson's triumphant celebration of "creativity" crowds out any recognition of that same empire's extraordinary (and no less ubiquitous) powers of destruction, but it also removes from view the multiple parts played by other actors – "subalterns" – in furthering, resisting, and reworking the projects of empire. Secondly, as that patronizing nod to native names and Indians reveals, self-constructions require constructions of the other. To return to Borges's world, it is through exactly this sort of logic that philosopher Enrique Dussel identifies 1492 as the date of modernity's birth. That fateful year saw both the Christian Reconquista that snuffed out Islamic rule in Andalusia and Columbus's voyage to the Americas. It was only then, so Dussel says, with Europe advancing against the Islamic world to the east and "discovering" the Americas to the west, that Europe was able to reposition itself as being at the very center of the world. More than this, he argues that the sectarian violence that was unleashed in the closing stages of the Reconquista was the model for the colonization of the New World. By these means, he claims, Europe "was in a position to pose itself against an other" and to colonize "an alterity [otherness] that gave back its image of itself."[10]

The Present Tense

The story of those European voyages of discovery (or self-discovery) can be told in many different ways. Joseph Conrad once distinguished three epochs in the history of formal geographical knowledges. He called the first "Geography Fabulous," which mapped a world of monsters and marvels. It was "a phase of circumstantially extravagant speculation which had nothing to do with the pursuit of truth." It was succeeded by "Geography Militant," which was advanced most decisively by Captain Cook and those who sailed into the South Pacific in his wake. By the nineteenth century, exploration by sea had given way to expeditions into the continental interiors. Conrad was fascinated, above all, by the replacement of the mythical geographies of Africa with "exciting pieces of white paper" – "honest maps," he called them – that were the paper-trail of "worthy, adventurous and devoted men" who had "nibbled at the edges" of that vast continent, "attacking from north and south and east and west, conquering a bit of truth here and a bit of truth there, and sometimes swallowed up by the mystery their hearts were so persistently set on unveiling." But by the early twentieth century this heroic age of exploration had yielded to "Geography Triumphant." Exploration had been replaced by travel, and even travel was being tarnished by tourism. The world had been measured, mapped, and made over in the image not only of Science but also of Capital.[11] Conrad's was not an innocent narrative, of course, even if he described geography as "the most blameless of sciences." Although his own *Heart of Darkness* illuminated the menace of Geography Triumphant with a brilliant intensity, his threnody for Geography Militant should blind us neither to the predatory designs advanced through those colonial cultures of exploration nor to their continuing impress on our own colonial present.

In his spirited reflection on these matters, Felix Driver writes about the "worldly after-life" of Geography Militant. This turns on what he calls "trading in memory," but these selective exchanges involve more than the cargo cult of relics and fetishes ("cultural forms") that he describes with such perspicacity. It is not just that our investments in these objects are, as he says, "thoroughly modern": "financial, emotional, aesthetic."[12] For we invest in more than objects. *We also invest in practices and dispositions.* "Culture" and "economy" are intimately intertwined and, as Nicholas Thomas reminds us, "relations of cultural colonialism are no more easily shrugged off than the economic entanglements that continue to structure a deeply asymmetrical world economy."[13] One way to persuade ourselves otherwise is to agree with L. P. Hartley that "The past is another country; they do things differently there." In some respects, so they do: distance conveys difference. But we should also listen to the words of another novelist, William Faulkner, writing about the American South. "The past is not dead," he remarked. "It is not even past."

What, then, are we to make of the *post*colonial? How are we to make sense of that precocious prefix? My preference is to trace the curve of the postcolonial from the inaugural moment of the colonial encounter. To speak of an "inaugural moment" in the singular is a fiction – there have been many different colonialisms, so that this arc is described in different histories and different geographies – but it is none the less an effective fiction. From that dispersed moment, marked by the "post," histories and geographies have all been made in the shadow of colonialism. To be sure, they have been made in the shadow of other formations too, and it is extremely important to avoid explanations that reduce everything to the marionette movements of a monolithic colonialism. Seen like this, histories and geographies are always compound, at once conjunctural and foliated. The French philosopher Louis Althusser wrote about the impossibility of cutting a cross-section through the multiple sectors of a social formation so that their connections could be displayed within a single temporality. It was necessary, he said, to recognize the coexistence of multiple temporalities. Or again, in a dazzling series of densely concrete experiments, Walter Benjamin demonstrated the need for a conception of history that could accommodate the spasmodic irruptions of multiple pasts into a condensed present. These two figures were not writing on the same page, and whether they belong in the same book is debatable. They were also working within a European Marxism that (for the most part) made little space for a critique of colonialism. But the importance of these ideas – in this, the most general of forms – is captured by Akhil Gupta when he argues that "the postcolonial condition is distinguished by heterogeneous temporalities that mingle and jostle with one another to interrupt the teleological narratives that have served both to constitute and to stabilize the identity of 'the West.' "[14]

To recover the contemporary formation that I have described as an intrinsically colonial modernity requires us to rethink the lazy separations between past, present, and future, and here modernism itself offers some guidance. Nineteenth-century modernism was haunted by the fugitive, the passing, the ephemeral, and had its face pressed up against the window of the future. But Andreas Huyssen has suggested that since the last decades of the twentieth century – in response to the vertigo of the late modern – the focus has shifted from "present futures to present pasts."[15] What has come to be called postcolonialism is part of this optical shift. Its commitment to a future free of colonial power and disposition is sustained in part by a critique of the continuities between the colonial past and the colonial present. While they may be displaced, distorted, and (most often) denied, the capacities that inhere within the colonial past are routinely reaffirmed and reactivated in the colonial present. There are many critical histories of colonialism, of course, and many studies that disclose its viral presence in the geopolitics and political economy of uneven development. But postcolonialism is usually distinguished from these projects by its central interest in the relations between culture and power. In fact, this is precisely how Said seeks to recover the past in the present. He warns against those radical separations through which "culture is exonerated from any entanglements with power, representations are considered only as apolitical images to be parsed and construed as so many grammars of exchange, and the divorce of the present from the past is assumed to be complete."[16] According to his contrary view, "culture" is not a cover term for supposedly more fundamental structures – geographies of politico-economic power or military violence – because culture is co-produced with them: culture underwrites power even as power elaborates culture. It follows that culture is not a mere mirror of the world. Culture involves the production, circulation, and legitimation of meanings through representations, practices, and performances that enter fully into the constitution of the world. Here is Thomas again:

> Colonialism is not best understood primarily as a political or economic relationship that is legitimized or justified through ideologies of racism or progress. Rather, colonialism has always, equally importantly and deeply, been a cultural process; its discoveries and trespasses are imagined and energized through signs, metaphors and narratives; even what would seem its purest moments of profit and violence have been mediated and enframed by structures of meaning. Colonial cultures are not simply ideologies that mask, mystify or rationalize forms of oppression that are external to them; they are also expressive and constitutive of colonial relationships in themselves.[17]

If postcolonialism is not indifferent to circuits of political, economic, and military power, its interest in culture – in the differential formations of metropolitan and colonial cultures – raises two critical questions. First, who claims the power to fabricate those meanings? Who assumes the power to represent others *as* other, and on what basis? Said's answer is revealed in the epigraph from Marx that he uses to frame his critique of Orientalism: "They cannot represent themselves; they must be represented." This attempt to muffle the other – so that, at the limit, metropolitan cultures protect their powers and privileges by insisting that "the subaltern cannot speak" – raises the second question. What is the power of those meanings? What do those meanings *do*? This double accent on power requires postcolonialism to be understood as a political as well as an intellectual project, and Robert Young is right to remind us that that the critique of

Table 1.1 Memory and the colonial present

	Colonial amnesia	Colonial nostalgia
Culture	Degradation of other cultures as "other"	Idealization of other cultures as "other"
Power	Violence and subjugation	Domination and deference

colonialism had its origins not in the groves of academe but in a tricontinental series of political struggles against colonialism.[18] Postcolonialism, we might say, has a constitutive interest in colonialism. It is in part an act of remembrance. Postcolonialism revisits the colonial past in order to recover the dead weight of colonialism: to retrieve its shapes, like the chalk outlines at a crime scene, and to recall the living bodies they so imperfectly summon to presence. But it is also an act of opposition. Postcolonialism reveals the continuing impositions and exactions of colonialism in order to subvert them: to examine them, disavow them, and dispel them. It for these reasons that Ali Behdad insists that postcolonialism must be "on the side of memory." Postcolonial critique must not only counter *amnesiac* histories of colonialism but also stage "a return of the repressed" to resist the seductions of *nostalgic* histories of colonialism.[19]

How, then, might one understand the cultural practices that are inscribed within our contemporary "tradings in memory?" In one of his essays on the haunting of Irish culture by its colonial past, Terry Eagleton describes the two moments I have just identified – amnesia and nostalgia – as "the terrible twins": "the inability to remember and the incapacity to do anything else."[20] If these are cross-cut with "culture" and "power" it is possible to use this rough and ready template to trace the arts of memory that play an important part in the production of the colonial present (see table 1.1).

On the one side, we too readily forget the ways in which metropolitan cultures constructed other cultures *as* "other." By this, I mean not only how metropolitan cultures represented other cultures as exotic, bizarre, alien – like Borges's "Chinese encyclopaedia" – but also how they acted as though "the meaning they dispensed was purely the result of their own activity" and so suppressed their predatory appropriations of other cultures. This is surely what was lost in Foucault's laughter.[21] We are also inclined to gloss over the terrible violence of colonialism. We forget the exactions, suppressions, and complicities that colonialism forced upon the peoples it subjugated, and the way in which it withdrew from them the right to make their own history, ensuring that they did so emphatically not under conditions of their own choosing. These erasures are not only delusions; they are also dangers. We forget that it is often ordinary people who do such awful, extraordinary things, and so foreclose the possibility that in similar circumstances most of us would, in all likelihood, have done much the same. To acknowledge this is not to protect our predecessors from criticism: it is to recall the part we are called to play – and continue to play – in the performance of the colonial present. We need to remind our rulers that "even the best-run empires are cruel and violent," Maria Misra argues, and that "overwhelming power, combined with a sense of boundless superiority, will produce atrocities – even among the well-intentioned." In other words, we still do much the same. Like Seumas Milne, I believe that "the roots of the global crisis which erupted on September 11 lie in precisely those colonial experiences and the informal quasi-imperial system that succeeded them." And if we do not successfully contest these amnesiac histories – in particular, if we do not recover the histories of Britain and the United States in Afghanistan, Palestine, and Iraq – then, in Misra's agonizing phrase, the Heart of Smugness will be substituted for the Heart of Darkness.[22]

On the other side, there is often nostalgia for the cultures that colonial modernity has destroyed. Art, design, fashion, film, literature, music, travel: all are marked by mourning the passing of "the traditional," "the unspoiled," "the authentic," and by a romanticized and thoroughly commodified longing for their revival as what Graham Huggan calls "the post-colonial exotic." This is not a harmless, still less a trivial pursuit, because its nostalgia works as a sort of cultural cryonics. Other cultures are fixed and frozen, often as a series of fetishes, and then brought back to life through metropolitan circuits of consumption. Commodity fetishism and cannibalism are repatriated to the metropolis.[23] But there is a still more violent side to colonial nostalgia. Contemporary metropolitan cultures are also characterized by nostalgia for the aggrandizing swagger of colonialism itself, for its privileges and powers. Its exercise may have been shot through with anxiety, even guilt; its codes may on occasion have been transgressed, even set aside. But the triumphal show of colonialism – its elaborate "ornamentalism," as David Cannadine calls it[24] – and its effortless, ethnocentric assumption of Might and Right are visibly and aggressively abroad in our own present. For what else is the war on terror other than the violent return of the colonial past, with its split geographies of "us" and "them," "civilization" and "barbarism," "Good" and "Evil"?

As Frances Yates and Walter Benjamin showed, in strikingly different ways, the arts of memory have always turned on space and geography as much as on time and history. We know that amnesia can be counteracted by the production of what Pierre Nora calls (not without misgivings) *lieux de mémoire*, while Jean Starobinski reminds us that nostalgia was originally a sort of homesickness, a pathology of distance. The late modern desire for memory-work – the need to secure the connective imperative between "then" and "now" – is itself the product of contemporary constructions of time and space that have also reconfigured the affiliations between "us" and "them." Hence Huyssen suggests that the "turn towards memory" has been brought about "by the desire to anchor ourselves in a world characterized by an increasing instability of time and the fracturing of lived space."[25] The kind of memory-work I have in mind is less therapeutic than Huyssen's gesture implies, but its insistence on the importance of productions of space is axiomatic for a colonialism that was always as much about making other people's geographies as it was about making other people's histories.

Fredric Jameson has offered a radically different gloss on claims like these. In his view, the delineation of what Said once called contrapuntal geographies was vital in a colonial world where "the epistemological separation of colony from metropolis, the systematic occultation of colony from metropolis" ensures that "the truth of metropolitan experience is not visible in the daily life of the metropolis itself; it lies outside the immediate space of Europe." In such circumstances, Said had proposed, "as we look back on the cultural archive," we need to read it "with a simultaneous awareness both of the metropolitan history that is narrated and of those other histories against which (and together with which) the dominant discourse acts."[26] In passing "from imperialism to globalization," however, Jameson claims that

What could not be mapped cognitively in the world of modernism now brightens into the very circuits of the new transnational cybernetic. Instant information transfers suddenly suppress the space that held the colony apart from the metropolis in the modern period. Meanwhile, the economic interdependence of the world system today means that wherever one may find oneself on the globe, the position can henceforth always be coordinated with its other spaces. This kind of epistemological transparency . . . goes hand in hand with standardization and has often been characterized as the Americanization of the world . . .[27]

I admire much of Jameson's work, but I think this argument – in its way, a belated version of Conrad's "Geography Triumphant" – is wholly mistaken. The middle passage from imperialism to globalization is not as smooth as he implies, still less complete, and the "new transnational cybernetic" imposes its own unequal and uneven geographies. The claim to "transparency" is one of the most powerful God-tricks of the late modern world, and Jameson's faith in the transcendent power of a politico-intellectual Global Positioning System seems to me fanciful. As Donna Haraway has shown with great perspicacity, vision is always partial and provisional, culturally produced and performed, and it depends on spaces of constructed visibility that – even as they claim to render the opacities of "other spaces" transparent – are always also spaces of constructed invisibility.[28] The production of the colonial present has not diminished the need for contrapuntal geographies. On the contrary. In a novel that has at its center the terrorist bombing of the US embassies in Dar es Salaam and Nairobi in 1998, Giles Foden writes about the "endless etcetera of events which led from dead Russians in Afghanistan, via this, that and the other, through dead Africans and Americans in Nairobi and Dar, to the bombardment of a country with some of the highest levels of malnutrition ever recorded."[29] Those connections are not transparent, as subsequent chapters will show, and the routes "via this, that and the other" cannot be made so by narratives in which moments clip together like magnets or by maps in which our unruly world is fixed within a conventional Cartesian grid. We need other ways of mapping the turbulent times and spaces in which and through which we live.

* * *

I have organized this book in the following way. I begin by clarifying what I mean by imaginative geographies, and illustrating their force through a discussion of the rhetorical response by politicians and commentators to the attacks on the World Trade Center in New York City and the Pentagon in Washington on September 11, 2001 (chapter 2). Others have described the consequences of those attacks for metropolitan America, but my own focus is different. The central sections of the book provide a triptych of studies that narrate the war on terror as a series of spatial stories that take place in other parts of the world: Afghanistan, Palestine, and Iraq (see figure 1.1). Each of these stories pivots around September 11, not to privilege that horrifying event (I don't think it marked an epochal rupture in human history) but to show that it had a complex genealogy that reached back into the colonial past and, equally, to show how it was used by regimes in Washington, London, and Tel Aviv to advance a grisly colonial present (and future).

The first story opens with the ragged formation of the modern state of Afghanistan, and traces the curve of America's involvement in its affairs from the Second World War through the Soviet occupation and the guerrilla wars of the 1980s and 1990s to the rise of the Taliban and its awkward accommodations with Osama bin Laden and al-Qaeda at the close of the twentieth century (chapter 3). Then I track forward from September 11 to the opening of the Afghan front in America's "war on terror," and its continuing campaign against al-Qaeda and the Taliban as they regroup on the Pakistan border (chapter 4).

The second story begins with European designs on the Middle East, and from this brittle template I trace the ways in which the formation and violent expansion of the state of Israel in the course of the twentieth century proceeded in lockstep with America's self-interest in its security to license successive partitionings of Palestine (chapter 5). Then I track forward from September 11 to show how the Israeli government took advantage of the "war on terror" in order to legitimize and radicalize its dispossession of the Palestinian people (chapter 6).

The third story describes British and American investments in Iraq from the First World War, when Iraq was formed out of three provinces of the Ottoman Empire, through the Iran–Iraq war of 1980–8, to the first Gulf War in 1990–1 and the international regime of sanctions and inspections that succeeded it (chapter 7). Then I track forward from September 11 to show how America and Britain resumed their war against Iraq in the spring of 2003 as yet another front in the endless and seemingly boundless "war on terror" (chapter 8).

Finally, I use these narratives and the performances of space that they disclose to bring the colonial present into sharper focus (chapter 9). It will be apparent that I regard the global "war on terror" – those scare-quotes are doubly necessary – as one of the central modalities through which the colonial present is articulated. Its production involves more than political maneuvrings, military deployments, and capital flows, the meat and drink

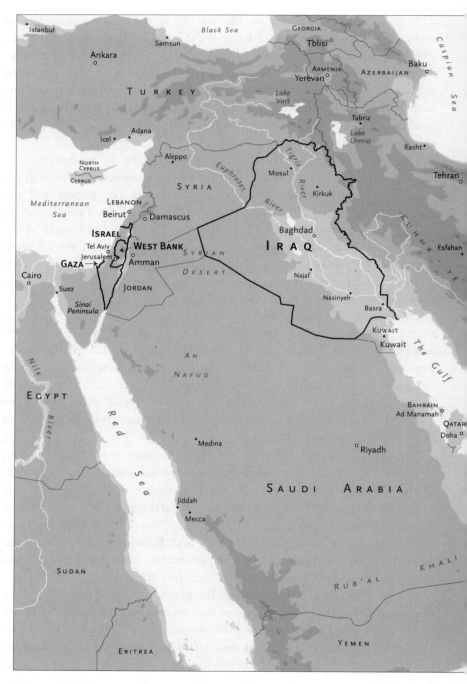

Figure 1.1 Afghanistan, Palestine, and Iraq

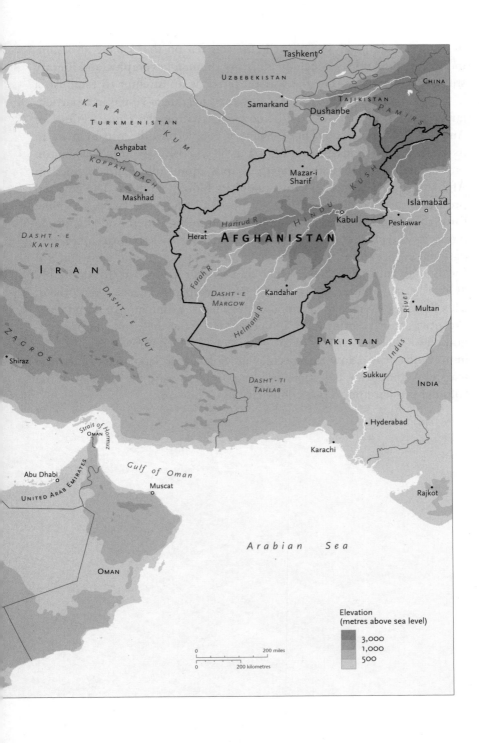

Tashkent

UZBEBEKISTAN

CHINA

KARA
KUM

TURKMENISTAN

Samarkand
Dushanbe

TAJIKISTAN
PAMIRS

Ashgabat

KOPPAH DAGH

Mazar-i
Sharif

HINDU
KUSH

Mashhad

Islamabad

Kabul
Peshawar

DASHT - E
KAVIR

Harirud R.
Herat
AFGHANISTAN

IRAN

ZAGROS

DASHT - E LUT

Farah R.

DASHT - E
MARGOW
Kandahar

Multan

Indus River

Helmand R.

PAKISTAN

Shiraz

DASHT - TI
TAHLAB

Sukkur

INDIA

Strait of Hormuz
OMAN

Hyderabad

Abu Dhabi

Karachi

UNITED ARAB EMIRATES

Gulf of Oman

Muscat

Rajkot

Arabian   Sea

OMAN

Elevation
(metres above sea level)

3,000
1,000
500

0   200 miles

0   200 kilometres

of critical social analysis, and it is for this reason that I have also sum-moned the humanities – including history, human geography, and literary studies – to my side. For the war on terror is an attempt to establish a new global narrative in which the power to narrate is vested in a particu-lar constellation of power and knowledge within the United States of America. I want to show how ordinary people have been caught up in its violence: the thousands murdered in New York City and Washington on September 11, but also the thousands more killed and maimed in Afghanistan, Palestine, and Iraq under its bloody banners. The colonial present is not produced through geopolitics and geoeconomics alone, through foreign and economic policy set in motion by presidents, prime ministers and chief executives, the state, the military apparatus and trans-national corporations. It is also set in motion through mundane cultural forms and cultural practices that mark other people as irredeemably "Other" and that license the unleashing of exemplary violence against them. This does not exempt the actions of presidents, prime minister, and chief executives from scrutiny (and, I hope, censure); but these imaginative geo-graphies lodge many more of us in the same architectures of enmity. It is important not to allow the spectacular violence of September 11, or the wars in Afghanistan, Palestine, and Iraq, to blind us to the *banality* of the colonial present and to our complicity in its horrors.

2 Architectures of Enmity

> And some of the men just in from the border say
> there are no barbarians any longer.
> Now what's going to happen to us without barbarians?
> Those people were a kind of solution.
>
> Constantine Cavafy, "Waiting for the Barbarians"

Imaginative Geographies

IN his critical discussion of Orientalism, Edward Said introduced the idea of imaginative geographies. These are constructions that fold distance into difference through a series of spatializations. They work, Said argued, by multiplying partitions and enclosures that serve to demarcate "the same" from "the other," at once constructing and calibrating a gap between the two by "designating in one's mind a familiar space which is 'ours' and an unfamiliar space beyond 'ours' which is 'theirs.'"[1] "Their" space is often seen as the inverse of "our" space: a sort of negative, in the photographic sense that "they" might "develop" into something like "us," but also the site of an absence, because "they" are seen somehow to lack the positive tonalities that supposedly distinguish "us." We might think of imaginative geographies as fabrications, a word that usefully combines "something fictionalized" and "something made real," because they are imaginations given substance. In Giles Foden's novel *Zanzibar*, a young American woman, Miranda Powers, newly arrived at the US embassy in Dar es Salaam, expresses what Said had in mind perfectly:

She'd realised a strong idea of America since coming to Africa. It was not a positive idea – since the country was too vast and complicated to be thought of in that way – but a negative one. Those shacks roofed with plastic bags, those pastel-paint signs in Swahili and broken English, that smell of wood smoke from the breakfast fires of crouched old women – those things all told her: this *isn't* home. This is far away. This is different.[2]

In their more general form these might seem strange claims to make in a world where, as anthropologist James Clifford once put it, "difference is encountered in the adjoining neighbourhood, the familiar turns up at the ends of the earth."[3] But that's really the point: distance – like difference – is not an absolute, fixed and given, but is set in motion and made meaningful through cultural practices.

Said's primary concern was with the ways in which European and American imaginative geographies of "the Orient" had combined over time to produce an internally structured archive in which things came to be seen as neither completely novel nor thoroughly familiar. Instead, a median category emerged that "allows one to see new things, things seen for the first time, as versions of a previously known thing." This Protean power of Orientalism is extremely important – all the more so now that Orientalism is abroad again, revivified and hideously emboldened – because the citationary structure that is authorized by these accretions is also in some substantial sense *performative*. In other words, *it produces the effects that it names*. Its categories, codes, and conventions shape the practices of those who draw upon it, actively constituting its object (most obviously, "the Orient") in such a way that this structure is as much a *repertoire* as it is an archive. Said said as much: his critique of Orientalism was shot through with theatrical motifs. "The idea of representation is a theatrical one," he wrote, and Orientalism has to be seen as a "cultural repertoire" through which, by the nineteenth century, "the Orient" becomes "a theatrical stage affixed to Europe" whose "audience, manager and actors are *for* Europe, and only for Europe."[4]

The repertory companies involved are now American as well as European, of course, but the theatrical motif is immensely suggestive. As one exiled Iraqi director puts it, the theater is a place where "one can perform this dividing line between fiction and reality, present and future."[5] The sense of performance matters, I suggest, for two reasons. In the first place, as the repertory figure implies, imaginative geographies are not only accumulations of time, sedimentations of successive histories; they are also *performances of space*. For this reason Alexander Moore's critique of Said seems to me profoundly mistaken. In Said's writings space is not "materialized as background" – "radically concretized as earth" – and it is wrong to use Soja's "illusion of opaqueness" – space as "a superficial materiality, concretized forms susceptible to little else but measurement and phenomenal description" – as a stick with which to beat him. For Said, too, space is an effect of practices of representation, valorization, and articulation; it is fabricated through and in these practices and is thus not only a domain but also a "doing."[6] In the second place, performances may be scripted (they usually are) but this does not make their outcomes fully determined; rather, performance creates a space in which it is possible for "newness" to enter the world. Judith Butler describes the conditional, creative possibilities of performance as "a relation of being implicated in that which one opposes, [yet] turning power against itself to produce alternative political modalities, to establish a kind of political contestation that is not a 'pure opposition' but a difficult labour of forging a future from resources inevitably impure." This space of potential is always conditional, always precarious, but every repertory performance of the colonial present carries within it the twin possibilities of either reaffirming and even radicalizing the hold of the colonial past on the present *or* undoing its enclosures and approaching closer to the horizon of the *post*colonial.[7]

In the chapters that follow I work with these ideas to sketch the ways in which "America" and "Afghanistan," "Israel" and "Palestine," were jointly (not severally) produced through the performance of imaginative geographies in the aftermath of the terrorist attacks on New York City and Washington on September 11, 2001. I also explore the ways in which America took advantage of those same attacks and mobilized those same imaginative geographies (or variants of them) to wage another war on Iraq in the spring of 2003. It has become commonplace to turn the events that took place in New York City and Washington on September 11, 2001 into "September 11" or "9/11" – to index the central, composite cluster of events by time not space – but this does not mean, as some commentators have suggested, that these were somehow "out-of-geography" events.[8] On the contrary, their origins have surged inwards and their consequences rippled outwards in complex, overlapping waves. The circuits that linked the military engagements launched in the dying months of that year by America against Afghanistan and by Israel against Palestine, and 18 months later by America and Britain against Iraq, cannot be exposed through any linear narrative. They were products of what Said would call "overlapping territories" and "intertwined histories," and so recovering these spatial stories and their contrapuntal filiations requires me to track backwards and forwards around September 11, connecting different places and combining different time-scales. Seen like this, as I hope to show, September 11 was a truly hideous event in which multiple geographies coalesced and multiple histories condensed in ways that have considerably extended the present moment of danger.[9]

These extensions have been made possible through the connective imperative between colonial modernity and its architecture of enmity. I borrow this phrase from political scientist Michael Shapiro, and it flows through much of my discussion in different forms and from different sources. "Geography is inextricably linked to the architecture of enmity," Shapiro writes, because it is centrally implicated "in how territorially elaborated collectivities locate themselves in the world and thus how they practice the meanings of Self and Other that provide the conditions of possibility for regarding others as threats or antagonists."[10] Architectures of enmity are not halls of mirrors reflecting the world – they enter into its very constitution – and while the imaginaries to which they give shape and substance are animated by fears and desires they are not mere phantasms. They inhabit dispositions and practices, investing them with meaning and legitimation, and so sharpen the spurs of action. As the American response to September 11 unfolded, and preparations were made for an armed assault on Afghanistan, James Der Derian cautioned that "more than a rational calculation of interests takes us to war. People go to war because of how they *see, perceive, picture, imagine and speak of* others: that is, how they construct the difference of others as well as the sameness of themselves through representation."[11]

"Why do they hate us?"

In the days and weeks that followed September 11, the asymmetry that underwrites the colonial production of imaginative geographies was end-lessly elaborated through the repetition of a single question. "Who hates America?" asked Michael Binyon in the London *Times* two days after the attacks. "What peoples, nations or governments are so twisted by loathing that they can concoct such an atrocity, plan its execution and dance in jubilation at the murder of thousands?" No government had expressed anything but horror and grief at the carnage, he went on, and no group had so far taken responsibility. "But the streets tell the story: rejoicing on the West Bank and in Palestinian refugee camps, 'happiness' in the mountains of Afghanistan, praise to Allah among Muslims in northern Nigeria. Overwhelmingly it is among the poor, the dispossessed and those who see themselves as victims that the rejoicing is heard." But these were different stories. Rejoicing and *Schadenfreude*: however reprehensible, the responses "on the street" are not in the same category as the planning and execution of acts of mass murder, and there is an important difference between those responsible for the attacks – who were far from being the wretched of the earth – and the infinitely larger (and poorer) audience for their actions, most of whom were surely horrified at the deaths of thousands of innocents.[12] But the difference was soon lost in the singularity of the question. On September 20 President George W. Bush appeared before a joint session of Congress and acknowledged the same, central question that came to dominate public discussion: "Americans are asking, 'Why do they hate us?' "[13]

Susan Buck-Morss maintains that the question was never intended to elicit an answer. "More than rhetorical question," she argued, "it was a ritual act: to insist on its unanswerability was a magical attempt to ward off this lethal attack against an American 'innocence' that never did exist." It was also an attempt to conjure up the specter not only of enmity but of evil incarnate which, as Hegel reminds us, resides in the innocent gaze itself, "perceiving as it does evil all around itself." As Roxanne Euben remarked, however, the question was itself a kind of answer, because it revealed "a privilege of power too often unseen: the luxury of not having *had* to know, a parochialism and insularity that those on the margins can neither enjoy nor afford."[14] It is this asymmetry – accepting the privilege of contemplating "the other" without acknowledging the gaze in return, what novelist John Wideman calls "dismissing the possibility that the native can look back at you as you are looking at him" – that marks this as a colonial gesture of extraordinary contemporary resonance. As Wideman goes on to say, "The destruction of the World Trade Center was a criminal act, the loss of life an unforgivable consequence, but it would be a crime of another order, with an even greater destructive potential, to allow the evocation of the word 'terror' to descend like a veil over the event, to rob us of the opportunity to see ourselves as others see us."[15]

And yet for the most part American public culture was constructed through a one-way mirror. The metropolis exercised its customary privilege to inspect the rest of the world. On October 15, 2001 *Newsweek* produced a thematic issue organized around the same question: "Why do they hate us?" The answer, significantly, was to be found among "them" not among "us": not in the foreign policy adventures of the USA, for example, but in what was portrayed as the chronic failure of Islamic societies to come to terms with the modern. The author of the title essay, Fareed Zakaria, explained that for bin Laden and his followers "this is a holy war between Islam and the Western world." Zakaria continued like this:

> Most Muslims disagree. Every Islamic country in the world has condemned the attacks. . . . But bin Laden and his followers are not an isolated cult or demented loners. . . . They come out of a culture that reinforces their hostility, distrust and hatred of the West – and of America in particular. This culture does not condone terrorism but fuels the fanaticism that is at its heart.[16]

This is an instructive passage because its double movement was repeated again and again over the next weeks and months. In the opening sentences Zakaria separates bin Laden and his followers from "most Muslims," who disagreed with their distortions of Islam and condemned the terrorist attacks carried out in its name. But in the very next sentences the partition is removed. Even those Muslims who disagreed with bin Laden and condemned what happened on September 11 are incarcerated with the terrorists in a monolithic super-organic "culture" that serves only to reinforce "hostility, distrust and hatred of the West" and to "fuel fanaticism." The culture of "Islam" – in the singular – is made to absorb everything, as though it were a black hole from whose force field no particle of life can escape. This is a culture not only alien in its details – its doctrines and observances – but in its very essence.[17] This culture (which is to say "their" culture) is closed and stultifying, monolithic and unchanging – a fixity that is at the very heart of modern racisms – whereas "our" culture (it goes without saying) is open and inventive, plural and dynamic. And yet, as Mahmood Mamdani asked in the wake of September 11,

> Is our world really divided into two, so that one part makes culture and the other is a prisoner of culture? Are there really two meanings of culture? Does culture stand for creativity, for what being human is all about, in one part of the world? But in the other part of the world, it stands for habit, for some kind of instinctive activity, whose rules are inscribed in early founding texts, usually religious, and museumized in early artefacts?[18]

If our answer is yes, then we are saying that "their" actions do not derive from any concrete historical experience of oppression or injustice, or from the imaginative, improvisational practices through which we ceaselessly elaborate our world. "Their" actions are simply dictated by the very nature of "their" culture. When Zakaria rephrased his original question it was only to make the same distinction in a different way. "What has gone wrong in the world of Islam?" he asked. To see that this *is* the same distinction one only has to reverse the question: "What has gone wrong in America?" From Zakaria's point of view, the only answer possible would be "the terrorist attacks on New York City and Washington." Not only is culture partitioned; so too is causality. "America" is constructed as the normal – because it is assumed to be the universal – and so any "attack on America" can only have arisen from the pathologies that are supposed to inhere within "the world of Islam."

In a subsequent essay Zakaria made his base assumption explicit: "America remains the universal nation, the country people across the world believe should speak for universal values."[19] This was not an exceptional view, and it was reinforced by the events of September 11. Anthropologist Veena Das drew attention to the way in which America was constructed as "the privileged site of universal values."

> It is from this perspective that one can speculate why the talk is not of the many terrorisms with which several countries have lived now for more than thirty years, but with one grand terrorism – Islamic terrorism. In the same vein the world is said to have changed after September 11. What could this mean except that while terrorist forms of warfare in other spaces in Africa, Asia or the Middle East were against forms of particularism, the attack on America is seen as an attack on humanity itself. . . . It is thus the reconfiguration of terrorism as a grand single global force – Islamic terrorism – that simultaneously cancels out other forms of terrorism and creates the enemy as a totality that has to be vanquished in the interests of a universalism that is embodied in the American nation.[20]

In case my comments are misunderstood, I should say that there are indeed substantial criticisms to be made of repressive state policies, human rights violations, and non-democratic political cultures in much of the Arab world. But many (most) of those regimes were set up or propped up by Britain, France, and the United States. And it is simply wrong to exempt America from criticism, and to represent its star-spangled banner as a universal standard whose elevation has been inevitable, ineluctable: in a word, simply "natural."[21] As novelist Arundhati Roy asked: "Could it be that the stygian anger that led to the attacks has its root not in American freedom and democracy, but in the US government's record of commitment and support to exactly the opposite things – to military and economic terrorism, insurgency, military dictatorship, religious bigotry and unimaginable genocide?"[22] This was a difficult, even dangerous question to pose immediately after September 11 when attempts at explanation risked being condemned as exoneration.[23] And yet, precisely because these are simultaneous equations in what Roy called "the fastidious algebra of infinite justice," Bush's original question – "Why do they hate us?" – invited its symmetrical interrogatory. When ordinary people cowered under the US bombardment of Baghdad in 1991, they had surely asked themselves, with Iraqi artist Nuha al-Radi, "Why do they hate us so much?" Sadly, the question never went away, and must have been repeated countless times in Afghanistan and elsewhere in the world.[24]

It is not part of my purpose to adjudicate between these questions and counter-questions because it is the dichotomy reproduced through them that I want to contest. As Said argues, "to build a conceptual framework around the notion of us-versus-them is in effect to pretend that the principal consideration is epistemological and natural – our civilization is known and accepted, theirs is different and strange – whereas in fact the framework separating us from them is belligerent, constructed and situational."[25] It is precisely those belligerencies, constructions, and situations that preoccupy me in these pages. The architecture of enmity – like all architectures – is produced and set to work through a repertoire of practices that have performative force. To blunt that force and deflect its violence requires, among other things, an analysis of the dispersed construction sites where the architecture of enmity is put in place and put into practice.

September 11

The terrorist attacks on New York City and Washington on the still morning of September 11, 2001 were so novel and so explosive that they soon became, in a jolting twist, one of the most thoroughly familiar and long-lingering after-images of contemporary history. The same narrative clips dominated television and computer screens around the world in real time and in an endlessly haunting replay: the two hijacked aircraft gliding into the twin towers of the World Trade Center; the booming fireballs and the

Figure 2.1   The skyline of Lower Manhattan on September 11, 2001 (© Mark Ludak/Topham/ImageWorks)

giant plumes of smoke rising high into the sky over Manhattan; the tiny figures tumbling to their deaths; the collapse of the towers in nightmare clouds of dust and debris; the gray outlines of survivors groping their way out of the scene; and the shocking, smoldering crater of "Ground Zero" (figure 2.1).

It is significant that these images all relate to the attacks on New York City. They rapidly eclipsed the other images of a third aircraft which was crashed into the Pentagon, and of a fourth aircraft that seems to have been bound for the Capitol or the White House but which, as a result of a struggle by the passengers against the hijackers, was crashed into a field 80 miles south of Pittsburgh. The concentration of the global gaze in this way reveals much about the mediatization of terror. Images of the collapse of the World Trade Center and the remains of "Ground Zero" became iconic not only by virtue of the scale of death and destruction that took place there, nor because they represented uniquely civilian casualties (unlike the Pentagon), but also because they conveyed with such visual, visceral power the eruption of spectacular terror in the very heart of metropolitan America. In doing so, they reactivated an urban imaginary from the early twentieth century which, as many observers remarked, was mobilized through a quintessentially cinematic gaze.[26] But it was a cinematic gaze with a difference. It was of course intensified; it dissolved the boundaries between fact and fiction, and projected horror beyond endurance. But most of all, through the confusion of raw, immediate, and unedited images, through the replays, jump-cuts and freeze-frames, through the jumbling of amateur and professional clips, through the juxtaposition of shots from multiple points of view, and through the agonizing, juddering close-ups, this was a cinematic gaze that replaced optical detachment with something much closer to the embodied, corporeal or "haptic" gaze.[27] It was by this means – through this medium – that the horror of September 11 reached out to *touch* virtually everyone who saw it.

I was deeply affected by what I saw that morning. So much so, that it was three months before I could begin to formulate a response – this response – and many more before I completed these essays. Even then, I have not addressed the intimate consequences of these attacks for the residents of New York City and Washington and those elsewhere in the world who lost family or friends in these appalling acts of mass murder. And since I do not dwell on the loss of 3,000 innocent lives from some 80 countries, on the thousands more who were seriously injured or traumatized, on their relatives, companions, and friends whose own lives were turned upside-down by grief, or on the heroic efforts of rescue workers on the ground, I need to say as clearly as I can that this is not because I have any wish to minimize the horror of what happened. Far from it. Equally, in making September 11 the fulcrum of my discussion I do not mean to marginalize the terrors that have ended or disfigured the lives of countless others elsewhere in the world. As Samantha Power pointedly remarked, in 1994 Rwanda "experienced the equivalent of more than two World Trade Center attacks every single day for one hundred days." When America "turned for help to its friends around the world" after September 11, she continued, "Americans were gratified by the overwhelming response. When the Tutsi cried out, by contrast, every country in the world turned away."[28] To make such comparisons and connections is not to diminish the enormity of what happened in New York City and Washington, nor is it to still what novelist Barbara Kingsolver described as that "pure, high note of anguish like a mother singing to an empty bed." Writing in the *Los Angeles Times* on September 23, she expressed something of what I mean like this:

[I]t's the worst thing that's happened, but only this week. Two years ago, an earthquake in Turkey killed 17,000 people in a day . . . and not one of them did a thing to cause it. The November before that, a hurricane hit Honduras and Nicaragua, and killed even more, buried whole villages and erased family lines, and even now people wake up there empty-handed. Which end of the world shall we talk about? Sixty years ago, Japanese airplanes bombed Navy boys who were sleeping on ships in gentle Pacific waters. Three and a half years later, American planes bombed a plaza in Japan where men and women were going to work, where schoolchildren were playing, and more humans died at once than anyone thought possible. Seventy thousand in a minute. Imagine. Then twice that many more, slowly, from the inside.

There are no worst days, it seems. Ten years ago, early on a January morning, bombs rained down from the sky and caused great buildings in the city of Baghdad to fall down – hotels, hospitals, palaces, buildings with mothers and soldiers inside – and here in the place I want to love best, I had to watch people cheering about it. In Baghdad, survivors shook their fists at the sky and said the word "evil." When many lives are lost all at once, people gather together and say words like "heinous" and "honor" and "revenge," presuming to make this awful moment stand apart somehow from the ways people die a little each day from sickness or hunger. They raise up their compatriots' lives to a sacred place – we do this, all of us who are human – thinking our own citizens to be more worthy of grief and less willingly risked than lives on other soil.[29]

In one sense, Kingsolver is surely right. There is something distasteful about cherry-picking among such extremes of horror. And yet in another sense, as I think she recognizes in her last sentence, each one of the dreadful events she describes – and those she doesn't, including the genocides in Nazi-occupied Europe, Cambodia, Iraq, Rwanda, and Bosnia that preoccupy Power – was understood in different ways and produced different responses in different places. This is why an analysis of the production of imaginative geographies is so vitally important. As Stephen Holmes puts it in his review of Power's indictment of indifference (at best inattention) to so many of these contemporary genocides, the distinction between "us" and "them" has consistently overshadowed any distinction between "just" and "unjust." Gilbert Achcar describes this more generally as a "narcissistic compassion," rooted in a humanism that masks a naked ethnocentrism: a form of empathy "evoked much more by calamities striking 'people like us,' much less by calamities affecting people unlike us."[30]

My purpose has thus been to try to understand what it was that those events in New York City and Washington triggered and, specifically, how they came to be shaped by a cluster of imaginative geographies into more or less *public* cultures of assumption, disposition, and action. Put most starkly: how did those imaginative geographies solidify architectures of enmity that contrived to set people in some places against people in other places? My comments cannot provide a full account of the geopolitical configurations, economic alignments and cultural formations that were mobilized during the months that followed September 11, and I have confined myself to three propositions. First, the military campaigns launched by America against Afghanistan, by Israel against Palestine, and by America and Britain against Iraq, were wired together. They became different parts of the same mechanism. Secondly, the architecture of enmity forwarded through the actions of America, Israel, and Britain turned on the cultural construction of their opponents in Afghanistan, Palestine, and Iraq as outsiders. Seen as occupying a space beyond the pale of the modern, their antagonists were held to have repudiated its moral geography and for this reason to have forfeited its rights, protections, and dignities. Thirdly, the extension of global order (as an asymmetric system of power, knowledge, and geography) was made dramatically coincident with a projection of the colonial past into what seems to me a profoundly colonial present.

In advancing these claims I follow the standard convention of using "America," "Israel," and "Britain," "Afghanistan," "Palestine," and "Iraq" as shorthand expressions. In fact they are of course cover terms for complex networks that spiral through state and para-state, military and para-military apparatuses. This much is familiar. But I need to emphasize that the networks also spiral beyond those apparatuses. In December 1998, on the morning after the United States and the United Kingdom had begun to rain laser-guided bombs and cruise missiles on Baghdad – even as the UN Security Council was meeting in emergency session to discuss the Iraq crisis – I was wandering through the streets of Cairo, sick at heart, when I was approached by an elderly Egyptian who asked me if I was an American. I began to explain that I was British, but even as the words left my lips I realized that this was neither consolation nor excuse. Before I could finish my sentence, the old man took me gently by the arm and said: "It doesn't matter. We just want you to know that we understand that it's governments that do these terrible things, not ordinary people. You are very welcome here." At the time I was (and I remain) astonished by his act of grace and generosity. And yet "ordinary people" were (and are) involved in these actions too, and in so far as so many of us assent to them, often by our silence, then we are complicit in what is done in our collective name. *The networks spiral beyond those apparatuses.* To be sure, there are political differences and divisions within each of the cover terms I have listed above. None of them is monolithic, and for this reason I have tried to listen to other voices inside America, Britain, and Israel, as well as the voices of Afghanis, Palestinians, and Iraqis. In consequence it now seems markedly less useful to me to think of "America," "Britain," and "Israel," "Afghanistan," "Palestine," and "Iraq" as cover terms and more important to reveal just what it is that they cover.

3 "The Land Where Red Tulips Grew"

The blind war has crushed all the tulips,
And inside the blood-stained ruins,
Mourning, the wind echoes . . .
Weeping, weeping . . .

Donia Gobar, *Home*

Great Games

AFGHANISTAN has endured a long history of foreign intervention and domestic turmoil. In the nineteenth and early twentieth centuries Britain fought three bloody Afghan wars in order to beat back the influence of tsarist Russia and secure the borders of its Indian Raj. When Captain Arthur Connolly, a young British officer who served in both Afghanistan and India from 1823 to 1842, wrote home of his hopes for a "great game," even a "noble game," to be played out in these extraordinary lands, he can have had no idea how his words – if not his aspirations – would echo down the centuries. His phrase was popularized by Rudyard Kipling in his novel *Kim* (1901), which, as Edward Said notes, treats service to empire "less like a story – linear, continuous, temporal – and more like a playing field – many-dimensional, discontinuous, spatial."[1] It was for precisely this reason that the Great Game was a favorite image of Lord Curzon, later Viceroy of India:

Turkestan, Afghanistan, Transcaspia, Persia – to many these words breathe only a sense of utter remoteness, or a memory of strange vicissitudes and of moribund romance. To me, I confess they are pieces on a chessboard upon which is being played out a game for the domination of the world.

This was an extraordinarily instrumental view of a land and its peoples, but it was also an accurate summary of the imperial imaginary. Between the formal campaigns of the Afghan wars an undeclared war of influence and infiltration – the Great Game – continued between the two imperial powers. It was these international geopolitical maneuvrings that shaped the formation of the modern state of Afghanistan – a "purely accidental" territory, Curzon called it – out of the shards of rival tribal fiefdoms and ethnic loyalties (figure 3.1).[2] This was a complex and uneven process, and given the indifferent proclivities of colonial cartography it is scarcely surprising that deep fractures remained. Of particular significance was the Durand Line, an arbitrary border between Afghanistan and British India that was drawn with a cavalier flourish by Sir Mortimer Durand, the Foreign Secretary of the colonial government of India. The Durand Line proved to be much more difficult to delineate on the ground than on a desk; it was finally surveyed in 1894–5, slicing through tribes and even villages, and cutting the territories of the Pashtun in two. After India's independence and partition in 1947, the line became the border between Afghanistan and Pakistan, but these fractures neither severed trans-border connections among the Pashtun nor shattered the dream of a united "Pashtunistan."

Within its tensely bounded space, the instrumentalities of the Afghan state developed at different rates, and their geographies had to accommodate not only the diffuse powers of a multiplicity of local political networks but also the deadly serious "games" that continued to be played by other states through the twentieth century and beyond.[3] The two principal foreign actors were the USA and the USSR. American involvement in Afghanistan began in the years after the First World War and accelerated soon after the Second World War. In 1946 the Helmand project, a vast hydraulic regime loosely based on the Tennessee Valley Authority, was set in motion in southern Afghanistan. With American aid and expertise, public and private, its object was, as historian Nick Cullahas puts it, "to translate Afghanistan into the legible inventories of material and human resources in the manner of modern states" and, through this, to intensify the centralizing, surveillant power of the Pashtun majority in Kabul.[4] But

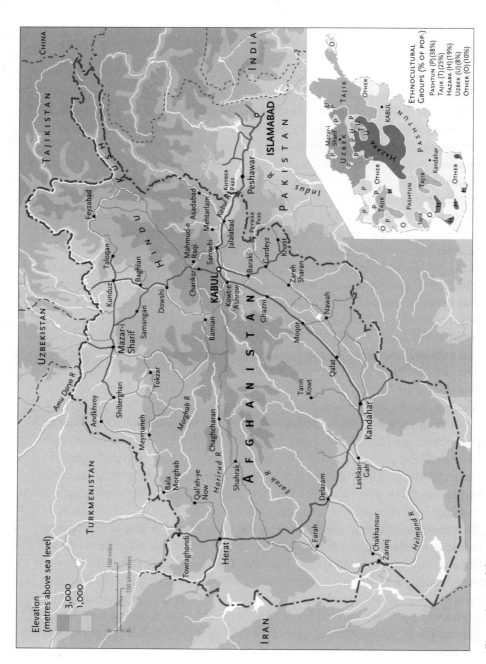

Figure 3.1 Afghanistan

in 1950 Pakistan, stung by repeated cross-border attacks by militants demanding the creation of an independent Pashtunistan, temporarily suspended its oil exports to Afghanistan; Pakistan was allied with the United States, and as part of its response to this dislocation Kabul crossed the street, so to speak, and signed major trade and aid agreements with the Soviet Union. From then on both the USA and the USSR used their aid programs as counters in the Cold War. Between 1956 and 1978 Afghanistan received $1.26 billion in economic aid and $1.25 billion in military aid from the USSR and $53 million from the USA. As these figures suggest, Kabul enjoyed an increasingly close relationship with Moscow. In 1973 Mohammed Daoud Khan – the king's brother-in-law, the former prime minister, and an American-educated technocrat – seized power and abolished the monarchy. He persuaded the United States to continue the Helmand project, and at first enjoyed the support of the largely urban-based faction of the Marxist-Leninist People's Democratic Party (PDP), the Parcham (the Party of the Flag), for his program of continued modernization. But it was an increasingly coercive regime – the government built the largest prison in Asia – and Daoud eventually purged Parcham from his administration. In 1977 he announced a new constitution that established a one-party system and set about persecuting Marxist and Islamic nationalists alike.

Parcham joined with Khalq (the Party of the People), whose base was largely in the countryside, in an uneasy coalition that reactivated the PDP. In April 1978 the party seized power in a military coup, the so-called Saur revolution, and American involvement in Helmand and in Afghanistan came to an abrupt end. The new administration declared the foundation of the Democratic Republic of Afghanistan and signed a new concordat with the USSR. It was now the turn of Khalq to gain the upper hand: following a purge, the surviving leadership of Parcham fled to Moscow. Khalq, backed by its own repressive and ruthless security apparatus, initiated a far-reaching program of social change and land reform that was a direct challenge to the patriarchal authority of the traditional elites – religious, tribal, landlord – that had ruled the countryside for generations. When these reforms were resisted, the Khalq regime responded with exceptional brutality. Mass arrests, summary executions, and massacres provoked an ever-widening spiral of rebellions and state reprisals. In a matter of months, Afghanistan was in turmoil, and by December of the following year the government held only the cities.[5]

The USSR, already perturbed by the spread of Islamicism through central Asia in the wake of the Iranian revolution that had toppled the Shah in 1978–9, was thoroughly alarmed at the prospect of armed resistance spilling over its southern border. On December 27, 1979 Moscow invoked its treaty with Afghanistan and airlifted Soviet troops into Kabul to install Parcham as a client regime. The new government sought to crush the uprisings by a renewed round of mass arrests and summary executions, backed by brutal military raids and pulverizing air strikes. Throughout the 1980s Kabul was shielded from the worst effects of the war by heavily protected "security belts," and those who supported Parcham received considerable Soviet subsidies (which is why Kabul was later reviled by the Taliban as a city of collaborators). But the countryside was ravaged by bombs and land-mines: agricultural production plummeted, and famine was widespread. Hundreds of thousands were killed in the widening conflict, and hundreds of thousands more fled the country.

The state's continued campaign of forced secularization and violent repression fanned the flames of a resistance movement that drew tens of thousands of Muslims to Afghanistan – many of them from Pakistan and Saudi Arabia, others from Egypt, Algeria and elsewhere in the Arab world – to join a *jihad* against the Soviet occupation and its client government. *Jihad* is a complex concept whose multiple meanings have been the subject of much debate throughout the history of Islam. It carries no necessary implication of violence or "holy war" (the usual translation in North America and Europe). In the early chapters of the Koran, promulgated when the Prophet Mohammed was still in Mecca, *jihad* often conveys a personal struggle to overcome passions and instincts, the effort to live in the way that God intended; in the later chapters, promulgated in Medina when Mohammed had become the head of a state, *jihad* does frequently mean an armed struggle to protect and defend the lands of Islam. It was in this second sense that these young fighters referred to themselves as *mujaheddin* or "holy warriors."[6] They had no central command, but they had much in common. Many of them had been shaped by the hybrid, exilic, and profoundly patriarchal culture of the refugee camps on the border around Peshawar in north-west Pakistan. They were "orphans of the war," growing up "without women – mothers, sisters, cousins," in an intensely masculinist culture where the space for the participation of women in almost every area of non-domestic life (including education) was severely restricted. As the conflict widened and deepened, they were also affected by – and implicated in – the intensifying militarization of the region. There were many different groups and factions, but their common faith and their common experience gave them a fierce determination to end the occupation of Afghanistan by non-believers.[7]

Others had a keen interest in their struggle too. The United States, mapping the fluctuating fortunes of the Marxist-Leninist government and the involvement of the USSR through its "red template," saw the Soviet intervention as opening another front in the Cold War that presented a direct threat to its own interests in the petro-world of the Gulf. The Carter administration had already tried to exploit the rivalries between Afghanistan's two communist factions, and had been secretly aiding the insurgents for six months before the Red Army arrived in Kabul. According to Carter's National Security Adviser, it was this covert operation that drew the Russian bear into what he called "the Afghan trap." The day Soviet troops crossed the Afghan border, he told the president that the United States finally had a chance to entangle the USSR in "its own Vietnam war."[8]

Pakistan and Saudi Arabia were watching too. The call for *jihad* had been transmitted through transnational Islamic networks, and this gave both states a powerful incentive to direct and contain the scope of the *mujaheddin* militias. These considerations were enhanced by geopolitical calculations that were, in each case, at once transnational and domestic. Pakistan sought to pursue what it called "strategic depth" by preventing instability on its north-west frontier from compromising its undeclared war with India along its eastern border. For this reason it looked to the victory of the *mujaheddin* to put an end to Khalq and Parcham – both predominantly Pashtun – and so to any prospect of a transborder Pashtunistan. (Sunni) Saudi Arabia was keen to enhance its credentials as the center of the Islamic world against the aggressive claims of its rival, (Shi'a) Iran, but the House of Saud had its own domestic concerns too: the precarious alliance between the ruling oil oligarchy and the religious schools and mosques was coming under increasing pressure, and the Saudi government attempted to solve these twin equations by sending thousands of young Islamic activists, who were increasingly critical of the corruption and materialism of the royal dynasty, to join the *jihad* against the Soviet occupation of Afghanistan.[9]

These multiple geopolitical considerations had two vital consequences. In the first place, the Afghan resistance was supported throughout this period in part by aid from the United States, whose Central Intelligence Agency (CIA) covertly supplied arms (including, from 1986, Stinger missiles) and provided military training to the *mujaheddin* through Pakistan and its

InterServices Intelligence Directorate (ISI). The overall cost has been estimated at $500 million for each year of the conflict, which was matched by Saudi Arabia from both official and clandestine sources. In the second place, much of this aid was channeled by the ISI to the more extremist and authoritarian militias; foremost amongst them was Gulbuddin Hekmatyar's Hizb-i-Islami. These groups were, for the most part, pursuing an Islamicist rather than a nationalist agenda that had no space for the creation of any independent state of Pashtunistan, which not only satisfied Pakistan's rulers but also conformed to the expedient logic of the House of Saud.[10]

Uncivil Wars and Transnational Terrorism

The triangulation of the Afghan civil war by these three states was to have fateful consequences for each of them. Among the young Muslim radicals who were recruited and trained through the CIA/ISI pipeline was Osama bin Laden, whose multi-millionaire father owned one of Saudi Arabia's largest construction companies. He first made contact with the *mujaheddin* in Peshawar in 1980, and returned to the border several times with donations for the Afghan resistance from various Saudi sources. He worked closely with one of his former professors, Abdullah Azzam, a Palestinian who had taught him at university in Jeddah. Azzam had set up the Maktab al-Khidamat, or Bureau of Services, across the border in Peshawar to provide medical services and rest-houses for the international volunteers and to channel money to them and their families. Although bin Laden took part in several skirmishes against the Soviet army, his major role seems to have been financial and logistical. He made repeated journeys between Afghanistan, Pakistan, and Saudi Arabia, and in 1986 brought civil engineers and heavy construction equipment back with him to build roads, training camps, and tunnel complexes for the *mujaheddin*. Azzam envisaged the extension of their struggle beyond Afghanistan, and in 1987 called for the creation of a revolutionary vanguard – in Arabic, "al-Qaeda al-Sulbah," which means "the solid base" or "strong foundation" – to carry forward an avowedly transnational Islamicist project. Then, in 1988, bin Laden established a computerized system – in Arabic this is also "al-Qaeda," "the [data]-base" – to keep track of all the volunteers who passed through the training camps and the Bureau of Services.[11]

So successful was the Afghan guerrilla campaign that by the late 1980s the Soviet-backed regime once again held only the cities, and even those precariously. In February 1989 the USSR, mired in what had indeed become its own Vietnam, finally withdrew all its 115,000 troops from Afghanistan. The US administration, confident that the balance of powers had been restored, withdrew its involvement too. Afghanistan "fell off the [American] map" and there was no concerted attempt to rebuild its ravaged economy or society. But both Pakistan and Saudi Arabia continued to keep a watchful eye on events.[12]

The bloody conflict ground on, and volunteers continued to stream across Afghanistan's borders to join the *mujaheddin*. By 1992 a loose confederation of militias had emerged (the "Northern Alliance"). The two largest groups were the Tajik Jamiat-i-Islami, led by Ahmad Shah Massoud, whose forces controlled most of the north-eastern provinces, and the Uzbek Junbish-i-Milli, led by Abdul Rashid Dostum, who had defected from the government army. They agreed to set their differences on one side in order to destroy what was left of the tottering communist government and to establish in its place an Islamic State of Afghanistan. Their eventual success marked not so much an end to the affair, however, as a reversal of forces. The Northern Alliance met with suspicion and hostility from members of the other ethnic groups, especially the Pashtun, but the coalition was itself unstable and the fighting between its factions, together with their horrific depredations on the civilian population, provoked widespread anger and despair. In the civil war that continued without pause, thousands of people were abducted and killed, refugees streamed across the borders, and cities and villages were left in ruins.[13]

The most successful militia commanders became local warlords. Much of their internecine fighting centered on Kabul, which fell to a joint force of Tajiks and Uzbeks in April 1992. As soon as their armies entered the city, they were at one another's throats. "Factions set up roadblocks every 100 meters, dividing the city into a mosaic of conflicting territories, and embarking on a spree of looting, rape and summary executions against their ethnic rivals." From the outlying districts to the south of Kabul, Gulbuddin Hekmatyar's Pashtun Hizb-i-Islami militia launched rockets and missiles into the heart of the city. Thousands were killed, thousands more injured, and hundreds of thousands fled, while the *mujaheddin* perpetrated such gross and systematic violations of the human rights of unarmed civilians (especially women) that Amnesty International declared Kabul "a human rights catastrophe." In Kandahar, too, the city was divided among different armed factions, and Human Rights Watch reported that its civilian inhabitants "had little security from murder, rape, looting or extortion."

The rural areas were largely spared the bombings and shellings – though not the sowing of land-mines – and in the north and west of the country a measure of stability was eventually achieved around Mazar-i-Sharif and Herat. But the Alliance effectively fell apart, while the south and east remained prey to a violent warlordism whose depredations remained unchecked.[14]

Meanwhile bin Laden's energies had been directed elsewhere. Azzam had been assassinated in 1989, and bin Laden had taken over the work of the Bureau of Services and redefined its role. The purpose of this new network – which Gilles Kepel describes as "an organizational structure built around a computer file," redeeming the double meaning of "al-Qaeda"[15] – was to continue the groundwork of raising money, but to use this to bring together Arab veterans of the Afghan campaigns in order to conduct *jihad* far beyond the boundaries of Afghanistan. Bin Laden had returned to Saudi Arabia after the Soviet withdrawal from Afghanistan, and new targets soon presented themselves. In 1990 Iraq invaded Kuwait, and bin Laden offered to mobilize 10,000 *mujaheddin* to liberate the kingdom from its occupation by Saddam Hussein's secular Ba'athist regime. The offer was, in one sense, fanciful, because there were not thousands of Islamic fighters at bin Laden's command. What underwrote bin Laden's proposal was less his own associates and resources than the extraordinary success of the Afghan *jihad*, and for this reason he was aghast when the Saudi royal family allowed the United States to intervene instead. Just as he had earlier opposed the presence of Soviet troops in Afghanistan, so bin Laden now opposed the presence of American troops at bases in Saudi Arabia. His was not a lone voice; many Islamic scholars agreed that it was forbidden for non-Muslim troops to be stationed in the holy lands of Mecca and Medina. Opposition increased when American troops failed to withdraw after the Gulf War, and bin Laden became increasingly outspoken in public addresses which he gave in person and on audio-tapes that were circulated widely in Saudi Arabia.[16]

In 1991 he was expelled for his activities and, after a few months in Peshawar took refuge in Sudan, where an Islamicist regime had been in power since a coup d'état in 1989. Its leader, Hassan al-Turabi, was resolutely opposed to the US–Saudi alliance and had some success in orchestrating a rival international Islamicist coalition. It was in Khartoum that the transnational mission of al-Qaeda gathered momentum. It is necessary to understand the context in which this mission was formulated and the many groups with which bin Laden had connections. It would be a serious mistake to exaggerate the unity of political Islam by conjuring up a vast, transnational Islamicist conspiracy orchestrated by a single, charismatic leader. As Omayma Abdel-Latif cautions, such a fantasy is "a product of the Western imagination," at once a Hollywood conceit and, as he says, "the result of a deep phobia that renders Islam both unknown and mysterious." Instead, al-Qaeda needs to be understood as a network of networks that neither stands and falls around bin Laden nor exists independently of the various political crises that have shaped and continue to shape its formation. In a helpful analysis of a complex field, Jason Burke distinguishes between a core group gathered round bin Laden himself – many of them Afghan veterans who (re)joined bin Laden in the Sudan and later in Afghanistan to serve as administrators, recruiters and trainers: Azzam's "vanguard" – and the scores of other militant Islamicist groups with their own leaders and their own struggles, who relate to bin Laden and his associates in diverse ways. The two clusters are linked, so Burke argues, by an intensely radical version of Islamicism. This includes, as a minimum, a profound sense of injustice inflicted on Muslims, an embrace of political violence as a means toward restitution, and a commitment to martyrdom in the cause of *jihad*. Perhaps most important of all is a belief in the importance of other Muslims inside and outside these groups bearing witness to the depth of their faith, so that what Burke calls "spectacular theatrical violence" is seen as both the ultimate testimony of their submission to the will of Allah and a powerful message to be delivered to a transnational audience. In accordance with these beliefs, bin Laden determined that *jihad* was now to be waged not only against the new army of "infidels" – the "American Crusaders" as bin Laden called them – but also against the "heretics," those compliant regimes in Saudi Arabia and elsewhere that supported the continued presence of American bases in the region.[17] Bin Laden set up trading and engineering companies in Khartoum, together with training camps for his "Afghan Arabs" and others. During this period American intelligence sources alleged that bin Laden's network was involved, directly or indirectly, in attacks on US troops in Somalia and in bombings in Saudi Arabia. Mounting American and Saudi pressure finally forced the Sudanese to expel him, and in the summer of 1996 bin Laden and several hundred of his closest associates returned to Afghanistan.[18]

By that time a considerable group of Muslim fighters, drawn mainly from the Pashtun majority, had become disillusioned with the Islamic State of Afghanistan and the brutalities, persecutions, and licenses it perpetrated in the name of Islam. Many of them were former students from the *madrassas*, religious schools that had been set up in Afghan refugee camps in Pakistan and in Kandahar. They were known collectively as the Taliban (which means "religious students" or "seekers of knowledge"), and they sought to restore law, order, and stability to Afghanistan through the removal of the warlords and the imposition of a radically purified Islam. This was a version of Deobandism which, like the Wahhabism that held sway in Saudi Arabia, had its foundations in Sunni literalisms, which held that the meaning of the Koran was so unambiguous that its teachings had to be put directly into practice. There was no intervening place for interpretation: teaching and practice were indissoluble and incontrovertible. The classical tradition of jurists debating the laws of Islam was dismissed as a corrupting intellectualism, and the complex trajectory of clarification and accommodation that had occurred during the historical development of Islamic societies was repudiated. Adherents retreated into the supposedly stable and secure "haven of the text."[19]

By 1994 Taliban troops had seized Kandahar, their spiritual home and effective capital, and severed the supply lines between the Islamic State of Afghanistan and its arch-protagonist, Iran (an action endorsed and even encouraged by the United States). The Taliban subjected Kabul to a renewed and relentless barrage of rocket attacks and ground assaults. In that year alone, 25,000 people, mainly civilians, were killed, and one-third of the city was reduced to rubble (figure 3.2). The Taliban finally forced Massoud's fighters out of Kabul in September 1996. Faced with such a resounding defeat, Massoud formally resurrected the Northern Alliance as the United Islamic and National Front for the Salvation of Afghanistan (though it continued to be widely known by its old name). But the rival militias had little immediate success, beaten back on front after front, and as the Taliban advanced they implemented their own exceptionally stringent interpretation of Islamic law. Most of them were from rural areas in the south-east, though many of them had never known ordinary village life – their homes, fields, and livelihoods had been destroyed by years of fighting – and the cities bore the brunt of their oppressions. Herat and Kabul in particular were treated as occupied zones. They were doubly alien to the Taliban. Their inhabitants were drawn primarily from non-Pashtun groups, and these cities were seen as the sites of a residual modernity whose corruptions (and, for that matter, collaborators) had to be purged from a properly Islamic Afghanistan. Harsh restrictions were imposed on the lives of the people. Girls' schools and colleges were closed; women were

Figure 3.2   Kabul, July 1996 (Profile Press/Rex Features)

not allowed to work outside the home; a strict dress code was enforced; most ordinary entertainment – even traditional music and kite-flying – was banned; and brutal punishments were meted out to those who disobeyed.[20]

When its troops entered Mazar-i-Sharif in May, only to lose it several days later, the governments of Pakistan, Saudi Arabia, and the United Arab Emirates recognized the Taliban as the legitimate government of Afghanistan. This was more than diplomatic show. Pakistan continued to pursue its policy of strategic depth, and in addition to its desire to contain nationalist ambitions for an independent Pashtunistan had, since 1990, been prepared to support any regime that would allow guerrilla fighters to train in Afghanistan for its covert war with India over Kashmir. "Of all the foreign powers involved in efforts to sustain and manipulate the ongoing fighting," Human Rights Watch reported, "Pakistan is distinguished both by the sweep of its objectives and the scale of its efforts, which include soliciting funds for the Taliban, bankrolling Taliban operations, providing diplomatic support as the Taliban's virtual emissaries abroad, arranging training for Taliban fighters, recruiting skilled and unskilled manpower to serve in Taliban armies, planning and directing offensives, providing and facilitating shipments of arms and fuel, and on several occasions apparently directly providing combat support." Once Pakistan threw its support behind the Taliban, "Saudi aid increasingly followed suit."[21]

In October the Taliban declared the foundation of the Islamic Emirate of Afghanistan. Throughout the following year the Taliban made repeated attempts to push further into the territories into which the Northern Alliance had withdrawn, and several hundred members of al-Qaeda fought alongside Taliban troops. The scale of the violence, and of the exaction and repression visited upon the civilian population by all sides, was stunning. By the end of 1998, when the Taliban controlled perhaps 90 percent of the country, Afghanistan was virtually destroyed, its civil society shattered. Kabul and other major cities were battered and beaten. When writer Christopher Kremmer visited the capital, he found "a demoralized and desperately poor city. The ruins of its buildings stretched for blocks, and people with dead eyes roamed about in tatters." According to one report, the only productive factories in the country were those making artificial limbs, crutches, and wheelchairs for the international aid agencies. Agriculture was devastated too, fields bombed and sown with mines. Taxes on the export of opium had become the mainstay of a war-torn economy that had been extensively criminalized. Heavy fighting continued in the north-east across a wavering zone of destruction, and streams of refugees continued to flee the grinding struggle between the Northern Alliance and the Taliban.[22]

The Taliban's original orientation was profoundly insular. They were deeply suspicious of the apparatus of the modern state, so much so that they destroyed most of its existing institutions. As Gilles Kepel explains, their vision of Afghanistan was simply that of "a community swollen to the dimensions of a country." Accordingly, "their *jihad* was primarily directed against their own society, on which they sought to impose a rigorous moral code: they had no taste for the state or for international politics."[23] This meant that there were serious cultural, political, and ideological differences between the Taliban and al-Qaeda. Bin Laden did not return to Afghanistan at the invitation of the Taliban. The Taliban were parochial, traditional; bin Laden and his associates were much more worldly, even "modern," and the "Afghan Arabs" regarded the Afghans as "unlettered and uncivil."[24] Although bin Laden worked hard to establish good relations with the Taliban – with partial success – he never made any secret of his larger aims. In 1996 he published a "Declaration of *Jihad* against the Americans occupying the lands of the two Holy Places" – Mecca and Medina in Saudi Arabia – in which the Saudi royal family was also indicted for its complicity in continuing to allow infidel troops to be stationed on holy ground. In 1998 another proclamation, issued with other Islamicist groups under the banner of the "World Islamic Front," repeated that "for more than seven years, the US has been occupying the lands of Islam in the holiest of places, the Arabian peninsula, plundering its riches, dictating to its rulers, humiliating its people, terrorizing its neighbours, and turning its bases into a spearhead with which to fight neighbouring Muslim peoples." This was accompanied by a *fatwa*, an injunction to all Muslims "to kill the Americans and their allies, civilians and military" – "Satan's troops and the devil's supporters allied with them" – "in any country in which it is possible to do so."[25] This was completely beyond the horizons of the Taliban. Far from endorsing these edicts their spiritual leader, Mullah Mohammed Omar, was displeased by many of them. In June 1998 he apparently agreed to return bin Laden for trial in Saudi Arabia once a proper legal justification had been formulated by Afghan and Saudi clerics.[26]

Two months later, US embassies in Nairobi and Dar es Salaam were bombed by al-Qaeda. Over 200 people were murdered and more than 4,500 injured in the twin terrorist attacks. In retaliation, the United States launched Operation Infinite Reach and, as Burke observes, this changed everything: but not in the way that the White House intended. Cruise missiles struck a pharmaceutical factory in Khartoum, mistakenly thought to be owned by bin Laden and linked to the production of chemical weapons. The destruction of the factory had a devastating effect on the people of Sudan, who were deprived of affordable drugs to treat malaria, tuberculosis, and other deadly diseases, and of veterinary drugs to kill the parasites that passed through the food chain, a leading cause of infant mortality. Thousands of people died within a year of the attack. All of this intensified regional opposition to America's global dispositions. Cruise missiles also struck six al-Qaeda bases in Afghanistan, and Omar ruled that bin Laden's extradition to Saudi Arabia was now out of the question.[27]

Positions were hardening everywhere. Prompted by the United States, the United Nations Security Council issued a stream of resolutions that expressed grave concern at both the continuing conflict and the intensifying humanitarian crisis in Afghanistan, and demanded that the Taliban "stop providing sanctuary and training for international terrorists." At the end of the following year the Security Council required the Taliban to turn over bin Laden "to a country where he has been indicted" (the United States was now the prime candidate) or face "smart sanctions" directed at their financial resources.[28] These diplomatic maneuvrings heightened the Taliban's sense of isolation and pushed them closer to al-Qaeda. Relations between Omar and bin Laden warmed considerably, and al-Qaeda's pan-Islamic ideology now made considerable headway with the Taliban, who became increasingly outspoken in their criticism of both the United States and Saudi Arabia. None of these measures sensibly diminished the activities of al-Qaeda either. On the contrary, it was almost certainly instrumental in the terrorist attack on an American warship, the USS *Cole*, while it was being refueled in Aden in October 2000. Two months later the United Nations Security Council was even more specific in its response. It deplored "the fact that the Taliban continues to provide safe haven to [O]sama bin Laden and to allow him and others associated with him to operate a network of terrorist training camps from Taliban-controlled territory and to use Afghanistan as a base from which to sponsor international terrorist operations." The Taliban were required to "cease the provision of sanctuary and training for international terrorists," to turn over bin Laden, and "to close all camps where terrorists are trained within the territory under its control."[29] But targeting bin Laden in these ways consolidated his iconic status so that he became a larger-than-life figure for many Muslims – even a hero – which in turn served only to increase his influence with the Taliban.

The Sorcerer's Apprentices

Soon after September 11, Max Boot, a features editor from the *Wall Street Journal*, claimed that Afghanistan was "crying out for the sort of enlightened foreign administration once provided by self-confident Englishmen in jodhpurs and pith helmets," and in Britain's *Independent* Philip Hensher declared that Afghanistan's problem was precisely that it had never been colonized. If only its people "had been subjugated as India was," he sighed.[30] In the face of these bugle calls from both sides of the Atlantic, it is necessary to emphasize that the relentless destruction of Afghanistan that I have summarized in these pages emerged out of a series of intimate engagements with – *not estrangements from* – modern imperial power. "Given to a highly decentralized and localized mode of life, the Afghani people have been subjected to two highly centralized state projects in the past several decades," Mamdani observes, "Soviet-supported Marxism, then CIA-supported Islamicization."[31]

As I have shown, Afghanistan was as much the object of international geopolitical maneuvrings in the late twentieth century as it had been in the nineteenth. Both the Soviet Union and the United States treated Afghanistan as another extra-territorial arena in which to fight the Cold War and, as Charles Hirschkind and Saba Mahmood have argued, Afghanistan was transformed by the role it was recruited to play: "The vast dissemination of arms, military training, the creation of a thriving drug trade with its attendant criminal activity, and all this in circumstances of desperate poverty, had a radical impact on the conditions of moral and political action for the people in the region."[32] By the 1990s Russia and the United States had moved on to a new "Great Game" in which the stakes were those of political economy rather than ideology. Each maneuvered to construct and control oil and gas pipelines from the Caspian Basin to the Indian Ocean. They both had considerable interests in securing Afghanistan on their own terms, and between 1994 and 1997 Russia, together with Iran and other central Asian states, supported the Northern Alliance, while the United States, together with its Saudi and Pakistani allies, tacitly supported the Taliban in an attempt to secure pipeline contracts for a consortium involving US-based Unocal and Saudi Arabia's Delta Oil Company.[33] These involvements were abruptly terminated in 1998 when al-Qaeda bombed US embassies in East Africa and the United States attacked al-Qaeda bases in Afghanistan.

But what is all too easily lost from view in grand narratives of this sort – one Great Game dissolving into another – is the multiple, conditional, but none the less powerful agency of those whose destinies these foreign players sought to manipulate; their intrigues and interventions sustained what Suchandana Chatterjee calls "a consciousness that was antipathetic, if not absolutely belligerent, towards colonial rule."[34] Several commentators have argued that the United States unwittingly "spawned a monster" through its entanglements: not only the Taliban but also the hydra-headed al-Qaeda. The language of the monstrous is significant, because colonial imaginaries typically let monsters loose in the far-away. But we need to remember that they also mirror metropolitan conceits. As Jasbir Puar and Amit Rai have shown, "discourses that mobilize monstrosity as a screen for otherness are always involved in circuits of normalizing power as well." In this case, they tied the figure of the Islamic terrorist, through a series of displaced racializations and sexualizations, to the counter-figure of the white, heterosexual patriot.[35] And yet, as Anthony Barnett properly reminds us, the repugnant terrorism of al-Qaeda "was not just an evil 'other' that the West could triumphantly eradicate thereby vindicating its own goodness." The fact of the matter is that "it was, and is, *also* our own Frankenstein."[36] The added emphasis is mine, and it carries a double charge. The United States was indeed centrally involved in the rise of a violent Islamicism in Afghanistan, and its connections with bin Laden and others cannot be conveniently forgotten or wished away. But those who think that September 11 can be laid at the door of the American political and military establishment alone need to remember that, however great those provocations, bin Laden and al-Qaeda were the result of more than the American pursuit of its own "Great Game." There is certainly no absolute opposition between "us" and "them" – the lines of filiation and connection are too complicated and too mutable for that – and, as I have tried to show, many other threads, at once ideological and material, were woven into the varied articulations of Islamicism. Those who enlisted in the civil wars in Afghanistan, from inside its borders and beyond them, were not pawns on the chessboards of the United States, Pakistan, and Saudi Arabia, any more than those who resisted British and Russian imperialism in the nineteenth century were pawns on Curzon's lordly chessboard. These fighters had their own agency: conditional, as I've said, but none the less irreducible to the determinations of other states. Similarly, the terrorism of al-Qaeda cannot be reduced to the manipulations of the CIA (or the ISI) or the short-lived triumph of the Taliban, significant though each of these were. It has its own objectives, and in appealing to hundreds, perhaps thousands, of people around the world the local and the transnational are woven into its operations in complex and contingent ways.

4 "Civilization" and "Barbarism"

There is no document of civilization which is not at the same time a document of barbarism.

Walter Benjamin, *Theses on the Philosophy of History*

The Visible and the Invisible

WITHIN hours of the attacks on New York City and Washington on September 11 the US government named Osama bin Laden as its prime suspect.[1] Nineteen young men involved in the hijacking of the four aircraft were identified. They were all Arab nationals. None were Afghan; most of them were Saudi citizens. They were all linked to al-Qaeda. Faced with the sudden irruption of *jihad* in the heart of America – "the homeland" – America declared its own holy war. This is no exaggeration. The sanctuary, even the sanctity, of the Republic had been breached by the terrorist attacks. Almost immediately President George W. Bush announced that "barbarians had declared war" on America. In the days and weeks that followed he repeatedly described the "civilized world" rallying to the American flag and what at first he called its "crusade" against transnational terrorism. It was, as he admitted later, an unfortunate choice of words, but it was also a revealing one. For the language of the president, his inner circle of advisers, and many media commentators was increasingly apocalyptic. They proclaimed that America had embarked on "a war to save civilization" that was presented as a series of Manichean moral absolutes: good against evil, "either you are with us or you are with the terrorists."[2] The Afghan front of this war was originally launched as an extension of Operation Infinite Reach (above, p. 43) and codenamed Operation Infinite Justice, whose eschatology also offended Muslims since they believe that only Allah can dispense infinite justice. The president constantly fulminated against "the Evil One" and the "evil-doers" and once the initial assault on Afghanistan was over, in an unmistakable echo of President Reagan's characterization of the USSR as an "evil empire," Bush posited an extended "axis of evil" made up of "regimes that sponsor terror": Iran, Iraq, and North Korea.[3]

These responses mimed the rhetoric of the Cold War with uncanny precision. As David Campbell has shown, the Cold War mapped a series of boundaries between "civilization" and "barbarism" whose inscriptions had performative force. They conjured up not only an architecture of enmity but what Campbell calls "a geography of evil." During the 2000 presidential election campaign, Bush had recalled growing up in a world where there was no doubt about the identity of America's "Other." "It was 'us' versus 'them,' and it was clear who ['they'] were," he said. "Today, we're not so sure who the 'they' are: but we know they're there." After September 11 Bush was sure who "they" were, and his new-found certainty – as Campbell also points out – reactivated the interpretative dispositions of the Cold War: "the sense of endangerment ascribed to all the activities of the other, the fear of internal challenge and subversion, the tendency to militarize all responses, and the willingness to draw the lines of superiority and inferiority between us and them."[4]

This is hardly surprising. As Jacques Derrida notes, September 11 was, in part, a "distant effect of the Cold War itself," and its genealogy can be traced back to US support for the *mujaheddin* against the Soviet intervention in Afghanistan.[5] But these are also the dispositions of colonial power, aggrandized and emboldened, set in motion by imaginative geographies that work silently to sever its "others" from the situations and circumstances that shape *their* dispositions. This was precisely why one commentator questioned Bush's Manichean cartography with such passionate lucidity:

[B]ombast about evil individuals doesn't help in understanding anything. Even vile and murderous actions come from somewhere, and if they are extreme in character we are not wrong to look for extreme situations. It does not mean that those who do them had no choice, are not answerable, far from it. But there is sentimentality too in ascribing what we don't understand to "evil"; it lets us off the hook, it allows us to avoid the question of what, if anything, we can *recognize* in the destructive act of another. If we react without that self-questioning, we change nothing.[6]

And yet that was precisely the point of the geography of evil – and fear – activated by Bush's rhetoric. It was a cartography designed to bring relief to "us" while bringing "them" *into* relief; at once a therapeutic and a vengeful gesture, its object was to reveal the face of the other *as* other. It was, as Stephen Bronner points out, a classic illustration of an argument originally proposed by the deeply conservative German philosopher Carl Schmitt, who claimed that the fundamental principle of politics was the distinction between "us" and "them," "friend" and "enemy": the sharper the distinction, so he believed, the more likely the success. I doubt that Bush was aware of the intellectual lineage, but Schmitt's ghost seems to stalk the corridors of Republican power (in several ways, as we will see), and Bush's strategy depended on techniques of projection, hysteria, and exaggeration that would have been familiar to Schmitt and his heirs. What is significant, however, is that Schmitt's writings sought to fuse political philosophy with political theology, because Bush's Manichean map of "the Enemy" as "Evil" cloaked its cartographers in righteousness.[7] If those who perpetrated the atrocities of September 11 could be seen as Lucifer's messengers, as composer Karlheinz Stockhausen suggested, those who set themselves against formless evil were then ineluctably cast as messengers of the divine. American troops were no longer fighting enemies; they were casting out demons.[8]

This theocratic image was refracted in a thousand different ways, but time and time again in the holy communion of the colonial present it oscillated between light and darkness, between the visible and the invisible. "To this bright capital," novelist Salman Rushdie wrote from New York, "the forces of invisibility have dealt a dreadful blow."[9] As Bush himself declared, "this is a conflict with opponents who believe they are invisible. Yet they are mistaken." To demonstrate their mistake – to *make* them visible – involved a number of different measures, and I want to consider these in turn.

Territorialization, Targets, and Technoculture

The first move was to identify al-Qaeda with Afghanistan – to fold the one into the other – so that it could become the object of a conventional military campaign. This entailed two peculiar cartographic performances. The first was a performance of sovereignty through which the ruptured space of Afghanistan could be simulated as a coherent state. As Simon Dalby explains, "the cartography of violence in the places that are still designated Afghanistan, despite the absence of most of the normal attributes of statehood, illustrates the continuing fixation of a simple cartographic description in circumstances where sovereignty has to be intensely simulated to render the categories of political action meaningful."[10] The second was a performance of territory through which the fluid networks of al-Qaeda could be fixed in a bounded space. I describe these as peculiar performances with good reason. Afghanistan was, in Washington's terms, a "failed state," and its sovereignty was thus rendered conditional (not least by the United States itself). And al-Qaeda is part of a distributed network of loosely articulated groups supposedly operating in over 40 countries, a network of networks with neither capital nor center, so that its "radical non-territoriality" renders any conventional military response problematic.[11] And yet, if one of the most immediate consequences of September 11 was a visibly heightened projection of America as a national space – closing its airspace, sealing its borders, and contracting itself to "the homeland"[12] – then its counterpart was surely the construction of a bounded locus of transnational terrorism. The networks in which al-Qaeda was involved, rhizomatic and capillary, were folded into the fractured but no less visibly bounded space of Afghanistan. It was an extraordinary accomplishment to convince a sufficient public constituency that these transnational terrorist networks could be rolled into the carpet-bombing of Afghanistan. Yet to commentators like Charles Krauthammer it was axiomatic. "The terrorists need a territorial base of sovereign protection," he wrote. "If bin Laden was behind this, then Afghanistan is our enemy."[13]

Terry Jones followed this principle of territorialization to its absurdist, Pythonesque conclusion: the British bombing Dublin, New York, and Boston to wage war on the IRA.[14] Derrida rehearsed the same deconstructive argument:

> The United States and Europe . . . are also sanctuaries, places of training or formation and information for all the "terrorists" of the world. No geography, no "territorial" determination is thus pertinent any longer for locating the seat of these new technologies of transmission or aggression. . . . The relationship between . . . *terra*, territory and terror has changed, and it is necessary to know that this is because of . . . technoscience.[15]

All this may be granted. But the Bush administration's territorial logic was not an awkward miscalculation: it derived from the very idea of waging a war on *terrorism*. William Pfaff was right to say that "Afghanistan has been substituted for terrorism, because Afghanistan is accessible to military power, and terrorism is not."[16] And yet even this is only part of the answer; territorialization was more than an instrumental expediency. Frédéric Mégret showed that by constructing its response to September 11 as a *war* on terrorism the United States necessarily co-constructed other *states* as its adversaries.[17] Bush's "axis of evil" projected this political geography beyond Afghanistan, and in so doing it – not incidentally – fulfilled the cartographic imperatives of the neo-conservative "Project for the New American Century." The Project had been established in 1997, and its protagonists included key members of Bush's new administration: Vice-President Richard Cheney, Secretary of Defense Donald Rumsfeld, and Under-Secretaries Paul Wolfowitz (Defense) and John Bolton (State). In January 1998 the Project wrote to President Clinton urging him to undertake political and military action aimed "at the removal of Saddam Hussein's regime from power." The argument was restated in the Project's *Rebuilding America's Defenses* (2000), which claimed that the imperative for a substantial American military presence in the Gulf "transcends the issue of the regime of Saddam Hussein." The review's authors conceded that the process of military expansion required to secure American global hegemony would be a long one without "some catastrophic and catalyzing event – like a new Pearl Harbor."[18] September 11 was just that event. If Afghanistan was now, perforce, to be the first target, it was clear that Iraq would be the second. A territorial logic – what Neil Smith would call the raw *geography* of American Empire[19] – was not incidental but integral to the historical horizon of the Project. Indeed, within 24 hours of the attacks on New York City and Washington, Rumsfeld argued that Iraq should be a "principal target" of the "first round" of the war on terrorism. The connection between the Islamicist al-Qaeda and Saddam Hussein's secular Ba'athist regime was stupefyingly opaque: bin Laden's immediate response to Iraq's occupation of Kuwait had been to offer to raise an army of *mujaheddin* to repel the invaders (above, p. 38). Nevertheless, Bush directed the Pentagon to prepare options for an invasion of Iraq on the same day that he endorsed the plan for a military assault on Afghanistan.

Within five days of the terrorist attacks, American combat and support aircraft had been dispatched to the Middle East and the Indian Ocean, and a large naval task force had put to sea. One by one, under American pressure, all six neighboring states closed their borders with Afghanistan. Refugees fleeing the coming conflict were trapped, and the lifelines of international aid on which so many of them depended were snapped one by one. Invoking the terms of earlier United Nations resolutions, Bush demanded that the Taliban close all al-Qaeda training camps and hand over its leaders. "These demands are not open to negotiation or discussion," he warned: "Hand over the terrorists, or suffer their fate." The Taliban temporized; their leadership condemned the attacks on America but insisted on evidence that bin Laden had been involved in them. On October 7 US air strikes were launched against Kabul and Kandahar in what Bush called "carefully targeted actions designed to disrupt the use of Afghanistan as a base of terrorist operations, and to attack the military capability of the Taliban regime." Two days later the Pentagon announced that US forces had achieved "aerial supremacy" over Afghanistan (it could have said exactly the same on September 10, of course, but braggadocio knows no bounds).[20]

These twin cartographic performances had other consequences. Much of the work of territorialization was conducted in a technical register that was always more than technical: it was techno*cultural*. Advanced systems of intelligence, interception, and surveillance were mobilized to produce an imaginative geography of al-Qaeda and the Taliban in Afghanistan. On October 5 a Keyhole photo-electronic satellite had been launched to join six other imaging satellites already in orbit for the US military. The circulation of this imagery was restricted, but not only for reasons of national security. After reports of heavy civilian casualties in Jalalabad appeared in the press, the US National Imagery and Mapping Agency (NIMA), which provides combat support to the Department of Defense, bought exclusive rights on a month-by-month basis to all commercial images of Afghanistan taken by Ikonos-2, an advanced civilian satellite owned by Space Imaging of Denver, whose client base included many news organizations. The resolution level of Ikonos-2 was as much as ten times inferior to that of the military satellites, but it could resolve objects less than 1 meter across in black and white and 4 meters in color, which would have been sufficient to identify bodies on the ground. While the Defense Department has the authority to exercise shutter control over civilian satellites, any such order is subject to legal challenge; the decision to use commercial powers to restrict public access to the images circumvented that possibility. The spaces of visibility constructed in this technical register were thus also spaces of carefully constructed *in*visibility, and Reporters Sans Frontières protested that this was censorship for political rather than military reasons.[21]

Throughout the first phase of high-level aerial bombardment the conflict remained a "war without witnesses" and its narrative progress was punctuated less by first-hand reporting than by long-range photography. As journalist Maggie O'Kane put it, she and her colleagues could only "stand on mountain tops and watch for puffs of smoke." They were denied access to American troops in the field "to a greater degree than in any previous war involving US military forces," Robert Hickey reported, in large measure because the Pentagon feared "that images and descriptions of civilian bomb casualties – people already the victims of famine, poverty, drought, oppression and brutality – would erode public support in the US and elsewhere in the world."[22] This was in striking contrast to the live, close-up coverage of the attacks on the World Trade Center and the Pentagon itself, and of the minute-by-minute attempts at rescue and recovery at "Ground Zero." Involvement and engagement saturated one theater of operations; detachment and disengagement ruled the other. The objective of news management was to produce a space within which those held responsible for these attacks would appear as nothing more than points on a map or nodes in a network: in short, as targets.[23] This was not confined to the political and military apparatus, of course. Many of these restrictions were self-imposed by the media (or their owners), and it would be foolish to minimize the complicity and the jingoism of many American media organizations.[24]

Those most directly involved in fighting the air war were also disposed to see Afghanistan as an abstract, de-corporealized space. Weeks before they took to the skies, American pilots had flown virtual sorties over "Afghanistan," a high-resolution three-dimensional computer space produced through a mission rehearsal system called Topscene (Tactical Operational Scene). It combined aerial photographs, satellite images, and intelligence information to produce a landscape so detailed that, according to Michael Macedonia, the technical director of the US army's Simulation Training and Instrumentation Command, "pilots could visualize flying from ground level up to 12,000 meters at speeds up to 2,250 km/hour," and plot the best approach to "designated targets." In late modern warfare the interface between computerized simulation and computerized mission had become so wafer-thin, he said, that from the pilot's point of view "a real combat mission feels much like a simulated one." Zygmunt Bauman described the likely consequences: "Remote as they are from their 'targets,' scurrying over those they hit too fast to witness the devastation they cause and the blood they spill, the pilots-turned-computer-operators hardly ever have a chance of looking their victims in the face and to survey the human misery they have sowed."[25]

These are easy jibes to make from a desk, but the media did much to confirm – and, for that matter, celebrate – their accuracy. To members of the 391st Fighter Squadron, "gods of the night sky" as Mark Bowden, the author of *Black Hawk Down*, hailed them, combat was "a procedure, deliberate and calculated, more cerebral than visceral." As they performed their grotesque "Kabul-ki dance" over the already eviscerated Afghan capital, Bowden suggested that their main bodily concern was whether they could endure such inhumanly long hours in the air without soiling themselves. I doubt that they were so inured, at least in their private moments of reflection. But what is significant is the imagery that Bowden used to represent their experience to his (primarily) American audience. Fusing the media and the military into the promoters of a visual spectacular, his language at once sanitized and legitimized through its own optical detachment, so that war seemed to become a purely technical exercise of calibration (figure 4.1).[26]

Modern cartographic reason, including its electronic, mediatized extensions, relies on these high-level, disembodied abstractions to produce the illusion of an authorizing master-subject. It deploys both a discourse of objectivity – so that elevation secures the higher Truth – and a discourse of object-ness that reduces the world to a series of objects in a visual plane. Bombs then rain down on co-ordinates on a grid, letters on a map, on 34.518611N, 69.15222 E, on K-A-B-U-L; but not on the city of Kabul, its buildings already devastated, its population already terrorized. Ground truth vanishes in the ultimate "God-trick," whose terrible vengeance depends on making its objects visible and its subjects invisible. Allen Feldman usefully brings these claims together and wires them to the imaginative geographies of Orientalism:

> Saturated areal bombing in Afghanistan . . . is a new Orientalism, the perceptual apparatus by which we make the eastern Other visible. Afghanis are being held accountable for the hidden histories and hidden geographies that are presumed to have assaulted America on September 11. . . . We displace our need for a transparent explanation of the World Trade Center attack onto our panoptical bomb-sights/sites that have turned Afghanistan into an open-air tomb of collateral damage.[27]

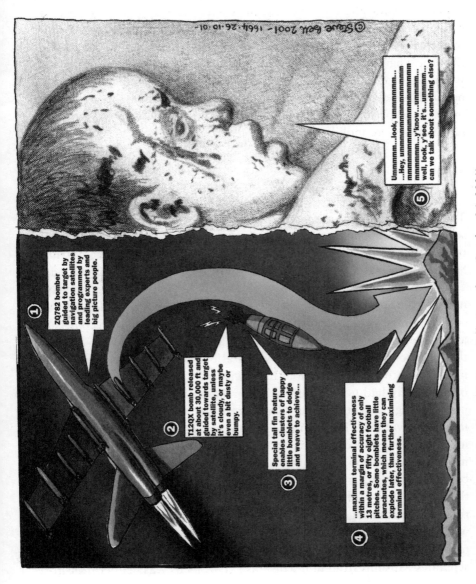

Figure 4.1 "Optical detachment" (Steve Bell, *Guardian*, October 26, 2001)

But "making the enemy visible" was more than a technocultural achievement, and it required the production and performance of other imaginative geographies. This became all the more urgent once the next, combined, air and ground phase of the assault was under way and reporters and camera-crews were able to cover the intimate effects of the war. "In order to recognize the enemy," Slavoj Žižek explains, "one has to 'schematize' the logical figure of the Enemy, providing it with the concrete features which will make it into an appropriate target of hatred and struggle." And, as he emphasizes, such recognition of "the enemy" is always at once imaginative *and* performative.[28] To this end, as I must now show, two main schematics were mobilized.

Deadly Messengers

The most common gesture was to represent the terrorists as deadly messengers heralding an imminent "clash of civilizations." This thesis had its origins in an essay by Orientalist Bernard Lewis, which political scientist Samuel Huntington had recast in a more general form.[29] Huntington argued that the question of collective identity – "Who are we?" which is made to turn on "Who are they?" – had assumed a special force in the contemporary world because everyday life had increasingly become subject to the upheavals and uncertainties of a globalizing modernity. He saw this question as a fundamentally cultural one whose answer was almost invariably provided by religion. In his view, the supposedly secular world of modernity had not triumphed over religion but, on the contrary, was now reaping the whirlwind of "God's revenge" in the form of a global religious revivalism.[30] Religion was the primary basis on which Huntington identified "seven or eight" major "civilizations" – the hesitation, Hegelian in its condescension, was over Africa – and on which he explained the conflicts emerging along the "fault-lines" between them. Although this thesis was supposed to be a generalization of Lewis's polemic on "the roots of Muslim rage," it had precisely the same destination. "The overwhelming majority of fault-line conflicts," Huntington concluded, "have taken place along the boundary looping across Eurasia and Africa that separates Muslims from non-Muslims." This locus was neither transitory nor contingent. It derived from what Huntington saw as "the Muslim propensity toward violent conflict." "Wherever one looks along the perimeter of Islam," he wrote, "Muslims have problems living peaceably with their neighbours." Indeed, he claimed that since the Iranian revolution in 1979 that toppled the Shah and installed an Islamicist regime in his place, a "quasi-war" had been in progress between Islam and the West. It was, so he said, wrong to think this was the work of a minority of "fundamentalists" whose "use of violence is rejected by the great majority of moderate Muslims." "This may be true," he conceded, "but evidence to support it is lacking." Huntington's skepticism produced a chillingly absolutist conclusion. "The underlying problem for the West is not Islamic fundamentalism," he declared. "It is Islam, a different civilization whose people are convinced of the superiority of their culture and are obsessed with the inferiority of their power."[31]

These are at once extraordinary and dangerous claims. They are extraordinary because they erase the ways in which cultures, far from being bounded totalities, interpenetrate and entangle with one another. Culture, as Said has reminded us, has always been syncretic. "What culture today has not had long, intimate, and extraordinarily rich contacts with other cultures?" In refusing this question, Huntington reaffirms the myth of the formation of "the West" as a process of auto-production, innocent of violence and immune from engagements with other cultures.[32] The victims of September 11 themselves give the lie to these claims. Even in the World Trade Center, those murdered by al-Qaeda were not all masters of the universe. They included "Puerto Rican secretaries, Sri Lankan cleaners, Indian clerks and Filipino restaurant workers as well as Japanese corporate executives and Italian-American bond traders. . . . Fifteen hundred Muslims came to pray in the building's mosque every Friday."[33] As Paul Gilroy wrote,

> The ordinary dead came from every corner and culture, north and south. Their troubling manifestation of the south inside the north . . . destabilizes the Manichean assumptions that divide the world tidily into "us" and "them." Under the profane and cosmopolitan constellation their trans-local lives and ethnic affiliations construct for us, remembrance of them might even be made to yield up a symbol of how exposure to difference, to alterity, can amount to rather more than the experience of loss with which it has been so easily and habitually associated. Their untidy, representative diversity might then be valued as . . . a civic asset that corrupts the sham unity of supposedly integral civilizations.[34]

Claims like Huntington's are also dangerous because, in proposing that the world is riven into implacable and opposing blocs, in fabricating that "sham unity," they participate in a "word politics" that opens some rhetorical spaces and closes others, which in turn prepares the ground for the construction of its architecture of enmity as material fact. That is, of course, precisely why these claims are so often activated in moments of crisis: as Shapiro puts it, they enable the state to construct "the worlds of danger to its coherence," to conjure a menacing Other that *requires* its own consolidation as a unitary and cohesive master-subject.[35]

In the wake of September 11, this imaginative geography helped to define and mobilize a series of publics within which popular assent to – indeed, a demand for – war assumed immense power. For many commentators, the attack on America was indeed a "clash of civilizations." In an interview Huntington himself argued that bin Laden wanted to unleash a war "between Islam and the West," and in a subsequent essay described the events of September 11 as an escalation "of previous patterns of violence involving Muslims."[36] Although he now connected the rise of Islamicism to the repressions of domestic governments and the repercussions of US foreign policy in the Middle East, other commentators used Huntington's repeated characterizations of Muslims and "Muslim wars" to degrade the very idea of Islam as a civilization. To them, the Islamic world – in the singular – was degenerate, a throwback to feudalism, and hence incapable of reaching an accommodation with the modern world (no less singular but prototypically American). This was Orientalism with a vengeance, in which the progressive "West" was set against an immobile "Islam" that was, if not a barbarism, then the breeding-ground of barbarians.[37]

For military historian Sir John Keegan, for example, Huntington did not go far enough. He had overlooked a fundamental difference in ways of waging war:

> Westerners fight face to face, in stand-up battle, and go on until one side or the other gives in. They choose the crudest of weapons available, and use them with appalling violence, but observe what to non-Westerners may well seem curious rules of honour. Orientals, by contrast, shrink from pitched battle, which they often deride as a sort of game, preferring ambush, surprise, treachery and deceit as the best way to overcome an enemy.

On September 11, he continued, the "Oriental tradition" was reasserted with a vengeance. "Arabs, appearing suddenly out of empty space like their desert raider ancestors, assaulted the heartlands of Western power in a terrifying surprise raid and did appalling damage." The image of Timothy McVeigh, who was responsible for the terrorist carnage in Oklahoma City in 1995, as a latterday Lawrence of Arabia is hardly compelling, but in Keegan's view the appropriate response to September 11 was to reassert the supremacy of the "Western tradition": "to launch massive retaliation and to persist relentlessly." He explained that the difference between the two modes of warfare had its roots in a much deeper divide. "Peoples of the desert and the empty spaces," Keegan insisted, do not exist on "the same level of civilization" as those of the West (I am not making this up) and – even as he protested that he was not deploying stereotypes – he drew a grotesque distinction between the "predatory, destructive Orientals" (all of them) and the "creative, productive" peoples of the West (all of them).[38] Keegan's view of "Western" warfare was not only ethnocentric; it was also hopelessly dated. Contemporary wars are, in a vital sense, nomadic not sedentary. Here, for example, is Zygmunt Bauman:

> The new global powers rest their superiority over the settled population on the speed of their own movement; their own ability to descend from nowhere without notice and vanish again without warning; their ability to travel light and not to bother with the kind of belongings which confine the mobility and the maneuvring potential of sedentary people.[39]

It is only necessary to reflect on the reluctance of the US to commit its own troops to ground offensives – let alone "pitched battles" – in Afghanistan and elsewhere and its reliance instead on spectacular bombardments from the air, to realize the absurdity of Keegan's characterizations.

A more sophisticated but no less rebarbative argument was advanced in the *Newsweek* essay that I cited earlier, in which September 11 was attributed to a collision between modernity and much of the Islamic world. Zakaria (a former student of Huntington's) argued that Indonesia, Pakistan, and Bangladesh had all "mixed Islam and modernity with some success"; after Indonesia's assault on East Timor, one wonders what would count as failure in his vision of the world. But "for the Arab world" – which Zakaria took to include Iran, a lazy generalization that betrayed his misunderstanding of the cultural history of the region – "modernity has been one failure after another." This collective inability to reach an accommodation with modernity was made even more humiliating, so he said, when juxtaposed with "the success of Israel." Again, "success" was unquestioned: Israel's modernization has not been achieved without extra-ordinary American aid, and the Palestinian people have paid an equally exorbitant price for that "success." But such matters were side issues to Zakaria. As a direct result of these failures and humiliations, "in Iran, Egypt, Syria, Iraq, Jordan, the occupied territories and the Persian Gulf" he claimed that "the resurgence of Islamic fundamentalism is virulent, and a raw anti-Americanism seems to be everywhere." Then: *"This is the land of suicide bombers, flag-burners and fiery mullahs."* In one astonishing sentence the various, vibrant cultures of the region were fixed and frozen into one diabolical landscape. One might just as easily (and accurately) say that America is the land of serial killers, neo-Nazi militias, and Christian fundamentalists.[40]

Reductive maneuvers like Zakaria's set in motion a metonymic relation-ship between territorialization and terrorism, in which each endlessly stands for the other: "terrorism" is made to mean these territories, and these territories are made to mean terrorism. Even as Bush and his European allies insisted that their quarrel was not with Islam, therefore, and even as the White House worked to include Islamic states in its international coalition and to reach out to American Muslims, "the clash of civiliza-tions" and its mutations served to confirm that America was engaged in a holy war against its enemy – a mirror-image of bin Laden's *jihad* – and to imply that, as geographer John Agnew put it, "vice and virtue have geo-graphical addresses":

> Bin Laden's is a cultural war, not an economic one. He does not worry about the starvation of the Afghan masses among whom he lives. The economy of the Middle East is definitely not his priority, as long as he can exploit credit card fraud and his inherited investments to fund his political activities. His writings and pronouncements do not give pride of place to the Palestinian struggle. . . . Bin Laden is the Samuel Huntington of the Arab world. . . . He offers a mirror-image security mapping of the world to that offered by Huntington and other prophets of the "clash of civilizations." Like the Western pundits, bin Laden collapses ontology into geography, the key move of the modern geopolitical imagination.[41]

But this is not only or even quintessentially a modern gesture. In a video broadcast on al-Jazeera in October 2001 bin Laden invoked the classical Islamic distinction between the House of Islam, where Islamic govern-ments rule and Islamic law prevails, and the House of War, whose lands are inhabited by infidels. For bin Laden, the world was still divided into

Figure 4.2   "The clash of fundamentalisms" (Mr Hepburn). This montage of Bush and bin Laden was used as the cover image for Tariq Ali's *The Clash of Fundamentalisms*

two zones: "one of faith where there is no hypocrisy, and another of infidelity." The parallels with Bush's own Manichean geography explain why Tariq Ali was able to describe this as a "clash of fundamentalisms" (figure 4.2). Each "perpetuates the anti-modern impulse of aggression and reinforces the stubborn nature of cultural opposition."[42]

Spaces of the Exception

The other schematic deployed to identify "the enemy" confirmed this as a holy war, but its imaginative geography had a radically different address. In a critical reflection on the unmarked powers of democratic politics, which was in part provoked by Schmitt's political theology, Italian philosopher Giorgio Agamben insisted that the formation of a political community turns not on inclusion – on "belonging" – but on exclusion. His argument radicalizes the imaginative geographies that Said described in *Orientalism*. In accentuating their performative force – and their coercive power – Agamben drew attention to the figure of *homo sacer* ("sacred man"). *Homo sacer* was a position conferred by Roman law upon those who could not be sacrificed according to ritual (because they were outside divine law: their deaths were of no value to the gods) but who could still be killed with impunity (because they were also outside juridical law: their lives were of no value to their contemporaries). Agamben connects this position to Schmitt's key claim: "Sovereign is he who decides the exception." For Agamben, these wretched figures were subjected to a biopolitics in which they were marked as outcasts through the operation of sovereign power.[43] For my present purposes the significance of *homo sacer* is threefold.

First, *homo sacer* emerged at the point where the law suspended itself, its absence falling as a shadow over a zone not merely of exclusion but a zone of abandonment that Agamben called the *space of the exception*. What matters is not only those who are marginalized but also, crucially, those who are placed beyond the margins. The exception – *ex-capere* – is literally that which is "taken outside" and, as this suggests, it is the result of a process of boundary promulgation *and* boundary perturbation. The juridico-political ordering of space is not only a "taking of land," Agamben continues, but above all "a 'taking of the outside,' an exception." As Andrew Norris explains, "the [sovereign] decision and the exception it concerns are [thus] never decisively placed within or without the legal system *as they are precisely the moving border between the two*." The mapping of this juridico-political space requires a topology that can fold its propriety into its perversity – a sort of Möbius strip marking "a zone of indistinction" – since, in Agamben's own words, "the exception is that which cannot be included in the whole of which it is a member and cannot be a member of the whole in which it is always already included." In effect, *homines sacri* are included as the objects of sovereign power but excluded from being its subjects. They are the mute bearers of what Agamben calls "bare life," deprived of language and the political life that language makes possible.[44]

Secondly, this paradoxical spacing – for it is an operative act – is performed through relays of delegations. While "the sovereign is the one with respect to whom all men are potentially *homines sacri*," Agamben insisted that *"homo sacer is the one with respect to whom all men act as sovereigns."* Their actions constantly enact a threshold that can neither be maintained nor eliminated – "a passage that cannot be completed" – and its instantiation and instability are sustained through multiple iterations that reach far beyond (and below) the pinnacle of sovereign power.[45]

Thirdly, as the term *homo sacer* implies, these spacings are sanctioned not only by the juridical (which is thus not the only basis for sovereign power) *but also by the sacred*: "an invisible imperative that inaugurates authority." Agamben accounts for "the proximity between the sphere of sovereignty and the sphere of the sacred" by arguing that "sacredness" is "the originary form of the inclusion of bare life in the juridical order." "To have exchanged a juridico-political phenomenon (*homo sacer*'s capacity to be killed but not sacrificed) for a genuinely religious phenomenon is," so he claims, "the root of the equivocations that have marked studies both of the sacred and of sovereignty in our time."[46]

This is a highly abstract philosophico-historical argument, and I have cruelly abbreviated Agamben's presentation of it. Some critics have urged caution about its purchase – how can Roman law be made to bear on our own times? – but in a fundamental sense this is precisely Agamben's point. His is an argument about the *metaphysics* of power. My own aims are more limited, however, and while I will refer to Agamben's arguments in a series of concrete cases throughout the discussions that follow I make no claims about their foundational importance (but I acknowledge that this apparent modesty introduces its own problems). Here I want to suggest, like several other commentators, that during the assault on Afghanistan and its aftermath – which, let me emphasize again, the alliance between neo-conservatives and evangelical Christians validated as much by the sacred as the juridical: America's "holy war" – Taliban fighters and al-Qaeda terrorists, Afghan refugees and civilians, were all regarded as *homines sacri*.

In November 2001 thousands of Taliban troops were captured in an operation directed by the Fifth US Special Forces Group around Kunduz. Four hundred of them were taken to Qala-i-Jhangi fortress on the outskirts of Mazar-i-Sharif, a town once before and now again ruled by Abdul

Rashid Dostum and his Jimbish-i-Milli, the second largest group in the Northern Alliance. When their Northern Alliance guards started to tie their hands together, the prisoners apparently feared they were about to be executed and a revolt broke out. American airstrikes were called in, and missiles and bombs pulverized the building; British SAS and US Special Forces troops then arrived to direct a ferocious ground assault by Northern Alliance militias. When the dust finally settled, reporter Luke Harding found "a death scene that Dante or Bosch might have conjured up" (figure 4.3). International law requires a proportionate military response to such incidents: "Instead there was an avalanche of death from the sky." Several hundred of those who died still had their hands tied.[47] Thousands more Taliban captives were sent to another prison compound at Shiberghan. They were loaded into sealed freight containers and the trucks left to stand in the sun for several days. Finally they left under the escort of Northern Alliance militias. "The prisoners, many of whom were dying of thirst and asphyxiation, started banging on the side of the trucks," George Monbiot reported. "Dostum's men stopped the convoy and machine-gunned the containers." By the end of the journey as many as 2,000–3,000 of the prisoners were dead, some from lack of air and water, others from their wounds. Their bodies were hurriedly buried in unmarked mass graves apparently under the supervision of US troops. The stench of secrecy that continues to surround these episode and the lack of importance attached to their investigation are in stark contrast to official responses to the deaths of coalition troops from so-called "friendly fire." In April 2002, for example, two US pilots attached to the 332nd Air Expeditionary Group mistook ground fire from a Canadian training exercise near Kandahar for a hostile attack. They released a laser-guided bomb in response, and four Canadian soldiers were killed and eight others wounded. Within one week of the incident a joint US–Canadian inquiry was in session, and within three months of its report the pilots had been charged with involuntary manslaughter, aggravated assault, and dereliction of duty. The difference makes it hard to avoid the conclusion that the Taliban troops were summarily dispatched as so many *homines sacri*. As journalist Jonathan Freedman pointedly asked, how can any of this be reconciled with international law on the treatment of prisoners of war?[48]

Sir John Keegan had no time for such questions, and briskly defended the summary execution of the "Afghan Arabs." If they surrendered, he demanded, where could they be sent? While "a desert island would be the best solution," a more immediate expedient was at hand:

Figure 4.3 Northern Alliance fighter at Mazar-i-Sharif, November 2001
(AP Photo/Darko Bandic)

Mr Rumsfeld, in his recent statements, has made it clear that swift, local brutality may cause the problem to disappear. Better not to speculate about the detail. We are dealing with the modern equivalent of pirates or bandits, whose fate was sealed historically by peremptory measures. That may be the best way out.[49]

So that's all right then. But even Rumsfeld drew back from endorsing this as a concerted course of action and, as it happens, he hit upon Keegan's alternative solution.

The first stage was to define many of the fighters who were detained by US troops not as enemy soldiers but as "unlawful combatants." In Žižek's terms, they constituted "the political Enemy excluded from the political arena" who, by virtue of this exception, were deemed beyond the scope of international law. Prisoners of a war on terrorism who were not thereby prisoners of war, the protections of the Geneva Conventions were summarily withdrawn from them. Amnesty International objected that the US military commissions to be set up to try the detainees were discriminatory: they allowed a lower standard of evidence than federal courts (including hearsay) and provided no right of appeal to an independent and impartial court. They were not independent of the executive, which had the right to name those to be tried by the commissions, to appoint the members of the commissions, and to make the final decision, so that it was exceptionally prejudicial for the president and his Secretary of Defense to refer repeatedly to the detainees as "killers" and "terrorists" before any trial or judicial determination.[50]

The second stage was to mark the "extra-territoriality" of these detainees by transporting many of them to a "non-place," at once outside Afghanistan and outside the continental United States (and so beyond the reach of US law). Not quite Keegan's "desert island," this was Camp X-Ray within the US naval base at Guantánamo Bay on Cuba. The subject position of these captives had its origins in the statements of Bush and Rumsfeld, but it was reiterated through the delegated actions of their agents. The status of the detainees was expressed with brutal concision by a staff writer from the Florida *St Petersburg Times* who witnessed the arrival of the first contingent at Guantánamo Bay. As soon as the heavy transport plane comes to a stop, he wrote, "the freak show begins." The manacled men, in blacked-out goggles and ear-muffs, white surgical masks and bright orange jumpsuits, shuffle slowly down the ramp. "The detainees don't look natural," he reported: "They look like giant bright orange flies."[51] The dehumanizing metaphor was not confined to observers, and neither was it merely a metaphor. The first four prisoners to be released – in October 2002 – had been so isolated that one of them wrote to his family: "I'm half an animal now. After a month I'll be a complete animal."[52] They might have been treated better had they been animals. The Geneva Convention only allows "close confinement" where this is necessary to safeguard the health of prisoners, whereas former Sing Sing correctional officer Ted Conover reported that the "supermax model of solitary confinement" is the norm, and prisoners are allowed out of their cells just three times a week for twenty minutes of solitary exercise in a large, concrete-floored cage (figure 4.4). There were 10 suicide attempts in 2002, and another 14 in the first three months of 2003.[53]

There are grounds for suspecting that prisoners who have remained at US bases in Afghanistan, who have been transported to other extra-territorial facilities made available to the US military (like the British base on Diego Garcia), or who have been handed over to foreign intelligence agencies in Saudi Arabia, Morocco, and elsewhere for "stress and duress" interrogation ("torture by proxy"), have fared even worse. At Bagram

Figure 4.4   Camp X-Ray, Guantánamo Bay, Cuba, March 2002
(AP Photo/Tomas van Houtryve)

airbase north of Kabul, for example, where prisoners are also kept in metal shipping containers, it has been alleged that "detainees are chained to the ceiling, shackled so tightly that the blood flow stops, kept naked and hooded [or in spray-painted goggles], and kicked to keep them awake for days on end." Two prisoners who died at Bagram in American custody were found to have suffered "blunt force injuries." All of this, of course, is a far cry – literally so – from the provisions of international law, and when two reporters referred to Bagram's "forbidden zone" as a space where "the lines between right and wrong, legal and inhuman" are blurred, they limn Agamben's space of the exception with precision.[54]

The war also displaced hundreds of thousands of Afghan civilians not only from their homes but also from the protections of international law. They became the mute bearers of what Agamben calls "bare life," excluded from both "politically qualified life" and, in many cases, from the actions of international aid agencies or even the scrutiny of the international media.[55] At the very beginning of the conflict, Felicity Lawrence drew attention to the absence of images of its victims. There were already vast numbers of refugees without food, water or medicine, she wrote, but within the space of constructed invisibility:

> [W]e can't see them; they have no face. They have not so far massed shockingly in front of the cameras, because the borders to neighbouring countries remain closed. They have fled to villages in the mountains, where aid agencies fear they will starve slowly, in pockets, away from the fences where photographers can bear witness."[56]

Lawrence's sense of this first phase of the attack on Afghanistan as "a war depersonalized and a narrative detached" eventually gave way, however, as the different imaginative geographies being mobilized by America and its allies confounded and ultimately perforated one another. The military assault could never be confined to the sanitized, surgical procedures conjured up by Bush's "carefully targeted actions," and most of the Afghan people were never able to appreciate what he called "the generosity of America and [its] allies." "As we strike military targets," the president had reassured his audience before the bombing began, "we will also drop food, medicine and supplies to the starving and suffering men and women and children of Afghanistan."[57] This was a tacit admission that territorialization was an imperfect schematic, and that "al-Qaeda" and "Afghanistan" were not coincident. Indeed, Žižek suggested that "perhaps the ultimate image of the 'local population' as *homo sacer* is that of the American war plane flying above Afghanistan: one can never be sure whether it will be dropping bombs or food parcels."[58]

The strategy was a cruel tokenism. The parcels were intended primarily for domestic consumption – and perhaps to rally America's allies – since the airdrops were so pitifully inadequate to the scale of the swelling humanitarian crisis.[59] But historian Niall Ferguson none the less approvingly quoted Kipling's *White Man's Burden*. America was waging a "savage war of peace," he wrote, while filling "full the mouths of Famine." And he tried to silence any dissenters by declaring that "Kipling would certainly have grasped the rationale of simultaneously dropping cluster bombs and food parcels," which makes one wonder if the appalling man had any idea of the sheer number of those "mouths of Famine" or what cluster bombs *do*.[60] For the record: each cluster bomb contains several hundred bomblets, and when each bomblet explodes hundreds of steel fragments shoot out at high velocity to kill or maim anyone within a radius of 100 meters from the point of detonation. Those that do not explode lie buried in the earth, even more dangerous than conventional land-mines: all the

Figure 4.5   Kabul, winter 2001–2 (AP Photo/Wolfram Steinberg)

more so in Afghanistan since many of them were yellow – the same color as the food parcels.[61]

"Territory," as Homi Bhabha once observed in a remark that Kipling would no doubt also have endorsed, derives from both *terra* (earth) and *terrere* (to frighten), from which we derive *territorium*, "a place from which people are frightened off."[62] And so it proved, as the crumpled folds between al-Qaeda and Afghanistan came undone. As the re-empowered Northern Alliance swept south, supported by massive high-level aerial bombardments, so streams of refugees headed for the borders, terrified by the prospect of another round of death and destruction. Many of them, disaffected with the Taliban, had suffered vicious reprisals from the retreating troops, but – as my narrative in the previous chapter has shown – they also had good reason to fear the Northern Alliance once again ruling their lives.[63] During the night of November 12/13 the Taliban abandoned Kabul, and the next day the city was occupied by Alliance troops. John Lee Anderson, a reporter for the *New Yorker*, surveyed what he called "a Daliesque panorama of wholesale destruction"; Kabul had been battered by so many different warlords that "all of the devastation had a name attached to it" (figure 4.5). By December 22 a new, interim administration had been installed in the capital, but this did not end the fighting or the suffering of the civilian population. This was in part the consequence of the sheer scale of devastation. Anderson described "a vast mud Chernobyl" stretching north across the Shamali plain from Kabul to the former front line, pockmarked by "roofless and crumbling adobe farm houses, collapsed walls and battered fields." But the continued humanitarian crisis was also the product of the US decision to rely on the militias of the Northern Alliance for most of the ground fighting. Millions of dollars were expended in wholesale bribery to persuade them to fight the Taliban, which minimized American casualties but also ensured that the warlordism that had disfigured Afghanistan for decades would resurface as soon as their opponents had fled. Human Rights Watch documented appalling atrocities inflicted by these militias on Pashtun civilians in particular: extortions and looting, sexual violence, beatings, and killings.[64]

The high-level war from the air also took a heavy toll of the population. By May 2002 it was estimated that 1,300–3,500 civilians had died and 4,000–6,500 civilians had been injured, many of them seriously, as a direct result of American bombs and missiles (figure 4.6). Probably another 20,000 civilians lost their lives as an indirect consequence of the American-led intervention; this includes thousands who died when relief columns from international aid agencies were halted or delayed, and others who died through the secondary effects of targeting civilian infrastructure (especially electrical power facilities vital for hospitals and water-supply systems).[65] Most of these men, women, and children were killed or maimed "not by design," as a horrified Noam Chomsky put it, "but because it [did not] matter": "a deeper level of moral depravity" mined by the ghosts of *homo sacer*.[66] The numbers of these nameless victims and what Marc Herold grimly calls their "unworthy bodies" do matter. But they matter not because "deaths directly attributable to US foreign policies are to be weighed against the deaths the US has suffered, somehow leaving the recipients of its imperial and post-colonial aggression in moral credit." It is not about making cruel comparisons, which is exactly what Arundhati Roy criticized as the algebra of infinite justice: "How many dead Afghans for every dead American?" Insisting instead on the absolute significance of these deaths disrupts those simultaneous equations and unsettles what Gilroy calls "the imperial topography which dictates that deaths are prized according to where they occur and the [racial markings] of the bodies involved."[67] We need to record these numbers, and to think about the destroyed lives that they represent even in excess of these numbers,

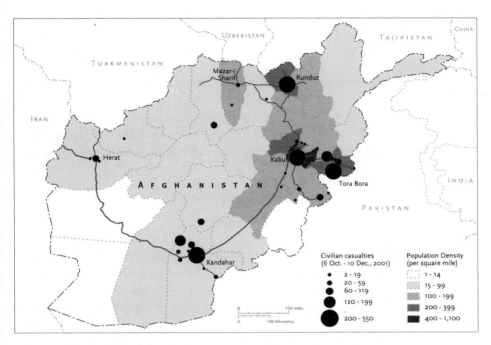

Figure 4.6   Civilian casualties in Afghanistan (after Marc Herold and
Steve Cater)

the friends and families pummeled by inconsolable loss, because no supposedly "sacred mission" – *jihad* or crusade – can provide a warrant for
this indiscriminate killing.

In all of these ways, then, the imaginative geographies of a colonial
past reasserted themselves in the colonial present. What Gilroy describes,
appropriately, as at once "old, modern notions of racial difference" were
activated within a differential calculus according to which "some human
bodies are more easily and appropriately humiliated, imprisoned, shackled, starved and destroyed than others." He continues:

These fine ethnic distinctions effectively revive a colonial economy in which
infrahumanity, measured against the benchmark of healthier imperial standards,
diminishes human rights and can defer human recognition. The native, the
enemy, the prisoner and all the other shadowy "third things" lodged between
animal and human can only be held accountable under special emergency
rules and fierce martial laws. Their lowly status underscores the fact that

they cannot be reciprocally endowed with the same vital humanity enjoyed
by their well-heeled captors, conquerors, judges, executioners and other racial
betters.[68]

The sovereign powers and delegations that decreed that the lives and deaths
of all these people were of no account – who claimed to wage a war of
"civilization" against "barbarism" within the spaces of their own exception – must surely be called to account and made to reflect on the meanings of the wretched colonial antinomies through which they preach
vengeance and retribution.

Deconstruction

The numbers of victims continue to grow as I write. While US bombing
raids continue and on the ground US troops still seek out al-Qaeda and
Taliban fighters – with decidedly mixed results – there have been repeated
incidents in which civilians have become targets of their military operations. Robert Fisk documented a particularly shocking case in which the
southern village of Hajibirgit was attacked by US Special Forces in the
middle of the night. More than one hundred families were forced out of
their homes by stun grenades, the women's hands were bound and their
burqas removed, and one child, fleeing in terror, stumbled into the village
well and drowned. The village elder was shot dead, and 55 other men were
seized, handcuffed, and blindfolded, and flown by helicopter to Kandahar.
There they were tied and shackled and had thick sacks placed over their
heads; they were stripped naked, had their beards shaved, and were inter-
rogated. Finally they were "issued with bright-yellow clothes and taken
to a series of wire cages laid out over the sand of the airbase – a minia-
ture version of Guantánamo Bay – where they were given bread, biscuits,
rice, beans and bottled water." The villagers were held in the cages for
five days before they were released and flown home accompanied by apologies. When they arrived they found that in their absence Hajibirgit had
been pillaged by a local warlord, and that most of the inhabitants had
fled into the hills.[69]

Neither the violence of the initial assault nor the lawlessness that followed is exceptional. US Special Forces have reportedly stormed through
other villages "as if bin Laden was in every house."[70] In July 2002 an Islamic
Transitional Authority replaced the interim administration, but the

warlords have grown bolder every day, settling old scores, extending their own networks of patronage, building their own political constituencies, and running end-games around an administration in Kabul that still struggles to extend its patchwork authority beyond the capital. Cluster bombs buried beneath the ground continue to explode, killing and maiming innocent civilians.[71] Every month, in what has become one of the most heavily mined countries in the world, between 150 and 300 people are killed by landmines. Countless more become sick or die from polluted water, disease, or malnutrition. Six million people are at risk from hunger and starvation. The difficulties of rebuilding this broken land are enormous, and yet the promised international aid is desperately slow to arrive. "This is what we returned to!" one anguished – and angry – young man told journalist Polly Toynbee in November 2002.

> We were promised by the world that if we fought the Russians for you, you would look after us. But you didn't. Then we fought the Taliban and al-Qaeda, and now look at us, here on this hillside in the mud, the winter coming and our children will die of cold. Where is your help now?[72]

Six months later one shocked journalist reported: "Afghanistan is no longer a country at all."[73]

Without sustained reconstruction of the Afghan economy, and without a concerted effort to establish the institutions of a genuinely civil society, the same matrix that supported the growth of al-Qaeda will reassert itself. As one minister in the transitional administration warned,

> You have a population of professional warriors who are poor and will do anything for money. These people will find their way back into global terrorism. If the West turns its back on Afghanistan it will be writing its own suicide note. How many 11 Septembers do you want to happen?[74]

But the White House preferred what Michael Ignatieff calls "nation-building lite," and American priorities remain fastened on military objectives. "We're not here because of the drought and the famine and the condition of women," the head of programs for the United States Agency for International Development in Afghanistan admitted. "We're here because of 9/11."[75] The international aid agencies and NGOs are troubled by the "gray area" that they say the United States has sought to establish between military operations and humanitarian aid – bombs and food parcels all over again – and they are understandably worried by the danger to their own staff should they be mistaken for US military personnel.[76] The agencies have started to make inroads here and there, but the humanitarian situation remains critical and refugees (many of whom have been forcibly returned to Afghanistan) are subjected to ferocious deprivation. In the summer of 2002 Fisk found 60,000 of them "rot[ting] along their frontier with Pakistan"; but "Pakistan no longer wants this riff-raff of poor and destitute on its squeaky clean border" and so "a second circle of hell" had been created for them 40 miles west of Kandahar, "a grey, hot desert, reached through minefields and shot through with blow-torch winds and black stones."[77]

During the winter of 2002/3 an ad hoc alliance emerged between the renegade *mujaheddin* of Gulbuddin Hekmatyar's Hizb-i-Islami militia, groups of al-Qaeda stragglers, and remaining Taliban fighters, and these factions achieved a considerable degree of operational cohesion. In the border towns and refugee camps of north-west Pakistan, one journalist reported, "the talk is of war and of the return of the Taliban to Afghanistan." When the militias descend on the refugee camps in Quetta, Peshawar, and Karachi to recruit new members they point to the violence and destruction of continuing US military operations and the broken promises of reconstruction and development. Politically, they display a new confidence in calling for a "holy war" against the occupying "crusaders" and their "puppet regime," and militarily their guerrilla operations against US forces have intensified along the border with Pakistan.[78] By the spring of 2003 US forces had little to show for their continuing operations. "Nearly every day," the *New York Times* reported, "there are killings, explosions, shootings, and targeted attacks on foreign aid workers." When troops turn villages upside down in their search for weapons caches or make repeated arrests, ordinary Afghans are markedly unimpressed: many are left humiliated and angry at the disruption of their lives. The people from Lejay were so furious at the conduct of US Special Forces who spent ten days searching through their village, that they wrote an open letter to the United Nations mission in Afghanistan. "They did not find Mullah Omar, they did not find Osama bin Laden, and they did not find any Taliban," the petition reads. But "they arrested old men, drivers, and shopkeepers, and they injured women and children."

This is all troubling enough. But the United States has also allowed the warlords that it enlisted in its war against the Taliban to assume control of much of the country outside Kabul, and even Hamid Karzai's brother,

Ahmed Wali Karzai, has been moved to say that it is like "seeing the same movie twice and no one is trying to fix the problem. What was promised to Afghans with the collapse of the Taliban was a new life of hope and change. But what was delivered? Nothing. Everyone is back in business."[79]

The warlords were incorporated into the post-war government – where many of them have ministerial positions – but they retained their own fiefdoms. "While each expediently mouths allegiance to President Hamid Karzai in Kabul, they still maintain their own militaries and collect their own revenues." They also play a leading role in redistributing reconstruction assistance, which further consolidates their regional powers.[80] The links between the interim government and the warlords are thus at once close and strained – Afghanistan is, once again, a forcefield of contending powers – and this intimate tension extends beyond struggles over political authority, financial resources, and military muscle. The civilian population continues to suffer extraordinary depredations: armed robberies, extortion, and kidnappings; arbitrary arrest and beatings; the rape of women, girls, and boys: all have become commonplace. Human Rights Watch reports that both the warlords and officials in the interim government are implicated in these abuses: "These violations have been carried out by people who would not have come to power without the intervention and support of the international community."[81]

As America's imaginative geographies of "friend" and "enemy" spin like the tumblers on a slot machine, therefore, it is not surprising that so many Afghanis become cynical. "I have a problem with your definition of 'enemy' and 'friend,' " one *mujaheddin* leader from the 1980s told an American agent in Jalalabad:

> In the 1980s, when you first came to Afghanistan, you also introduced Osama [bin Laden] to me, saying he was a great man and would be very useful to me. I always mistrusted foreign fighters in my country. I was told from all sides to accept Osama and his other lunatic friends. Then your best friends were also the likes of Hekmatyar, Rabbani and others. If you remember I told you they were very dangerous people. Your then best friends are now your worst enemies, and you are asking me to do the impossible, keep following your chain of thought.[82]

The expedient rotations of the imaginative geographies set in motion by the Bush administration thus not only have performative force: they also have extraordinarily destructive power.

5 Barbed Boundaries

All the birds that followed my palm
To the door of the distant airport
All the wheatfields
All the prisons
All the white tombstones
All the barbed boundaries
All the waving handkerchiefs
All the eyes
were with me
But they dropped them from my passport.
Mahmoud Darwish, *Passport*

America's Israel

THROUGH the events of September 11 the arc that I have been tracing between America and Afghanistan intersected with a second terrifying trajectory that speared Israel and the occupied territories of Palestine. This second trajectory reaches back far beyond the formation of the state of Israel to the European conquest of North America itself, which in many of the eastern colonies was inflected by a Judaeo-Christian imaginary within which the continent appeared as the new "Promised Land" whose settlement was to be illuminated by a beacon on a hill, the foundation of a "New Jerusalem." In 1850 Hermann Melville famously described Americans as "the peculiar, chosen people – the Israel of our time," and these affiliations were strengthened by American travelers who journeyed to Palestine in ever-increasing numbers after the Civil War and whose writings, paintings, and photographs enabled a domestic audience to reaffirm a vicarious identification with the region. Indeed, as John Davis has shown, many of those travelers claimed to understand the landscape so much better than those who lived there that the Holy Land became, imaginatively and ideologically, "American." While American (like European) travelers registered the presence of Arabs, these remained marginal figures: it was the landscape itself that was central to their collective gaze.[1] From the closing decades of the nineteenth century this marginalization – eventually studied erasure – of the Arab population assumed a starkly physical form as American Jews joined those from other lands to establish the first modern Jewish settlements in Palestine.[2] There were, of course, reverse ties too. In the middle decades of the nineteenth century hundreds of thousands of German Jews crossed the Atlantic to America, and from the 1880s on into the early twentieth century millions of Polish and Russian Jews fled the pogroms and restrictions imposed on them in the Pale of Settlement for sanctuary in the United States. Together these movements laid the foundations of Zionism's political constituency within the United States.

These cultural connections were subsequently reinforced by a series of geopolitical filiations. Following the formation of the state of Israel in 1948, Perry Anderson claims that Zionism "relied on a carapace of American power."[3] But American interest in Israel was fitful, negotiating an awkward passage between its dependence on Middle East oil and its determination to counter Soviet influence during the Cold War. Three moments were of decisive importance. First, the victory of Israel in what it called the Six Day War in 1967 clearly impressed an America whose forces were not only being defeated but also humiliated in Vietnam. President Lyndon B. Johnson took what has been described as "vicarious pleasure" from Israel's ability "to thwart an Arab war of national liberation not unlike the one the United States faced in Vietnam." Egypt's President Nasser had embraced the Viet Cong struggle and encouraged the Palestinians to launch their own war for national liberation; but Johnson's reaction was about more than unaffected pleasure and Israel was not a passive partner in the consummation of this "special relationship." With their victory in 1967, "the Israelis positioned themselves to become a strategic asset [against the spread of communism] at precisely the moment when the debacle in Southeast Asia was tempting the United States to limit its involvement in the Middle East." After the 1967 war France suspended arms shipments to Israel, and Egypt and Syria began to rebuild their armies through a closer relationship with the USSR, and so the Israeli government, in concert with major American Zionist organizations, worked to ensure that the United States would offer Israel unconditional support.[4] It was therefore increasingly seen as desirable for America to act not only like Israel but also *with* Israel: so much so, indeed, that throughout the 1970s Israel's military audacity attracted "increased US investment in an image of a militarized Israel that represented revitalized masculinity and restored national pride."[5]

The violent response of the Palestine Liberation Organization to Israel's occupation of Gaza and the West Bank encouraged further US aid and assistance, but the PLO was a secular organization and it was not until the American hostage crisis in Iran between 1979 and 1981 – the second moment – that a conjunction between "Islam" and "terrorism" was established within American public culture through which many Americans and Israelis were able to find a common language and a common cause. In fact, on the day that the hostages were released, President Ronald Reagan announced that terrorism would replace human rights as America's primary foreign policy concern.[6] The alliance between America and Israel has varied in its intensity, but Israel has been the largest cumulative recipient of US aid since the Second World War – between 1949 and 2001 it received between $90 and $100 billion – and aid to Israel now accounts for around 30 percent of the total US foreign aid budget.[7]

The third decisive punctuation point in this special relationship was September 11, but, as I must now show, to understand its present significance it is necessary to return to the colonial past.

Diaspora, Dispossession, and Disaster

The Zionist dream of uniting the diaspora in a Jewish state was by its very nature a colonial project.[8] In a gesture that had been repeated time and time again since the European conquest of the New World, the discourse of modern Zionism constructed Palestine as a space empty of its native Arab population. A series of campaigns – at once political and military, economic and cultural – was waged to establish this imaginary as brute "facts on the ground." Beginning in 1878 European Jews had already started to purchase a patchwork of agricultural land in Palestine, then still part of the crumbling Ottoman Empire, and by the final years of the nineteenth century these holdings were seen, under the sign of Zionism, as small stepping-stones toward the reclamation of the biblical Land of Israel (Eretz Israel). In *Der Judenstaat*, a pamphlet published in 1896, Theodor Herzl argued that it was only through the birth of their own nation-state that Jews would emerge into the world of modernity. Until then, they would live at best provisionally, so to speak, enduring a double exile from their land and from their destiny. Their "return" – in Hebrew, *aliyah* (ascent) – to the Land of Israel would thus signify their re-entry into history (or, rather, History). The Zionists knew very well that Arabs lived on the land; they knew, too, that they would not give it up willingly. But – in another quintessentially colonial gesture – the indigenous population was reduced to the mute *object* of history, people who merely have things done *to* them, and never recognized as one of its active *subjects*. According to Zionism, it was given to the Jews alone to reclaim "the wilderness," to make the desert bloom so that the land once again flowed with milk and honey – to make the very earth come alive again. As historian Gabriel Piterberg puts it, it was as though "the land, too, was condemned to an exile so long as there was no Jewish sovereignty over it: it lacked any meaningful or authentic history, awaiting redemption with the return of the Jews."[9]

In the following decades thousands more Jewish immigrants arrived to claim a place in Palestine. Arab farmers and laborers saw this as a creeping dispossession, and the new settlers were met with animosity and eventually resistance. Most of their early settlements were built along the coastal plains and in the northern valleys, and they found it much more difficult to secure toeholds in the mountainous heartland of Palestine. In the years that followed, the immigrants formed armed militias so that their colonization of the land could proceed behind what Ze'ev Jabotinksy called "an iron wall" that the Arabs would be powerless to breach. These beginnings were crucial, because they forged a triple imperative that has shaped Zionist ideology ever since. Settlement, security, and sovereignty were fused in an essential union that has continued to function as something far deeper than any political and military objective, something much closer to an existential imperative.[10]

Herzl had located the Zionist project within the larger framework of European colonialism and imperialism. A Jewish state in Palestine would form "part of a rampart for Europe against Asia," he wrote, "an outpost of civilization as opposed to barbarism." This bellicose and brutalizing image would be repeated throughout the next century and beyond. During the First World War – hardly a vindication of European "civilization" – British foreign policy toward Palestine was Janus-faced. In 1915–16 Britain persuaded Husayn ibn 'Ali, the grand sheriff of Mecca and head of the Hashemite family, to lead the Arabs in an uprising against the increasingly secular regime of the Ottoman Empire which had aligned itself with Germany. His reward was to be the foundation of a single, unified and independent state in the Arab provinces of the defeated empire. In 1917 the British government also affirmed, through the Balfour Declaration, that it viewed with favor "the establishment in Palestine of a national home for the Jewish people." It promised to use its "best endeavours to facilitate the achievement of this object," but wanted it clearly understood "that nothing shall be done which may prejudice the civil and religious rights of existing non-Jewish communities in Palestine." It is hard to imagine how these vicious circles, intersecting in Palestine but drawn by the warped power-geometries of European imperialism, could ever have been squared.

At the end of the war, following the collapse of the Ottoman Empire, Britain occupied Palestine and in 1920 received a Mandate from the League of Nations to administer the territory. The mandate system entrusted to "advanced nations" the "tutelage" of those peoples who were "not yet able to stand by themselves under the strenuous conditions of the modern world." The Mandate for Palestine showed little regard for its indigenous inhabitants even by the colonialist tenor of this framing legislation and its enfeeblement of subaltern populations. Instead, the Mandate repeated the terms of the Balfour Declaration. A "Jewish national home" would be established in Palestine, and the Mandatory authority was required to "facilitate Jewish immigration" and encourage its "close settlement on the land."[11] In 1921 Britain detached "Transjordan" in order to establish a Hashemite state east of the River Jordan; after the ratification of the British Mandate in the following year, Jewish settlement west of the Jordan accelerated (figure 5.1). Although it was buttressed by British military and police forces, the situation in Mandatory Palestine was fraught and unstable. Confrontations between Jews and Arabs became increasingly violent, and when the so-called "Arab Revolt" broke out in 1936 the British government established a Royal Commission under Lord Peel to inquire into the circumstances of the unrest. When they visited Palestine, Chaim Weizmann, president of the World Zionist Organization, told the commissioners that "the revolt" was merely "the old war of the desert against civilization": "On one side, the forces of destruction, the forces of the desert, have arisen, and on the other side stand firm the

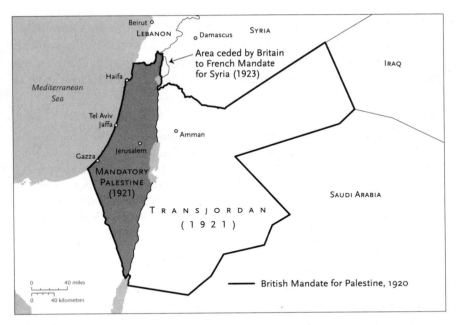

Figure 5.1 The British Mandate for Palestine (1920) and Mandatory Palestine (1921) (after H. M. Sacher/Palestinian Society for the Study of International Affairs)

forces of civilization and building." The commissioners were impressed by Weizmann's testimony. They declared that "the Jewish National Home is no longer an experiment," and drew a "striking" contrast between "the modern democratic and primarily European character of the National Home and that of the Arab world around it." The representation of Jewish colonization as modernization was a tenacious stratagem, and many politicians used it, then and since, to legitimize the dispossession of the Palestinians. There was no injustice in removing Arabs from their land, Churchill told the Peel Commission: "The injustice is when those who live in the country leave it to be desert for thousands of years." Colonial modernity was seen by its advocates as the life-blood of a renewed Palestine, and Judaicization was to be the means of its transfusion. The commissioners used a similar pathological metaphor to conclude that the conflict between Jews and Arabs was irrepressible within the body of a single state. Palestine was "diseased," they wrote, and a "surgical operation" was required: they recommended partition.[12]

According to the Commission's proposals, the Jews would receive 20 percent of Mandatory Palestine (figure 5.2). Even before the Commission completed its deliberations, however, Jewish settlers were busily working to extend the visible perimeter of their territorial claims by building "tower and stockade" settlements. These fulfilled the existential imperative of Zionism with a raw power. Here is one witness:

> By late afternoon, a new Jewish village had sprung up. Bungalows had been erected, barricades run up around the boundaries, and the wooden watch-tower, complete with lamp and dynamo, put in position. When night fell the lamp was switched on amid dead silence. It threw a powerful beam across the surrounding waste. Its symbolism was apparent to all. . . . It was the light of a new life and a new era. An area from which civilization had departed 2,000 years before was being reclaimed. [13]

The performance of this imaginative geography, with its colonial couplets of darkness and light, waste and civilization, proved to be a model for subsequent conquest and settlement. At the time, the Jewish Agency had serious reservations about the Peel Commission's proposals, and its chief negotiator with the Mandatory Authority, Moshe Sharratt, objected that "the proposed Jewish state territory would not be contiguous; its boundaries would be twisted and broken" and "the frontier line would separate villages from their fields." Although the Jewish Agency accepted the proposals as a basis for negotiation, therefore, its leaders regarded the recommendations as interim measures that would eventually deliver the whole country to the Jews. Many of them fastened on the Commission's proposals for the transfer of the Arab population out of its new state. "If the settlement is to be clean and final," the commissioners wrote, then 225,000 Arabs living in the area to be allocated to the Jewish state would eventually have to be to be "re-settled." The concept of transfer was central to the Zionist vision of the Land of Israel as a state with both territorial and cultural integrity.[14] But some militant Zionist factions – notably the Irgun, led by Menachem Begin – rejected any such temporizing and denounced the proposals outright. "The partition of Palestine is illegal," Begin fumed, and "Eretz Israel will be restored to the people of Israel. All of it. And for ever." The Arab Higher Committee, which represented the Palestinian Arabs, viewed partition as illegal too but for diametrically opposite reasons, and dismissed the plan as "absurd, impracticable and unjust."[15]

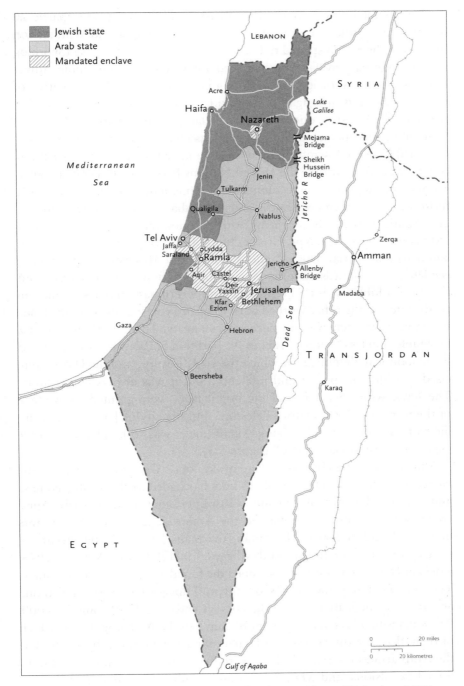

Figure 5.2 The Peel Commission's plan for the partition of Palestine, 1937

There seemed no way out of the impasse, and the prospect of partition dimmed still further with the approach of the Second World War. As the horrors of the Shoah started to become known, the Zionist case for a permanent sanctuary in Palestine achieved a new and desperate momentum. But this was not sufficient to produce a political resolution, and with terrorist attacks and riots against its Mandate increasing in severity, Britain devolved the Palestine question to the fledgling United Nations. A Special Committee was appointed, and following its report, in the autumn of 1947, a divided General Assembly passed Resolution 181 in favor of the partition of Palestine. At that time the United Nations had only 56 member states: 33 of them supported the recommendation (including the USA; the USSR; most European member states; and Australia, Canada, New Zealand, and South Africa, all of them British dominions); 13 voted against (Afghanistan, Cuba, Egypt, Greece, India, Iran, Iraq, Lebanon, Pakistan, Saudi Arabia, Syria, Turkey, and Yemen); and 10 abstained (including the UK). A two-thirds majority was required to implement partition, and the Zionist lobby with US President Harry S. Truman on one side and the Arab states on the other worked hard to secure votes: in the end, the resolution narrowly achieved the necessary majority. There was thus nothing inevitable, still less "natural," about the partition of Palestine; it was framed by geopolitical alignments in which the USA, Europe, and the USSR exercised considerable power and influence, and it was always contentious. The Jews, with 35 percent of the population, were granted 56 percent of the territory of Mandatory Palestine, and the city of Jerusalem, in the light of its transnational religious significance, was to be placed under a "special international regime" (figure 5.3).[16]

Almost immediately, civil war broke out. Guerrilla attacks were launched by Arabs and by Jews. Both sides blockaded roads, planted bombs, and murdered unarmed civilians. Hostilities intensified in early April when Begin's Irgun militia entered the Arab village of Deir Yassin and massacred 250 civilians.[17] Haganah, the main Jewish militia, began to seize Arab cities and destroy Arab villages.[18] In Tel Aviv on May 14, 1948 a defiant David Ben-Gurion proclaimed the foundation of the state of Israel. The very next day the armies of Egypt, Transjordan, Syria, Lebanon, and Iraq invaded. By the time the conflict ended in 1949 some 750,000 Palestinians had been displaced, more than half the Arab population. Most of them fled as a direct result of Israeli military action, much of it before the Arab armies intervened; there were massacres of Palestinian villages, forced expulsions, and wholesale intimidation of the civilian population.

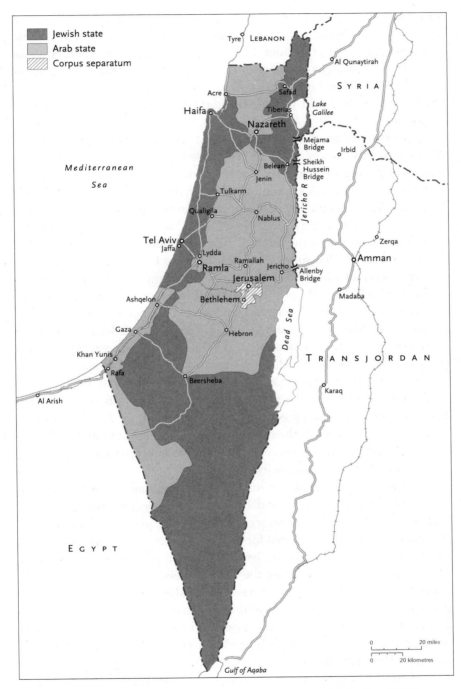

Figure 5.3   The United Nations' plan for the partition of Palestine, 1947

Many people sought refuge in Gaza and the West Bank, while others fled
to Transjordan, Syria, Lebanon, and Egypt. Wherever the refugees found
themselves, however, they found no sign of any Palestinian state. After an
armistice had been concluded with Egypt and Jordan, establishing a series
of so-called "Green Lines," the coastal plain around Gaza was administered by Egypt, and East Jerusalem and the West Bank were administered
by Jordan.[19]

To the Palestinians this was a compound catastrophe of destruction, dispossession, and dispersal – what they called *al-Nakba* ("the disaster") –
which has proved to be an ever-present horizon of meaning within which,
in Mahmoud Darwish's haunting phrase, the Palestinian people have
been cast into "redundant shadows exiled from space and time." "The
Nakba," Darwish wrote over 50 years later, "is an extended present that
promises to continue in the future."[20] To the Israelis, however, all this was
the sweet fruit of what they called their "War of Independence." And yet,
as Joseph Massad asks, "from whom were the Zionists declaring their independence?" This is a sharp question: the British had withdrawn from the
Mandate before the war broke out, and Israel continued to depend on imperial sponsorship after it ended. Massad argues that the invocation of
"independence" was an attempt to rehabilitate the intrinsically colonial
project of Zionism by establishing Israel as a *post*colonial state. And yet
this new state had emerged not only flushed with victory but with far more
land – other people's land – than had been granted to it by either the Peel
Commission or the United Nations. Israel now held not 20 percent or 56
percent but 78 percent of the territory that had been Mandatory Palestine
(figure 5.4), including 95 percent of the arable land that had been classi-
fied by the Mandatory authority as "good."[21]

But within those engorged boundaries the land that was legally owned
by Jewish property-holders and organizations, together with land that
had been held by the Mandatory Authority and over which Israel now
assumed ownership, accounted for only 13.5 percent of the total. As soon
as the war was over, therefore, Israel initiated a massive transfer of land
ownership and sought to erase the Arab presence from the landscape in
order to establish not only its sovereignty but also its patrimony. This took
place in legal, statistical, and cultural registers. The Israeli legal system
consistently used procedural and evidential rules to limit the possibility
of Arab residents retaining their land: "It created a legal geography of
power," Alexandre Kedar concludes, "that contributed to the dispossess-
sion of Arab landholders while simultaneously masking and legitimating

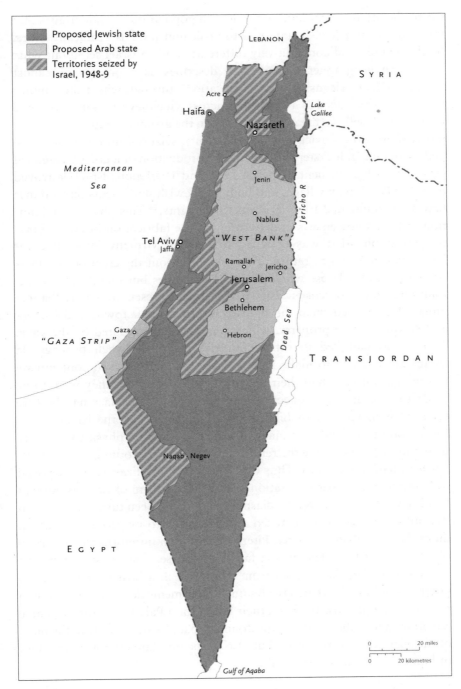

Legend:
- Proposed Jewish state
- Proposed Arab state
- Territories seized by Israel, 1948-9

LEBANON

SYRIA

Acre

Haifa

Lake Galilee

Nazareth

Mediterranean Sea

Jenin

Jericho R

Nablus

"WEST BANK"

Tel Aviv
Jaffa

Ramallah

Jericho

Jerusalem

Bethlehem

Dead Sea

"GAZA STRIP"

Gaza

Hebron

TRANSJORDAN

Naqab · Negev

EGYPT

0   20 miles
0   20 kilometres

Gulf of Aqaba

Figure 5.4   Palestinian territories seized by Israel, 1948–9 (after PASSIA)

the reallocation of that land to the Jewish population."[22] Said argues that
the creation of a Jewish state had to posit non-Jews as "radically other,
fundamentally and constitutively different," and so Israel set about what
Palestinian geographer Ghazi Falah describes as a process of almost
ritually violent "cleansing" or "purification" through which the country
was to be reenvisioned as a blank slate across which Jewish signatures could
be written at will. To create such "facts on the ground" required immense
physical erasures – evictions, displacements, seizures, and demolitions –
and, marching in lockstep with them, the production of a greatly extended
grid of Jewish settlement. Between 1948 and 1950 alone Israel destroyed
over 400 Palestinian villages and built 160 Jewish settlements on land that
had been confiscated from its former occupants.[23] This physical elaboration of Israeli power was underwritten by the fabrication of an imaginative geography that was designed to make it virtually impossible for
Palestinian refugees to return. This too was about the creation of "facts
on the ground." Those who had left their homes but remained in Israel
found that the new census designated them as "present absentees," a formula which denied them the right to return to their towns and villages
and repossess their property, which was then appropriated by the state.
Those who had fled to other countries faced an Israeli propaganda
campaign designed to make it impossible for them even to contemplate
returning. Not only had their property been seized, but they were to be
made to give up their collective memory too. Arabic place-names were
replaced with Hebrew or biblical ones, and images of the Israeli transformation of the land – its massive scale and its brute physicality – were
disseminated to persuade the refugees that there was nothing recognizable
left for them to return to. Thus was Israeli territorialization firmly yoked
to Palestinian de-territorialization. The Zionist dream of Eretz Israel that
had been sustained across the diaspora had finally been turned into a reality, but Palestine was de-realized and presented to its people as nothing
more than a chimera, as what Piterberg calls "an unreturnable and irrec-
ollective country."[24] The project failed, of course. The Palestinian people
had most of their land taken from them, but in a host of ways – from
poetry to politics[25] – they have retained their memories of the Palestinian
past and, as I propose to show, their hopes for a Palestinian future. These
retentions and elaborations are profoundly spatialized, not only in the sense
of the space of Palestine itself but also in the intimate microtopographies
of homes, fields, and cemeteries.

Occupation, Coercion, and Colonization

On June 5, 1967 Israel launched pre-emptive strikes against Egypt and Syria, and by the end of the morning – fatefully for the Palestinians – Jordan also entered the war. Six days later Israel had seized the Sinai peninsula and Gaza from Egypt, and the Golan Heights from Syria. Still more significantly, Jordan had been displaced from the West Bank, so that Israel now effectively controlled 100 percent of the area of Mandatory Palestine. The victory was soon invested with religious, even messianic, importance. Just as the world was supposedly made after the six days of Creation, so Eretz Israel was made whole after what came to be called the "Six Day War."

By the end of June hundreds of Arab families had been summarily evicted from East Jerusalem, which was annexed by Israel, and in September the Israeli government endorsed the first Israeli "settlement" on the West Bank and expropriated all state-owned land there. The transfer of any part of a civilian population into territory occupied by a foreign power is expressly forbidden under Article 49 of the Fourth Geneva Convention relative to the Protection of Civilian Persons in Time of War (1949), and in November 1967 the UN Security Council passed Resolution 242 that emphatically reminded Israel of "the inadmissibility of the acquisition of territory by force," required it to withdraw "from territories occupied in the recent conflict," and affirmed the right of every state "to live in peace with secure and recognized boundaries free from threats or acts of force." The English text did not refer to "all the territories" or even "the territories," which enabled successive Israeli administrations and their apologists to exploit what they chose to regard as an ambiguous space for interpretative wrangling. Against this, however, lawyer John McHugo has presented a compelling counter-argument. He makes three submissions. First, the resolution is framed by a preamble that expressly notes "the in-admissibility of the acquisition of territory by force" which is plainly a general not a selective principle. As McHugo notes, this has implications for the territories seized by Israel in 1948 as well as those occupied in 1967. His second submission rests on a commonsense analogy: no reasonable person could construe (for example) "Dogs must be kept on a leash" to mean only *some* dogs must be kept on a leash so that, by extension, the resolution must require Israel to withdraw from all the occupied territories.

McHugo's final submission moves beyond the hermeneutics of the text to reconstruct the drafting process and the debate within the Security Council, which confirms his central claim: that absence of the word "all" does not imply that "some" was intended.[26]

Israel ignored the resolution, however, refusing to withdraw its troops and declining to fix its boundaries. The Israeli government justified its actions by claiming that Gaza and the West Bank were not "occupied" since they had never been part of the sovereign territory of Egypt or Jordan. Israel was thus an "administrator" not an occupier (so that the Geneva Conventions were out of place), and accordingly these were deemed "administered territories" whose final status had yet to be determined. This argument was as bogus as it was self-serving. The principles of belligerent occupation, including Article 49 of the Fourth Geneva Convention, apply "whether or not Jordan and Egypt possessed legitimate sovereign rights in respect of those territories. Protecting the reversionary interest of an ousted sovereign is not their sole or essential purpose; the paramount purposes are protecting the civilian population of an occupied territory and reserving permanent territorial changes, if any, until settlement of the conflict."[27]

For the first weeks of the occupation the Israel Defence Forces (IDF) had a nominal policy of "non-interference" – so far as possible, everyday life in the territories was to be "normalized" – but Israeli political and military actions soon gave the lie to these promises. The economies of Gaza and the West Bank were rapidly fused with that of Israel in a dependent and thoroughly exploitative relationship, through which they became cheap labor pools and convenient export markets for Israeli commodity production. These colonial economic structures, together with systems of direct and indirect taxation, enabled the occupiers to transfer the costs of occupation to the occupied. Everyday life was increasingly constrained by the grid of occupation. Palestinians were caught in a network of identity papers and travel permits, roadblocks and body searches. Palestinian nationalism was criminalized; freedom of expression and association were denied; and collective punishments like curfews, border closures, and house demolitions were regularly imposed on the population at large. Like all military occupations, Israeli historian Benny Morris concludes, "Israel's was founded on brute force, repression and fear, collaboration and treachery, beatings and torture chambers, and daily intimidation, humiliation and manipulation."[28]

This program of state coercion emerged in an ad hoc, hit-and-miss fashion. Its ostensible purpose was to maintain (Palestinian) public order and (Israeli) security, but as it became more systematic so it became covertly directed toward encouraging Palestinians to leave the occupied territories. This policy of renewed cleansing was reinforced by a second, overt strategy of dispossession, as hundreds of thousands of Israeli settlers were moved into the occupied territories in a sustained violation of international law. The ideological importance of the settlements was explained by the Minister of Defence, Moshe Dayan, who conceded that "without them the IDF would be a foreign army ruling a foreign population." This was not much of a concession, since the IDF plainly remained a foreign army ruling a foreign population: its mandate was provided by colonial power not international law. The Israeli cabinet considered two options for the colonization of the West Bank. The plan proposed by the Minister of Labour, Yigal Allon, fastened on the eastern and western margins (figure 5.5(a)). It called for the annexation of the Jordan Valley and an area around Jerusalem through the renewed extension of the grid of Jewish settlement; the core area of the Palestinian population, the mountain spine running from Jenin in the north to Hebron in the south, would be granted limited autonomy or confederated with Jordan. The rival plan proposed by Moshe Dayan reversed this geography. It proposed punching "four fists" along the central ridge; each would consist of a military base surrounded by a circle of Jewish settlements linked directly to Israel by a network of main roads. The cabinet decided to compromise. Dayan's proposals for military bases along the ridge were accepted, but civilian settlement would take place under the aegis of the Allon Plan. Ten years later, when the right-wing Likud party took power from Labour in 1977, there were 16 illegal Israeli settlements in Gaza and 36 in the West Bank.[29]

Ironically, Labour's hold over Israeli politics had been weakened by the very developments it promoted. A war of position was fought over the basic template of Israel, in which Zionism's redemptive mythologies were mobilized by Labour's opponents to focus not on the boundaries, citizens and laws of the state of Israel but on the spiritual and existential completion of the *Land* of Israel.[30] The new prime minister, former terrorist leader Menachem Begin, wanted "nothing less than the hegemonic establishment of a new Zionist paradigm," as Ian Lustick notes, and he fulfilled his party's election manifesto to the letter. The West Bank was formally renamed "Judea and Samaria," and since for Jews these constituted the

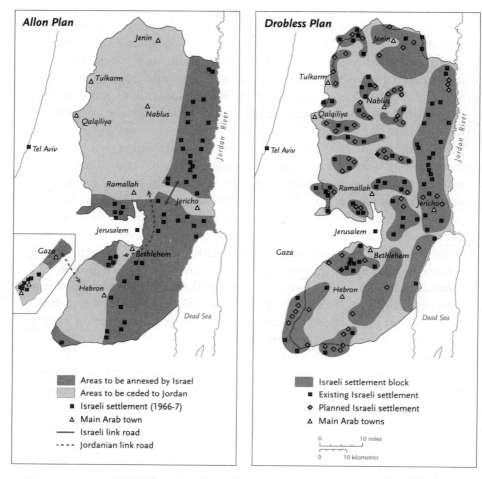

Figure 5.5 (a) The Allon Plan for the Israeli settlement of the occupied West Bank; (b) The Drobless Plan for the Israeli settlement of the occupied West Bank (after Meron Benvenisti, Eyal Weizman)

spiritual heart of Eretz Israel the territories were redefined as neither occupied nor even administered but "liberated." Once again, the existential imperative of Zionism was translated directly into a territorial imperative that severed the Palestinian people from their land. For it was plainly not the Palestinian people who were "liberated" by the Israeli occupation: how could it have been? *It was the land itself.* Under international law a civilian population has the right to resist military occupation but, following the same Orwellian logic, all Palestinian acts of resistance to "liberation" were now counted as acts of "terrorism."[31] While Begin was prepared to consider "full cultural autonomy" for the Palestinians, therefore, this could only ever take the form of administrative authority rather than legislative or territorial sovereignty. Begin remained implacably opposed to the formation of a Palestinian state. "Between the sea and the Jordan," he affirmed, "there will be Jewish sovereignty alone."[32]

Not only was it impossible for Begin to contemplate Israeli withdrawal from Gaza and the West Bank, he was committed to erasing the significance of the Green Line, increasing the number of illegal settlements in the occupied territories, and extending the colonial grid up into the mountains. This was, in part, a spiritual project – a climactic *aliyah* as Jewish settlement finally reached what the leader of Gush Emunim, "The Block of Faith," called "the sacred summits" – but it was also a political strategy designed to provide a constituency for Likud that would rival and ultimately replace Labour's in the earlier kibbutzim. Accordingly, Begin was determined to create "facts on the ground" that would make it virtually impossible for any future government to disengage from these territories. The new plan drawn up in 1977–8 by Matityahu Drobless, co-chairman of the World Zionist Organization's Land Settlement Division, envisaged "the dispersion of the [Jewish] population from the densely pop-ulated urban strip of the central plain eastward to the presently empty areas of Judea and Samaria." These areas could only be seen as "empty" from the most extreme Zionist optic, but the intention, as Drobless explained, was to establish Jewish settlements not only around those of what he termed (outrageously) "the minorities" – the Arabs – but also "in between them," in order to fulfill Begin's ultimate objective: to deny the Palestinians a con-tinuous territory that could provide the basis for an autonomous state (figure 5.5(b)). Protestations from the UN and even the United States notwith-standing, the number of illegal settlements soared.[33]

By 1981, when Likud had been re-elected for a second term, all pre-tense that this was a temporary occupation had been dropped. Drobless's scheme was reaffirmed in a plan proposed by Ariel Sharon, Minister of Agriculture and subsequently Minister of Defence, which proposed con-ceding at most a few, scattered pockets to the Palestinians: Israel would eventually annex most of the West Bank. It was now official Israeli policy to establish what historian Avi Shlaim calls "a permanent and coercive jurisdiction over the 1.3 million Arab inhabitants of the West Bank and

Gaza." By 1990 there were 120,000 Israelis in East Jerusalem, and 76,000 Israeli settlers in Gaza and the West Bank, where their illegal settlements had spread, as planned, from the periphery to the densely populated (far from "empty") Arab spine.[34] Some of the settlers were motivated by religious ideology, but major financial incentives were used to attract other settlers, many of whom elected to move to illegal settlements that had been established within commuting range of the metropolitan areas of Tel Aviv and Jerusalem. These subsidies, grants, loans, benefits, and tax concessions to Israelis were – and remain – in stark contrast to the restrictions imposed on the Palestinians.[35] Can there be any doubt that this was – and remains – colonialism of the most repressive kind? "We enthusiastically chose to become a colonial society," admits a former Israeli Attorney-General,

> ignoring international treaties, expropriating lands, transferring settlers from Israel to the occupied territories, engaging in theft and finding justification for all these activities. Passionately desiring to keep the occupied territories, we developed two judicial systems: one – progressive, liberal – in Israel; the other – cruel, injurious – in the occupied territories.[36]

It was the trauma of colonial occupation and renewed dispossession that reawakened Palestinian nationalism and shifted its center of gravity from the Palestine Liberation Organization, which had been exiled first in Jordan, then in Lebanon and finally in Tunis, to the occupied territories themselves. A popular uprising broke out in Gaza and the West Bank in December 1987. Its origins lay in the everyday experience of immiseration and oppression, but it developed into a vigorous assertion of the Palestinian right to resist occupation and to national self-determination. It became known as the Intifada (which means a "shaking off") and, as Said remarks, it was one of the great anti-colonial insurrections of the modern period.[37] It was met with a draconian response from the IDF, which imposed collective punishments on the Palestinians. The physical force of these measures and the economic dislocation that they caused were intended to instill fear in the population and to leave "deterrent memories" in their wake. Communities in Gaza and the West Bank were subjected to closures and curfews on an unparalleled scale; there were arbitrary arrests and detentions; people were beaten on the street and in their homes, and their property was vandalized; food convoys were prevented from entering refugee camps, and when Palestinians sought to disengage from the Israeli economy and provide their own subsistence the IDF uprooted trees, denied villagers access to their fields, and imposed restrictions on grazing, herding, and even feeding their livestock.[38] In the course of these struggles there were two major victories: Jordan renounced its interest in the West Bank, and the Palestinians were finally recognized as a legitimate party to international negotiations.

Compliant Cartographies

In 1991 the administration of President George H. W. Bush brokered a peace conference in Madrid, followed by further rounds in Washington, in which Palestinian representatives from the occupied territories insisted that any discussion had to be based on the provisions of the Fourth Geneva Convention and on UN Security Council Resolutions 242 and 338. The United States accepted these stipulations, but Israel rejected them outright. Even when Labour replaced Likud the following year, no agreement could be reached. By the fall of 1992, Shlaim reports, it was clear that "the Palestinians wanted to end the occupation" while "the Israelis wanted to retain as much control for as long as possible." In order to circumvent this impasse, and to steal a march over those who had the most direct experience of the occupation, Israel opened a back-channel to Yasser Arafat's exiled PLO leadership in January 1993. Many of the Palestinians who took part in these secret discussions in Oslo were unfamiliar with the facts on the ground that had been created by the occupation – as Said witheringly remarked, "neither Arafat nor any of his Palestinian partners with the Israelis has ever seen an [illegal] settlement" – and crucially, as Allegra Pacheco notes, they were also markedly less familiar with "the political connection between the human rights violations, the Geneva Convention and Israel's territorial expansion plans." By then a newly elected President Clinton had reversed US policy, setting on one side *both* the framework of international human rights law, so that compliance with its provisions became negotiable, *and* the framework of UN resolutions, so that Gaza and the West Bank were made "disputed" territories and Israel's claim was rendered formally equivalent to that of the Palestinians. Israel naturally had no difficult in accepting any of this, but when the Palestinian negotiators in Oslo fell into line they conceded exactly what their counterparts in Madrid had struggled so hard to uphold.[39] The "Declaration of Principles on Interim Self-Government Arrangements" that was finally agreed between Israel and the PLO promised a phased Israeli military withdrawal from the territories and the establishment of an elected Palestinian Authority in Gaza and the West Bank. This was, as Said noted, merely a "modified Allon Plan" that aimed to keep the territories "in a state of permanent dependency." But the devil was not only in the details, which remained to be worked out; it was also in the postponement of two crucial issues: the fate of the Palestinian refugees huddled in camps in Gaza, the West Bank, and beyond; and the fate of the illegal settlements that Israel had established outside the Green Line.[40]

Two years later an interim agreement was signed at the White House ("Oslo II") that incorporated and superseded these preliminary understandings. The occupied territories were divided into three areas – "Area A," "Area B," and "Area C" – whose alphabetical rather than geographical designations confirmed them as topological abstractions produced by a strategic-instrumental discourse of political and military power. Area A was to be under exclusive Palestinian control (but its exits and entrances remained under Israeli control); Area B was to be under dual control, with a Palestinian civil authority and an Israeli security authority; and Area C was to be under exclusive Israeli control, and included all those lands and reserves that had been confiscated by the Israelis for military bases, settlements, and roads (figure 5.6). The Israeli concessions were minimal – during the first phase the Palestinian Authority would exercise full control over just 4 percent of the territory – and the preceding history of occupation and dispossession ensured that any lands ceded to the Palestinians would be bounded by Israel and never contiguous so that they seemed much more like a series of South African bantustans limned by a new apartheid than the basis for any viable state.[41] The basic principles of the Oslo accords were thus unacceptable to many Palestinians; but they were nevertheless accepted by the PLO, and its leader was elected to head the Palestinian Authority. As Said put it, "Arafat and his people [now] rule over a kingdom of illusions, with Israel firmly in command." Arafat's rule was palpable enough; protracted exile had estranged the PLO leadership from the emergent civil society in the occupied territories, as the divisions between Madrid and Oslo had revealed, and on his return Arafat moved to install a regime characterized by a mix of personalization and authoritarianism buttressed by an elaborate security apparatus.[42] But it was a rule of opportunism that constituted a mere shadow of a state with neither depth nor substance. It nullified the Intifada, transforming the resistant contours of an anti-colonial struggle into a compliant cartography drawn in collaboration with an occupying army and, as Salah Hassan has argued,

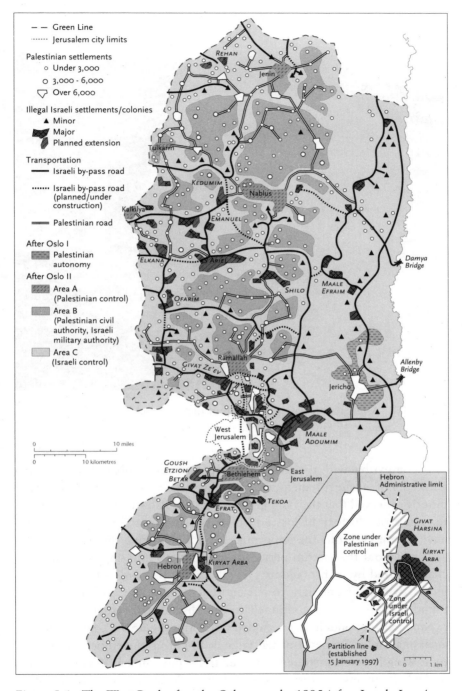

Figure 5.6 The West Bank after the Oslo accords, 1995 (after Jan de Jong/
PASSIA/Foundation for Middle East Peace/*Le Monde diplomatique*)

Figure 5.7   Ariel Sharon points at a map of the occupied West Bank at Beit Arieh, November 1995 (AP Photo/Nicolas B. Tatro)

fully compatible with the colonizing imperatives of globalization. Its map marked not a site of memory, therefore, but a site of amnesia. Said bitterly observed that the Oslo process required Palestinians "to forget and renounce our history of loss and dispossession by the very people who have taught everyone the importance of not forgetting the past."[43]

Throughout the interim period of negotiations and implementations – characterized by its protagonists as "the peace process" – Israeli governments switched from right to left and back again, but both Labour and Likud administrations continued to establish illegal settlements and to expand existing ones in the occupied territories (figure 5.7). Soon after the assassination of Prime Minister Yitzhak Rabin in November 1995, by a right-wing Israeli law student opposed to his government's "concessions" to the Palestinians, the threadbare election of Benjamin Netanyahu's Likud government in May 1996 was the single most significant setback to the entire process. Netanyahu had nothing but contempt for the Palestinians and did everything in his power to subvert the Oslo accords. Pledges to redeploy the IDF from Palestinian areas were not honored; the demolition of Palestinian homes was stepped up; and illegal settlements were aggressively expanded in what Netanyahu called "the battle for Jerusalem." In May 1998 a further agreement was brokered by Clinton between Israel and the Palestinian Authority. This Wye River Memorandum did not materially improve the prospects for a Palestinian state, and yet Shlaim concludes that Netanyahu immediately emptied the accord of any real meaning and initiated "a renewed spurt of land confiscation," while "the Palestinians scrupulously adhered to the course charted at Wye."[44] The landslide election of Ehud Barak's Labour government in 1999 promised to resume the dialogue between Israel and the Palestinians. And yet, throughout the Oslo process, including the administrations on either side of Netanyahu's, not a single illegal settlement was abandoned; the only prohibitions on building contained in the various agreements were on Palestinian construction. Between 1992 and 2001 the Jewish population in East Jerusalem rose from 141,000 to 170,000. Over the same period the population in the illegal settlements in Gaza and the West Bank rose from 110,000 to 214,000. While the built-up area of the illegal settlements occupied less than 2 percent of the West Bank, their boundaries were over three times the size (to allow for "natural growth"), and through a network of so-called "regional councils" they controlled planning and environmental policy in another 35 percent: in total, 42 percent of the West Bank was under the control of illegal settlements (figure 5.8).[45]

These illegal settlements were linked to one another and to Israel by a new highway network. The Trans-Israel Highway scored the border of the West Bank and moved Israel's center of gravity decisively eastward, while a system of "bypass roads" around Palestinian towns and villages reserved contiguity for Israelis alone: "Vehicles of Palestinian residents will not be permitted to travel on these strategic routes." By these means over 400,000 illegal settlers enjoyed freedom of movement throughout the occupied territories and into Israel, whereas 3 million Palestinians were confined to isolated enclaves separated by illegal settlements and their land reserves and by a series of Israeli military checkpoints. Camille Mansour calculated that a Palestinian leaving Jenin in the north would have to change zones 50 times in order to reach Hebron in the south – although both towns are in Area A – whereas an Israeli could cross the entire West Bank from

Figure 5.8 Efrat, Israeli settlement on the occupied West Bank (© David Wells/ Topham/ImageWorks)

north to south or east to west without ever leaving Area C. "Instead of returning the population to civilian life after more than thirty-six years of occupation," Mansour continued, "this cartography scarred their daily landscape with countless signs of military control: watchtowers, barbed wire, concrete block barriers, zigzagging tracks, forced detours, flying checkpoints."[46] This fractured Palestinian landscape, wrenched by brutal spatial torsions, afforded a dizzyingly surreal contrast to the centrifugal space reserved for Israelis, where the labor of representation invested in the bypass road network produced its own symbolic power. Like the German *Autobahnen* the new highway network was a means to conquer distance "that also transformed the meaning of the territory it traversed"; it too was "a powerful allegory for continuity and progression, a historical teleology and vision of the future *projected into the landscape itself*."[47] The *Israel Yearbook and Almanac* for 1998 offered a still more surreal rendering of the lie of the land: "The Palestinian Authority has built its own bypasses – crude paths usable for creating territorial facts and rushing suspected terrorists to refuge" – while "rank-and-file Palestinians have carved their own bypasses, which circumvent IDF checkpoints and make a farce of security quarantines."[48] The farce, such as it is, lies in such a shockingly perverted gloss on the intrinsic violence of colonial occupation.

In the course of constructing this landscape of colonial modernity, integrating and differentiating a space of hideous Reason, tens of thousands of acres of fertile Palestinian farmland were expropriated and 7,000 Palestinian homes were demolished, leaving 50,000 people homeless in addition to the millions in the refugee camps. During the Oslo process the contraction of the Palestinian economy was accelerated; as its territorial base fragmented, perforated by illegal settlements and scissored by Israeli closures, so it became disarticulated. The corruptions, monopolies, and profiteering of the Palestinian Authority played their part in this state of affairs, but the primary reason was Israel's policy of periodically closing its borders to the movement of labor and goods from Gaza and the West Bank. Unemployment soared and living standards plunged. Palestinians were subject to routinized humiliation and their human rights were violated day after day. By 2000 Israel was still in full control of 60 percent of Gaza and the West Bank. Far from setting in train a process of de-colonization, the accords had enabled Israel to intensify its system of predatory colonialism over Gaza and the West Bank. "The Oslo process actually worsened the situation in the territories," Shlaim concludes, "and confounded Palestinian aspirations for a state of their own."[49]

Camp David and Goliath

The crisis came to a head at a series of meetings between Barak and Arafat convened by Clinton at Camp David in Maryland in July 2000. Israel insisted that the issues to be resolved had their origins in 1967, in its "Six Day War" that resulted in the occupation of Gaza and the West Bank, whereas the Palestinians argued that the roots lay in 1948, in *al-Nakba* and the dispossession and dispersal of the Palestinian people. The distinction is crucial, and it turns not on amnesia but on active repression. In effect, the Israeli position valorizes a selective past:

> While the events which preceded and led to the foundation of modern Israel in 1948 not only remain unquestioned, but are in fact justified, those following 1967 and the continued Israeli occupation of the territories conquered during this period (that is, the West Bank and Gaza) are deemed unacceptable. . . . Jews are the victims of the earlier and more distant chapter, while Palestinians are the victims of its more recent chapter.[50]

The questions silenced by this (left) Israeli argument are ones of great and grave substance. What of the Arab refugees who fled in 1948? What of the expropriation of their land and property? The thrust of the negotiations at Camp David was to rebut these questions and to secure the Israeli position on a post-1967 accord on three fronts.[51]

In the first place, there was no movement on the question of Palestinian refugees post-1948, and Israel flatly refused to provide any compensation for the appropriation of their property. "The most we can do," the Palestinian delegation was told, "is to express our sorrow for the sufferings of the refugees, *the way we would for any accident or natural disaster.*"[52] The dispossession of the Palestinian people was deemed "accidental," even "natural," rather than the deliberate consequence of geopolitical strategy and military and paramilitary violence. Its effects were accordingly supposed to be short-lived. In fact, Barak likened Palestinians to salmon returning to spawn: in the fullness of time, he argued, "there will be very few salmon around who still want to return to their birthplace to die."[53] In one casual metaphor Palestinians' desire to return to their homeland was dehumanized and recast as transitory, yet it would have been unthinkable for Barak to have described diasporic Jews in such terms.

Then, since the Six Day War all six US administrations had more or less consistently adhered to UN Resolution 242 and its central thesis –

that peace for Israel would be guaranteed by its withdrawal from the occupied territories – but Clinton obtained a Palestinian commitment to peace with Israel while continuing to treat Gaza and the West Bank as "disputed" territories whose final shape was to be determined through negotiations.[54] Barak made a series of territorial proposals that ultimately envisaged the IDF withdrawing from 88–94 percent of the West Bank and parts of Gaza.[55] At the same time, Israel insisted on consolidating or "thickening" its main blocs of illegal settlement, which would have confirmed the dismemberment of the West Bank into three almost completely non-contiguous sections connected by a narrow thread of land. *This was a territorial formation that Israel had explicitly rejected for itself* because its boundaries would have been "twisted" and "broken" and many of its villages would have been separated from their fields (above, p. 82). And yet the "peace process" produced exactly the same torsions and severations. It depended on what Israeli architect Eyal Weizman calls "an Escher-like representation of space," a "politics of verticality" in which Palestine was to be splintered into a territorial hologram of six dimensions, "three Jewish and three Arab." Projecting this topological imaginary onto the ground, a baroque system of underpasses, overpasses, and even a viaduct from Gaza to the West Bank would make it possible to draw a continuous boundary between Israel and Palestine *without dismantling the blocs of illegal settlements*.[56]

Finally, the territory that Israel insisted on retaining constituted what Israeli anthropologist Jeff Halper calls "a matrix of control" that Israel had been laying down since 1967 and which would have left Israel in effective control of East Jerusalem and the West Bank yet relieved it of any direct responsibility for their 3 million inhabitants. "It's like a prison," Halper explained. If prisoners occupy (on the most generous estimate) 94 percent of the area – cell-blocks, exercise yards, dining-room, workshops – and the prison administration occupies just 6 percent, this does not make the place any less of a prison. The proposed Palestinian configuration was even more restrictive than this comparison implies, however, because the politics of verticality projected the matrix of control both above and below ground. Israel required Palestinian airspace to be brought beneath Israeli airspace, so that it would continue to command the skies above Palestinian buildings and low-flying helicopters, and Israel also demanded "subterranean sovereignty" over the mountain aquifer beneath the West Bank. The result would have been the institutionalization of a carceral archipelago, an ersatz Palestine controlled by Eretz Israel.[57]

The Palestinians were not blind, and even Arafat finally seemed to understand that his kingdom of illusions was vanishing. As one Israeli commentator put it, "the prospect of being able to establish a viable state was fading right before their eyes. They were confronted with an intolerable set of options: to agree to the spreading occupation, to set up wretched Bantustans, or to launch an uprising."[58] In September 2000 a new Intifada (the al-Aqsa Intifada) broke out. It was precipitated by the provocative visit of Ariel Sharon, by then the new leader of Likud, to one of the holiest places in Arab East Jerusalem.[59] But like the first Intifada it had deeper origins in the protracted experience of occupation and dispossession made still more melancholy by the despair produced through the "peace process."[60] The IDF responded with astonishing violence; no Israeli civilians were killed by Palestinians until November, but by October Israel had already deployed high-velocity bullets, helicopter gunships, tanks, and missiles against the Palestinian population, and so the al-Aqsa Intifada increasingly turned into an armed revolt. The IDF's tactics were calculated to goad Palestinians into a response whose violence could then "justify" – and be trumped by – the Israeli military's own ferocious actions. One Israeli commentator described the violence of Palestinian resistance as "a direct response to the violence of the occupation." Occupation *is* violence, of course, but the Israeli occupation has consistently ratcheted up the level of violence to the point where the IDF's operations have to be seen as proactive not reactive measures in a long-term military strategy that is expressly designed to undermine the Oslo process and any negotiations whose terminus is the formation of a sovereign and independent Palestinian state.[61]

There was a final, desperate attempt to find a peaceful solution at Taba in late January 2001, when the prospect of an imminent Israeli election underscored the urgency of reaching an agreement. Significantly, Israeli and Palestinian negotiators accepted that Resolution 242 should be reinstated as the framework for any agreement. Gaza was to be sovereign Palestinian territory, with all illegal settlements evacuated, but Israel proposed to annex 6 percent of the West Bank for its illegal settlements there, which it planned to develop further, and insisted that it was "entitled to contiguity between and among them": an argument that mimicked the Palestinian case for territorial contiguity while maintaining the Israeli matrix of control. Little or no progress was made on the question of Palestinian refugees or on the Palestinian claim to East Jerusalem. Critics claimed that all of this was merely an election ploy, but it is hard to know what Barak had in mind. He withdrew his negotiators from the discussions, and the meeting ended on January 27 without an agreement. Ten days later Barak was resoundingly defeated by Ariel Sharon, who lost no time in denouncing the "concessions" that had been offered by his predecessor.[62]

Sharon's election as prime minister fanned the flames of Palestinian revolt (and revulsion), but the gravity of the situation was exacerbated by a dramatic rise in so-called "suicide bombing" attacks on Israeli civilians. The first attack had taken place in 1994. By September 2000 there had been 14 other such bombings, but in 1998–9 the Palestinian Authority had moved against the two main organizations that claimed responsibility and the level of violence had been contained. Hamas returned to suicide bombings in January 2001, Islamic Jihad soon after, and from December 2001, when the number of murders spiked sharply upward, their twin campaigns were joined by attacks carried out by the al-Aqsa Martyrs' Brigade. These "martyrdom operations," as many Palestinians prefer to call them, reveal an ongoing Islamicization of the local population – and of the Intifada itself – that has been fostered, at least in part, by Israel's marginalization of the secular Palestinian Authority. Some Israeli politicians have sought to reduce these terrorist attacks to a culture of violence that they claim inheres within Islam. The only way to "cleanse" the space of Reason from these "irrational" irruptions, so they argue, is to remove the Palestinians from Gaza and the West Bank.[63] But it seems to me that quite another removal is called for. These attacks, and the heightened militarization of the al-Aqsa Intifada more generally, are the product of a profound, desperate anger born out of the sustained and asymmetric violence of Israel's continuing military occupation of Gaza and the West Bank.[64] The youth culture from which many suicide bombers have emerged, especially in the camps, is both communal and competitive. Ghassan Hage suggests that there is a sort of jockeying for symbolic capital among those for whom most other opportunities for recognition and worth have been systematically withdrawn. More recent suicide bombers have been middle-aged as well as young, married as well as unmarried; many are well educated. But Hage's point remains a sharp one: it is through the colonial circulation of affect – through the continuous accumulation of the countless hurts and humiliations of occupation – that martyrdom becomes a way for some individuals to commit themselves to what they believe will be a worthwhile symbolic life after the end of their physical life.[65]

All that said, however, the scale and the systematicity of these terrorist attacks render them crimes against humanity, and culpability is of course neither a purely individual nor an exclusively Israeli affair. Militant organizations provide an operational matrix that at once encourages and enables these crimes to be carried out. While international law upholds the right of any people to struggle against colonial domination or foreign occupation, the Fourth Geneva Convention (on which the Palestinians quite properly rely for much of their case against Israel's illegal settlement and occupation) distinguishes between civilians and combatants and requires every effort to be made to protect the former from harm; its prohibitions against targeting civilians cannot be set aside by the actions of adversaries. Human rights organizations emphasize that Arafat's security apparatus did little or nothing to rein in the organizations that claimed responsibility for these attacks in 2001, before Israeli military incursions rendered it virtually incapable of doing so, and the continued bombing campaign threatens to disfigure a struggle for liberation which, as Said and others have repeatedly insisted, is pre-eminently about life not death. I am aware that the IDF had done much to provoke these attacks, and that it has capitalized on them in its own murderous campaign of terror and intimidation. And, as I must now show, it also capitalized on the mass murders of September 11 to continue its own atrocities. But, as Mahmoud Darwish wrote in the wake of the attacks on New York City and Washington,

> No cause, not even a just cause, can make legitimate the killing of innocent civilians, no matter how long the list of accusations and the register of grievances. Terror never paves the way to justice, but leads down the shortest path to hell. . . . For a victim is a victim, and terrorism is terrorism, here or there.[66]

6   Defiled Cities

Can defiled cities be
the outcome of our struggle?
Have years of suffering,
long days of vigilance
in trenches, on hills
and in tattered tents
led to this?
Harun Hashim Rasheed,
Raise Your Arms

Ground Zeros

WHEN the Bush administration assumed office on January 20, 2001 its foreign policy was, at least outwardly, one of disengagement. Palestine was no exception. Faced with the new Intifada and the rapidly escalating spiral of violence, the White House closed its doors and opted for minimal involvement. Within days of the terrorist attacks on New York City and Washington, the intensity of Israeli incursions into the West Bank was stepped up. Tanks drove into Jenin, Jericho, and Ramallah, supported by helicopter gunships; houses were demolished, trees uprooted, and civilians killed and injured. Palestinians claimed that Sharon was using the attacks on America as a pretext "to enter the endgame" against them. "He thinks that the dust in New York and Washington will cover up Israeli actions here," one Palestinian official explained. "He is taking advantage of the fact that no one is watching."[1] But constructing such a space of invisibility required the substitution of another, carefully constructed space of visibility so that the attacks on the World Trade Center and the Pentagon would serve not only as a distraction from but also as a justification for Israeli actions. And so a political offensive was launched alongside the military one. "Acts of terror against Israeli citizens are no different from bin Laden's terror against American citizens," Sharon insisted. "The fight against terror is an international struggle of the free world against the forces of darkness who seek to destroy our liberty and our way of life."[2]

Edward Said, himself a New Yorker and deeply affected by the attacks on his city, was not alone in protesting that Israel was "cynically exploiting the American catastrophe by intensifying its military occupation and oppression of the Palestinians" and justifying its actions by representing "the connection between the World Trade Center and Pentagon bombings and Palestinian attacks on Israel [as] an absolute conjunction of 'world terrorism' in which bin Laden and Arafat are interchangeable entities."[3] The White House also rejected Sharon's diversionary tactic, and dismissed his substitution of Arafat for bin Laden as inaccurate and unhelpful. If America were to secure the support of Islamic states like Saudi Arabia and Pakistan for its military response to September 11 – both of them allies in its previous interventions in Afghanistan – the Bush administration understood that it would have to re-engage with the Palestinian question on terms that were markedly less partisan than those of the past. A fragile ceasefire was cobbled together on 17–18 September, and Sharon reluctantly agreed to withdraw Israeli tanks and troops from the areas nominally under Palestinian jurisdiction.[4] A truce was signed on September 26, but it ended within days of Bush announcing his support for the foundation of a Palestinian state. Sharon knew very well what the White House was about. Furious, he compared its attempt to include the Arab world in the American-led coalition to British and French appeasement of the Nazis in 1938 – a comparison that was as odious to the Arabs as it was to the Americans – and he warned the White House: "Do not try to placate the Arabs at Israel's expense. We are not Czechoslovakia."[5] Bush, equally angry, denounced the comparison as unacceptable, and when Sharon renewed the military offensive the White House repeatedly criticized the Israeli campaign of intimidation and incursion.[6]

One incident disturbed this carefully calculated American approach. Exactly one month after the terrorist attacks, Alwaleed bin Talal, a member of the Saudi royal family, arrived in New York City to present Mayor Rudolph Giuliani with a $10 million check for the Twin Towers Fund established by the mayor principally to support the families of firefighters, police officers, and other rescuers who lost their lives when the buildings collapsed. The prince fiercely criticized Osama bin Laden and unreservedly condemned "all forms of terror"; but in an accompanying press release he also drew attention to Sharon's diversionary tactics and the way in which Israel had intensified its aggression toward the Palestinians. "While the United Nations passed clear resolutions numbered 242 and 338 calling for the Israeli withdrawal from the West Bank and Gaza Strip decades ago," he noted, "our Palestinian brethren continue to be slaughtered at the hands of Israelis while the world turns the other cheek." Giuliani was incensed at any attempt to diminish the singularity of 9–11. He refused any linkage between the attacks on New York City and Washington and events in Gaza and the West Bank, and promptly returned the check. "There is no moral equivalent to this attack. Not only are those statements wrong," he declared, "they are part of the problem."[7]

Throughout October Sharon defied American demands to retreat from nominally Palestinian-controlled areas of the West Bank. In fact, Israel repeatedly identified its attacks on the occupied territories with America's assault on Afghanistan, and Sharon instructed the actions of the Israeli military – the IDF – to be "packaged" so that "the elimination of the Taliban and the elimination of the Palestinian Authority" would be seen as "two parallel goals." "We are doing precisely what the US is doing in Afghanistan," an Israeli spokesman explained to CNN. But the comparison failed to convince many in its target audience. "We are not out to destroy this extremist menace [in Afghanistan] so that Israel will be free to build more [illegal] settlements or to eat up more Palestinian land," Thomas Friedman wrote in the *New York Times*. "Mr Sharon needs to realise that we are out to make the world safe for Israel to be free, not safe for Israel to occupy the West Bank according to his biblical map."[8] The Bush administration also rejected Sharon's tactic. As tanks drove into the heart of West Bank cities and scores of Palestinians were killed, the State Department was moved to "deeply regret and deplore Israeli army actions that have killed numerous Palestinian civilians."[9] Washington was hardly on the side of the Palestinian Authority, but relations with Tel Aviv were so close to collapse that by October 30 it was possible for one commentator to suggest that the sea-change in superpower sensibilities meant that "the cruel calculations of geopolitics [would] continue to make Afghanistan's loss into Palestine's gain."[10]

But the world began to turn in the dying weeks of November. By then, to the evident surprise of America and its coalition partners, the Northern Alliance was sweeping southwards through Afghanistan, and the Taliban forces were in full retreat. On November 23 the IDF assassinated Mahmoud Abu Hanoud, Hamas's military leader in the West Bank, and several Israeli commentators warned that this was certain to provoke a violent retaliation. They also claimed that such an eventuality had explicitly been taken into consideration by the military and political apparatus, and the act was either recklessness or a cold-blooded attempt to scuttle any projected ceasefire.[11] In any event the response was not long in coming. On November 29 Sharon arrived in New York City and made what he called a "solidarity visit" to Ground Zero. Over that weekend, as the Jewish sabbath was coming to an end on the night of December 1–2, two suicide bombs and a car bomb exploded outside a café in a crowded district in the heart of West Jerusalem. Ten Israelis were murdered and over 170 injured. Soon after, another suicide bomb exploded on a bus at Haifa, murdering 15 Israelis and injuring 40 others. Sharon cut short his visit, but before he flew back to Israel he reminded Bush that the deaths of 25 Israelis were equivalent to the deaths of 2,000 Americans. The significance of the comparison was lost on nobody. Sharon insisted that the weekend's events had made it apodictically clear that America and Israel were engaged in "the same war" on terrorism, and if America had been justified in its military retaliation against al-Qaeda and the Taliban in Afghanistan, then Israel was justified in launching its helicopter gunships against Hamas, Islamic Jihad, and the Palestinian Authority in Gaza and the West Bank.[12]

Israeli attacks on the occupied territories immediately intensified. Missiles were launched against Gaza and the West Bank, helicopter gunships struck at the Palestinian Authority's compound in Ramallah, tanks moved into the scattered districts of Area A (which was supposedly under full Palestinian control), and the IDF blockaded Palestinian towns and villages. But Bush now firmly resisted calls to restrain Sharon. "Israel has a right to defend itself," a White House spokesman explained, "and the President understands that." The focus was, relentlessly, on the Palestinian Authority and its security apparatus. The attacks threatened to bring down Arafat's tottering – "cash-strapped, ineffectual and deeply unpopular" – regime. The onus was repeatedly placed on the Palestinian Authority to "end terror," even as its own security apparatus was destroyed by the IDF so that it was now virtually impossible for it to act against the militant organizations (Hamas and Islamic Jihad in particular) which had claimed responsibility for the suicide bombings. And there was neither admonishment nor caution from the White House over Israeli actions. On the contrary, senior US officials, speaking off the record, freely compared Palestinian attacks in Israel to al-Qaeda's attacks on America.[13]

On December 7 Giuliani, by then the outgoing mayor of New York City, together with his successor Michael Bloomberg and George Pataki, the governor of the state of New York, were invited to visit Jerusalem. They toured an illegal settlement on the outskirts of the city and visited the scene of the weekend's suicide bombings. Weeks earlier Giuliani had denounced any attempt to draw parallels with the attacks on America. Now he had no hesitation in drawing a reverse parallel of his own:

> The people of Jerusalem and the people of New York City, and the people of America and the people of Israel, are shoulder-to-shoulder in the fight against terrorism. We feel a great kinship with the people of Israel. We always have, and I think since September 11 and what's happened here in Israel, we're even closer.

The efforts to consolidate the bonds between America and Israel were gathering momentum.[14]

As the New Year wore on, the militarization of the occupation and of the Intifada reached new heights (or depths). On January 17, 2002 a Palestinian gunman murdered six Israelis at a bar mitzvah party in Hadera; in response, Israeli jets destroyed the Palestinian Authority's police station in Tulkarm and its tanks and troops entered the city, imposing a curfew and conducting house-to-house searches. This was the first time that the IDF had occupied an entire Palestinian city. It would not be the last. Bush accused Arafat of "enhancing" terrorism, and the White House granted Israel its widest freedom of military action since the Reagan administration had turned a blind eye to Sharon's invasion of Lebanon in 1982: "Israel is seen as the equivalent of New York and the Pentagon."[15] In February, following more suicide bombs and the launch of two home-made "Qasram-2" missiles from Gaza (which landed in open fields), the IDF launched a massive air and ground operation against Palestinian towns and refugee camps in Gaza. The scope of the incursions steadily widened as the IDF mounted a series of ferocious assaults in both Gaza and the

West Bank. Tanks rolled into Jabalya refugee camp north of Gaza City, and into Jenin refugee camp and Balata refugee camp south-east of Nablus, the largest in the West Bank. Alleys and cinderblock houses were shelled from the air and from the surrounding hills; tanks patrolled the main streets; and holes were blown in the walls of houses as the army swept through the camps. In the middle of March, 20,000 troops reinvaded camps in Gaza and reoccupied Ramallah in what was claimed to be the largest Israeli offensive since its invasion of Lebanon.[16]

By the end of the month even that benchmark was passed. On March 27, as they sat down for a Passover *seder* in Netanya, 28 Israelis were murdered and 140 injured by a suicide bomb. For American columnist Charles Krauthammer this atrocity was *"Kristallnacht* transposed to Israel" and "Israel's September 11, a time when sporadic terrorism reaches a critical mass of malevolence that war is the only response." Within 24 hours the IDF had called up 20,000 reservists, its largest mobilization since 1967, and what Tanya Reinhart describes as its long-awaited and carefully planned offensive, Operation Defensive Shield, was under way. Tanks smashed into Arafat's compound and troops stormed into the offices of the Palestinian Authority in Ramallah. How often "defensive," in the official Israeli lexicon, means "offensive." "As with the American attack on Afghanistan," Krauthammer argued, "Israel is going into Palestinian territory to destroy the terrorists and the regime that sponsors them." Krauthammer was simply repeating Sharon's own claims. In a calculated echo of Bush's rhetoric the Israeli prime minister had hailed the operation as the first stage of a "long and complicated war that knows no borders." He declared that "Arafat, who has formed a coalition of terror against Israel, is an enemy" and he vowed to eliminate the "terrorist infrastructure" that he claimed the Palestinian Authority had put in place.[17] Whatever Sharon understood "terrorist infrastructure" to mean, the IDF had so far concentrated its efforts on destroying the Palestinian Authority's police and paramilitary security installations. With Sharon's encouragement, however, the IDF now targeted the Palestinian Authority's *civilian* infrastructure. First it shelled the buildings. "All night," Palestinian lawyer Raja Shehadeh wrote in his diary, "I heard the Israeli bombardment of Palestinian institutions built after Oslo." Then its troops rampaged through the offices to destroy the record – the very archive, the institutional memory – of Palestinian civil society. "From the second week onward," Rema Hammami reported, "the invasion saw daily rounds of blasting entrances followed by ransacking, aimed at everything from the Legislative Council offices to the Ministries of Education, Finance, Agriculture, Trade and Industry to municipal buildings and chambers of commerce."[18] Uri Avnery contemptuously identified the real objective. "The lists of terrorists were not hidden in the land registration books, the inventory of bombs was not tucked away among the list of kindergarten teachers. The real aim is obvious: to destroy not only the Palestinian Authority but Palestinian society itself."[19] In spite of this new and malignant focus – Amnesty International concluded that the military offensive aimed at the collective punishment of all Palestinians, which is illegal under international law[20] – the White House still refused to condemn the Israeli attacks and incursions.

The military campaign escalated throughout April. At the beginning of the month helicopter gunships, tanks, and armored bulldozers launched an assault on Bethlehem, and witnesses described close-quarter fighting in the city. Many of its residents were deprived of food, water, electricity, and medical supplies. Religious leaders pleaded with the White House to use its influence over Israel to halt what they called "the inhuman tragedy that is taking place in this Holy Land."[21] Undeterred, the IDF pushed on into Nablus, Hebron, and Jenin. At last Bush told Sharon that "enough is enough" and urged him to withdraw his troops from Palestinian towns "without delay"; he was ignored. His Secretary of State, Colin Powell, took a week to make a staged journey to Tel Aviv; not surprisingly, when he finally arrived he too was ignored. The military invasion extended and tightened its grip and yet, with Israel in control of six out of eight Palestinian cities, the White House press secretary could still announce that "the President believes that Ariel Sharon is a man of peace."[22]

As the attacks wore on – and Tel Aviv and Washington turned "peace" into a synonym for war – one of Palestine's most prominent painters and sculptors, Nabil Anani, drew attention to the grotesque reversal by erecting a mock "Statue of Liberty" with its torch reversed on the roof of Arafat's ruined compound in Ramallah (figure 6.1). The pointed juxtaposition of "Liberty" with American endorsement of Israel's attacks on Palestine activated another irony. The Statue of Liberty was designed by Frédéric-Auguste Bartholdi, who had intended it to be raised at the Mediterranean entrance to the Suez Canal as a symbol of the nineteenth-century expansion of Europe; it was to be called *Egypt Carrying Light to Asia*, in which a colonized Egypt was cast as the handmaiden of the West and itself-validated "mission" to bring enlightenment to the Orient. The distress and deceit symbolized by the reversed torch in Ramallah thus illuminated yet another nadir of Orientalism.

Figure 6.1   Palestinian artists erect a "Statue of Liberty" (with the torch reversed) on top of a damaged building at Yasser Arafat's compound, Ramallah, October 2002 (AP Photo/Nasser Nasser)

In the spring the IDF was already busily demolishing houses in Jenin refugee camp and clearing paths for tanks and troops with giant Caterpillar D-9 bulldozers. When 13 Israeli soldiers died in a booby-trapped building on April 9, the scale of destruction intensified, and the center of the camp was painstakingly reduced to rubble (figure 6.2). "I had no mercy," a driver of one of the armored bulldozers declared.

> I would erase anyone with the D-9 just so that our soldiers wouldn't expose themselves to danger. . . . For three days I just destroyed and destroyed. The whole area. Any house that they fired from came down. And to knock it down, I tore down some more. They were warned by loudspeaker to get out of the house before I came, but I gave no one a chance. . . . Many people were inside houses we started to demolish. . . . I didn't see with my own eyes people dying under the blade of the D-9, and I didn't see houses falling down on live people. But if there were any, I wouldn't care at all. I am sure people died inside these houses. . . . I found joy with every house that came down, because I knew they didn't mind dying, but they cared for their homes. If

Figure 6.2 Jenin refugee camp, aerial view, April 2002 (© David Silverman/ Reuters)

you knocked down a house, you buried 40 or 50 people for generations. If I am sorry for anything, it is for not tearing the whole camp down.[23]

Almost a fortnight later the army began to withdraw, but international aid agencies and human rights workers continued to be denied access to the camp for nearly a week after the fighting had ended. When reporters were finally allowed in, they found "a silent wasteland, permeated with the stench of rotting corpses and cordite." "The scale is almost beyond imagination," wrote Suzanne Goldenberg, gazing out over "a vast expanse of rubble and mangled iron rods, surrounded by the carcasses of shattered homes" that became known locally as "Ground Zero" (figure 6.3). "Rarely in more than a decade of war reporting from Bosnia, Chechnya, Sierra Leone and Kosovo" had Janine di Giovanni seen "such deliberate destruction, such disrespect for human life":

Sofas and satellite dishes hang from the crevices of third-floors of what were once family homes. A red curtain, peppered with bullet holes, flaps in the breeze. This is what war does: it leaves behind imprints of lives. A sewing

Figure 6.3　Jenin refugee camp, April 2002 (© Reinhard Krause/Reuters)

machine with a girl's dress still under the needle inside a house with the walls blown out. A goosedown pillow, ripped, the feathers fluttering. A photograph of a child with a bird hangs on a partly demolished wall.

Thousands of houses had been destroyed; scores of bodies were buried beneath the ruins; 16,000 people had fled in terror, and those who remained were left to survive without running water or electricity.[24] The International Committee of the Red Cross, Human Rights Watch, and Amnesty International all accused Israel of breaching the Geneva Convention by recklessly endangering civilian lives and property during its assault on the camp. Israel was undeterred, insisting that its operations were necessary, professional, surgical, and that no massacre had taken place. "Like everything else in our corrupted life," wrote Israeli commentator Yitzhak Laor, "it comes down to the number of dead: ten dead Israelis are a massacre; 50 Palestinians not enough to count."[25] This is another version of the algebra of infinite justice, and the United States endorsed the same grisly equation: it first supported, then moved to disrupt, and finally blocked any attempt at an inquiry by the United Nations.[26]

Besieging Cartographies

There were geopolitical reasons that allowed the Bush administration to reaffirm American support for Israel: most immediately, the fall of the Taliban had terminated the necessity for an international military coalition in Afghanistan; more generally, the territorial designs for American Empire that had been mapped out by the Project for a New American Century had returned the Middle East to the center of the neoconservative stage. But what gave this reaffirmation its teeth – what gave it both voice and bite – was a series of parallels between the imaginative geographies deployed by America in its military assault on Afghanistan and those deployed by Israel in its military operations in the occupied territories of Palestine. The Palestinians were also reduced to targets, to barbarians, and to *homines sacri*: I will consider each in turn.

Palestinians were reduced to targets through what Camille Mansour calls a "besieging cartography" that was sustained by an intricate system of monitoring. This involved passive sensors, observation towers equipped with day/night and radar surveillance capabilities, and satellite images and photographs from reconnaissance planes that were fed through electronic communications systems into computerized data banks for storage, retrieval, and analysis. This formidable arsenal was largely funded by American aid, and much of it was provided by American manufacturers.[27] As the assault on the occupied territories intensified, however, Stephen Graham showed that the conflict was transformed into "an urban war in which the distance between enemies [was] measured in metres." Orientalist tropes were invoked to render Palestinian towns and cities as "impenetrable, unknowable spaces" whose close quarters were beyond "the three-dimensional gaze of the IDF's high-technology surveillance systems." As surveillance at a distance became markedly less effective, therefore, so "a new family of Unattended Aerial Vehicles (UAVs) and camera-carrying balloons was deployed to permit real-time monitoring of the complex battles within the cities, and to track the movements of key Palestinian fighters and officials so that missiles could target and kill them."[28] This was a strategically vital arm in the realization (and radicalization) of Israel's politics of verticality. "Every floor in every house, every car, every telephone call or radio transmission can be monitored," explains Eyal Weizman. "These eyes in the sky, completing the network of observation that is woven throughout the ground, finally iron out the folded surface and flatten the terrain." The opacity of supposedly alien spaces is thus rendered transparent, and their complexities reduced to a series of objects in a purely visual plane.[29]

An example will serve to show what this means. In July 2002, when it became known that Hamas was about to announce a suspension of attacks inside Israel, Sharon and his Minister of Defence authorized the IDF to execute Salah Shehadeh, the leader of Hamas's military wing. This was a rerun of the assassination of Mahmoud Abu Hanoud eight months earlier, but with a savage twist. On this occasion an IDF F-16 was ordered to drop a one-ton bomb on a densely crowded neighborhood in Gaza. The raid leveled an entire city block and killed not only its intended target but also 16 others and injured 140 more. The pilot was protected by his aircraft and its armaments and also by the armature of cartographic reason: its doctrines of "objectivity" and "object-ness." Asked what he felt when he released the bomb over a residential area, he replied: "I feel a slight ping in the aircraft, the result of releasing the bomb. It passes a second later, and that's it. That's what I feel." He was not alone in his reduction of ordinary Palestinians to targets. Sharon described the atrocity as "one of our greatest successes," and President Bush merely complained that the attack was "heavy-handed."[30]

But the disembodied abstractions produced within such an enhanced technocultural sphere have been perforated by imaginative geographies that activate other, intensely corporeal registers. For Palestinians, of course, the distance between detachment and engagement has always been vulnerable to unpredictable, hideous collapse. Walking the streets of Ramallah, Hanan Elmasu recalled wondering "if suddenly the drone of the reconnaissance planes that are often circling above us will disappear and be replaced by an Apache attack helicopter beginning to rain down bullets from the sky as I am walking to my friend's home."[31] But some Israeli pilots have also been troubled by the same perforations, and they have found it difficult to sustain the optical detachment achieved by some of their colleagues and by their counterparts in America's "Kabul-ki dance" (above, p. 54). One fighter pilot urged those who flew Israel's deadly F-16s "to think about what a bombing operation would be like in the city they live in." He explained what he meant with an immediacy that provides a pointed contrast to the chilling detachment that I have just described: "I am talking about bombing a densely populated city. I am talking about liquidating people on the main street."[32]

The ground war involved the performance of highly abstract spacings too, in which every Palestinian was reduced to a threat and a target. One reporter described how, at the height of Operation Defensive Shield in Tulkarm, a reserve detachment of Paratrooper Reconnaissance Commandos operated in "a peculiar state of sensory deprivation." Occupying a house seized from its Palestinian owners, the soldiers lived "in a kind of perpetual shadow," he wrote, "behind drawn curtains and under dim lighting, rarely venturing out except at night and then only in tanks or the windowless A[rmored] P[ersonnel] C[arriers]. Their knowledge of the battlefield [*sic*] is largely limited to the maps they study or the tiny corner of land they view when the [APC] door opens, and so anyone who crosses their path is viewed as a potential life-and-death threat." Yet here too the abstractions were qualified, their imaginative geographies perforated by much more intimate engagements, and many of the soldiers interviewed saw the military occupation as unsustainable on humanitarian rather than narrowly logistical grounds.[33] It was not only the aggrandized violence of offensive operations like Defensive Shield that convinced some reservists to become conscientious objectors. It was also the everyday exercise of the power to humiliate at what Meron Benvenisti calls "the checkpoints of arrogance" that turned their stomachs. Benvenisti is a former deputy mayor of Jerusalem, and he explains that the function of the checkpoint "is to send a message of force and authority, to inspire fear, and to symbolize the downtrodden nature and inferiority of those under the occupation." Some conscientious objectors came to see that humiliation saturates both sides of the barrier. For the checkpoint also degrades those who are enrolled in its operations: "You become a machine of the checkpoints" (figure 6.4).[34]

For all these reasons, over 500 reserve soldiers have refused to serve in the occupied territories since February 2002. Eight of them petitioned the Israeli Supreme Court to have their refusal to serve beyond the Green Line recognized as a matter of conscience. They claimed that the aim of IDF operations in Gaza and the West Bank has been to damage "the entire civil fabric" of Palestinian society and "to dominate, starve and humiliate an entire people." Their submission charged the IDF with systematically violating the most fundamental human rights of the Palestinian people, and argued that the Israeli occupation is itself illegal.[35] Significantly, the court declined to rule on the legality of the occupation. While it accepted that the reservists' objections were moral ones it nevertheless upheld the prison sentences that had been imposed upon them for refusing to serve in the occupied territories. This decision tacitly recognized that the reservists' refusal to fight what they call "the War of the Settlements" presents a much

Figure 6.4   Israeli checkpoint, Tulkarem (© AP Photo/Mohammed Azba)

more serious threat to the legitimacy of Israel's politicomilitary strategy than conscientious objectors who refuse to serve in the IDF at all. For theirs is a *selective* refusal that exposes the territorial underbelly of Israel's aggressions. As Susan Sontag observed, "the soldiers are not refusing a particular order. *They are refusing to enter the space where illegal orders are bound to be given.*"[36]

The production of this space – its articulation and legitimation – was reinforced by the deployment of other imaginative geographies that also mirrored those used by America in its military assault on Afghanistan. The "clash of civilizations" was rarely invoked directly. Huntington himself had said remarkably little about Palestine, apart from the monstrous perversion that the "fault-line war" in Gaza and the West Bank showed that "Muslims have problems living peacefully with their neighbours." He did acknowledge, in passing, the role of the European powers in setting the stage for the conflict, but said nothing at all about Israel's predatory actions. Robert Wistrich, a professor of modern European history at the Hebrew University, was more forthright. "It *is* a clash of civilisations," he wrote in the *Jerusalem Post* soon after September 11. Not only had radical Islam devastated New York City ("the largest Jewish city on the planet") but it continued to threaten the survival of the state of Israel. Columnist Thomas Friedman, writing in the *New York Times* six months later, invoked Huntington too, but drew a markedly different conclusion: "What Osama bin Laden failed to achieve on September 11 is now being unleashed by the Israeli-Palestinian war in the West Bank: a clash of civilizations." But this had to end, so he insisted, in an Israeli withdrawal from the occupied territories.[37]

These straws in the wind were blowing in different directions, but the imaginative geography that dominated Israeli policy dispensed with their dualisms altogether. Instead, it resurrected the opposition between "civilization" and "barbarism" that had been a foundational weapon of Zionism and which the White House had also deployed in its "war on terrorism." Palestinians were represented as denizens of a barbarian space lying *beyond* the pale of civilization. When Barak had described Israel as "a villa in the middle of the jungle" and as "a vanguard of culture against barbarism," he was not only degrading and brutalizing Palestinian culture and civil society: he was also rendering its spaces inchoate, outside the space of Reason.[38] What Sharon sought to do was to establish these linguistic claims in acutely physical terms. As Lena Jayyusi wrote from Ramallah, "There is no constative any longer: only the pure performative."[39] This is the heart of the matter because, as I have repeatedly insisted, representations are not mere mirrors of the world. They enter directly into its fabrication. Israel's offensive operations were designed to turn the Palestinian people not only into enemies but into aliens, and in placing them outside the modern, figuratively and physically, they were constructed, like whole sections of the population in Afghanistan, as *homines sacri* from whom the rights and protections of international law could be systematically withdrawn. The process was already in train, of course, but by invoking the global "war on terrorism" Sharon and his government were able to radicalize its effects. As the siege of Ramallah intensified, Shehadeh recognized that, to the Israelis,

> We the Palestinians are terrorists and therefore anything they do to us is legitimate. We are treated as *homo sacer* – to whom the laws of the rest of humanity do not apply. . . . There is something pornographic about Sharon's repetition of the word terrorist. . . . Isn't pornography the denigration of the human being into a mere object, a mere body, and a toy to which things can be done? So with the Palestinians, who are now dubbed terrorists. They can be killed, disposed of like flies by the army's big machines without second thought.[40]

It will be recalled that, for Agamben, *homo sacer* is constituted through the production and performance of the space of the exception, but in Palestine this process assumes an ever more physical form.[41] On one side, a strategy of consolidation and containment continues to bind Israel to its illegal settlements and to separate both from the remainder of the occupied territories; on the other side, a strategy of cantonization institutionalizes the siege of Palestinian towns and villages.

The first objective had already been secured in Gaza during the first Intifada. "Surrounded by electronic fences and army posts," Reinhart reported, "completely sealed off from the outside world, Gaza has become a huge prison."[42] Barak had proposed the construction of a similar fence for the West Bank, but in June 2002 Sharon announced the construction of a much more formidable barrier network (figure 6.5). For most of its length this will be an electronic fence but in places it will solidify into a concrete or steel wall 8 meters high: Jabotinsky's "iron wall" materialized, malevolent (figure 6.6). The line will be flanked by a 50–100 m security zone, edged with concertina wire, trenches, and patrol roads, and monitored by watchtowers, floodlights, electronic sensors, and surveillance cameras. Barak wanted the fence to run along the Green Line, which is 360 km long, but under Sharon the barrier will be 1,000 km long and much of it will run far to the east of the Green Line. It follows no natural contour (and in any case armored bulldozers are supremely indifferent to topography). Instead, as Uri Avnery remarks, "it twists like a snake according to a single principle: most of the [illegal Israeli] settlements must remain on the western side of the wall" (figure 6.7). Thousands of hectares of some of the most highly productive Palestinian farmland will be on the Israeli side too, with implications not only for the beleaguered Palestinian economy but also for the subsistence of the Palestinian population. During the first phase of construction at least 15 Palestinian villages will be on the Israeli side, while others will be cut off from their fields and wells, so that Israel will extend its control over the crucial central aquifer. The barrier is also intended to consolidate Israel's stranglehold over East Jerusalem, where again it runs deep into Palestinian territory and cuts off hundreds of thousands of Palestinians (many of whom do not have Israeli residency) from the West Bank. In March 2003 Sharon announced plans for a second barrier to be built around the eastern foothills and along the Jordan Valley, to connect with the first and so encircle the West Bank like Gaza. The Israeli Defence Minister has persistently represented the barrier as a security measure whose sole objective is to deny suicide bombers access

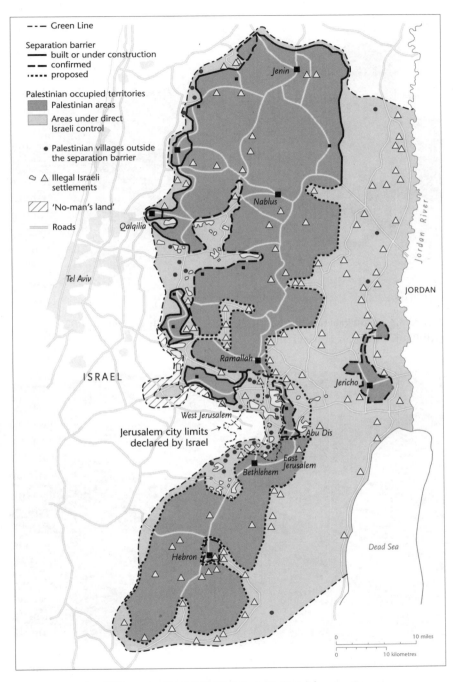

Figure 6.5 Ariel Sharon's "Iron Wall" (after *Yediot Aharonot*)

Figure 6.6 Construction of the "Iron Wall," Qualqilya, August 2002
(AP Photo/Brennan Linsley)

Figure 6.7 The West Bank: Palestinian village, the "separation barrier," and
an illegal Israeli settlement, July 2003 (AP Photo/Lefteris Pitarakis)

to Israel from the West Bank. The route of the first barrier and the plan for a second make a nonsense of these claims, and when the minister adds that "this not a border between political entities or sovereign territories," it becomes crystal clear that the only sovereign power to be recognized is the state of Israel. What lies beyond the line is not the (future) semi-state of Palestine – confined to just 42 percent of the West Bank – but what Agamben would call the (present) space of the exception.[43]

This is the point at which the analogy between occupied Palestine and the prison breaks down, for this carceral archipelago limns the dispersed site not of the prison but of the camp. Agamben explains the difference:

> While prison law only constitutes a particular sphere of penal law and is not outside the juridical order, the juridical constellation that guides the camp is martial law and the state of siege. . . . As the absolute space of the exception, the camp is topologically different from a single space of confinement.[44]

On that other side of the line, therefore, Israel has set about the proliferation of zones of indistinction in which, as the reservists who refuse to serve in the occupied territories claim, "the legal and the lawful can no longer be distinguished from the illegal and unlawful."[45] The baroque geography of the Oslo process has been swept away; the quasi-sovereignty of Area A has been terminated, and all that remains is another Escher-like system of exclusion and inclusion in which Palestinian towns and villages are severed from one another and placed under constant siege from a military force that has now twisted the topologies of occupation into new and even more grotesque forms. In his original discussion of *homo sacer*, Agamben suggested that the space of the exception – and here we should remind ourselves that he was arguing in general terms because the concordance with the occupied territories is agonizingly close – traces a threshold through which "outside and inside, the normal situation and chaos, enter into those topological relations that make the validity of the juridical order possible."[46] A delegation from the International Writers Parliament visited the West Bank in March 2002, at the invitation of Mahmoud Darwish, and their reports described the installation of these new topologies – the performance of their collective *danse macabre* – with shivering immediacy:

> The landscape of the West Bank and Gaza Strip has been ripped and torn like cloth made from strips of different materials. Barbed wire surrounds

Israeli settlements and military posts and the areas theoretically controlled by the Palestinian Authority: it protects and excludes, *unites separated zones and separates adjacent territories, weaves in between a labyrinth of islands that are mutually repelled and attracted.* A complex circulatory system of capillary veins demonstrates the occupier's desire to split the territory into slices, remnants, tracts that seemingly impact on each other and yet remain mutually unaware. . . . The landscape of settlements, frequently constructed on the ruins of Palestinian villages, evokes yet again the chess-board of reciprocal exclusion between the former and what remains of the autonomous areas, to the point of *confusing the inexpert visitor as to what they encompass and limit, the "interior" and the "exterior."*[47]

More prosaically, the military correspondent for *Ha'aretz* reported in April that "there is [now] only one area and that area is controlled by the IDF without Palestinian intermediaries." As far as the military was concerned, Amir Oren explained, there was no longer any difference between Areas A, B, and C: "The IDF is doing as it pleases in all of them." Israel had established a series of "security zones" throughout the West Bank (figure 6.8), so that Palestinians were now confined and corralled, subject to endless curfew and closure, whereas the IDF had complete freedom of movement and action.[48] As the Israeli Minister of Internal (*sic*) Security put it, "They are there, but we are here *and there as well.*"[49]

The occupied territories have been turned into twilight zones, caught in a frenzied cartography of mobile frontiers rather than fixed boundaries. These enforce a violent fragmentation and recombination of time and space, which is nothing less than a concerted attempt to disturb and derange the normal rhythms of everyday Palestinian life. During the first Intifada many Palestinians elected to "suspend" everyday life as a political strategy. This was a way of reminding one another that these were not normal times, a way of reasserting their collective power and, by calling attention to their actions, also a way of narrativizing the occupation: all of which actively sustained the process of Palestinian nationalism.[50] What I am describing here, in contrast, is the violent *annulment* of everyday life by the IDF through a series of military operations that is intended to paralyze Palestinian agency and – through its physical assaults on the Palestinian archive – to erase Palestinian memory.

These deformations involve deliberate twistings – torsions – of both time and space. Time is at once calibrated and indeterminate: the occupying army pulverizes Palestine into a landscape where everything is temporary except the occupation itself. In one sense, of course, Palestinians have had

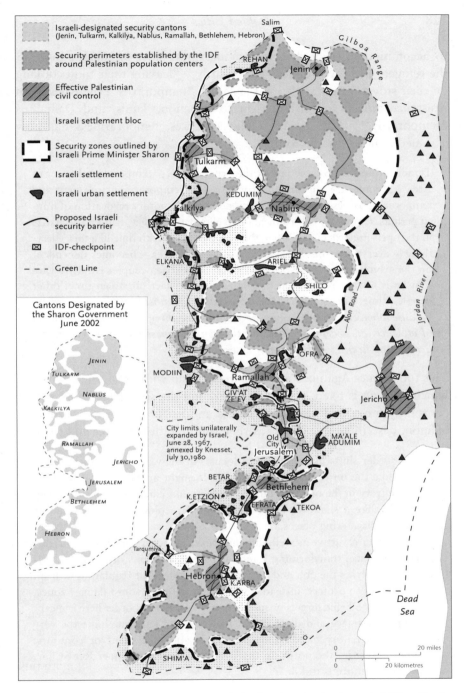

Legend:

- Israeli-designated security cantons
  (Jenin, Tulkarm, Kalkilya, Nablus, Ramallah, Bethlehem, Hebron)
- Security perimeters established by the IDF
  around Palestinian population centers
- Effective Palestinian
  civil control
- Israeli settlement bloc
- Security zones outlined by
  Israeli Prime Minister Sharon
- ▲ Israeli settlement
- ◆ Israeli urban settlement
- Proposed Israeli
  security barrier
- ⊠ IDF-checkpoint
- – – – Green Line

Cantons Designated by
the Sharon Government
June 2002

JENIN
TULKARM
NABLUS
KALKILYA
RAMALLAH
JERICHO
JERUSALEM
BETHLEHEM
HEBRON

Map labels: Salim, Gilboa Range, REHAN, Jenin, Tulkarm, KEDUMIM, Nablus, Kalkilya, ELKANA, ARIEL, SHILO, Alon Road, Jordan River, MODIIN, OFRA, Ramallah, GIV'AT ZE'EV, Jericho, MA'ALE ADUMIM, Old City Jerusalem, BETAR, Bethlehem, K.ETZION, EFRATA, TEKOA, Tarqumiya, Hebron, K.ARBA, SHIM'A, Dead Sea

City limits unilaterally
expanded by Israel,
June 28, 1967,
annexed by Knesset,
July 30, 1980

0   20 miles
0   20 kilometres

Figure 6.8   Israeli security cantons and checkpoints in the occupied West Bank, 2002–3 (after Jan de Jong/Foundation for Middle East Peace)

to accommodate themselves to temporariness since *al-Nakba*. In 1948 the refugees fled their homes "temporarily," "leaving their food cooking on their stoves"; they settled in the camps "temporarily"; the Palestinian resistance moved to Jordan, then to Lebanon, Tunis, and Damascus "temporarily."[51] But, as Adi Ophir observes, temporariness has now assumed a more volatile form.

> Temporariness is now the law of the occupation . . . temporary takeover of Area A, temporary withdrawal from Area A, temporary encirclement and temporary closures, temporary transit permits, temporary revocation of transit permits, temporary enforcement of an elimination policy, temporary change in the open-fire orders. . . . When the occupier plays with time like this, everything – everything that moves, everything that lives – becomes dependent on the arbitrariness of the occupier's decisions. The occupier is fully aware that he is always playing on borrowed time, in fact on stolen time, other people's time. *This occupier is an unrestrained, almost boundless sovereign, because when everything is temporary almost anything – any crime, any form of violence – is acceptable, because the temporariness seemingly grants it a license, the license of the state of emergency.*[52]

This too mimics Agamben's nightmare scenario with precision: a world in which nothing is fixed, nothing is clear, and the spaces of the exception constantly move and multiply. Here is another of the writers, Christian Salmon, describing its borders as they roll in with the night and the fog:

> [T]he border shifts like a swarm of locusts in the wake of another suicide attack, like the onset of a sudden storm. It might arrive at your doorstep like a delivery in the night, as quickly as the tanks can roll in; or it may slip in slowly, like a shadow. The border keeps creeping along, surrounding villages and watering places . . .
>
> The border is furtive as well: like the rocket launchers, it crushes and disintegrates space, transforming it into a frontier, into bits of territory. This frontier paralyses the ebb and flow of transit instead of regulating it. It no longer serves to protect, instead transforming all points into danger zones, all persons into living targets or suicide bombers. . . . The border here is meant to repress, displace and disorganize. In Israel and Palestine alike the very concept of territory has become hostile, devoid of content or contours, making insecurity the norm. In the words of the French poet Reni Char, "To stifle distance is to kill."[53]

Within these zones of indistinction the provisions of the Geneva Conventions that prohibit Israel from transferring its civilian population to the occupied territories continue to be disregarded. The same protocols that are supposed to protect Palestinians from torture, illegal detention, house demolition, deportation, and degradation remain suspended. And still this is not enough. In June 2002 the Knesset passed the Imprisonment of Illegal Combatants Law, which allowed for indefinite detention without charge or trial of anyone believed to have taken part in hostile activity against Israel, directly or indirectly. The symmetry with America's designation of captives from its war in Afghanistan as "unlawful combatants" was deliberate, and extended the parallels that the Sharon regime has been determined to draw between Palestine and Afghanistan. These new measures considerably widened the scope of existing provisions for administrative detention, which by the end of the year were being used to hold over 1,000 Palestinians in custody.[54] And in a further, shocking show of contempt for the law, Israel continues to carry out what it calls "extrajudicial killings." The policy was initiated by Barak but it has intensified under Sharon. Between early November 2000 and the end of April 2003 the IDF is alleged to have carried out 175 attempts at liquidation – one every five days – in which 235 Palestinians have been killed and 310 injured. Here too the parallels with America's "war on terrorism" are dreadfully instructive. Although the State Department has criticized Israel's policy of assassinations, other US agencies have taken a different view and carried out summary executions of suspected al-Qaeda members outside Afghanistan.[55]

Under international law the occupying power is responsible for the welfare of the local population. But the Oslo agreements transferred this responsibility to the Palestinian Authority, whose capacity to act has been severely compromised by the concerted actions of the IDF. Israel acts as a sovereign power in the occupied territories, therefore, even as it destroys the very fabric of civil society.

> The Palestinians are expected to obey military orders from the State of Israel, as if they were the laws of a Palestinian state. But the state that imposes those orders and whose army controls the territories, the land, the water resources, is not responsible for the welfare of the Palestinians living in those territories. It need not behave like a normal state . . .[56]

In this world wrenched upside down, Israel extends its illegal settlement of the occupied territories and asserts its monopoly of violence there even as it criminalizes any act of Palestinian resistance to its illegal operations and its state terrorism.

The logic of *homo sacer* is clearly discernible in the way the Western media report from the occupied West Bank: when the Israeli army, in what Israel itself describes as a "war" operation, attacks the Palestinian police force and systematically destroys the Palestinian infrastructure, their resistance is cited as proof that we are dealing with terrorists. This paradox is inscribed into the very notion of a "war on terror" – a strange war in which the enemy is criminalized if he defends himself and returns fire.[57]

What can this be other than the space of the exception? Within its weasel boundaries, crisis becomes routine and the exceptional becomes the normal. As Hass explains,

> Calamities – when the lives of a person, a family, a society, are turned upside down – are enormous, unusual, once-in-a-lifetime events. The opposite of routine. But the nature of the Palestinian effort to cope with the series of IDF raids means adapting to a routine of disaster after disaster. There's no time to get used to the results of one disaster before the next one comes. And every day that routine gets worse.[58]

The space of the exception is not so much punctuated by crises as produced through them, and these ever-present emergencies force a mutation in the position of those who are made subject to them. Abu Audah has argued that, long before the Oslo process, but intensified by its accommodations, Israel sought "to transform the Palestinian people into inhabitants." The difference, he explained, "is that people have national rights of sovereignty over their land, identity, independence, and freedom, while inhabitants constitute a group of people with interests not exceeding garbage collection and earning a daily living."[59] But now even the elemental forms of bare life are under acute threat.

In the countryside, Palestinian villages and fields have been pulverized by the military: houses demolished, reservoirs destroyed, olive groves uprooted. The writers' delegation visited a village razed to the ground by the IDF and walked among the rubble of bulldozed homes:

> Exercise books, kitchen utensils and a toothbrush were strewn about, signs of life reduced to pieces. One woman told us that residents were given five minutes to leave their homes in the middle of the night. The bulldozers returned several times to "finish the job" . . . Mounted high atop the watchtowers, infrared machine guns watch over the wasteland. There are no soldiers about. At night the guns fire automatically as soon as any lights are turned on.[60]

This is a bleak reversal of the imaginary of the original tower and stockade settlements (above, p. 82). The land that the Zionists believed they would transform from "wilderness" into "civilization" has been laid waste by their own (armored) bulldozers. It is as though the very earth has been turned into an enemy.[61]

Since 1967 Israel has demolished 8,000 Palestinian homes in the occupied territories, 2,000 of them between the start of the al-Aqsa Intifada and the "re-occupation" that began in the spring of 2002. The raw numbers of buildings destroyed do not – cannot – convey the emotional damage. "It would be hard to overstate the symbolic value of a house to an individual for whom the culture of wandering and of becoming rooted to the land is deeply engrained in tradition," Benvenisti emphasizes, "for an individual whose national mythos is based on the tragedy of being uprooted from a stolen homeland."[62] The demolition of Palestinian homes proceeded under the cover of the law – Israel's "law" – and yet most of the so-called outposts established by illegal settlers without permission from Israel's supposedly "civil administration" in the occupied territories have not only been left alone: they have been provided with military protection. "In a normal country," Yuli Tamir remarks, "criminals and security forces are on opposite sides of the fence [*sic*] and do not coordinate their activities." Yet in Israel these criminals do not offer protection, they demand it: and get it. "The new settlers don't seize the land in any official way," one observer explains. "They simply uproot Palestinians' trees or shoot in the air at any Palestinian who comes close."[63]

Palestinian towns and cities have fared no better. They have been smashed by Israeli missiles and bombs, by tanks and armored bulldozers. The objective is to suppress what Henri Lefebvre called "the right to the city" through a campaign of coerced de-modernization. "Urbicide is Sharon's war strategy," argues Graham. "His main purpose is to deny the Palestinian people their collective, individual and cultural rights to the city-based modernity long enjoyed by Israelis."[64] In the past this process had proceeded by stealth, through a series of discriminatory planning and building regulations that prevented Palestinian construction and authorized demolition of Palestinian homes. Under this asymmetric system of law enforcement, Palestinian "facts on the ground" were erased with almost machine-like efficiency: coolly, dispassionately, ruthlessly. But since the spring of 2002 the legal fictions that permitted these erasures have increasingly been dispensed with. In the space of the exception the law – even discriminatory law – suspends itself. Serge Schlemann reported that

the IDF's spasm of destruction had created a landscape of devastation from
Bethlehem to Jenin. "There is no way to assess the full extent of the latest
damage to the cities and towns – Ramallah, Bethlehem, Tulkarm, Qalqilya,
Nablus and Jenin – while they remain under a tight siege," he continued,
"but it is safe to say that *the infrastructure of life itself* and of any future
Palestinian state – roads, schools, electricity pylons, water pipes, telephone
lines – has been devastated."[65] Since then, the destruction has continued:
in Nazlat Issa, for example, 60 shops, a pharmacy, and a medical center
were destroyed in a single military operation.[66] As one young American
activist wrote to her parents from the town of Rafeh in Gaza in the spring
of 2003, these are violent assaults not only on buildings and property but
on the labor of the past and on the dreams of the future that had been
invested in them:

> If any of us had our lives and welfare completely strangled, lived with chil-
> dren in a shrinking place where we knew, because of previous experience,
> that soldiers and tanks and bulldozers could come for us at any moment
> and destroy all the greenhouses that we had been cultivating for however
> long, and did this while some of us were beaten and held captive with 149
> other people for several hours – do you think we might try to use some-
> what violent means to protect whatever fragments remained? I think about
> this especially when I see orchards and greenhouses and fruit trees destroyed
> – just years of care and cultivation. I think about you and how long it takes
> to make things grow and what a labour of love it is.

The words are those of Rachel Corrie, a peace activist from Olympia,
Washington. Three weeks later she was murdered by the Israeli driver of
an armored bulldozer – which drove over her, reversed, and then drove
over her again – when she tried to prevent the demolition of Palestinian
homes.[67] The significance of her death, and those of others killed in
similar IDF operations, extends beyond the feral violence of Israel's war
on the occupied territories and the arbitrary, asymmetric enforcement and
suspension of its own laws. These demolitions contravene the Geneva
Conventions, and it is the responsibility of the High Contracting Parties
– the signatory states and their representatives – to compel Israel to honor
its legally binding obligations. As Laurie King-Irani insists, "it is their duty,
not that of college students from Olympia" to safeguard the rights – and
lives – of those under military occupation: and yet, like the state of Israel,
these sovereign powers have elected to suspend the law and to allow Israel
to extend the space of the exception. For the most part, they have also elected

to ignore the continued assault by the IDF on international observers, including journalists, in Gaza and the West Bank. As Justin Podur asks: "When all the witnesses are murdered or driven out, what will go on in the occupied territories?" To Palestinian writer Elias Sanbar, this studied indifference is inscribed within "the global construction of the new empire," which makes it possible "not just to violate international law, already a common practice, but to proclaim loudly and clearly that one is working outside the parameters of the law without being ostracised by other nations."[68]

Taken together, these collective assaults in city and in countryside are not only assaults on what Agamben calls politically qualified life, on the integrity of Palestinian civil society, and on the formation of a Palestinian state, but assaults on what he calls "bare life" itself. As Darwish declared, "the occupation does not content itself with depriving us of the primary conditions of freedom, but goes on to deprive us of *the bare essentials of a dignified human life*, by declaring constant war on our bodies, and our dreams, on the people and the homes and the trees, and by committing crimes of war. . . ."[69]

The hideous objective of Sharon's government, which it scarcely bothers to hide any longer, is to reduce *homo sacer* to the abject despair of *der Muselmann*. This is truly shocking. *Der Muselmann* is a figure from the Nazi concentration camps – it means, with deeply depressing significance, "the Muslim" – who was reduced to mere survival. Following Primo Levi's horrifying memorial of Auschwitz, Agamben writes that *der Muselmann*

> no longer belongs to the world of men in any way; he does not even belong to the threatened and precarious world of the camp inhabitants. . . . Mute and absolutely alone, he has passed into another world without memory and without grief. He moves in an absolute indistinction of fact and law, of life and juridical rule.[70]

The Sharon regime would understandably not invoke this figure by name: and yet it is exceptionally difficult to avoid seeing its haunted, hollowed-out shadows flickering in the darkness of the zones of indistinction that have been so deliberately, systematically, and cruelly produced in the occupied territories. To say this is not to collapse one world into the other. I agree with Sara Roy on the importance of acknowledging the very real differences in volume, scale, and horror between the Holocaust and the occupation. But I also agree with her on the importance of "recognizing the parallels where they exist." To acknowledge them is *not* to be

Figure 6.9 IDF armored bulldozer demolishing Palestinian houses at Balata refugee camp near Nablus, November 2002 (AP Photo/Nasser Ishtayeh)

anti-Semitic; instead it is to try to honor the lives of all those who perished in the Holocaust and whose legacy is sullied by these statements and these actions. The parallels include the systematic campaign of violence, humiliation, and degradation that I have described here, which works toward the deliberate dehumanization of its victims.[71] There are other, even more awful parallels. Some of those most closely identified with the Sharon regime have used biomedical metaphors that would have been only too familiar to the Nazis (and their victims) to characterize Palestinians as a "cancerous tumor" that is "destroying the ordered host," and to prescribe aggressive "chemotherapy" to "cleanse" the body politic, while the IDF has not hesitated to draw lessons for its own urban operations from the Wehrmacht's ghastly assault on the Warsaw Ghetto.[72]

It is in the Palestinian refugee camps, the *nomos* of Israel's colonial present, that this project finds the purest expression of its violence (figure 6.9). In one of her letters from Ramallah, written as she waited for the next Israeli attack, suspended in the silence that terrifies by the certainty that it will be shattered, Jayyusi anticipated the even greater terror that awaited those in the refugee camps:

> Down there in the refugee camps they will receive the fury that inhabits the fear – and animates the will to crush – that the colonizer always vents. They will receive the depleted uranium, the heavy missiles, the columns of tanks smashing through the small alleys, the army which will bore through the walls of the close bordered houses; down there the real battle, the big toll will be had.
>
> The refugee camps are the very mark of our condition. They are the sign of the original deed which catapulted us all into this unending journey, the embodiment of what might have been, what was, what could be, the body which must be dismembered for so many to breathe lightly, rest back in comfort. This body within our body is the representation of our memory. . . .
>
> Who will lie bleeding tonight while ambulances are prevented from reaching them? How many will die here? How many will be led away, like they were yesterday in Qalqilya; all males between the ages of fifteen and fifty rounded up, blindfolded, their arms marked with numbers. Always the marking. Stripped, interrogated and beaten, led away for more to the place of concentration.[73]

As I have shown, successive Israeli politico-military apparatuses have attempted to efface Palestine from the map altogether. Here is Barghouti in 1996, allowed to cross to the West Bank for the first time in 30 years, no longer sure what to call his land:

> And now I pass from my exile to their . . . homeland? My homeland? The West Bank and Gaza? The Occupied Territories? The Areas? Judea and Samaria? The Autonomous Government? Israel? Palestine? Is there any other country in the world that so perplexes you with its name?[74]

This is not an arbitrary inventory; Israel has redistributed the splinters of Palestine into a series of abstract categories located in a purely topological imaginary. These redistributions – or "spacings," since they have performative force – possess such consistency and systematicity that they amount to a concerted project to fold the sacralization of the land of Israel – and particularly of "Judea" and "Samaria" – into the reduction of the Palestinian people to so many *homines sacri*. As Bargouti says, "they took the space with the power of the sacred and with the sacredness of power, with the imagination, and with geography." And by these means, through these fractures and torsions, "Palestine has been pushed to the edge of history, the edge of hope and the edge of despair, present and unreachable, fearful and afraid, and ragged into zones A, B and C. . . ."[75] (figure 6.10).

The horror is redoubled when one realizes that, for many Palestinians, the dispossessed and the dispersed, Palestine has indeed become an abstract space. Forbidden to travel to Palestine for many years, the anguish of exile that marks Said's *After the Last Sky* is, precisely, the anguish of abstraction. So too for Barghouti:

> Each time Husam asked me about a house, a landmark, a road, an event, I quickly replied "I know." The truth is I did not know. I no longer know.
>
> How did I sing for my homeland when I did not know it? . . . Israel succeeded in tearing away the sacred aspect of the Palestinian cause, turning it into what it is now – a series of "procedures" and "schedules" that are usually respected only by the weaker party in the conflict. . . . The Occupation has created generations without a place whose colors, smells and sounds they can remember; a first place that belongs to them, that they can return to in their memories and in their cobbled-together exiles. . . . The Occupation has created generations of us that have to adore an unknown beloved, distant, difficult, surrounded by guards, by walls, by nuclear missiles, by sheer terror.[76]

This was 1996, and since then the violence of abstraction has folded into itself an ever more profound de-corporealization of place and space. The detentions and demolitions, the collective punishments and individual humiliations, grind on. The killing grounds fill with their victims: colonial *Lebensraum* turned into *Todesraum*. Between September 2000 and January 2003 B'Tselem estimated that more than 1,700 Palestinians had been killed by the IDF in the occupied territories, and a further 25 by illegal Israeli settlers.[77] The splinters of Palestine have thus been formed into a scattered, shattered space of the exception, punctuated by the power-topologies of what Achille Mbembe calls a colonial necropolitics, "a generalized instrumentalization of human existence and the material destruction of human bodies and populations."[78] The so-called "road map to peace" proposed by the Quartet in the spring of 2003 was another exercise in abstraction. Said described it as "an unsituated document, oblivious of its time and place," and so it was. Its proposals preferred "performance-based" criteria to any engagement with the material performances of occupation, separation, and exception on the ground.[79]

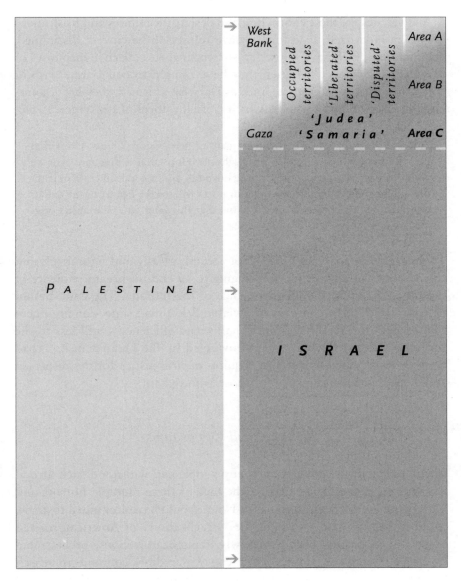

Figure 6.10 The abstract spaces of Palestine

And yet, despite these enormities, and despite the failures and frustrations of the Intifada itself, Palestinians have refused to be cowed, disciplined, dehumanized; they have refused to surrender their collective memories or to silence their collective grief; they have refused to collaborate with or consent to their own erasure. And, as Darwish affirmed, they are – somehow – still animated by hope, which is itself a form of resistance:

> Hope in a normal life where we are neither heroes nor victims. Hope that our children will go safely to their schools. Hope that a pregnant woman will give birth to a living baby, at the hospital, and not a dead child in front of a military checkpoint; hope that our poets will see the beauty of the colour red in roses rather than in blood; hope that this land will take up its original name: the land of love and peace.[80]

To enlarge that space of hope – not metaphorically and figuratively but concretely – is fundamental to bringing to an end the greater violence of the occupation and the lesser violence of the Intifada. The issue cannot be contracted to the contours of a viable Palestinian state – an argument that reduces too readily to functionality and efficiency – still less to the strange, "quasi-sovereign" object envisaged by the Quartet in its "road map" toward peace. For it also requires *justice*: justice for the dispersed and dispossessed, and justice for those who remain.

Identities and Oppositions

It is hard for me to imagine how any people can withstand such atrocities, but it beggars belief that, in the face of these multiple horrors and humiliations, American support for Israel should have continued to grow: so much so that Said speaks of the "Israelization" of American foreign policy.[81] This has not been a narrowly Republican response orchestrated by the White House alone. "How can we credibly continue to search for and destroy the remaining al-Qaeda terrorists in Afghanistan and throughout the world," Senator Joseph Lieberman asked a Democratic convention in Florida, "while demanding that the Israelis stop doing exactly that?" At a pro-Israel rally in Washington in the middle of April 2002, Giuliani shared the platform with Netanyahu, and hailed Sharon as "a very close friend." He described Israel as "an oasis of freedom in a desert of authoritarianism," and yet he could not bring himself to utter a single word about the IDF laying waste the West Bank – turning its olive-groves into "desert" – nor about its own brutal "authoritarianism" in the occupied territories. Deputy Secretary of Defense Paul Wolfowitz attended the demonstration at the request of the White House. "On September 11," he told the crowd, "every American understood what it is like to live in Jerusalem or Netanya or Haifa." But when he added that "Israelis are not the only victims of the violence in the Middle East," that "innocent Palestinians are suffering and dying in great numbers as well," he was booed and jeered.[82] Finally, on May 2, 2002, the Senate and the House of Representatives (Area D?) passed motions expressing solidarity with Israel (by 94:2 and 352:21 respectively). The then Democrat-led Senate affirmed that the United States and Israel "are now engaged in a common struggle against terrorism"; condemned Palestinian suicide bombings; supported Israeli incursions into Palestinian towns and refugee camps as "necessary steps to provide security to its people by dismantling the terrorist infrastructure in the Palestinian areas," and called upon the Palestinian Authority to fulfill its commitment to do the same; and declared that the US would "continue to assist Israel in strengthening its homeland defenses." Lieberman was explicit: "Israel has been under siege from a systematic and deliberate campaign of suicide and homicide attacks by terrorists. *Their essence is identical to the attacks on our country of 11 September.*"[83]

The claim to an identity has had exceptionally grave consequences. There are fundamental differences between (for example) al-Qaeda and Hamas, between the Taliban and the Palestinian Authority. Al-Qaeda is a transnational terrorist network and its patronage systems, such as they are, do not reach beyond its immediate circles, whereas Hamas, which does have an armed terrorist wing, also provides a local matrix of welfare and social institutions – including schools and clinics – often miserably absent from the programs of central administrations. It is in part through its various charitable arms that Hamas has sought to reclaim space not only from Israel but also from the Palestinian Authority. Unlike al-Qaeda, which eventually enjoyed a close relationship with the Taliban, Hamas remains implacably hostile to the Palestinian Authority. The Taliban prosecuted a radical Islamicism and in many respects shunned the trappings and responsibilities of a modern state, but the Palestinian Authority is a profoundly secular organization committed to the formation of an independent state within the territories occupied by Israel since 1967. Hamas is opposed to both planks of this platform: it is an Islamicist movement that rejects the legitimacy of the state of Israel altogether.[84]

These differences are strikingly significant. And yet the rhetorical fusion of America's September 11 and Israel's December 2 (or March 27) through the proliferating "war on terrorism" has given Bush and Sharon *carte blanche* to erase them. As a result "terrorism" has been made polymorphous. Without defined shape or determinate roots, its mantle can be cast over *any* form of resistance to sovereign power. This has allowed the Sharon regime to advance its colonial project not through appeals to Zionism alone, to the messianic mission of "redeeming" the biblical heartlands of Judea and Samaria (though this has by no means lost its ideological force) but also – crucially for its international constituency – as but another front in the generalized, rationalized "war on terrorism." This has in turn sustained the deception, so assiduously fostered by right-wing ideologues, that terrorism can be suppressed without reference to the historico-geographical conditions that frame it. Netanyahu's repeated insistence that "the root cause of terrorism lies not in grievance but in a disposition toward unbridled violence" – itself an attempt to align his own war on the Palestinians with the previous "war on terrorism" declared by President Ronald Reagan – has been reaffirmed by both the Bush and Sharon administrations. It conveniently exempts their own actions from scrutiny and absolves them of anything other than a restless, roving military response.[85]

In consequence, Gaza and the West Bank – the tattered remnants of Palestine – are placed under erasure within the dominant American and Israeli imaginaries, hollowed out figuratively and physically, so that US Defense Secretary Donald Rumsfeld can then refer to them as the "so-called occupied territories" and reduce the meaning of their occupation to "a loss of real estate" – the only "value" he seems capable of recognizing.[86] The existential meaning of the land is systematically denied to the Palestinians even as it is consistently upheld for the Israelis. This too is the pure performative, and performance here as elsewhere resides in the spacing between what happens and what does not happen, between what is seen and what is not seen. Said puts this with desperate clarity. Through these gestures, he writes,

> Palestinian violence, the response of a desperate and horribly oppressed people, has been stripped from its context and the terrible suffering from which it arises. . . . [T]he location of Palestinian terror – of course it is terror

– is never allowed a moment's chance to appear, so remorseless has been the focus on it as a phenomenon apart, a pure gratuitous evil which Israel, supposedly acting on behalf of pure good, has been virtuously battling.[87]

It is as though, by virtue of the de-realization of Palestine, a project reaching back over 50 years, the roots of Palestinian violence – the dispossession of the Palestinian people, the dispersal of Palestinian refugees, and the horrors of military occupation – have been torn up with their olivegroves. Violence must be lodged in their genes not the geographies to which they have been so brutally subjected. It is not only Palestinians who see this as sophistry. As Hass recognizes,

> It's so easy and comforting to think of the entire Palestinian society as primitive, bloodthirsty terrorists, after the raw material and product of their intellectual, cultural, social and economic activity has been destroyed. That way, the Israeli public can continue to be deceived into believing that terror is a genetic problem and not a sociological and political mutation, horrific as it may be, derived from the horrors of the occupation.[88]

This legerdemain is designed to distract attention from the occupation of Gaza and the West Bank. Just as for some commentators after September 11 "what had gone wrong" in America could only be the attacks on New York City and Washington (above, p. 23), so too "what has gone wrong" in Israel can only be Palestinian attacks on its citizens. The misadventures of American foreign policy; Israel's continuing colonial dispossession of the Palestinians; and most of all the connections between the two: none of these has a place in the calculated abstractions of righteousness. The Bush and Sharon administrations continue to perform their own "God-trick" of seeing the face of Evil everywhere except in their own looking-glasses.

This not only mirrors bin Laden's ideology. It also ultimately serves the interests of al-Qaeda. Neither September 11 nor December 2 marked the end of transnational terrorism. In October 2002 a discotheque and a crowded nightclub were bombed at Bali's Kuta Beach, murdering over 180 people and injuring 300 more. Most of the victims were young Australian tourists. Reports suggested that the attack was probably the work of Jemaah Islamiyah, a militant group with links to al-Qaeda that seeks to establish by violent means a pan-Islamic state in South-East Asia. Less than two

Figure 6.11 "Shake hands and be friends" (Steve Bell, *Guardian*, July 2, 2003)

weeks later Chechen guerrillas took hundreds of hostages in a Moscow theatre, demanding the withdrawal of Russian troops from their homeland: special forces stormed the building, killing all 41 guerrillas and leaving more than 120 hostages dead from the effects of narcotic gas. At the end of November an Israeli-owned hotel in Mombasa was bombed; 18 people were murdered, including three Israeli tourists. Two missiles were also fired at an Israeli charter jet in an unsuccessful attempt to bring it down as it took off for Tel Aviv from Mombasa. A previously unknown group calling itself the "Army of Palestine" claimed responsibility, but it was widely reported that the twin attacks were the work of al-Qaeda affiliates in East Africa. On the same day, at Beit She'an in northern Israel, two Palestinian gunmen murdered six Israelis and wounded many more as they waited to vote in a Likud primary. After these atrocities an Israeli government spokesman affirmed: "Whether in New York or Washington, Bali or Moscow, Mombasa or Beit She'an, terrorism is indivisible, and all attempts to understand it will only ensure its continuation."[89]

On the contrary. It is precisely the failure to discriminate, the refusal to understand – worse, the determination to discredit and disable any attempt to understand – that will ensure the continuation of terrorism. Terrorism cannot be reduced to circumstances; but neither can it be severed from them. All political violence – including transnational terrorism and state terrorism – is intimately involved in the local; it requires a matrix out of which volunteers or informants can be recruited and through which material and ideological support can be provided. As Jason Burke observes, shutting down al-Qaeda's bases in Afghanistan does not remove the reasons that motivated so many young men to travel there.[90] And detaining, imprisoning, and liquidating Palestinian fighters, and demolishing the homes of their families, does not lessen the desire of Palestinians to fight against colonial dispossession and occupation. Understanding those reasons is unlikely to move in the Euclidean space of the hermeneutic circle. Instead it will move in the folds and torsions of the power-topologies that I have described here. Jonathan Freedland once described the Israelis and Palestinians as inhabiting "parallel universes, where the same set of facts has two entirely different meanings depending where you stand."[91] But this assumes that "different meanings" are somehow separable from the differential elaborations of power in which they are involved. It substitutes an equivalence ("parallel universes") for the palpable asymmetry between the military and economic might of Israel, supported by American aid and armaments, and the broken-backed, rag-tag resources left for the Palestinians (figure 6.11). Until these differences are recognized, Bush and Sharon will continue to fight their mirror-wars with impunity, believing – like bin Laden and others like him – in the indiscriminate categorization of whole populations and in the indiscriminate use of violence against them.

7 The Tyranny of Strangers

Like molten bronze and iron shed blood
pools. Our country's dead
melt into the earth
as grease melts in the sun, men whose
helmets now lie scattered, men annihilated

by the double-bladed axe. Heavy, beyond
help, they lie still as a gazelle
exhausted in a trap,
muzzle in the dust. In home
after home, empty doorways frame the absence

of mothers and fathers who vanished
in the flames remorselessly
spreading claiming even
frightened children who lay quiet
in their mothers' arms, now borne into

oblivion, like swimmers swept out to sea
by the surging current.
May the great barred gate
of blackest night again swing shut
on silent hinges. Destroyed in its turn,

may this disaster too be torn out of mind.
        Tom Sleigh, *Lamentation on Ur, 2000 BC*[1]

"Not as conquerors or enemies . . ."

WHEN American and British forces launched a joint invasion of Iraq in the spring of 2003, the narrative arcs that I have traced in the previous chapters intersected in another constellation of colonial power and military violence. Jonathan Raban captured the explosive force of their crossing and the physical intimacy of their connection for Muslims around the world:

> Never has the body of believers been so vitalised by its own pain and rage. The attacks on Gaza and the West Bank by Israeli planes and tanks, the invasion of Afghanistan and the invasion of Iraq are seen as three interlinked fronts of the same unholy project. Each magnifies and clarifies the others.[2]

This was not the first time that the shadows of British and American power had fallen across the region. In the First World War the British army had advanced into the lands between the Tigris and the Euphrates – Mesopotamia – and it was a British colonial administration that created the modern state of Iraq out of shards of the broken Ottoman Empire (figure 7.1). After the Second World War the United States intervened time and time again in the political economy of Iraq, with increasing force and increasing British complicity. These joint legacies were invested in the Gulf wars fought since 1990, and it is impossible to revisit the sites of those previous involvements without recognizing the ironies that attended the production of the colonial present in Iraq in 2003. The parallels will become clear as I proceed, and I will not need to underscore them. As historian Charles Tripp observes, they are drawn not by "some irreducible essence of Iraqi history" but by the logics of colonial and imperial power. For this very reason they were studiously disregarded – even denied – by the new masters of war. "Led by the United States of Amnesia," columnist Gary Yonge wrote, it became a commonplace to dismiss the past as an inconvenience. Instead, we were supposed to live "in the ever-evolving present and its ever-changing enemy."[3] Against this, I propose to show that the war in Iraq is one more wretched instance of the colonial present.

In November 1914, days after Turkey entered the First World War on the side of Germany, the British government moved to secure its interests in the region. Foremost among them were the land bridge to British India and the likelihood of major oil resources in Mesopotamia. "Archaeological" missions had scoured the deserts before the war broke out, and the

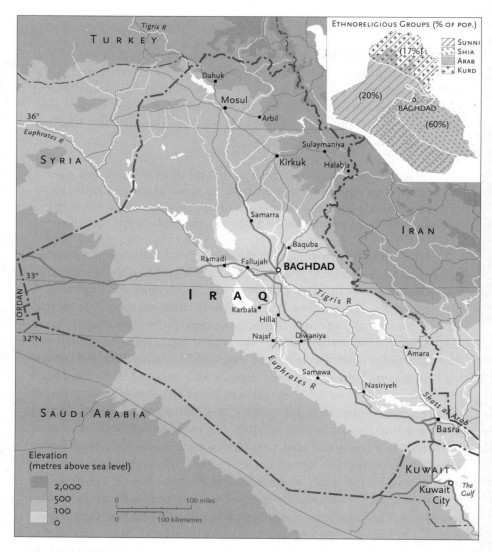

Figure 7.1   Iraq

Turkish Petroleum Company – a joint venture between Britain, Germany, and Turkey – had been established in 1912 to consolidate the process of exploration. With the outbreak of war, the company and its operations were paralyzed at the very moment when oil was assuming considerable strategic significance. As the Royal Navy switched from coal, the Admiralty had became gravely concerned about the need to guarantee un-fettered access to oil for the fleet. An Indian Expeditionary Force was accordingly dispatched to seize the Ottoman province of Basra. When the troops attempted to move north from Basra – largely to forestall the threat of a Russian advance southwards – they met with fierce resistance, and it was not until the winter of 1916 and the arrival of reinforcements from Britain that they were able to continue their advance through the province of Baghdad.[4] In March 1917 its capital city fell, and Lieutenant General Sir Stanley Maude issued a proclamation to its citizens:

> Our military operations have as their object the defeat of the enemy, and the driving of him from these territories . . . [O]ur armies do not come into your cities and lands as conquerors or enemies, but as liberators.
>
> Since the days of Halaka your city and your lands have been subject to the tyranny of strangers, your palaces have fallen into ruins, your gardens have sunk in desolation, and your forefathers and yourselves have groaned in bondage. Your sons have been carried off to wars not of your seeking, your wealth has been stripped from you by unjust men and squandered in distant places.[5]

It was probably clear, even then, that the plunderers of colonial modernity would always prefer to march under the meretricious banners of "liberation." In October 1918 all Ottoman garrisons in Mesopotamia were ordered to surrender, and British troops renewed their advance north into the Ottoman province of Mosul. The General Staff had not been convinced that this would serve any discernible military purpose, but the Secretary to the War Cabinet had explicitly identified control of all the region's oil resources as a vital objective. "The retention of the oil-bearing regions in Mesopotamia and Persia in British hands . . . would appear to be a first-class British war aim," he wrote. "[W]e should obtain possession of all the oil-bearing regions in Mesopotamia and Southern Persia." The area he had in mind included Mosul – which was part of neither Mesopotamia nor Persia – and in November, a few days after the war had ended, the Ottoman garrison was forced to withdraw from that province too.[6]

In 1919 the League of Nations – "the shell of respectability under which the victors of the war attempted to hide their avarice"[7] – conferred a mandate on Britain for the administration of Mesopotamia, which was ratified in the following year. The first British administration was drawn from the Indian Political Service – an expatriate colonial apparatus based in Delhi – which assumed that the model Britain had developed for India was equally relevant to the lands between the two rivers. This was inflected by an Orientalism that divided Mesopotamia between cities supposedly "corrupted" by the "despotism" of the Ottoman Empire and a country-side which was believed to be the preserve of the "true Iraqi" who was, none the less, backward, even prelapsarian, and irrational. This simple-minded and offensive dualism ensured that indigenous voices would not be listened to and indigenous agency denied. Not surprisingly, such an occu-pation (and "tutelage") sparked a smoldering resistance. "Even at its most benign," Tripp explains, "it seemed to many of the former officials of the Ottoman Empire, as well as to a number of notable families, that the idea was deeply contemptuous of their own administrative and political experi-ence."[8] It was not only the Sunni, who had formed the administrative elite since the Ottomans captured Mesopotamia in 1638, who were affronted; so too were the Shi'a majority. When mass meetings were held in Baghdad to protest the mandate, people gathered at Sunni and Shi'a mosques alike in a symbolic demonstration of an alliance between the two schools of Islam forged in the crucible of independence. By June 1920 civil dissent had turned into armed revolt that spread rapidly from Baghdad through the Shi'a heartlands of the south. The cost of occupation weighed heavily on Britain's Minister for War and Air, Winston Churchill, whose preferred solution was to rely not on the massive deployment of ground troops but on mechanized forces and airpower to bring the insurgents to heel. Britain deployed a formidable arsenal, against which the tribespeople had little or no defense. There were pulverizing bombing raids, heavy artillery bombardments, and gas attacks – "I am strongly in favour of using poison gas against uncivilized tribes," Churchill declared – and by the end of these counter-insurgency operations more than 9,000 people had been killed.[9]

In late August Churchill was still raging against the cost of the military operation, and he bitterly regretted that Britain should have been "com-pelled to go on pouring armies and treasure into these thankless deserts." "It is an extraordinary thing," he continued, "that the British civil admin-istration should have succeeded in such a short time in alienating the whole country to such an extent that the Arabs have laid aside the blood feuds they have nursed for centuries and that the Sunni and Shi'a tribes are working together." And then the ultimate irony: "We have been advised locally that the best way to get our supplies up the river would be to fly the Turkish flag, which would be respected by the tribesmen."[10] Soon after he became Colonial Secretary, Churchill convened a meeting of British political and military advisers – the "Forty Thieves" – who met in Cairo in March 1921 to resolve the continuing crisis. On the recommendation of Sir Percy Cox, the British High Commissioner, and Cox's Oriental Secretary Gertrude Bell, it was agreed that predominantly Arab Mesopotamia (Basra and Baghdad) should be conjoined with predominantly Kurdish Mosul to form the state of Iraq, which would be presided over by a client Hashemite monarchy and administered by the Sunni political and military elite that had managed the affairs of the Ottoman provinces in the past.[11]

But Iraq's northern border could not be ruled with the geometric precision of a colonial straight-edge: it was a ragged zone whose inhabitants were largely hostile to Turkish or British control. Both Turkey and Britain were determined to see off any prospect of an independent Kurdistan, which had been provided for by the treaty of Sevres in 1920, and when the Kurds rebelled Britain deployed its air force against them in another series of exemplary assaults. "They now know what real bombing means, in casualties and damage," one officer recalled. "They now know that within 45 minutes a full-sized village can be practically wiped out and a third of its inhabitants killed or injured by four or five machines that offer them no real target, no opportunity for glory as warrior, no effective means of escape."[12] Political observers were impressed too. In the high summer of 1924, Gertrude Bell attended a "bombing demonstration" by the Royal Air Force:

> They had made an imaginary village about a quarter of a mile from where we sat on the Diyala [Sirwan] dyke and the two first bombs, dropped from 3,000 ft, went straight into the middle of it and set it alight. It was wonderful and horrible. They then dropped bombs all round it, as if to catch the fugitives and finally firebombs which even in the bright sunlight, made flares of bright flame in the desert. They burn through metal, and water won't extinguish them. At the end the armoured cars went out to round up the fugitives with machine guns. "And now" said the A[ir] V[ice] M[arshal] wearily, "they'll insist on getting out and letting of[f] trench mortars. They are really no good, but the men do love it so that I can't persuade them not to." Sure enough they did. I was tremendously impressed. It's an amazingly relentless and terrible thing, war from the air.[13]

It was not only the Kurds in the north who suffered these terrors – which in their case were only too real – and the significance of "war from the air" extended far beyond its palpably asymmetric disposition. For the air force was used not only to put down insurgencies but also as an arm of government itself, and this corroded the very core of the state apparatus. Shi'a tribespeople in the south were bombed merely for withholding their taxes and, as historian Peter Sluglett puts it, with such formidable powers at its disposal the administration "was not encouraged to develop less violent methods of extending its authority."[14]

In 1925 the League of Nations agreed that the province of Mosul should be formally incorporated within Iraq. Mosul was not prized for its oil reserves alone – the legendary "Nebuchadnezzar's furnace" – which were thought to be considerable. In fact, Britain's Foreign Secretary, Lord Curzon, disingenuously claimed that "the question of oil" had "nothing to do" with Britain's case for its retention of the province.[15] Be that as it may – and it wasn't – Britain also hoped that the inclusion of Mosul's Sunni Kurds within Iraq would allow the Sunni Arab minority to counterbalance the Shi'a majority. Power was to be held at the center, in the cities, by the Sunni, and it was assumed that most of the Kurdish and Shi'a populations would be locked in their own intensely tribal societies. Bell had no doubt that "that the final authority must [remain] in the hands of the Sunnis, in spite of their numerical inferiority, otherwise you'll have a . . . theocratic state, which is the very devil."[16] The same sentiments would be repeated down the years, but by 1930 another intrepid and outspoken Englishwoman, Freya Stark, thought it absurd to worry over much about the political constitution of the fledgling state:

> I don't know why one should bother so much about how Iraq is governed. The matter of importance to us is to safeguard our own affairs. It is only because we assume that the two are bound together that we give so much weight to the local politics. It seems to me that the one only vital problem is to find out how the things we are interested in can be made safe independently of native politics. If this was solved, all the rest would follow – including as much Arab freedom as their geography allows: for I imagine no one would wish to stay here for the mere pleasure of doing good to people who don't want it.[17]

This was at least a frank recognition of the importance Britain attached to its own interests, and its "informal empire" remained intact after Iraq's formal independence in 1932.

By then oil loomed even larger in Britain's calculus. There had been a concerted effort to keep American companies out of the region, which had incurred the wrath of Washington, but in 1928 – one year after oil had been discovered near Kirkuk – the reconstituted Iraq Petroleum Company (IPC) agreed to divide its principal shares equally among Britain's Anglo-Persian Oil Company, the Anglo-Dutch company Shell, the Compagnie Française des Pétroles, and the Near East Development Corporation (a consortium representing the five major American oil companies and spearheaded by Standard Oil). Commercial production began in 1934, following the completion of a pipeline from Kirkuk to Haifa in Palestine and Tripoli in Lebanon.[18] In 1937 Freya Stark flew south from Baghdad to visit "the little buffer state of Kuwait." At the time, it was "nothing but desert and sea," she wrote; the mainstays of its economy were herding, trading, and pearl-diving. Drilling for oil had started the previous year, however, and Stark predicted that

> In a few years' time oil will have come to Kuwait and a jaunty imitation of the West may take the place of its desert refinement. The shadow is there already, no bigger than a man's hand – a modest brass plate on a house on the sea-front with the name of the Anglo-American K.O.C., Kuwait Oil Company. . . . Civilization will come tempered, more like a Marriage and less like a Rape.[19]

Coups and Conflicts

After the Second World War America's geopolitical interest in Iraq increased, but for the most part it preferred to work behind the scenes. In 1958 Iraq's compliant monarchy was overthrown in a military coup led by Free Officers inspired by Egyptian president Gamal Abdul Nasser's potent mix of Arab nationalism and anti-imperialism. Most Iraqis greeted the fall of the Hashemites with enthusiasm, though popular participation in the coup was largely gestural, but the new republican government was met with growing alarm in London and Washington. Their list of concerns was a long and lengthening one. The new government closed British bases in Iraq, and opposed the pro-Western regime of Mohammad Reza Shah Pahlavi in Iran (who had been restored to the Peacock Throne with British and American help in 1953). It re-established close relations with the USSR, and withdrew from the Baghdad Pact with Britain, Iran, and Turkey (which had been instituted in 1955 in an attempt to contain Soviet expansionism). It renewed Iraq's claims for sovereignty over Kuwait (which had been part of Basra province but signed a protectorate agreement with Britain at the end of the nineteenth century). Finally, it moved to curtail Western interests in Iraq's oil (by convening a meeting of oil-producing states in Baghdad which established the Organization of Petroleum Exporting Countries (OPEC), and by taking back most of the prospecting rights that had been vested in IPC).[20]

Almost immediately American troops were deployed in Lebanon and British troops in Jordan to secure what were seen as vulnerable regimes. In 1961, following Kuwait's independence, Iraqi troops moved to the border and Britain sent warships from Hong Kong and Singapore and landed 6,000 troops to defend its former protectorate. It was also in Kuwait that the United States, with British and Israeli support, set up a clandestine operation led by the CIA to monitor Iraqi military communications and to coordinate an insurgency in Iraq. This culminated in a new military coup in 1963 led by army officers in the Ba'ath party. Ba'ath ("Re-birth" or "Renaissance") was a political movement that had been founded by two young Syrian intellectuals during the Second World War. It was driven by a vision of pan-Arab unity, of a single Arab state that would be delivered not only from colonialism but also from tribalism and sectarianism. The Ba'ath project was thus constructed independently of and largely outside Islam, but it is also important to recognize its roots in Arab culture and history, which have been profoundly influenced by Islam: Fred Halliday thus emphasizes Ba'athism's "cult of war as the purgative fire, its obsession with the strong man, the knight or *faris* on horseback, who will deliver the Arab nation, and its explicit valorization of *al-qiswa* (harshness) as a tool of government control."[21] Although theirs was nominally a socialist project, it owed much more to European fascism, and as soon as they seized power the Ba'athists launched a bloody purge of the Iraq Communist Party, the largest in the Middle East, which had been a rallying-ground for many disadvantaged Kurds and Shi'as. The scale and systematicity of the arrests and executions made many historians suspect that the new regime was working from lists supplied by the CIA. The Ba'athists also used pan-Arabism to wage a war against the Kurds and their guerrilla armies, the *peshmergas*, but the Kurds succeeded in establishing a precarious autonomy over parts of the north. The Ba'athist regime quickly unraveled in a series of factionalisms, but in 1968 the Ba'ath party seized power again with renewed CIA support, and it was through its system of populism, patronage, and repression that Saddam Hussein rose to the pinnacle of absolute power. Mass arrests, torture, and imprisonment of opponents of the regime resumed, and thousands of communists fled into exile. A new offensive was launched against the Kurds, for which Iraq sought military aid from the USSR. America, seeing the shadows of the Cold War lengthening again, responded by supplying military aid to the Kurds through its twin proxies: Israel and Iran.[22]

But the Shah's Iran was far from stable, and Saddam was well aware of the danger posed to his own secular regime by the rise of Islamicism. When the Shah had expelled the Ayatollah Ruhollah Khomeini from Iran in 1964 the cleric had taken refuge in the Shi'a holy city of Najaf, from where he issued repeated calls for a rebellion against the Shah. In response to pressure from Tehran, Saddam expelled Khomeini from Najaf in 1978, but after the Shah had been driven from power in the following year Saddam moved to forestall the prospect of an alliance between the new Islamic Republic of Iran and Iraq's own Shi'a majority.[23] His main worry was that Iraq would disintegrate into Sunni, Shi'a, and Kurdish fractions. At first, his interventions were cautious and conciliatory, but after an attempt on the life of his deputy prime minister, Tariq Aziz, Saddam went on the offensive. He ordered mass arrests and executions of Shi'a clerics, and in September 1980 – after a series of bloody border skirmishes – launched what he insisted was a pre-emptive attack on Iran. Viewed from Baghdad, revolutionary Iran appeared to be on the brink of chaos: unrest in the provinces, factionalism at the center; a military corps weakened by a purge of thousands of officers trained by the US army, a military machine seizing up for the lack of American-made spare parts. Although the situation was ripe for Iraqi intervention, Saddam's initial objectives seem to have been limited. As the war dragged on, however, the conflict turned into what Sandra Mackey rightly calls "a war of identity." Saddam himself came to describe the conflict as a war against "the concerted machinations of the forces of darkness," a war to reclaim what he assiduously cultivated as "the civilization of Mesopotamia" that he said had "illuminated the world when the rest of mankind was living in darkness," and a war to recover sole Arab sovereignty over the Shatt al-Arab waterway that controlled access to the Gulf.[24]

The Iran–Iraq war lasted eight years, and each side suffered horrific casualties: 1 million dead, over 2 million wounded, and millions more made refugees. At the outset a debilitating stalemate seemed likely – Iran had a much larger population (45 million against 15 million) but Iraq's military was now much better equipped – and the rest of the world seemed content to let each side grind the other down. It took the UN Security Council days to agree on a resolution calling for a ceasefire, which neither condemned Iraq for its aggression nor called upon Iraq to withdraw. Although the United States proclaimed its neutrality, it was in fact playing a deadly and devious game. The administration of President Jimmy Carter had been deeply dismayed at the replacement of the Shah's militarist regime by a clericist regime that constantly railed against the United States as "the Great Satan," and thoroughly humiliated by the taking of American hostages at the American embassy in Tehran. By contrast, Saddam's regime was not only secular; it was also increasingly vocal in its opposition to the spread of communism, which Saddam described as "a yellow storm" plaguing Iraq. There are good reasons for believing that the Carter administration tacitly condoned and even encouraged the Iraqi invasion of Iran, and as the war ground on, the White House increasingly took the part of the supposedly "moderate" and "pragmatic" Saddam.[25]

This policy intensified following the installation of President Ronald Reagan in January 1981. The next year Iraq was removed from the State Department's list of states supporting international terrorism, which allowed it to purchase "dual-use" technology that was capable of both civilian and military use. From 1983 Washington supplied Baghdad with satellite intelligence on Iranian military dispositions and, no less crucially given that Iraq faced the virtual disappearance of commercial sources for unsecured credit, with credit guarantees through the US Department of Agriculture's Commodity Credit Corporation for the purchase of American agricultural products. In the same year Iraq began to use chemical weapons against Iranian troops, first mustard gas and then, two years later, the deadly nerve gas tabun. Although Iran protested at these deployments, there was little reaction from Washington – "it was just another way of killing people," one defense intelligence officer observed, "whether with a bullet or [gas], it didn't make any difference" – and the United States blocked condemnation of Iraq's actions in the Security Council. American air force and army officers were seconded to work with their Iraqi counterparts and to assist them in selecting targets and devising battle plans. At the time, Donald Rumsfeld was Reagan's special Middle East envoy, and amid what Michael Dobbs calls "a flurry of reports that Iraqi forces were using chemical weapons," he flew to Baghdad in December 1983 to assure Saddam that Washington was ready to resume full diplomatic relations.[26] By 1984 the war was on a knife-edge. Iran had suffered heavy casualties but had also made a series of significant advances. Washington immediately sharpened the edge. It pressurized its allies to stop supplying arms to Tehran and then, in an attempt to secure the release of American hostages held in Beirut by the pro-Iranian Hezbollah, a Shi'a guerrilla organization, Reagan authorized the covert shipment of anti-aircraft and anti-tank missiles to Tehran. At the same time the United States granted export licenses that allowed Iraq to accelerate and intensify its chemical and biological weapons programs. In 1986 the American trade with Iran was exposed, and the administration's predicament was made all the more humiliating when it was revealed that some of the profits from the deal had been illegally diverted to provide military aid to the Contras who were conducting a guerrilla war against the Sandinista government in Nicaragua.[27] Reagan now frantically scrambled to recover credibility with the Arab states by visibly and dramatically intervening on the side of Iraq. As Gabriel Kalko puts it, "the United States was Iraq's functional ally and encouraged it to build and utilize a huge army with modern armor, aviation, artillery and chemical and biological weapons." Some 60 American, British, and French warships patrolled the Gulf, while American armed forces blew up two Iranian offshore oil platforms and destroyed an Iranian frigate: all of which, as Dilip Hiro says, was "tantamount to opening a second front against Iran." The US Center for Disease Control and Prevention and the American Type Culture Collection were both authorized by the administration to send chemical and biological agents to Iraq, including precursor chemicals for the production of mustard gas and strains of anthrax, botulinum toxin, and botulinum toxoid. In 1988, as Iraq's use of chemical weapons increased, Washington provided Tehran with "crop-spraying" helicopters, which Iraq used to deliver chemical agents on the battlefield, and also authorized major enhancements for Iraq's missile procurement agency. In the spring of that same year, Iraq used mustard gas, tabun, sarin, and VX gas against Kurdish civilians in Halabja, killing 3,000–5,000 people and leaving thousands more with grave long-term health problems: the United States tried to claim that Iran was partly responsible for the atrocity. Iraq then launched another Kurdish offensive, al-Anfal ("the spoils of war"), which was designed to inspire terror as much as to achieve any coherent military objective. This was another instance of a "war on terror" waged through terror itself. Areas in which Kurdish guerrilla organizations operated – or, in the terms used by other administrations in other places, areas "harboring" them – were subjected to a scorched earth campaign. At the end of al-Anfal over 1,200 villages had been destroyed, over 100,000 men, women, and children killed, and another 300,000 people displaced; the use of chemical weapons also had serious consequences for the survivors and their families. Yet there was little sustained criticism from the Reagan administration, which had repeatedly resisted attempts by Congress to impose sanctions on Saddam's regime for its serial violations of human rights and now frustrated attempts to have the Security Council conduct an investigation into Iraq's use of chemical weapons. Even when it was revealed that Iraq had diverted a substantial proportion of its American agricultural credits to the purchase of military equipment – a distorted mirror of the Iran–Contra deal – the administration authorized new loans to Iraq totaling $1 billion, and American exports to Iraq with dual military and civilian use doubled.[28]

For all this meddling the conflict remained, as Mackey says, "a war in which neither side could win and neither side was willing to surrender."[29] By the time a fragile ceasefire had been signed in August 1988, Iraq was virtually bankrupt and heavily indebted to Saudi Arabia and Kuwait. Its vulnerability was made worse because by June the following year, in open defiance of OPEC quotas, Kuwait had increased its oil production by 40 percent and the United Arab Emirates by 30 percent. The prolonged collapse in oil prices that resulted had a catastrophic impact on the Iraqi economy. Saddam described it as a form of economic warfare, which he claimed was aggravated by Kuwait slant-drilling across the border into Iraq's Rumaila oil field. Kuwait had been part of the Ottoman province of Basra, and although its ruling dynasty, the al-Sabah family, had concluded a protectorate agreement in 1899 that assigned responsibility for its foreign affairs to Britain, it did not make any attempt to secede formally from the Ottoman Empire. For this reason successive Iraqi governments had always refused to accept Kuwait's independence, and its borders were never clearly defined or mutually agreed. This is scarcely surprising, because when Britain's High Commissioner drew his original lines in the sand – little more than rough approximations in any case – he deliberately constricted Iraq's access to the ocean so that any future Iraqi government would be in no position to threaten Britain's domination of the Gulf.[30] These were real if contentious grievances, and Saddam invoked both the integrity of Iraq's economy and the integrity of Iraq's territory when his troops invaded Kuwait on August 2, 1990.

Desert Storms and Urban Nightmares

Tripp suggests that Saddam regarded Kuwait as a commodity to be retained or exchanged for substantial concessions, but whatever the merits of this interpretation it seems clear that Saddam seriously misread the likely response of his erstwhile allies, both the United States and other Arab states. Within hours of the invasion the UN Security Council passed Resolution 660 demanding Iraq's immediate and unconditional withdrawal from Kuwait, and on August 6 followed up with Resolution 661 imposing comprehensive economic sanctions until Iraq complied.

Although the United Nations was involved with the crisis from the very beginning, the prime mover in orchestrating the international response was the United States. On August 5 President George H. W. Bush sent his Secretary of Defense, Richard Cheney, with Under-Secretary of Defense Paul Wolfowitz and the commander-in-chief of US Central Command (CENTCOM), General Norman Schwarzkopf, to Riyadh to persuade Saudi Arabia to accept American military assistance to defend the kingdom against future Iraqi aggression. They were so successful in their presentation of an imminent threat to the kingdom that the very next day, as John Bulloch and Harvey Morris put it, the Saudis "asked for the help the Americans were determined to give." As soon as Riyadh formally requested military assistance from Washington, the United States set in motion Operation Desert Shield. Carrier battle groups were deployed to the Gulf; combat aircraft, infantry, and armored divisions were dispatched to bases in Saudi Arabia; and Washington began to assemble an international military coalition. Its object was "wholly defensive," Bush insisted. "The acquisition of territory by force is unacceptable," he declared, and the intention of the military build-up was solely to "deter Iraqi aggression" against Saudi Arabia. The coalition would eventually include 34 states providing military or other forms of support – the alphabetical list was headed by Afghanistan – but 500,000 of the 600,000 troops deployed were from the United States and Schwarzkopf was appointed Supreme Allied Commander.[31]

None of this occurred in an infrastructural vacuum. Between 1970 and 1979 Saudi Arabia had purchased American weapons and military services totaling $3.2 billion and American defense contractors had built military installations across the kingdom. The Iran–Iraq war gave the United States leverage to extract what Joel Stork and Martha Wenger describe as "a more intimate Saudi collaboration with US military power." They continue:

> The centrepiece of this effort was the sale of five AWACS planes and a system of bases with stocks of fuel, parts and munitions. . . . Over the course of the decade, Saudi Arabia poured nearly $50 billion into building

a Gulf-wide air defense system to US and NATO specifications, and ready for US forces to use in a crisis. By 1988 the US Army Corps of Engineers had designed and constructed a $14 billion network of military facilities across Saudi Arabia.[32]

Throughout the crisis the White House constantly emphasized not only the invasion of Kuwait but also what it represented as the imminent threat to Saudi Arabia. "Iraq has amassed an enormous war machine on the Saudi border," Bush told the nation in a televized address on August 8, and "the sovereign independence of Saudi Arabia is of vital interest to the United States."

It was indeed, and for reasons that were both crude and dark. If the principal export from Saudi Arabia (or Kuwait) was oranges, one American diplomat noted, "a mid-level State Department official would have issued a statement and we would have closed down for August." But the Gulf states accounted for 62 percent of known global oil reserves. The Bush administration was oil-savvy, and charted a slippery course between two undesirable extremes. On the one side, its relations with Iran and Iraq were in tatters, and both of these states had a clear interest in raising oil prices as high as possible in order to meet their internal responsibilities and external debts. On the other side, the White House had no interest in slashing oil prices as low as possible because it wanted to ensure that America's own, high-cost oil industry remained competitive. This sector was dominated not by the multinational companies, which had multiple sources of supply, but by independent American companies, operating out of Texas and pumping oil from the Gulf of Mexico. This is why Saudi Arabia was vital. Its massive production capacity – around 10 million barrels per day – "gave it the unique ability to operate as a 'swing' producer, switching its surplus on and off to discipline other producers who tried to exceed their production quotas." Viewed thus, Saudi Arabia was crucial to the United States not only in the absolute sense of its reserves being "pivotal for the supply of oil to the world economy," as Paul Aarts and Michael Renner argue, but also in the relative sense of its regulation being pivotal for sustaining "the system of scarcity," as Timothy Mitchell explains, so that the price of oil would conform to American political and commercial interests.[33]

Faced with a joint diplomatic offensive and military coalition formed not only by the United States and its immediate allies but also by other Arab states, Iraq reaffirmed the legitimacy of its double case against

Kuwait. But it now made two additional stipulations that Saddam must have thought would redeem Iraq's position within the Arab world. First, it insisted that the Arab League should condemn not Iraq but Saudi Arabia for allowing non-Muslim troops to set foot on the holy lands of Mecca and Medina. This may have been a cynical maneuver – like so many of Saddam's sudden professions of faith – but, as Gilles Kepel remarks, it had remarkable force because "it did not come from a [Shi'a] Persian but from a Sunni Arab – from the very heart of the Islamic zone that Riyadh had marked out with such painstaking effort and expense." This was the single point at which, in purely formal terms, Saddam's position coincided with that of Osama bin Laden, who was aghast when his offer to raise an army of *mujaheddin* to put to flight the armies of the "apostate" Saddam was refused in favor of the United States sending its "infidel" troops to Saudi Arabia.[34] Second, if "the acquisition of territory by force" were indeed unacceptable, as Bush repeatedly proclaimed, then Iraq insisted that any resolution of its occupation of Kuwait should be linked to Israel's occupation of Arab territories in Palestine, Syria, and Lebanon. Perhaps Saddam should have offered to withdraw from 42 percent of Kuwait, excluding its capital city, its main highways, and the most productive oil-wells. Neither the United States nor other Arab states were disposed to accept the linkage, but the statement won Saddam considerable support on the Arab street and, above all, in Gaza and the West Bank.[35]

On September 11, 1990 Bush addressed a joint session of Congress. Again, he raised the specter of an imminent Iraqi invasion of Saudi Arabia. "Within three days, 120,000 Iraqi troops with 850 tanks had poured into Kuwait and moved south to threaten Saudi Arabia," he told his audience. "It was then that I decided to act to check that aggression." Even so, Bush argued that the crisis in the Gulf was also a moment of opportunity. "Out of these troubled times," he declared, "a new world order can emerge," one in which "the rule of law supplants the law of the jungle." He described Iraq's invasion of Kuwait as "the first assault" on this emergent order. As Gearóid Ó'Tuathail explains, Bush's speech reinscribed a colonial discourse of "wild, untamed spaces" in which "civilization" was menaced by a reversion to "barbarism."[36] A fortnight later the French president François Mitterrand proposed that the United Nations substitute what he called a "logic of peace" for a "logic of war." The crux of his proposal was that a peaceful resolution of the Kuwait crisis should be followed by a comprehensive Middle East peace conference. The White House was far from happy at Mitterrand's intervention, which appeared to endorse Saddam's own proposal, but Bush was now obliged to confront the charge that he was applying double standards to the belligerent occupation of territory. In his own speech to the UN General Assembly on October 1 the president held out the hope that a successful resolution of the crisis would make it possible "for all the states and the peoples of the region to settle the conflicts that divide the Arabs from Israel." But the burden of his remarks concerned the return of the past rather than the realization of a future. The imagery of reversion – and above all, of the First World War – haunted his presentation. Two months ago, he said, "the vast beauty of the peaceful Kuwaiti desert was fouled by the stench of diesel and the roar of steel tanks. Once again the sounds of distant thunder echoed across a cloudless sky, and once again the world woke to face the guns of August." His words echoed the history of Iraq itself, which was a creation of those same guns, of the violence and duplicity of the war, and Bush pursued the theme with a vengeance. Iraq's raw aggression was a "throwback," he claimed, "a dark relic from a dark time" that threatened to turn the dream of a new world order into a nightmare "in which the law of the jungle supplants the law of nations."[37]

Given Bush's insistent characterization of Operation Desert Shield as defensive, it is important to scrutinize the immensity of the threat a "reversionary" Iraq was supposed to pose to Saudi Arabia and hence to the United States. This had at least two rhetorical dimensions. In the first place, the Pentagon claimed that its satellite photographs showed hundreds of thousands of Iraqi troops and tanks massing on the Saudi border. These threat assessments were used to persuade Riyadh to ask for US military assistance and to convince the allies and the American public alike that the danger of attack was substantial. But Jean Heller, an American journalist, subsequently obtained commercial photographs from a Soviet surveillance satellite for the crucial dates in August and September when the administration had made its boldest claims, and expert analysis showed no military build-up on the Iraqi side of the border, only roads covered with untracked sand and empty barracks. The only trace of a vast military concentration was on the Saudi side of the border, where the massive American deployments were clearly visible.[38] In the second place, the White House's geopolitical strategy depended on the hyperinflation of its adversary. With the collapse of the Soviet Union, the United States required a military and ideological Other whose stature was commensurate with its own self-image. Ironically, the withering of communism threatened the survival of the national security state itself, and its resuscitation – let alone its growth – required what Philip Golub called a "new demon" whose menace would be sufficiently grotesque to remind the American public of both "the meaningfulness *and* the precariousness of their culture and polity." The consolidation of the United States as a hyperpower required a hyper-villain – absolute Evil as its dark and constitutive Other – whose aggrandized threat legitimized the consecration of its own assumption of global hegemony.[39] This is not to deny the hideously repressive character of the Iraqi regime, but it is to call into question the exorbitant military threat that it was said to pose and the exorbitant military response that this supposedly justified.

On November 29, 1990 the United States extracted a new resolution from the Security Council through a mix of persuasion and coercion that was resisted only by Cuba (which had long since been placed beyond the American pale) and Yemen (which paid an enormous economic price for its impertinent independence). Resolution 678 demanded Iraq's unconditional withdrawal by January 15, 1991 and authorized the use of "all necessary means" if it failed to comply. In December the Bush administration seized upon a report from Amnesty International documenting human rights abuses in occupied Kuwait as confirmation of the barbaric cast of Saddam's regime. Amnesty objected that its report noted that these violations were "entirely consistent" with abuses known to have been committed in Iraq itself over many years. Not only had the administration said next to nothing about those infractions, but earlier that year Bush had intervened (again) to secure a massive loan for the Iraqi regime. He signed an executive order waiving economic sanctions that had been approved by Congress precisely to protest the continued violation of human rights in Iraq.[40]

To some conservative commentators Iraq's invasion of Kuwait merely confirmed what Charles Krauthammer had identified earlier in the year as a "Muslim demand for hegemony" against which the West had to prevail: Saddam was positioning himself to assume the unchallenged leadership of a "global intifada."[41] Given the previous intimacy of the relations between Iraq and Britain, France, Russia, and the United States this was scarcely credible. But Saddam was always willing to conceal his thoroughly secular designs under the banner of Islam, and three days before the UN deadline for his troops to withdraw from Kuwait he had the Koranic injunction *Allahu Akbar* ("God is the greatest") emblazoned between the three stars on the Iraqi flag. Then, on January 16, 1991, the supposedly defensive Operation Desert Shield became the incontrovertibly offensive Operation Desert Storm.

As geographer James Sidaway shrewdly observes, throughout this escalation of events the constellation of forces that produced the war was contracted to Iraq alone – all the other states were airbrushed from the scene – and Iraq itself was contracted to Saddam Hussein. No longer "moderate" or "pragmatic," he was demonized as evil incarnate and painted in "the colours of Orientalist fantasies of sexual perversity and excess."[42] Iraq's invasion was also coded in starkly masculinist terms – Bush later spoke of Saddam's "ruthless, systematic rape of a peaceful neighbor" – and the "rape of Kuwait" became the pretext for what Ella Shohat and Robert Stam describe as "the manly penetration of Iraq":

> The metaphor of the rape of Kuwait, the circulating rumors about Iraqi rapes of Kuwaiti women, and the insinuation of possible rapes of American female soldiers by Iraqi captors became part of an imperial rescue fantasy. . . . At the same time, through a show of phallic vigor in the Gulf war, a senescent America imagined itself cured of the traumatic impotence it suffered in another war, in another Third World country – Vietnam.[43]

Whatever one makes of these metaphors – and metaphors are always more than figures of speech: they are also vehicles for action – the conduct of the war plainly involved a less figurative kind of pornography. Its first phase was an air war. For six weeks bombs and cruise missiles rained down on occupied Kuwait and on Iraq, targeting Iraq's command-and-control systems, military installations, and troop deployments and also its civilian infrastructure. An electronic conjunction of intelligence-gathering satellites and planetary television networks was mobilized so that Iraq was supposed to be made fully visible – transparent – and yet simultaneously reduced to a series of targets. The raw power of these objectifications, the sadistic union of the savage and the sensual, was made clear in a report by Maggie O'Kane from Baghdad:

> Some nights we climbed to the upper floors [of the Al Rashid hotel] for a better view of the show. Pointed out the targets to each other. *Front row seats at a live snuff movie, except we never saw any blood.* . . . There were flashes, red stains that crept past the censor, but mostly it was fun: stealth missiles, smart bombs, mind-reading rockets, flashes of tracer fire in the night. F16s and war games.[44]

By such means, Stam notes, "we were encouraged to spy, through a kind of pornographic surveillance, on a whole region, the nooks and crannies of which were exposed to the panoptic view of the military and the spectator." The use of the fictive "we" is deliberate; a vantage point was carefully constructed to both privilege and protect the (American) viewer through the fabrication of (American) innocence and the demonization of the (Iraqi) enemy. By conferring an instantaneous ubiquity upon the spectator, the circumference of this Americanocentric vision seemed to be projected from an Archimedean point in geosynchronous orbit above all partisan interests: a sort of universal projection. And, as Paul Virilio remarked, it also pulled off a God-trick. Proclaiming "ubiquity, instantaneity, immediacy, omnipresence, omnivoyance" it transformed the spectator into "a divine being, at once here and there."[45] From this position and perspective, war became "the remote controlled destruction of places whose only existence to military personnel was as electronic target coordinates on a screen," and Ó'Tuathail argues that the complicity between "the eye of the military's watching machine and the eye of the television camera" effaced both the materiality of places and the corporeality of bodies. What he calls this "electronic spatiality" presented the war to its audience "as live yet distant, as instantaneous yet remote, as dramatically real yet reassuringly televisual."[46]

As these vacillations suggest, voyeurism of this sort depends upon a peculiar torsion of time and space. Distance is compressed, so that the lustful eye gazes on the intimacies of death, and distance is expanded to remove the viewer from the full force of engagement. Even so, contrapuntal geographies have the power – on occasion – to call these distractions into question. On the very day that Bush delivered his triumphant State of the Union address in Washington, in which he hailed the imminent coalition victory "over tyranny and savage aggression," reflected on a "renewed America" illuminated by "a thousand points of light," and praised his nation for "selflessly confront[ing] evil for the sake of good in a land so far away," a thousand points of light were still bursting on that distant land. Here is Paul William Roberts writing on the same day, January 29, from the outskirts of Baghdad:

In places, not a building was left standing as far as I could see. By the roadside, at intervals, lying on makeshift beds in the misty, freezing damp, lay casualties crudely swaddled in bloodstained bandages. They were waiting, I learned later, for the few ambulances that daily made rounds, either treating the wounded where they were or carrying them off to overburdened, understaffed hospitals. Most doctors and nursing staff had been sent to the eastern front. So had all able-bodied men. We were bombing the defenseless, the old, women and children. . . .

Perhaps the description should be as *surgical* as the bombing was said to be. One girl, aged ten or so, with shrapnel wound to the abdomen, holding lower intestines in hands like snake's nest. Teenage boy, unconscious, head like a half-eaten boiled egg. Old woman coughing out spray of blood. . . .

A little later, Muhie and some of the soldier showed me an obliterated high-tech death-factory cunningly arranged to look as if it had been an elementary school. Scraps of kids' art projects fluttered beneath crumbling concrete slabs and twisted metal rods. A little exercise book lay stained by fire and rain, with the universal language of children's art and words etched in rudimentary English that were just too apt and too heartbreaking to be ever repeated.

> "Those who reject our signs
> And the meeting in the hereafter –
> Vain are their deeds:
> Can they expect to be rewarded
> Except as they have wrought?"[47]

The horror of these paragraphs is magnified by the connective dissonance between Washington and Baghdad. Even as the president spoke, America was being redeemed through spectacular violence: an ideology not a million light-years from Ba'athism.

On February 23 Iraq announced its unconditional withdrawal from Kuwait, but CENTCOM decided that the army was merely retreating and coalition forces were ordered "to block enemy forces from withdrawing into Iraq." They were to be harried by an all-out offensive from the air and, the very next day, by a punishing ground offensive (Operation Desert Sabre) that lasted 100 hours. The Iraqi army suffered far more casualties during this phase than it had during the protracted air war that preceded it. The front lines were held, for the most part, by thousands of ill-equipped young conscripts. Hundreds, perhaps thousands, of them were buried alive as heavy ploughs mounted on Abrams tanks smashed through their crude earthwork defenses: "The Abrams flanked the trench lines so that tons of sand from the plow spoil funneled into the trenches. Just behind the tanks, actually straddling the trench line, came M2 Bradleys pumping 7.62 mm machine gun bullets into the Iraqi troops." They were followed by Armored

Combat Earthmovers, vast machines relentlessly "leveling the ground and smoothing away projecting Iraqi arms, legs and equipment." Seventy miles of trenches were erased like this, and with them all trace of the bodies of the conscripts who had held them.[48]

Others were cut down ruthlessly as they tried to surrender or flee. "It's like someone turned on the kitchen light late at night, and the cockroaches started scurrying. We finally got them out where we can find them and kill them," remarked Air Force Colonel Dick "Snake" White. According to John Balzar of the *Los Angeles Times*, infrared films of the United States assault suggest "sheep, flushed from a pen – Iraqi infantry soldiers bewildered and terrified, jarred from sleep and fleeing their bunkers under a hell storm of fire. One by one they were cut down by attackers they couldn't see or understand."[49]

Iraqi troops withdrew from Kuwait not in ordered array but in uncoordinated panic. The fleeing soldiers had commandeered whatever vehicles they could find, but even Iraqi tanks were flying white flags and riding with their turrets open. Still coalition forces pressed forward relentlessly. It was "like a giant hunt," one journalist traveling with the US army noted, in which "the Iraqis were driven ahead of us like animals." These bestializing metaphors – reducing people to "cockroaches" and "sheep," and elsewhere to "sitting ducks," "rabbits in a sack," and "fish in a barrel"[50] – reached their ugly and only too physical climax in the "turkey shoot" on February 26. American planes cut the head and tail of retreating Iraqi military columns along Highway 60 from Kuwait City to Basra, and then firebombed the trapped troops in designated "kill-boxes" along what came to be known as "the Highway of Death" (figure 7.2). The scene resembled the hell of Hieronymus Bosch, horrified reporters wrote: "giant red flames" soaring into the sky, "weird contorted figures" and "wizened, mummified charcoal-men" on the ground.[51] Journalist Robert Fisk recalled seeing a camera crew later filming wild dogs savaging the corpses of Iraqi soldiers. "Every few seconds a ravenous beast would rip off a decaying arm and make off with it over the desert in front of us, dead fingers trailing through the sand, the remains of the burned military sleeve flapping in the wind." Yet he knew, like the camera crew, that the footage would never be shown. For casualties to be shown on screen, if they were shown at all, "it was necessary for them to have died with care" – "on their backs, one hand over a ruined face . . . benignly, and with no obvious wounds, without any kind of squalor, without a trace of shit or mucus or congealed

Figure 7.2 "Highway of Death," Kuwait City to Basra, February 28, 1991 (AP Photo/Laurent Rebours)

blood" – so that their bodies were romanticized and their audience anaesthetized. The watching – and, in their way, devouring – public had to be shielded from the vile sights that Fisk witnessed. They were protected by military and media censorship and by what he called "war's linguistic mendacity."[52]

But there were principled reporters – like Fisk himself – who worked to overcome this detachment, and to reveal the contrapuntal geographies that the coalition military and mainstream media were concerned to conceal. To take one of the most vivid examples, it was only outside the theater of war that the hegemonic gaze was allowed to linger on the intimate connections between soldiers and civilians. American and British viewers were constantly reminded of the families back home who anxiously waited for news or for the return of flag-draped coffins. But Maggie O'Kane showed, in one devastatingly simple paragraph, that Iraqi soldiers had families too:

> On the day the war ended, at a bus station south of Baghdad, dusk was falling and the road was covered with weeping women. The Iraqi survivors of the "turkey shoot" on the Basra road were crawling home with fresh running wounds. Their women were throwing themselves at the battered minibuses and trucks, pulling, pleading, begging: "Where is he, have you seen him? Is he not with you?" Some fell to their knees on the road when they heard the news. Others kept running from bus, to truck, to car, looking for their husbands, their sons or their lovers – the 37,000 Iraqi soldiers who did not come back. It went on all night and it was the most desperate and moving scene I have ever witnessed.[53]

Numbers like these were exceptionally hard to come by. While the coalition kept meticulous records of its own – low – casualties it consistently claimed that it had no record of Iraqi casualties. It had the technical capacity to evaluate the destruction caused by its bombs and missiles: the ability to do so is, after all, a necessary part of continuing military operations. It also had the legal responsibility to account for the casualties: the Geneva Conventions require belligerents "to search for the dead prevent their being despoiled," to record any information that might aid in their identification, and to forward to each other "authenticated lists of the dead"; they are also supposed to ensure that they are "honourably interred" and, as far as circumstances allow, to bury them individually in marked graves. Yet the Pentagon categorically refused to get into what General Schwarzkopf called "the body-count business." It wasn't just that people who weren't counted presumably didn't count – dispatched as so many *homines sacri* – but that this was made to seem the holiest of all possible wars: one in which virtually nobody died.[54]

President Bush ordered a ceasefire on February 27, 1991, but in April General Colin Powell, chairman of the Joint Chiefs of Staff, said that he still had "no idea" how many Iraqis had been killed, "and I really don't plan to undertake any real effort to find out." Fortunately others did. Greenpeace estimated that 70,000–115,000 Iraqi troops and 72,500–93,000 civilians had been killed during the conflict. Comparatively few of the civilian deaths were a direct result of injuries from bombs and missiles – Human Rights Watch thought the maximum was around 3,000 – but a vastly greater number were caused by the combination of continued UN sanctions and the allies' deliberate destruction of Iraq's civilian infrastructure: in particular, its food warehouses, its electricity generation and distribution network, and its water-treatment and sewage facilities.[55]

It was the supposedly "surgical" precision of its "smart bombs" that induced the coalition to target these critical junctions, but even where they hit their intended target (and 20 percent did not) the spillover effects were calamitous and by no means as circumscribed as the clean medical imagery implied. By the end of the war, electricity output had been reduced to less than 300 megawatts, about 4 percent of the pre-war capacity. Without power, water-treatment and sewage facilities shut down, and thousands of people (particularly children) died from diarrhea, dysentery and dehydration, gastroenteritis, cholera, and typhoid. Nor were these consequences unanticipated or unintended. The US Defense Intelligence Agency had estimated that "full degradation of the water treatment system" in Iraq would take at least six months, and that its destruction would cause serious public health problems. For this very reason, the Geneva Conventions affirm that "it is prohibited to attack, destroy or render useless objects indispensable to the survival of the civilian population," and Article 54 specifically includes "drinking water installations and supplies and irrigation works." All the same, in addition to coalition attacks on Iraq's electricity generation and distribution network that impacted directly on the system of water treatment and distribution (in such a flat land pumping is indispensable), eight major dams were repeatedly hit, four of seven major pumping stations were destroyed, and 31 water and sewage installations were put out of action, including 20 in the sprawling city of Baghdad alone. Water supplies were cut, raw sewage flowed into the rivers, and water-borne diseases became endemic and epidemic. These problems were particularly acute in the southern governorates of Basra, Diqar, Karbala, Najaf, and Nasit. And since hospitals were deprived of electrical power, they were left without reliable means of refrigeration. As vaccines and medicines deteriorated, many patients who could have been treated easily and effectively in normal circumstances died.[56] All of this, one needs to remember, was the result of "defense intelligence" and "smart bombs." The vast majority of bombs were not precision-guided, however, and over 75 percent of these "dumb bombs" missed their targets and killed thousands more in Baghdad, Basra, and other cities.[57]

Worse: the killing did not stop with the ceasefire. In a speech on February 15 that was broadcast to the Iraqi people, Bush had urged them "to take matters into [their] own hands to force Saddam Hussein, the dictator, to step aside." And in the jaws of defeat, as Faleh Abd al-Jabbar puts it, many Iraqis "reached out for victory inside their own wrecked and wretched nation." At the very end of February a Shi'a revolt began in Nasriyeh, and from there it spread rapidly to Basra, Najaf, and Karbala. By the end of the first week of March most of the main towns in the south were in revolt. The rebellion was spontaneous and seemed to have little or no central direction, though local clerics took part in various ways. The White House watched its development with growing unease. Many of the rebels were calling for an Islamic revolution and the establishment of an Islamic republic. Although Bush's National Security Adviser had thought it likely that Saddam would be deposed, he had not imagined the regime itself would be at risk: "I envisioned a post-war government being a military government," he explained. For the stony-faced men in the White House, that was evidently the preferred outcome. Then, in the middle of March, Kurdish guerrillas staged a rebellion in the north that was much more tightly orchestrated. Soon Saddam had effective control of only three of Iraq's 18 governorates – Baghdad, Tikrit, and Mosul – and the Bush administration was now as concerned as Saddam had been at the prospect of Iraq's disintegration. "I'm not sure whose side you'd want to be on," said Secretary of Defense Richard Cheney (really). This was the same logic that had forcibly created Iraq out of Kurdish, Shi'a, and Sunni fractions in the first place, the colonial logic of "divide and rule." The capital retained an uneasy calm as rumors of the uprisings spread, and the Republican Guard moved quickly to crush the insurgency. First it seized the rebel cities in the south, inflicting massive physical destruction and killing tens of thousands of people. Some of the rebels found refuge in the marshes, the vast wetlands at the confluence of the Tigris and Euphrates, but thousands more fled to Saudi Arabia and Iran. Then the Republican Guard turned its attention to the north, where it inflicted heavy casualties and its depredations forced hundreds of thousands to flee to Iran and Turkey. And so it ended. The uprisings were "drowned in blood," al-Jabbar notes, and the rebel areas reduced to "a wonderland of terror."[58]

Throughout these struggles America and its allies did next to nothing. The only response was to condemn the regime's repression, and in April 1991 the allies (not the United Nations) established a "no-fly zone" above 36 degrees north to exclude Iraqi aircraft from the area. Its original purpose was to protect coalition aircraft dropping aid to the refugees, but the mission was then changed to one of protecting the surviving Kurds from renewed attacks by the Iraqi air force. But it did nothing to protect them from attacks by the Turkish air force: American and British pilots were regularly ordered to return to their base in Turkey to allow Turkish F-14s and F-16s to bomb the Kurds, and in 1999 separate pathways were established "so that US aircraft patrolling the no-fly zone would not cross paths with Turkish planes bombing alleged Kurdish terrorist bases." In August 1992 the United States and Britain established a second no-fly zone in the south, below 32 degrees (increased in September 1996 to 33 degrees), to protect the Shi'ia population in the southern marshes, the Ma'dan or "Marsh Arabs," from Iraqi military action. In December 1991 and January 1992 the Iraqi army had encircled the wetlands, which were used as a base by guerrillas continuing their "war of the fleas," and when the troops moved in they destroyed 70 villages and displaced around 50,000 people. But the southern no-fly zone did little to protect the Ma'dan from continued ground operations by government troops, still less to prevent the draining of 90 percent of the wetlands by vast civil engineering projects, which the government undertook with what Peter Clark calls a "punitive determination" that displaced at least 200,000 people. It seems clear that here too the allies' primary objectives were military and geopolitical, not humanitarian. The rules of engagement were progressively relaxed to permit American and British pilots to bomb any part of the Iraqi air defense system, not just those batteries that locked on to or fired on their aircraft, and the overall intention was simply to "keep Saddam in his box."[59]

Still the killing continued, but not only by the murderous Iraqi regime. In a hideously real sense the Gulf War that "never took place" never ended either, and it was continued even by the supposedly left-liberal governments that succeeded Bush and his principal ally. American and British aircraft continued bombing operations within – and beyond – the "no-fly

Figure 7.3 Missile strike, Baghdad, December 17, 1998 (AP Photo/Peter Dejong)

zones." Their raids intensified during and after Operation Desert Fox in December 1998 (figure 7.3).[60] The Iraqi government claimed that more than 300 civilians were killed and 960 injured in allied air attacks over the next two years. Soon American officials were boasting that they were running out of targets: "We're down to the last outhouse." Perhaps such sadistic delight in – or, at best, calculated indifference to – death and destruction explains an incident like the following, which took place in the spring of 2000.

> Suddenly out of a clear blue sky, the forgotten war being waged by the United States and Britain over Iraq visited its lethal routine on the shepherds and farmers of Toq al-Ghazalat about 10.30 a.m. on May 17. Omran Harbi Jawair, 13, was squatting on his haunches at the time, watching the family sheep as they nosed the hard, flat ground in search of grass. He wore a white robe and was bareheaded in spite of an unforgiving sun. Omran, who liked to kick a soccer ball around this dusty village, had just finished fifth grade at the little school a 15-minute walk from his mud-brick home. A shepherd boy's summer vacation lay ahead.

That is when the missile landed. Without warning, according to several youths standing nearby, the device came crashing down in an open field 200 yards from the dozen houses of Toq al-Ghazalat. A deafening explosion cracked across the silent land. Shrapnel flew in ever direction. Four shepherds were wounded. And Omran, the others recalled, lay dead in the dirt, most of his head torn off, the white of his robe stained red.

"He was only 13 years old, but he was a good boy," sobbed Omran's father, Harbi Jawair, 61. What happened at Toq al-Ghazalat, 35 miles southwest of Najaf in southern Iraq, has become a recurring event in the Iraqi countryside.[61]

Less than 18 months later, in the wake of September 11, military historian John Keegan would describe attacks where the perpetrators appear suddenly out of empty space, without warning, without provocation, as uncivilized, barbaric: in a word (his word) "Oriental" (see above, {p. 00}). By early 2001 the bombing of Iraq had lasted longer than the Vietnam war, and yet attacks like these were made to seem unremarkable, unexceptional, even banal. "They call it routine," wrote Nuha al-Radi from Baghdad in February 2001: "Since when can you call bombing a country routine?"[62]

The Iraqi people were not only dying from the unrelenting "post-war" bombing. They were also dying – as they will continue to die – from the legacy of the war itself. Cluster bombs and mines continued to kill and maim innocent civilians. Still more sinister, however, coalition forces had made extensive use of munitions coated with depleted uranium (DU) against Iraqi troops south of Basra. DU is uranium-238, the trace element that remains when fissionable material is extracted from uranium-235. Shells coated with this deadly waste product can penetrate layers of hardened steel, and on impact the DU ignites to create a fiery aerosol of uranium oxide. This fine dust can be dispersed by the wind over considerable distances; it can be inhaled or absorbed by the human body, and it can enter the food chain through contaminated water, plants, and animals. Once in the bloodstream, many medical scientists believe it leads to leukemia, lung and bone cancer, pulmonary and lymph node fibrosis, pneumoconiosis, and the depletion of the body's immune system. The fields south of Basra were saturated with DU shells during the ground war – a chillingly appropriate name for it – and these fields still produce tomatoes, onions, and potatoes, and support extensive herds of animals. Iraqi doctors are convinced that the four- or fivefold increase in cancers they have detected among children there can be attributed to the coalition's use of DU shells which turned fertile farmland into a vast killing field. The doctors also link DU to a significant rise in congenital birth defects in the same region. In 1980 there were 11 such cases per 1,000 live births in Basra; in 2001 this had soared to 116. Both American and British governments have doggedly rejected any connection between DU and these incidents – they have been locked into an interminable dispute with their own veterans over "Gulf War Syndrome" too – but it should be noted that the US army requires anyone who comes within 25 meters of equipment or terrain contaminated with DU to wear respiratory and body protection, and its manual warns that such contamination "will make food and water unsafe for consumption."[63]

And still the deaths continued. A UN mission visited Iraq in March 1991 and in its report warned that "the Iraqi people may soon face a further imminent catastrophe, which could include epidemic and famine, if massive life-support needs are not rapidly met." The response from the UN Security Council was twofold.

First, on April 3, 1991, UN Security Council Resolution 687 declared that sanctions would remain in place until Iraq formally accepted its border with Kuwait, paid war reparations, and returned all prisoners of war, and until it had eliminated its program for developing chemical, biological, and nuclear weapons, and dismantled its existing long-range missiles, which were seen as "steps towards the goal of establishing in the Middle East a zone free from weapons of mass destruction and all missiles for their delivery, and the object of a global ban on chemical weapons."[64] Iraq accepted the terms of this resolution, but in the years to come its resistance to the UN inspections regime, both overt and covert, through diplomatic challenges and active concealment, and the United States' misuse of the inspection teams to further its own aims of espionage and subversion in Iraq, mired the whole process in controversy and conflict. These difficulties were grave enough, but they were exacerbated by disagreements within the Security Council over the objective of sanctions. Some permanent members expected the formal requirements for suspension to be met reasonably rapidly; but Bush was determined that they would remain in place until Saddam was forced from power. Yet he had refused to come to the aid of the Shi'a and the Kurds when they responded to his call to do exactly that.[65]

Secondly, on April 5, 1991, UN Security Council Resolution 688 at once condemned and called for an end to the Iraqi regime's repression of its citizens, and demanded that the Iraqi government allow immediate access by international humanitarian organizations "to all those in need of assistance." Iraq saw this as an infringement of its sovereignty, and flatly refused to accept the terms In July, a UN mission reported that "for large numbers of the people of Iraq, every passing month brings them closer to the brink of calamity. As usual, it is the poor, the children, the widowed and the elderly, the most vulnerable amongst the population, who are the first to suffer." It calculated that $2.63 billion would be needed over a four-month period as an immediate, interim, and minimum emergency measure, and suggested that Iraq be allowed to use its oil revenues – through its existing bank accounts in the United States, which would be subject to rigorous UN scrutiny – for that purpose. The Security Council rejected the proposal and offered to allow Iraq to raise $1.6 billion over a six-month period; this was not only to pay for food and medical supplies but also to make reparations to Kuwait, and to pay for UN weapons inspections, boundary demarcation teams, and other administrative expenses. This would have left Iraq with $930 million over six months. The Security Council also attached a number of riders to its proposal – most significantly, revenues from the sale of Iraq's oil were to be deposited in an escrow account, which would be controlled directly by the UN – which seemed to be intended to humiliate the Iraqi government rather than to facilitate humanitarian assistance.[66]

By 1995, when the Iraqi government accepted a revised "oil-for-food program," the situation had deteriorated dramatically. That same year Paul Roberts returned to Baghdad:

> The early morning air reeked of decay and sewage. Wherever I looked there were tattered, crumbling buildings, so long neglected that it was hard to believe they weren't boarded up, let alone that they were still occupied, still in business. Rubble of many varieties sat in piles or splashed across rooftops or cascaded onto balconies. Some of it had been bulldozed into jagged heaps that were even, on closer inspection, impossibly *still dwellings* which has just suffered particularly unconscionable neglect or abuse. Wrecked but not ruined.
>
> I was shocked to the core. Those who won't give peace a chance should see what war actually achieves. What was once a rich and vibrant city, full of ambition, hope, discotheques and grandiose construction projects was now an ugly, battered Third World slum, with not a single redeeming thing of beauty to be found anywhere throughout all its many miserable square miles. Except the human spirit, which seems to thrive under such circumstances.
>
> And no city's circumstances . . . can hold a match to those circumstances now endured in Baghdad. Here the outer circumstances pale in comparison

with the inner carnage and horror. Not just the city has suffered from neglect and physical abuse: the minds of its inhabitants have been tampered with in an infinitely crueler, probably irreparable manner. For over twenty years, what has been happening in Iraq amounts to a psychological holocaust, an atrocity that almost no one in the west seems to grasp fully in its awful scope and complexity, since we are continuing to help make it even worse than it already was before Saddam Hussein attained demonhood in 1990.[67]

The political gulf between those who the sovereign powers of America and its allies deemed to matter and those who were excluded from politically qualified life was driven home to Roberts when he realized that:

> None of the Western countries – none of *our crowd* – had embassies in Baghdad. Only the other kind, *those* countries, the ones always in trouble, in debt, and usually in Africa, only *they* had embassies here now. It struck me that I was a stranger in a strange and parallel world, one where all the things that didn't matter much at all in mine were almost *all* that mattered – all there *was* to matter.[68]

The same Manichean geography was at work when, in January 1996, Bush's former National Security Adviser affirmed that "a thousand Iraqi lives [are] equal to one American," and in May of the same year when Madeleine Albright, appointed by President Clinton as the US permanent representative to the United Nations and soon to be his Secretary of State, was asked about a report that over 500,000 Iraqi children had died as a result of sanctions. She replied: "We think it's worth it." More recent estimates regard this figure as too high, though the margins of error are likely to be considerable, and suggest that by 2000 international sanctions had been responsible for the deaths of 350,000 Iraqi children. Those who are persuaded by Albright's scale of values will no doubt think this even more of a bargain but, as Wadood Hamad emphasizes, it is still a truly horrific figure. "Would any decent person" change their minds about the "murderous nature of the September 11 acts of terror," he asks, "when official death figures were recently revealed to be at least one-third lower than what was originally thought?"[69]

The effects of sanctions on the civilian population were only partially mitigated by the revised oil-for-food program, which did not become operational until December 1996. Since this was funded entirely by exports of Iraqi oil it was highly vulnerable both to the continued degradation of Iraq's industrial infrastructure and to any fall in global oil prices. In 1998 the

Table 7.1 "Oil for food" program allocations

	%
15 central and southern governorates	53*
3 northern governorates	13
Kuwait compensation fund	30*
UN administrative and operational costs	2.2
UN weapons inspection program	0.8

* In December 2000 the allocation to the central and southern governorates
  was increased to 59%, and the allocation to the compensation fund
  decreased to 25%.
Source: UN Office of the Iraq Program: <http://www.un.org/Depts/oip>.

ceiling for funds made available by the program was raised from $2 billion to $5.26 billion every six months, and in December 1999 the limits were removed altogether. Receipts were allocated as shown in table 7.1.

Adoption of this program did not mean that sanctions had lost their teeth or that the American and British governments had stopped tightening them. The power to monitor Iraq's imports was vested in the Security Council's "661 Committee," where the United States, often supported by Britain, fought aggressively to block or disrupt the entry of humanitarian goods into the country. Contracts were subjected to strict and protracted scrutiny. Many of them were rejected, and once American objections to a contract had been addressed it was not uncommon for the United States to change its grounds so that the whole review process had to be gone through again. Vaccines to treat infant hepatitis, tetanus, and diphtheria were denied, for example, because they contained live cultures that the United States alleged could be extracted for military use; United Nations agencies like UNICEF complained, and biological weapons experts flatly contradicted the claims, but the United States prevailed. Other contracts were selectively approved, so that Iraq "got insulin without syringes, blood bags without catheters, even a sewage treatment plant without the generator needed to run it." When goods that had been rendered useless in this way were stored in government warehouses, Iraq was criticized for "hoarding." Iraq's civilian infrastructure was also deliberately targeted:

electricity, water and sanitation contracts were routinely placed on hold. Most supplies needed to repair or maintain Iraq's power stations and its transmission system were blocked; in August 2001, for every water supply contract that was unblocked, three new ones were put on hold. The impact of these manipulations on Iraqi public health was catastrophic, and led many critics to condemn the sanctions as themselves weapons of mass destruction.[70]

When challenged over the effects of sanctions on the civilian population, successive American and British governments insisted that they had "no quarrel" with the Iraqi people (who must have wondered what their lives would have been like if America and Britain really *did* have a quarrel with them). Instead, both governments sought to shift responsibility for the cruel spikes in disease, death, and poverty onto Saddam Hussein alone. In their view, he was the single architect of the Gulf War; as I have noted, all the other states involved in this concatenation of events were excised from their record. Saddam was thus made single-handedly responsible for the imposition of sanctions, and he remained solely responsible for their continuation. Many commentators accepted these arguments. David Cortright agreed that the United States and Britain had "pursued a punitive policy that has victimized the people of Iraq in the name of isolating Saddam Hussein," for example, but he also found that the government of Iraq was culpable for its non-cooperation with the inspections regime that prolonged the sanctions, and its "denial and disruption of the oil-for-food humanitarian program." His central submission turned on the geography of infant and child mortality (table 7.2). Mortality rates for infants and for children under 5 declined in the three northern governorates, the autonomous Kurdish areas where food distribution was managed by the UN, whereas they increased sharply in the south and central districts, where distribution was managed by the Iraqi government. The contrast, Cortright concluded, "says a great deal about relative responsibility for the continuing crisis."[71]

But these are disingenuous arguments, no matter who makes them, because they ignore two key considerations. First, the geography of resources is itself uneven. The per capita allocation of funds to the northern governorates was 22 percent higher than in the south, and, as the Security Council itself acknowledged, the northern border was also "more permeable to embargoed commodities than the rest of the country." In any case, the north has far more agricultural resources, since it contains nearly 50 percent of the productive arable land of the country; much of this is rain-fed,

Table 7.2   Infant and child mortality in Iraq, 1984–1990

	Infant mortality per 1,000		*Under 5 mortality per 1,000*	
	1984–1989	*1994–1999*	*1984–1989*	*1994–1999*
north	64	59	80	72
south/centre	47	108	56	131

Source: based on data in Mohamed Ali and Iqbal Shah, "Sanctions and childhood mortality in Iraq," *The Lancet* 335 92000, pp. 1851–7.

whereas agriculture in the south is heavily dependent on a degraded irrigation system. The south suffered disproportionately more destruction during the war, and the "killing fields" around Basra have further increased mortality rates. It is certainly true that Saddam's patronage and client networks were extensively involved in the development of a black economy that sought to circumvent the embargo, and one could argue that the imposition of sanctions enhanced Saddam's ability to reward his followers and hence reinforced (rather than undermined) his power: by 1992 Iraq had "relapsed into family rule under a Republican guise." But the oil-for-food program operated outside the regime's webs of bribery and smuggling, and since the program started in 1996 international relief agencies have attested that the Iraqi government did not mishandle the distribution of aid in the center and south.

Second, the oil-for-food program was not intended to compensate fully for the effects of sanctions, which were supposed to do harm. That was the objective of the Security Council. As Cambridge University's Campaign Against Sanctions in Iraq put it: "*Suffering is not an unintentional side effect of sanctions. It is their aim.* Sanctions are instruments of coercion and they coerce by causing hardship."[72] But the coercion was double-edged. Saddam was undoubtedly skilled at manipulating the international sanctions regime, and he orchestrated an elaborate system of "dividends" and kickbacks from foreign contractors to line his own coffers. He diverted Iraq's diminished resources into displays of conspicuous consumption that were intended for his personal aggrandizement: great palaces and mosques that punched his power into the landscape. But he also had a vested interest in securing the food distribution system. Basic supplies were provided through a network of small government warehouses in each neighborhood – which created the impression that it was the benevolent Saddam who was feeding his people – while the rationing system in its turn provided the regime with a constantly corrected database on each individual citizen. As Hans von Sponeck bitterly observed, it was by these means that "local repression and international sanctions became brothers-in-arms in their quest to punish the Iraqi people for something they had not done."[73]

Two events in October 1998 revealed the Janus face of a sanctions regime that used "humanitarian assistance" for geopolitical purposes. At the beginning of the month UN Assistant General Secretary Denis Halliday, who had been coordinator of humanitarian aid for Iraq since 1997, resigned his post in protest at the impact of sanctions on the Iraqi people. "We are in the process of destroying an entire society," he wrote. "It is as simple and terrifying as that. It is illegal and immoral." In his first public speech after his resignation, Halliday affirmed that sanctions were destroying the lives and the expectations of the young and the innocent. And later he was even more direct: "We are responsible for genocide in Iraq."[74] Then, at the end of the month, President Clinton signed the Iraq Liberation Act. Its stated intention was to "support efforts to remove the regime headed by Saddam Hussein from power and to promote the emergence of a democratic government to replace that regime." The president was authorized to spend $97 million to train, equip, and finance an Iraqi insurgency, and a further $2 million was to be made available to Iraqi opposition groups for radio and television broadcasting. Funds were also to be channeled to the exiled Iraqi National Congress, led by Ahmed Chalabi: a group that, as the *New York Times* remarked, "represents almost no one." The newspaper's editorial was headlined "Fantasies about Iraq." But the fantasies were not Clinton's, and neither he nor his administration took the proposed measures seriously. The Republicans had pressured the president, who was simultaneously fighting impeachment and a mid-term election, to sign the Act. To the fury of its sponsors, he subsequently did little to activate its provisions. But, in the dog days of the Clinton presidency, Richard Perle railed against the persistent refusal to act. He also observed with relish that the Republican presidential candidate, George W. Bush, had said "he would fully implement the Iraq Liberation Act." And he added: "We all understand what that means."[75] I imagine most of us also understand what it means when genocide is made to march in lockstep with "liberation."

8   Boundless War

> Put your coffee aside and drink something else,
> Listening to what the invaders say:
> With Heaven's blessing
> We are directing a preventive war,
> Carrying the water of life
> From the banks of the Hudson and the Thames
> So that it may flow in the Tigris and Euphrates.
> A war against water and trees,
> Against birds and children's faces,
> A fire on the ends of sharp nails
> Comes out of their hands,
> The machine's hand taps their shoulders.
>
> Adonis, *Salute to Baghdad* (London,
> April 1, 2003), trans. Sinan Antoon

Black September

WHEN he addressed the General Assembly of the United Nations on September 12, 2002, President George W. Bush offered three main reasons for a military attack on Iraq. The first was that Iraq had persistently defied Security Council resolutions and, so he said, possessed weapons of mass destruction (WMD): nuclear, chemical, and biological. Bush represented this as a "defining moment" for the integrity of the United Nations. "Are Security Council resolutions to be honored and enforced," he demanded, "or cast aside without consequence?" The second reason was that the Iraqi government had persistently violated human rights, and routinely used torture and carried out summary executions. The third reason was that the regime of Saddam Hussein was implicated in transnational terrorism and, specifically, in the attacks on America on September 11.[1]

None of these charges was straightforward. To many Palestinians the first two confirmed America's partisan view of the Middle East. Israel has consistently refused to comply with United Nations Resolution 242, which required it to withdraw from the territories seized during the war of 1967, and Israel also possesses weapons of mass destruction, which contradicts the UN's declared goal "of establishing in the Middle East a zone free from weapons of mass destruction and all missiles for their delivery" and securing "a global ban on chemical weapons."[2] Israel has also persistently violated the human rights of Palestinians both within the state of Israel and within the occupied territories, and its armed forces frequently resort to torture and summary executions ("extra-judicial killings").[3] And yet, far from calling Israel to account before the United Nations, the United States has persistently protected Israel from sanction by the extensive use of its veto in the Security Council.[4]

These objections do not of course excuse Iraq from international sanction. But they surely raise questions about why Iraq should have been singled out on these grounds, and why it was supposed they demanded a military response. As Perry Anderson recognized, arguments about the war on Iraq need to address "the entire prior structure of the special treatment accorded to Iraq by the United Nations."[5] The answers are to be found in the narrative thread that I have traced in previous chapters, and in particular in the violent history of Anglo-American involvement in Iraq. None of this absolves the Iraqi government of responsibility. Saddam Hussein's regime was not the innocent party – not least because there were no innocent parties – but neither were its actions the single source of serious concern.

Weapons of mass destruction are, of course, matters of the gravest concern. Even Bush has described them, correctly, as "weapons of mass murder," though he seems strangely reluctant to think of America's arsenal in these terms. This matters because Iraq is not the only locus of their development, and it should not be forgotten that the only state to have used nuclear weapons is the United States itself (the Bush administration's disdain for international law and international conventions makes this of more than minor significance). Although Iraq persistently obstructed the work of UN weapons inspection teams, its actions were provoked, at least in part, by equally persistent attempts by the United States to subvert the integrity of the process.[6] Even so, by the beginning of 2003 those leading the searches in Iraq for nuclear weapons and for chemical and biological weapons – the International Atomic Energy Agency (IAEA) and the United Nations Monitoring, Verification and Inspection Commission (UNMOVIC) – both affirmed that a substantial degree of compliance had already been achieved, and attested that they would be able to complete their work within eight months. The evidence of WMD programs and capabilities that US Secretary of State Colin Powell presented to members of the Security Council on February 5, 2003 failed to persuade most of them that Iraq posed an imminent military threat to the security of any other state in the region or to the United States. Subsequently serious doubts were cast on both the provenance and probity of the intelligence assessments used by Washington and London to make their joint case for war. Reports revealed the use of documents shown to be forgeries and of plagiarized and out-of-date information; the politicization of intelligence through selective and partisan interpretations; the omission and suppression of counter-evidence; attempts to discredit both Mohammed El-Baradei, director-general of the IAEA, and Hans Blix, executive chairman of UNMOVIC; attempts to smear and intimidate credible media sources, including Dr David Kelly, a senior adviser with UNSCOM's biological weapons teams and special adviser to the director of Counter-Proliferation and Arms Control in Britain's Ministry of Defence, who was driven to take his own life in July 2003; and the systematic provision of disinformation.[7] None of this is surprising given that Saddam did not use weapons of mass destruction during the war, and that no trace of deliverable weapons has been found after the war.[8] Indeed, US Secretary of Defense Donald Rumsfeld admitted that they might have been destroyed before the war. As Britain's former Foreign Secretary Robin Cook remarked, "You have to admire his effrontery but not his logic." It beggars belief that Saddam would destroy his most lethal weapons on the eve of an invasion, and it is much more likely that he did not have large stockpiles of them to deploy in the first place.[9] Two American commentators concluded after a careful analysis of the evidence that Bush had "deceived Americans about what was known of the threat from Iraq, and deprived Congress of its ability to make an informed decision about whether or not to take the country to war."[10] In Britain, similar charges were made against Tony Blair's Labour government.[11] These are matters of the utmost gravity. A democratic politics requires the informed consent of its citizens, and a democratic state cannot go to war on a foundation of falsehoods.

Violations of human rights are also matters of the gravest concern. The Ba'athist regime in Iraq was, without question, savage and brutal, and identifying other regimes contemptuous of human rights does not exempt the Iraqi government from international sanction. The Annual Report from Human Rights Watch in 2002 confirmed, as it had year after wretched year, that the regime "perpetrated widespread and gross human rights violations, including arbitrary arrests of suspected political opponents and their relatives, routine torture and ill-treatment of detainees, summary executions and forced expulsions."[12] But to demonize Saddam Hussein as absolute Evil – to conjure an Enemy whose atrocities admit no parallel – is to allow what Tariq Ali called "selective vigilantism" to masquerade as moral principle. When Iraq was an ally of the United States, Saddam's ruthless suppression of dissent and his use of chemical weapons against the Kurds were well known; yet, far from protesting or proposing military action, the United States supplied Iraq with the materials necessary for waging biological and chemical warfare, and protected it from sanction by both Congress and the United Nations. When coalition troops uncovered mass graves of Iraqis who had been killed by Saddam's forces during the Shi'a uprisings in 1991, Blair claimed that this justified the war: and yet the United States had encouraged the rebellion and then did nothing to aid the rebels.[13] To suppress this recent history is to assemble a case for war out of a just-in-time morality: flexible, expedient, and eminently disposable. Both American and British governments had been presented with unflinching evidence of human rights abuses within Iraq for decades, and had been stoic in their indifference. "Salam Pax," the young Iraqi architect whose weblog from Baghdad attracted 20,000 visits a day during the war, expressed an understandable contempt for such "defenders" of human rights:

> Thank you for your keen interest in the human rights situation in my country. Thank you for turning a blind eye for thirty years. . . . Thank you for ignoring all human rights organizations when it came to the plight of the Iraqi people. . . . So what makes you so worried about how I manage to live in this shithole now? You had the reports all the time and you knew. What makes today different [from] a year ago?[14]

The answer, it seems, was "not much." In the months and even weeks before the conflict began, it was still being claimed that bloodshed could be averted if Iraq made a full and complete disclosure of its weapons of mass destruction, so that the resolve to come to the aid of the suffering Iraqi people was evidently less than steel-clad. Yet "liberty for the Iraqi people is a great moral cause," Bush told the UN General Assembly on September 12. "Free societies do not intimidate through cruelty and conquest." If we were wrong about weapons of mass destruction, Blair told the United States Congress in his post-war address, "history will forgive us [because we] have destroyed a threat that, at its least, is responsible for inhuman carnage and suffering."[15] Bush praised Blair's speech for its "moral clarity." And yet his argument – the high point of his address – not only slithered away from the *causus belli* that the two of them had declared before the war began; it also concealed their continuing complicity with serial abusers of human rights. If attacking Iraq was a humanitarian imperative, as both Bush and Blair claimed, then the inclusion of states such as Uzbekistan and Turkmenistan in the international coalition they cobbled together made a mockery of the moral purpose of the mission. In fact, of the 30 states willing to be identified as members of the coalition – 15 preferred to remain anonymous – the State Department's own survey of human rights identified no less than 18 as having "poor or extremely poor" records in the very area that was now supposed to have provided such compelling grounds for military intervention. Once again, as Amnesty International complained, human rights records were being used in a selective fashion to further political objectives and to legitimize military violence. Human Rights Watch was even sharper in its criticism. The organization had no illusions about Saddam's vicious inhumanity. It had circled the globe throughout the 1990s trying to find a government (any government) willing to institute legal proceedings against the Iraqi regime for genocide: but without success. Its executive director noted that the war was not primarily about humanitarian intervention, which was at best a subsidiary motivation, but he also argued that it did not meet the minimum standards necessary for military action on such grounds. Precisely because military action entails a substantial risk of large-scale death and destruction, he believed that it should only be undertaken as a last resort, when all other options have been closed off, and then only to prevent ongoing or imminent genocide or other forms of mass slaughter. It is simply wrong, he concluded, to use military action to address atrocities that were ignored in the past.[16]

The rhetorical force of Bush's first two charges was magnified by the third: the president represented an attack on Iraq as another front in the "war on terrorism" that he had declared after the attacks on the World Trade Center and the Pentagon. In the weeks after September 11 Rumsfeld asked the CIA on ten separate occasions to find evidence linking Iraq to the attacks on the World Trade Center and the Pentagon, and each time the agency drew a blank; Britain's Joint Intelligence Committee reached the same conclusion. Still, from the summer of 2002, as the administration started to agitate for "regime change" in Iraq, both the president and his Secretary of Defense made increasingly sweeping claims about connections between al-Qaeda and Saddam Hussein's regime until, by September, Bush was insisting that the two were "already virtually indistinguishable." "Imagine, a September 11 with weapons of mass destruction," Rumsfeld warned on CBS Television's *Face the Nation*. "It's not three thousand – it's tens of thousands of innocent men, women and children."[17]

It was thus no accident that the president elected to address the UN General Assembly on September 12, 2002, "one year and one day after a terrorist attack brought grief to my country and to many citizens of our world." Later in his speech Bush returned to the theme:

> Above all our principles and our security are challenged today by outlaw groups and regimes that accept no law of morality and have no limit to their violent intentions. *In the attacks on America a year ago, we saw the destructive intentions of our enemies.* This threat hides within many nations, including my own. In cells and camps, terrorists are plotting further destruction, and building new bases for their war against civilization. And our greatest fear is that terrorists will find a shortcut to their mad ambitions when an outlaw regime supplies them with the new technologies to kill on a massive scale. In one place – in one regime we find all these dangers, in their most lethal and aggressive forms. . . . Iraq continues to shelter and support terrorist organizations . . . and *al-Qaeda terrorists escaped from Afghanistan and are known to be in Iraq.*[18]

One month later Congress passed a joint resolution authorizing the use of United States Armed Forces against Iraq. The text of the resolution is instructive. It claimed that "Iraq both poses a continuing threat to the national security of the United States and international peace and security in the Persian Gulf region and remains in material and unacceptable breach of its international obligations by, amongst other things, continuing to possess and develop a significant chemical and biological weapons

capability, actively seeking a nuclear weapons capability, and supporting
and harboring terrorist organizations"; that "Iraq persists in violating resolutions of the United Nations Security Council by continuing to engage
in brutal repression of its civilian population"; that *"members of al Qaida,
an organization bearing responsibility for attacks on the United States, its
citizens and interests, including the attacks that occurred on September
11, 2001, are known to be in Iraq"*; that *"the attacks on the United States
of September 11, 2001, underscored the gravity of the threat posed by
the acquisition of weapons of mass destruction by international terrorist
organizations"*; and that there is a risk that "the current Iraqi regime will
either employ these weapons to launch a surprise attack against the United
States or its Armed Forces or provide them to international terrorists who
would do so." The resolution also noted that Congress had already taken
steps to pursue the "war on terrorism," including actions against "those
nations, organizations, or persons who planned, authorized or committed
or aided the terrorist attacks that occurred on *September 11, 2001,* or
harbored such persons or organizations," and that the president and
Congress were determined to continue "to take all appropriate actions
against international terrorists and terrorist organizations, including those
nations, organizations, or persons who planned, authorized or committed
or aided the terrorist attacks that occurred on *September 11, 2001,* or harbored such persons or organizations." Finally, the resolution empowered
the president to use the armed forces of the United States "as he deems
appropriate" on condition that he advised Congress that:

(1) reliance by the United States on further diplomatic or other peaceful means
alone either (A) will not adequately protect the national security of the United
States against the continued threat posed by Iraq or (B) is not likely to lead
to enforcement of all relevant United Nations Security Council resolutions
regarding Iraq; and

(2) *acting pursuant to this joint resolution is consistent with the United States
and other countries continuing to take all the necessary actions against international terrorists and terrorist organizations, including those nations,
organizations, or persons who planned, authorized or committed or aided
the terrorist attacks that occurred on September 11, 2001.*[19]

Bush made these twin declarations to Congress by letter on March 18,
2003.

I have italicized the passages in which September 11 was invoked as a justification for war on Iraq: their cumulative weight is astonishing, because there is no credible evidence that Iraq was involved in the attacks on the World Trade Center and the Pentagon. I have repeatedly underscored the hostility between Saddam and Osama bin Laden, and the ideological chasm between Ba'athism and Islamicism. Many of those who advocated military action against Iraq conceded as much. Kenneth Pollack, director of National Security Studies for the Council on Foreign Relations, was at the forefront of those who urged the Bush administration to launch "a full-scale invasion of Iraq to topple Saddam, eradicate his weapons of mass destruction, and rebuild Iraq as a prosperous and stable society for the good of the United States, Iraq's own people, and the entire region." The fulcrum of his case was the need for the United States to invade Iraq as a means of what he called "anticipatory self-defense" against the use of WMD, and Pollack advocated using United Nations weapons inspectors "to create a pretext." But he was equally clear that "as best we can tell, Iraq was not involved in the terrorist attacks of September 11, 2001. American intelligence officials have repeatedly affirmed that they can't connect Baghdad to the attacks despite Herculean labors to do so." Attempts to link Saddam to al-Qaeda fared no better: "Neither side wanted to have much to do with the other and they mostly went their separate ways. After all, Saddam Hussein is an avowed secularist who has killed far more Muslim clerics than he has American soldiers."[20]

In Pollack's view the significance of September 11 was strategic. It fanned the flames of domestic and international support – even enthusiasm – for military action against Iraq. The attacks on the World Trade Center and the Pentagon, and the war in Afghanistan, had prepared the ground for the American public to accept future military interventions with equanimity, and although Pollack was concerned that the window of opportunity might close, that "the sense of threat" might dissipate, the administration issued regular terrorism alerts and threat assessments that kept fear alive. "Fear is in the air," wrote Jacqueline Rose:

It is being manipulated to ratchet up the fever of war. . . . We are being asked to enter into a state of infinite war. . . . Fear of the unknown is, of course, the most powerful fear of all, because it tells us that we are vulnerable in ways that we cannot control. . . . Behind the argument for war, therefore, we can glimpse another fear – the fear of impotence.[21]

Pollack thought that September 11 would also dispose other governments to grant the Bush administration considerable freedom of action.
He argued that it would be much easier to capitalize on this new-found
tolerance "if the United States could point to a smoking gun with Iraqi
fingerprints on it." "Unfortunately" – his qualifier, not mine – "the evidence regarding the September 11 attacks continues to point entirely to
al-Qaeda." This was a crucial concession. While Pollack believed that
an invasion of Iraq was necessary, he accepted that the need to advance
the "war on terror" against al-Qaeda "should take precedence over invading Iraq." Not only were these separate objectives; the one trumped the
other.[22]

And yet the Bush administration systematically, deliberately, blurred
the lines between the two. In his State of the Union address on January
28, 2003 Bush again summoned the specter of September 11 to his aid.
"Imagine those 19 hijackers with other weapons and other plans – this
time armed by Saddam Hussein," he said. "It would take one vial, one
canister, one crate slipped into this country to bring a day of horror like
none we have ever known." As Robert Byrd put it in a speech to the Senate,
"the face of Osama bin Laden morphed into that of Saddam Hussein."[23]
One member of the United States diplomatic corps, John Brady Kiesling,
resigned his post for precisely these reasons:

> [W]e have not seen such systematic distortion of intelligence, such systematic
> manipulation of American public opinion, since Vietnam. . . . We spread dis-
> proportionate terror and confusion in the public mind, arbitrarily linking
> the unrelated problems of terrorism and Iraq. The result, and perhaps the
> motive, is to justify a vast misallocation of shrinking public wealth to the
> military and to weaken the safeguards that protect American citizens from
> the heavy hand of government. September 11 did not do as much damage
> to the fabric of American society as we seem determined to do ourselves.[24]

He was not alone in his skepticism. Among American cities passing resolutions opposing a pre-emptive strike on Iraq without the authority of the
United Nations were the twin targets of September 11: New York City
and Washington, DC.

When the war began, or more accurately resumed, on March 19, 2003,
the Bush administration accentuated the rhetorical connections between
Iraq and the terrorist attacks of September 11. In press briefings Iraqi resistance to the invading troops included "irregulars" who, when they used
subterfuge to attack American troops, suddenly became "terrorists." White

House press secretary Ari Fleischer claimed that "We're really dealing with elements of terrorism inside Iraq that are being employed now against our troops." The State Department defines terrorism as "premeditated, politically motivated violence propagated against noncombatant targets," however, so attacks on troops do not qualify. But describing Iraqi tactics in these terms artfully reinforced the claim that Iraq was connected to September 11. Then again, the Stars and Stripes draped over the face of Saddam Hussein as his statue was toppled before a crowd of journalists in Baghdad was said to have been the flag flying from the Pentagon when it was attacked on September 11. As one reporter wryly observed, this was by any measure an astonishing coincidence.[25] Finally, Bush's announcement of the end of "major combat operations" in Iraq on May 1, 2003 was staged to clinch the identification of Iraq with the war on terrorism. The president first made a dramatic tailhook landing on the deck of the USS *Abraham Lincoln*, which had returned from the Gulf and was lying off San Diego. Still dressed in his flying suit, Bush linked what he called "the battle of Iraq" to the "battle of Afghanistan." Both of them were victories in "a war on terror that began on September 11, 2001," he declared, "and still goes on." Characterizing Saddam as "an ally of al-Qaeda," Bush insisted that "the liberation of Iraq is a crucial advance in the campaign against terror." And he reassured his audience that "we have not forgotten the victims of September 11."[26] This speech – and its calculated staging – was perhaps the most cynical gesture of all. Here is Senator Byrd again:

> It may make for grand theater to describe Saddam Hussein as an ally of al-Qaeda or to characterize the fall of Baghdad as a victory in the war on terror, but stirring rhetoric does not necessarily reflect sobering reality. Not one of the 19 September 11th hijackers was an Iraqi. In fact, there is not a shred of evidence to link the September 11 attacks on the United States to Iraq . . . bringing Saddam Hussein to justice will not bring justice to the victims of 9–11. The United States has made great progress in its efforts to disrupt and destroy the al-Qaeda terror network. . . . We should not risk tarnishing these very real accomplishments by trumpeting victory in Iraq as a victory over Osama bin Laden.[27]

In these and other ways, as Richard Falk objected, September 11 was repeatedly appropriated by the Bush administration to further its own project: "Everything was validated, however imprudent, immoral and illegal. Anti-terrorism provided a welcome blanket of geopolitical disguise."[28]

When "major combat operations" had supposedly ended, Bush tired of toying under the covers. "We've had no evidence that Saddam Hussein was involved with September 11th," he admitted, and his Orwellian press secretary insisted that the White House had never claimed the existence of such a link.[29]

What, then, were the other grounds for war? Its critics identified two. The first was – inevitably – oil. Opponents claimed that the resumed war on Iraq was merely another move in the Great Game in which President Bush's father had been a key player in 1990–1, and which reached right back to the advance of British troops from Basra through Baghdad to Mosul in the First World War: in other words, "blood for oil." Iraq's proven oil reserves – over 112 billion barrels, around 11 percent of the world's total – are second only to those of Saudi Arabia, and new exploration technologies hold out the prospect of doubling this to around 250 billion barrels, which would allow Iraq to rival the petro-power of Saudi Arabia. Reversing the position of its predecessor in 1990–1, this was now an attractive proposition to the White House for two reasons. Since the fall in oil prices in 1998–9 Saudi Arabia had developed closer relations with Iran, and the two states had driven the price of oil above the threshold at which the US was comfortable. Saudi Arabia had signaled that its oil policy would no longer be subservient to American interests, and Washington's fears about the unreliability of the Saudis had been heightened by September 11. Most of the hijackers were Saudi citizens, and one Pentagon briefing paper claimed that "the Saudis are active at every level of the terror chain, from planners to financiers, from cadre to foot-soldier, from ideologist to cheer-leader."[30] These concerns were aggravated by signs of growing internal opposition to the Saudi regime and renewed doubts about its long-term stability. In these compounding circumstances, Iraqi oil came to be seen as a strategic asset that would enable a compliant successor-state to displace an increasingly volatile Saudi Arabia as the pivotal "swing" producer. Indeed, an influential American report, *Strategic Energy Policy Challenges for the Twenty-First Century*, noted in April 2001 that Iraq had already effectively become "a key 'swing' producer . . . turning its taps on and off when it has felt such action was in its strategic interest," and had warned that Saudi Arabia's role in countering these effects "should not be taken for granted."[31] It seemed like a "two-for-one sale," according to Thomas Friedman: "Destroy Saddam and destabilize OPEC."[32]

But the Bush II administration was not as oil-savvy as the Bush I administration. In principle, as the US Department of Energy noted,

Iraq's production costs are amongst the lowest in the world. Its fields can be tapped by shallow wells, and in their most productive phase the oil rises rapidly to the surface under pressure. In fact, however, on the eve of war Iraq had the lowest yield of any major oil producer – around 0.8 percent of its potential output; only 15 of its 74 known oilfields had been developed – and it was producing at most 2.5 million barrels per day (MBD). Washington hawks originally entertained fantasies of output rapidly soaring to 7 MBD, but this turned out to be an extremely expensive proposition. Rapid extraction had allowed water to seep into both the Kirkuk and Rumaila fields, and this had seriously compromised the reserves: recovery rates were far below industry norms. Repairing Iraq's existing oil wells and pipelines will cost more than $1 billion, and raising oil production to even 3.5 MBD will take at least three years and require another $8 billion to be invested in facilities and another $20 billion for repairs to the electricity grid that powers the pumps and refineries. There were certainly opportunities here for oil-service companies such as Halliburton and the Bechtel Group, which have close ties to senior members of the Bush administration, but multinational oil companies would require the formation of a stable and sovereign government in Iraq that could underwrite contracts and guarantee the security of these massive, long-term capital investments. It would be absurd to discount Iraqi oil altogether – as Paul Wolfowitz remarked, Iraq "floats on a sea of oil" – but it would be misleading to trumpet this as the sole reason for war.[33]

The other reason adduced by critics was the exercise of sovereign power itself. I say "reason," but for David Hare there *was* no reason: the Bush administration was "deliberately declaring that the only criterion of power shall now be power itself."[34] Or, more accurately perhaps, the only criterion of power would now be American power. This had been given formal expression in the *National Security Strategy of the United States*, published in September 2002. In his foreword, the president declared that "terrorists and tyrants" were the "enemies of civilization," repeated his concern that the one would be armed by the other with "catastrophic technologies," and vowed that the United States would act against "such emerging threats before they are fully formed." The last clause was crucial. Although the doctrine of deterrence had successfully contained the menace of the Soviet Union during the Cold War, the *Strategy* argued that it had no purchase on these new constellations whose reckless unreason required, in specified circumstances and in response to a "specific threat," a doctrine of "pre-emptive self-defence."[35] The *Strategy* recognized that

Table 8.1   Security Council vetoes, 1970–2002

Veto	1970–1979	1980–1989	1990–2002	Total
US alone	13	31	9	53
US/UK (and sometimes France)	8	15	0	23
USSR/Russian Federation	6 (+ 1 with China)	4	2	13
Total	28	50	11	89

such a doctrine transformed the concept of "imminent threat" on which international law was based. International law allows military force to be used in only two situations: either with the express authorization of the Security Council, or in self-defense when the attack is imminent and there are no other reasonable means of deterrence. The first provision is indeed problematic because it renders the permanent members of the Security Council "absolute custodians of the legitimization of international force," as Walter Slocombe puts it, but this was not the focus of the *Strategy*. On the contrary, the undemocratic powers of the permanent members never bothered the United States when it was exercising them. Given that the Bush administration was so angry at the prospect of two other permanent members, Russia and France, exercising their veto powers to withhold authorization for a military attack on Iraq, the full record of Security Council vetoes is instructive (see table 8.1). The figures in this table cast a revealing light on a dismissive remark made by Richard Perle, an influential member of the Defense Policy Board. "If a policy is right with the approbation of the Security Council," he asked, "how can it be wrong just because communist China or Russia or France or a gaggle of minor dictatorships withhold their assent . . . ?"[36] This, I think, is what is meant by *chutzpah*. The British poet Tom Raworth captured its chauvinism with a mordant brilliance in the opening lines of "Listen Up":

> Why should we listen to Hans Blix
> and all those foreign pricks[?][37]

Table 8.2 Global military expenditure, 2002

	$US billion 2000 constant $	% global military expenditure
1 USA	335.7	42.8
2 Japan	46.7	5.95
3 United Kingdom	36.0	4.58
4 France	33.6	4.28
5 China	31.1	3.96
6 Germany	27.7	3.53
7 Saudi Arabia	21.6	2.75
8 Italy	21.1	2.68
9 Iran (2001 figures)	17.5	2.23
10 South Korea	13.5	1.72
11 India	12.9	1.64
12 Russia	11.4	1.45
13 Turkey	10.1	1.28
14 Brazil	10.0	1.27
15 Israel	9.8	1.24

Source: Stockholm International Peace Research Institute.

All of this irritated the White House immensely, but the focus of the *Strategy* was on the second provision for authorizing the use of military force. To wait for an imminent attack was outdated, it was argued, and made absolutely no sense against "rogue states" (like Iraq) and "elusive," "stateless" terrorist organizations "of global reach" (like al-Qaeda), which threatened to use "weapons that can be easily concealed, delivered covertly, and used without warning." It was therefore vital for the United States to "reaffirm the essential role of American military strength" – to build defense capabilities beyond challenge ("full spectrum dominance") and to establish military bases around the globe – so that no adversary would ever equal "the power of the United States." Bush called this creating "a balance [*sic*] of power." For the record, global military expenditures in 2002 were around $784.6 billion US. The United States spent $335.7 billion, which exceeds the total spent by the next 14 states *combined* (see table 8.2).[38]

The *Strategy* was festooned with candy-floss concessions about "expanding the circle of development" – while "poverty does not make poor people into terrorists and murderers" it can make states "vulnerable to terror networks and drug cartels" – but at its hard core was a unilateral declaration that placed international law in abeyance.[39] The attack on Iraq was consistent with this doctrine, or at least with the administration's interpretation of it, but the fact remains that it was not consistent with international law. Perle subsequently said as much: "International law stood in the way."[40] For the war was not authorized by earlier Security Council resolutions and neither was it authorized by Resolution 1441, which had found Iraq in "material breach" of its disarmament obligations and imposed a "final deadline" for it to comply. The resolution required the Council to meet to consider the outcome and to determine future action, and this possibility had been foreclosed when the United States and Britain declined to submit a second resolution authorizing military action against Iraq for fear that it would be vetoed.[41] And most members of the Security Council were clearly not persuaded that Iraq – still less the fantasmatic conjunction of Saddam Hussein and Osama bin Laden[42] – posed a specific, clear, and credible threat to the United States that justified military action. In the event, only 4 out of 15 member states of the Security Council joined the coalition. Although the International Commission of Jurists warned that attacking without a UN mandate would constitute "an illegal invasion of Iraq which amounts to a war of aggression," the line between legal pre-emption and illegal aggression was to be drawn – unilaterally – by the United States. Edward Said effectively turned the *Strategy*'s indictment of rogue states against the United States to insist that its war on Iraq was "the most reckless war in modern times." It was all about "imperial arrogance unschooled in worldliness," he wrote, "unfettered either by competence or experience, undeterred by history or human complexity, unrepentant in its violence and the cruelty of its technology": in a word, unreason aggrandized.[43] But it was also, surely, about the assertion of American military power and geopolitical will. It is not enough for a hegemonic state to declare a new policy, Noam Chomsky explained. "It must establish it as a new norm of international law by exemplary action." Iraq presented the ideal target for such a project. It appeared strong – which explains, in some part, why the "threat" it posed was consistently talked up again – but in fact it was extraordinarily weak: enfeebled by the slaughter and destruction of the first Gulf War, by a decade of damaging sanctions, and by continuing air raids within and beyond the "no-fly zones." American victory would be swift and sure. The United States would have prevailed not only over Iraq but also over the rest of the world.[44] Sovereignty would be absolute for the United States but conditional for everyone else. As Salam Pax put it, "It's beginning to look like a showdown between the US of A and the rest of the world. We get to be the example."[45]

The strategy of the Bush administration was, once again, to present the United States *as* the world – the "universal nation" articulating universal values – and the war on Iraq became another front in its continuing fight against "the enemies of civilization": terrorists, tyrants, barbarians. There was something Hegelian about this materialization of a World Spirit – especially since Mesopotamia was one of the cradles of civilization – but the religious imagery invoked by Bush and others allowed many observers to see the coming conflict as another round in Samuel Huntington's "clash of civilizations." This impression was reinforced by the army of Christian fundamentalists, many of them with close ties to the White House, whose members were waiting in the wings to descend on Iraq as missionaries.[46] But most attention was directed toward the clash of more literal armies. Columnist Thomas Friedman argued that the shock of the war on Iraq to the Arab world could be compared only with the Israeli victory over the Arab armies in 1967 and Napoleon's invasion of Egypt in 1798.[47] Although he didn't say so, both of those violent conquests spawned a different violence, the violence of occupation and resistance. This did not perturb the indefatigable Sir John Keegan, of course, who believed that resistance to occupation was merely "Oriental" outrage at Western military superiority:

> Islam achieved its initial success as a self-proclaimed world religion in the seventh and eighth centuries by military conquest. It consolidated its achievement by the exercise of military power, which, perpetuated by the Ottoman Caliphate, maintained Islam as the most important polity in the northern hemisphere until the beginning of the 18th century. Islam's subsequent decline embittered Muslims everywhere, but particularly those of its heartland in the Middle East. Muslims, convinced of the infallibility of their belief system, are merely outraged by demonstrations of the unbelievers' material superiority, particularly their military superiority. The Ba'ath party, of which Saddam was leader in Iraq, was founded to achieve a Muslim renaissance.
>
> The failure of the Ba'athist idea, which can only be emphasised by the fall of Saddam, will encourage militant Islamic fundamentalists – who have espoused the idea that unbelievers' mastery of military techniques can be countered only by terror – to pursue novel and alternative methods of resistance to the unbelievers' power.

Western civilisation, rooted in the idea that the improvement of the human
lot lies in material advance and the enlargement of individual opportunity,
is ill-equipped to engage with a creed that deplores materialism and rejects
the concept of individuality, particularly individual freedom. The defeat of
Saddam has achieved a respite, an important respite, in the contest between
the Western way and its Muslim alternative. It has not, however, secured a
decisive success. The very completeness of the Western victory in Iraq ensures
the continuation of the conflict.[48]

Ba'athism was not about a "Muslim renaissance," however, but an *Arab*
renaissance, and its nationalist ideology was a secular one. It is true that
Saddam's exploitation of Islam had intensified since the Gulf War, and
that he used it to secure support for his regime both at home and abroad.
Saddam claimed to be descended from the Prophet Mohammed, and the
regime's rhetoric and its political iconography increasingly presented him
as a devout Sunni Muslim. He established a nationwide "Faith Campaign"
in the schools and the Saddam University of Islamic Studies. He embarked
on a monumental mosque-building campaign, including two vast mosques
in Baghdad that revealed how closely his promotion of Islam was entwined
with his own glorification. The Umm al-Ma'arik ("Mother of All Battles")
mosque was completed in 2001 to commemorate the Iraqi "victory" in the
Gulf War of 1991, and the Saddam Grand Mosque, which was projected
for completion by 2015, was intended to be the third-largest mosque in
the world after Mecca and Medina.[49] The regime portrayed the Anglo-
American invaders as "crusaders," and this view was shared by many
Muslims around the world and affected the sensibilities of a number of
prominent Islamic states. In marked contrast to its position in 1990–1,
Saudi Arabia refused to participate "under any condition or in any form"
in the war on Iraq, and announced that its forces would "under no
circumstance step even one foot into Iraqi territory."[50] This no doubt confirmed the American hawks' view of the unreliability of the Saudi regime
– US Central Command was obliged to establish its regional headquarters
in Doha, Qatar – but the House of Saud was acknowledging the anger of
its own subjects. Huntington himself – who as it happens opposed the war
and criticized the Bush administration – saw their point. "What we see as
the war against terrorism and against a brutal dictatorship," he noted in
a lecture at Georgetown University, "Muslims – quite understandably –
see as a war on Islam."[51] And in much of the Arab world, Susan Sachs
reported, the war was seen as a "clash of civilizations." "What is happening in Iraq is [seen as] part of one continuous brutal assault by America

and its allies on defenseless Arabs, wherever they are," she wrote, "a single bloodstained tableau of Arab grievance."[52] I don't think it surprising that Saddam's rallying-cry should have prompted young Muslims from the Lebanon, Saudi Arabia, Syria, and Yemen to journey to Iraq to fight. But most of them were not going to fight for Saddam and his regime; they were going to defend Islam and the people of Iraq.

And yet this was surely not a "clash of civilizations." Although Bush said as much, his protestations were hollowed out by senior members of his administration, who dismissed the prospect of an Islamic state arising out of the ashes of Ba'athism (or Baghdad): "It's not going to happen," Rumsfeld declared.[53] But it was the opponents of the war, not its orchestrators and cheerleaders, who gave the lie to these Manichean antagonisms. Global opposition to the war showed that Muslims and non-Muslims did not live in hermetic enclosures, "with malevolence their only messenger," as Yasmin Alibhai-Brown put it: "People otherwise divided" came together in solidarity "to reject the manufactured reasons for this invasion." Shahid Alam reached the same conclusion:

> If the thesis of an inevitable clash between the West and Islam still had any semblance of credibility, it was shredded by the global anti-war rallies of 15 February 2003. It is estimated that some 30 million people joined these rallies in more than 600 cities across the world. Significantly, the most massive of these rallies were staged in the capitals, cities and towns of Western countries.[54]

Those "manufactured reasons," as I have tried to show, confirmed that the attack on Iraq was an aggression of unprecedented cynicism.[55] But the cynicism of Bush and Blair in launching the war – and calling it Operation Iraqi Freedom to boot – was equaled by the cynicism of Saddam in using the genuine faith of millions of Muslims to try to see them off.

Killing Grounds

"What will follow will not be a repeat of any other conflict," Rumsfeld declared on March 20, 2003, as a second wave of cruise missiles rained down on Baghdad. "It will be of a force and a scope and scale that [will be] beyond what has been seen before." The war on Iraq thus began as a war of intimidation that always threatened to turn into a war of terror.

For what is a campaign of "shock and awe" other than a strategy designed to terrify? Its purpose was to use America's overwhelming military force in a sufficiently "intimidating and compelling" manner to force the Iraqis to accept the will and power of the United States. Robert Fisk watched one of Saddam's presidential palaces in the center of Baghdad explode in a cauldron of fire. "When the cruise missiles came in it sounded as if someone was ripping to pieces huge curtains of silk in the sky and the blast waves became a kind of frightening counterpoint to the flames." The message was clear: "the United States must be obeyed." As Aijaz Ahmad commented, the message was delivered not just to the regime but also to the Iraqi people at large. "The intent is simply to terrorize the population, to demonstrate that if the most majestic buildings in the city can go up in balls of fire and sky-high splinters of debris, then every one of the inhabitants of the city can also meet the same fate unless they flee or surrender immediately."[56]

But a different message had to be designed for American and British audiences, because it was not politically expedient for them to see this as a war *of* terror. In order to advance from the grounds for killing into the killing grounds themselves, imaginative geographies were mobilized to stage the war within a space of constructed visibility where military violence became – for these audiences at least – cinematic performance. I do not say this lightly. There were endless previews and trailers: drama at the Security Council, drumbeat scenarios of the conflict to come. The action movie mythology summoned up by the White House created heroes out of protagonists who not only broke the law – always to achieve a greater good – but who were above the law. Once the action started, there were special effects ("shock and awe") and artful cameos ("Saving Private Lynch"). There were clips and interactives on media websites, and a grand climax (the toppling of Saddam's statue in Baghdad). The Project for the New American Century's *The Building of America's Defenses* had described US forces overseas as "the cavalry on the new American frontier," and many commentators presented the war as a Hollywood Western (an impression that was reinforced when Bush gave Saddam 48 hours to get out of town). In December 2002 *Mad Magazine* parodied this cinematic ideology with a brilliant movie poster that its publishers will not allow me to reproduce here. "The Bush Administration, in association with the other Bush Administration, presents Gulf Wars, Episode II: Clone of the Attack." "Directed by a desire to win the November elections," its credits warned viewers that "the success of this military action has not yet been rated."[57]

For all that, wars are, of course, not movies. What is at issue here is the way in which the conduct of the war was presented to particular publics. I have repeatedly emphasized that spaces of constructed visibility are always also spaces of constructed invisibility. Presentation of the war was artfully scripted, and the 600 journalists who were "embedded" with coalition forces, together with the elaborately staged press conferences at CENTCOM's million-dollar media center in Doha (designed by a Hollywood art director) showed that lines of sight were carefully plotted too. But following the action on the Pentagon's terms is to lose sight of the role that the people of Iraq were cast to play. Above all, they were required to remain anonymous – merely extras, figures in the crowd, the collective object of a purportedly humanitarian intervention – because to do otherwise, to reveal the faces of the men, women, and children who were to be subjected to the pulverizing military assault, would have been to disclose the catastrophic scale of the suffering inflicted on them over the previous 12 years by the US-led sanctions and bombing regime. They were also required to remain invisible so that their country could be reduced to a series of "targets."

The focus was relentlessly on Iraq's cities. In part this reflected Iraq's high degree of urbanization; 70–75 percent of its population lives in towns and cities. But it also mirrored the specter raised by the Bush administration of mushroom clouds rising over American cities. It was as though one prospective nightmare could be made to disappear by the realization of another.[58] From the summer of 2002 American media were previewing scenarios of urban warfare and building their audiences for the coming conflict. In late November CNN's classroom edition included a special report on "Urban Combat." Students were asked to study cities in "global 'hot spots' of current conflict" to provide them with the basis for designing a simulated city to be used for war games. Among the activities suggested, two were particularly revealing. First, students were invited to "discuss the challenges foreign troops would face in combat" in their simulated city "and how knowledge of that particular urban setting could be a valuable weapon for both sides." Secondly, they were to devise "a plan to prepare the American people for the human costs of urban war while promoting support for such an effort." These may have been simulations and games, but anyone who assumed that the assignments were merely make-believe only had to read the key words at the end. They included only one real city: "ambush; anarchy; asymmetric; *Baghdad* . . ."[59]

The military is no stranger to simulations and war-games, of course, and it has paid increasing attention to urban combat.[60] Some of its training is in computer-generated virtual cities, but it also has a number of specialized training facilities. Perhaps the most sophisticated is the Zussman Mounted Urban Combat Training Center at Fort Knox, which was designed with the help of architects, and pyrotechnic and special effects experts from Disney World, Universal Studios, and Las Vegas themed casinos. It features a city whose identity can be changed from one part of the world to another, with pop-up targets, and fire and special effects (such as exploding gas lines, collapsing bridges) controlled by a computer system; troops' performance is monitored through the Multiple Integrated Laser Engagement System. My concern is not that the military should have called on these civilian experts; troops plainly need to have the most realistic and rigorous training possible. But, as I propose to show, when these militarized scenarios are returned to a nominally civilian public sphere in the form of media reports, computer games, or CGI animations in films, they hollow out specific conflicts, presenting them as disembodied games that, at the limit, bleed into voyeuristic entertainment.

Many of the scenarios that appeared in the media were based on the *Doctrine for Joint Urban Operations* prepared for the Joint Chiefs of Staff and published in September 2002. The report identified a distinctive "urban triad" that had significant effects on the battle space:

1   the three-dimensionality of urban terrain: "internal and external space of buildings and structures; subsurface areas; and the airspace above the topographical complex";
2   the interactivity of urban life: "The noncombatant population is characterized by the interaction of numerous political, economic and social activities";
3   the infrastructural networks that support the urban population.

The report argued that "understanding the urban battlespace calls for different ways of visualizing space and time." In particular, surveillance and reconnaissance "are hampered by urban structures, clutter, background noise, and the difficulty [of] seeing into interior space." Similarly, "the construction of urban areas may inhibit tactical movement and maneuvers above, below and on the ground, as well as within or among structures."

The emphasis throughout the report was on the city as an object-space – a space of envelopes, hard structures, and networks – that had to be brought under control for victory to be won.[61] A summary presentation of the study focused on one city alone: Baghdad. It mapped out the urban battle-space – the city's "geographic grids" – and then identified seven strategies in purely abstract, geometric terms: "isolation siege," "remote strike," "ground assault, frontal," "nodal isolation," "nodal capture," "segment and capture," "softpoint capture and expansion."[62]

Again, I'm not so much interested here in the military performances of space and time choreographed by the report, and the other briefing papers made available to the press, important though these are, as in the ways in which the report's imaginative geographies were mapped onto the American public sphere to align military and civilian geographical knowledge.[63] Here, for example, is journalist Ann Scott Tyson describing the deceptive geometries of Iraqi cities:

> Inside Iraqi cities, military operations would be vastly more complicated. Buildings constrict troop and tank maneuvers, interfere with radio communications, and limit close air support from helicopters and gunships. Dense populations make airstrikes – even precision ones – costly in civilian lives. From sewers to rooftops, cities are multilayered, like three-dimensional chessboards, creating endless opportunities for ambushes and snipers. . . . "Urban warfare is close, personal and brutal," says an Army report. "Tall buildings . . . sewer and storm drains, allow unobserved shifting of forces, and streets become kill-zones."[64]

Similarly, James Baker described the city as a space of objects ("things") whose "three-dimensionality" posed formidable problems: "Upper stories of buildings may be enemy observation and sniper posts. Sewers may be enemy communication tunnels and ambush bunkers. Buildings block line-of-sight communications, laser detectors and direct-fire weapons. *It is a terrain of tunnels, bunkers, twists and turns.*"[65] This is the language of object-ness again, cities as collections of objects not congeries of people.

But it is also the language of Vietnam. Baker's last sentence evoked the jungle war against the Viet Cong and their elaborate system of bunkers and tunnels, and in the fall Tariq Aziz had warned that Iraq aimed to create "a new Vietnam" for the United States in its cities: "People say to me you are not the Vietnamese. You have no jungles and swamps to hide in. I reply: Let our streets be our jungles, let our buildings be our swamps."[66]

Time enlarged this sense of threat in a graphical illustration of "The Perils" of the Iraqi city (singular). This showed a stylized, Orientalized street – hardly modern Baghdad – with "Iraqi soldiers disguised as civilians," "Iraqi soldiers faking surrender," tunnels and sewers "conceal[ing] Iraqi soldiers and arms," and "mosques, hospitals and historic buildings that US would prefer not to demolish [but] could hide soldiers or munitions" (figure 8.1). The Orientalist imaginary was more than scenography here. This was a city in which nothing was as it seemed, where deceit and danger threatened at every turn.[67]

And yet all of these hidden traps could be revealed – the Orientalist veil lifted – as they were in the print edition by the bright circle suggesting the powerful effects of night-vision goggles and in the interactive version on the web by rolling the mouse over the designated numbers. The American public was thus reassured that Baghdad would not be another Vietnam. But there was the real risk of another Jenin. An Israeli military historian advised readers of the *New York Times* that Operation Defensive Shield provided "a good model for military tactics" in Iraq. The Pentagon evidently agreed. The US Marine Corps had studied Israeli military tactics in the fall, just months after the IDF's ferocious assault on Palestinian towns and refugee camps in the West Bank, and officers had visited a mock-Arab town inside a military base in the Negev to see at first hand how Israeli troops learned to move from house to house by knocking holes through connecting walls, and how armored bulldozers were used to open up lines of sight and advance.[68] But there were other, less overtly physical ways to render the opaque spaces of Arab cities transparent to American armed forces. "Intelligence will be crucial," *Time* reported, and plans of the city's infrastructure and satellite photographs would bring the multiple geometries of the city into clear view. "The reason cities have been so militarily formidable has been that it is so hard to know where things are," Baker explained, and "in a battle, the side that knows the most about where things are has a huge advantage – particularly if that knowledge is comprehensive." That was precisely what gave the United States the advantage. For cities are systems – collections of objects, remember – in which "the buildings, streets, sewers, water lines, gas lines, telephone lines and electricity lines – all the things that distinguish a city – are tied together." It would be possible for American troops to see the fractured, fragmented city as a totality, Baker explained, because "there is more information about a given city block of Baghdad than for almost any other similar-sized area of nonurban terrain."

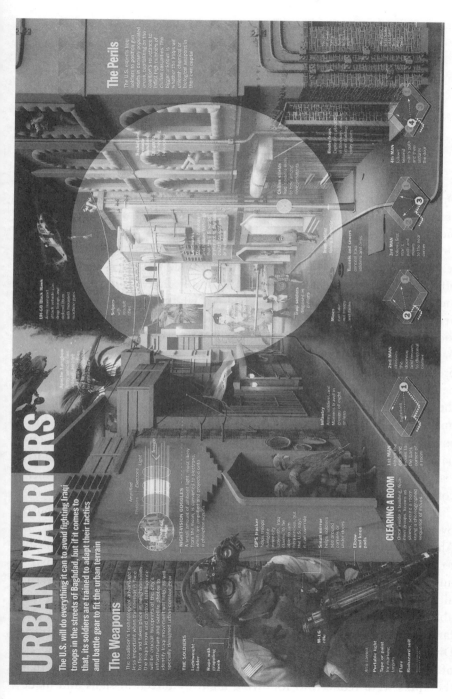

Figure 8.1 "Urban warriors" (*Time*, April 7, 2003)

The locations of buildings, sewers and telephone lines that have made urban terrain so formidable are recorded in blueprints, maps, maintenance records, photographs, directories, and scale models. And the US Geographical Information Systems – which combine traditional location information of recorded plans with up-to-date, highly precise radar-generated digital terrain-elevation data and other measurements – have grown dramatically over the past decade. . . . That's what offsets the street smarts of someone who has intimate knowledge of a room, building or neighborhood. *If the last battle is in Baghdad, the US will enter it knowing more about the terrain than the Iraqis do.*[69]

Once American troops were in the urban battle space they would also be able to see its configurations more clearly than Iraqi troops. The press made much of UAVs – Predator drones, and especially tiny drones such as the Dragon Eye that fit into a backpack – that could transmit high-resolution, real-time images that would enable American commanders to "tell their officers on the street where Iraqi soldiers and Fedayeen guerrillas are hiding – which rooftops they're crouched on, which windows they've been firing from, which alleyways are clear and which are deathtraps." This too was a lesson from Israeli military operations in Gaza and the West Bank. Cities reduce the effectiveness of many remote technologies, "compressing combat space and decision-making time-lines," but the left-hand pane of the *Time* graphic showed that American ground troops would have the advantage of "specially designed urban-combat gear" including thermal-imaging and night-vision goggles (so that they would "own the night," as one reporter put it) and GPS trackers and intranets "to help troops navigate the inner-city labyrinth." And the use of laser- and GPS-guided "smart bombs" would supposedly permit American forces to pinpoint their concealed targets with deadly accuracy.[70]

It never turned out quite that way. Most Iraqi cities were pounded by airstrikes before the ground troops swept in. The aim, according to Ahmad, was to turn Baghdad into "a city of corpses and ghosts" expressly to spare American troops the nightmare of urban combat.[71] Ahmad's imagery may be questioned – attempts were made to minimize civilian casualties – but the "pinpoint accuracy" of the strikes was equally questionable.[72] And once troops entered the city, the battle space turned out to be far from transparent. When the armored columns of the 3rd Infantry Division launched their "Thunder Run" through Baghdad in the first week of April, for example, their military maps had no civilian markings so that the tanks were reduced to following highway direction signs and made one wrong turn after another. High-level visuals were no better: "Satellite imagery didn't show bunkers or camouflaged armor and artillery," and field commanders had access to just one unmanned drone whose cameras "weren't providing much either."[73] In the months that followed, guerrilla warfare started against the occupying forces and their technological superiority counted for very little in the cities. The streets were transparent to Iraqis but still stubbornly opaque to American troops: "The daily attacks that use the urban landscape for concealment and flight have frustrated and frightened US forces in Baghdad."[74]

As these media reports showed, it was not just American armed forces who sought to peer into the opaque spaces of Iraqi cities. As the president of MSNBC put it, since the first Gulf War "the technology – the military's and the media's – has exploded." What he didn't say is that technologies had also become increasingly interchangeable. Media commentators described the Pentagon as "more creative" and "more imaginative" than it had been in the first Gulf War – "this may be the one time where the sequel is more compelling than the original" – and studio sets in their turn mimicked the military's command-and-control centers. The computer-generated graphics used by television news programs were created by the same satellite firms and defense industries that supplied the military. In the print media there were endless satellite photographs and maps too – and, on media websites, interactive graphics – to make these spaces transparent to viewers. Newspapers provided daily satellite maps of Baghdad as a city of targets (figure 8.2). On the web, *USA Today*'s interactive map of "Downtown Baghdad" invited its users: "Get a satellite-eye's view of Baghdad. Strategic sites and bombing targets are marked, but you can click on any quadrant for a close-up." The site also included imagery of the targets "before" and "after" the air strikes. The *Washington Post*'s interactives invited the viewer to "roll over the numbers to see what targets were hit on which day; click to read more about the targets."[75] It wasn't just that, through these means, the war in Iraq was presented as "the ultimate in reality television," as Michiko Kakutani has it, because the interactivity of these images on the web added another dimension. Their visuality was produced through the conjunction of sight and touch, eye and hand, the interface of screen and mouse, and this made it possible for the viewer to intervene and make the spaces transparent – to repeat the military reduction of the city to a series of targets, and so become complicit in its destruction – and yet at the same time to refuse the intimacy of corporeal engagement.[76]

Known bombing targets   Presidential complex   0   500M

1. Iraq air force headquarters
2. Central railroad station
3. TV centre
4. Ministry of Information
5. Ministry of Planning
6. Ministry of Industry and
   Military Industrialization
7. Council of Ministers

8. Special Security headquarters
9. Al Salam Palace
10. Al Sijood Presidential Palace
    (Hussein's official residence)
11. Baath Party headquarters
12. Baath Party Military Command headquarters
13. Republican Palace
14. 5th Battalion Special Republican Guard

Figure 8.2 Targeting Baghdad (Courtesy of Digital Global, after *Los Angeles Times*, March 29, 2003)

These effects were reinforced by a studied refusal to count – or even estimate – Iraqi casualties. The "kills" counted by coalition forces (for public consumption at any rate) were tanks, artillery, missile launchers – objects – not people. "We do not look at combat as a scorecard," the chief military spokesman at CENTCOM told the *New York Times*. "We are not going to ask battlefield commanders to make specific reports on enemy casualties." This is a strange claim to make, since the effective conduct of war evidently requires an assessment of the losses suffered by the enemy.[77] In fact some commanders estimated that 2,000–3,000 Iraqi fighters were killed during the first ground assault on Baghdad alone, and another report put the total number of Iraqi military casualties anywhere between 13,500 and 45,000.[78] Whatever the correct figure, the contrast with coalition casualties could not be plainer. These were much lower, precisely accounted for, and – significantly – linked to their families at home. Here is novelist Julian Barnes:

> The return of British bodies has been given full-scale TV coverage. . . . It thuds on the emotions. *But Iraqi soldiers? They're just dead.* The *Guardian* told us in useful detail how the British Army breaks bad news to families. What happens in Iraq? Who tells whom? Does news even get through? Do you just wait for your 18 year-old conscript son to come home or not to come home? Do you get the few bits that remain after he has been pulverized by our bold new armaments? There aren't many equivalencies around in this war, but you can be sure that the equivalence of grief exists.[79]

For American and British viewers, their troops had families and friends – *lives* – but Iraqi troops were without these affiliations. Cut free from the ties that bound them to others, they disappeared – neither bodies nor even numbers – but, as Barnes said, just *dead*.

The principle that if they had not been counted they did not count applied with equal force to civilian casualties. Colin Powell repeated the indifference he had shown during the first Gulf War: "We really don't know how many civilian deaths there have been, and we don't know how many of them can be attributed to coalition action, as opposed to action on the part of Iraqi armed forces as they defended themselves."[80] But the Pentagon must have had some idea because it made its own estimates in advance. Rumsfeld required all plans for air attacks likely to kill more than 30 civilians to be submitted to him for approval. Over 50 submissions were made; all of them were approved. None of the numbers were released. All estimates of casualties are bound to be contentious and, in the teeth of official opposition, are shot through with difficulties.[81] But there are some markers. A detailed examination of the records of 27 hospitals in Baghdad and the surrounding districts concluded that at least 1,700 Iraqi civilians had died and more than 8,000 were injured in the battle for the capital alone. Hundreds, even thousands of other deaths were undocumented, their bodies lying under tons of rubble, buried in makeshift graves all over the city, or marked only by scraps of black card fluttering on walls and doors.[82] The most systematic and scrupulous accounting concluded that 6,087–7,798 civilians had been killed and at least 20,000 injured (8,000 of them in Baghdad alone) between January 1 and August 1, 2003.[83]

The Pentagon's war without bodies was in stark contrast to the war seen by the Arab world. Arabic newspapers and news channels showed the bloody victims of Operation Iraqi Freedom, and the overwhelming grief of ordinary families who had been caught up in the violence of the war. These images had a terrifying impact on Iraqis waiting for the fighting to reach them. Here is Salam Pax writing from Baghdad:

> Today's (and last night's) shock attacks didn't come from airplanes but rather from the airwaves. The images *al-Jazeera* is broadcasting are beyond any description. . . . What was most disturbing [were] the images of civilian casualties from the hospitals [in Basra]. They are simply not prepared to deal with these things. People were lying on the floor with bandages and blood all over. If this is what "urban warfare" is going to look like we're in for a disaster.[84]

The same images reverberated around the rest of the Arab world. There were five Arabic all-news channels, but al-Jazeera led the field in both the quality of its reporting and its independence. Proceeding on the reasonable belief that the war was illegal, al-Jazeera consistently referred to American and British troops as "invading forces," and did not shrink from broadcasting what one of its senior editors described as "the horror of the bombing campaign, the blown-out brains, the blood-spattered pavements, the screaming infants and the corpses." In the eyes of the Pentagon al-Jazeera was "cinematic agitprop against American Central Command's Hollywood news producers," and on several occasions coalition forces took offensive action against its offices and staff, and against other so-called "unilateral" journalists who were supposedly reporting "from the enemy side."[85]

But the images shown by the Arabic media to their various audiences did much more than counter the Defense Department's preferred points of view and lines of sight. To Muslim viewers these scenes had a far more intense corporeality than substituting bodies for targets might seem to imply. In a brilliantly perceptive essay Jonathan Raban linked the sense of bodily assault and injury conveyed by images like these to the corporeality of Islam itself. Throughout the nineteenth century European Orientalists such as Edward Lane had marveled at the choreography of Islam's profession of faith, the intricate sequence of bodily gestures and movements repeated by Muslims all over the world as they face Mecca and pray five times a day.[86] Raban realized that the physical character of this prayer is unique to Islam, but he also recognized its extraordinary significance for the constitution of Islam as a political and cultural communion. As the world turns, he wrote, "the entire *ummah* [the global community of Muslims] goes down on its knees in a never-ending wave of synchronised prayer," and this endows the *ummah* – "a body literally made up of bodies" – with "a corporeal substance" that is utterly unlike "the airy, arbitrary, dissolving and re-constituting nations of Arabia." The space of the *ummah* is not empty, abstract, hollowed out; it has a palpable fleshiness, filled with and con-stituted through interconnected bodies whose affiliations cannot be sundered by the geometries of colonial power. Raban explained that this orchestrated performance of space, and the connectivities that are produced and validated through it, means that it is by no means "a far-fetched thought in the Islamic world" to see "the invasion of Iraq as a brutal assault on the *ummah*, and therefore on one's own person." On the contrary, "*Geographical distance from the site of the invasion hardly seems to dull the impact of this bodily assault.* It's no wonder the call of the *ummah* effortlessly transcends the flimsy national boundaries of the Middle East – those lines of colonial convenience, drawn in the sand by the British and the French 80 years ago." This way of seeing – and being in – the world involves a radically different conception of the self to the autonomous individual constructed under the sign of European modernity. Within the cultures of Islam, as Lawrence Rosen has shown with exemplary clarity, "the self is not an artifact of interior construction but an unavoidably pub-lic act." The consequences of all this are, as Raban emphasized, literally far-reaching:

> We're dealing here with a world in which a commitment to, say, Palestine, or to the people of Iraq, can be a defining constituent of the self in a way that westerners don't easily understand. The recent demonstrations against the US and Britain on the streets of Cairo, Amman, Sanaa and Islamabad may

look deceptively like their counterparts in Athens, Hamburg, London and New York, but their content is importantly different. What they register is not the vicarious outrage of the anti-war protests in the west but a sense of intense personal injury and affront, a violation of the self. Next time, look closely at the faces on the screen: if their expressions appear to be those of people seen in the act of being raped, or stabbed, that is perhaps closer than we can imagine to how they actually feel.[87]

There were also non-Muslim journalists, particularly the 2,000 "uni-lateral" ones disembodied from the coalition forces, whose reports brought home the horror of the attacks and the suffering of individuals and families. Suzanne Goldenberg went to an improvised mortuary in a Baghdad hospital and her account – the most awful still life I can imagine – has a visceral corporeality that continues to haunt me:

> Death's embrace gave the bodies intimacies they never knew in life. Strangers, bloodied and blackened, wrapped their arms around others, hugging them close. A man's hand rose disembodied from the bottom of the heap of corpses to rest on the belly of a man near the top. A blue stone in his ring glinted as an Iraqi orderly opened the door of the morgue, admitting daylight and the sound of a man's sobs to the cold silence within. . . . These were mere fragments in a larger picture of killing, flight and destruction inflicted on a sprawling city of 5 million. And it grew more unbearable by the minute.[88]

Until that pulverizing assault, Baghdad had seemed almost surreal. Fixed cameras transmitted the same endless pictures of near-empty streets in the central districts, traffic lights moving through their sequence time and time again. War, as Goldenberg put it, "arrived as a series of interruptions to daily life." But behind the scenes, in the outlying districts and as the war advanced, an altogether different story was unfolding. Reporters described scenes of incandescent horror: mutilated bodies, screaming children, and overworked doctors in ill-equipped hospitals performing operations using aspirin instead of anaesthetic.[89]

On occasion, media reports obliged the coalition forces and the distant governments that stood behind them to account for the consequences of their actions. I have space for only two examples. In the early evening of March 28 a missile struck the al-Naser market in the al-Shula district in north Baghdad, a poor Shi'a neighborhood of single-story corrugated iron and cement stores, tents, and two-room houses. The market was crowded with women, children, and the elderly. "The missile sprayed hunks of metal through the crowds – mainly women and children – and through the cheap brick walls of local homes, amputating limbs and heads." By the following day, at least 60 people had died; scores more were left with excruciating injuries. The immediate response from American and British sources was to suggest that the attack was the result of a malfunctioning Iraqi missile ("many have fallen back on Baghdad"). But an old man whose home was close to the crater retrieved a metal fragment minutes after the explosion. It was marked with a serial and a lot number, which enabled it to be traced to a HARM cruise missile (HARM stands for High-speed Anti-Radiation Missile, but the acronym is more accurate) whose warhead is designed to explode into thousands of aluminum fragments; it was manufactured by the Texas-based company Ray-theon, "the world's largest producer of 'smart' armaments," and sold to the procurement arm of the US navy. The response to these revelations, from Britain's Defence Secretary Geoffrey Hoon, was to claim that the fragment had been moved from elsewhere in the city and planted to discredit coalition forces. "We have very clear evidence immediately after those two explosions there were representatives of the regime clearing up in and around the market place," he said. "Now why they should be doing that other than to perhaps disguise their own responsibility for what took place is an interesting question." Presumably had their roles been reversed Mr Hoon's own reaction would not have been to see what he could do to help but instead to nip down to the East End with a fragment of Iraqi missile and find a senior citizen willing to foist it into the arms of a gullible journalist. An inquiry into the attack was promised – in fact, reporters were assured that it was ongoing – but this was a lie: several months later it was revealed that there had never been an inquiry.[90]

On April 7 four 2,000 lb satellite-guided "bunker-buster" bombs were dropped on the Baghdad suburb of Mansur. The target was the al-Sa'ah, a cheap restaurant where American intelligence believed Saddam and two of his sons were meeting with their aides. The "smart bombs" missed their target and instead destroyed four or five houses, pulverizing their inhabitants into "pink mist."

> The smouldering crater is littered with the artifacts of ordinary middle-class life – a crunched Passat sedan, a charred stove, a wrought-iron front gate, a broken bedhead and the armrest of a chair upholstered in green-brocade. The top floors of surrounding buildings are sheared off. Mud thrown by the force of the blast cakes what is left of those buildings. Nearby date palms

are decapitated. Bulldozers and rescue crews work frantically, peeling back
the rubble in the hope of finding survivors. Neighbours and relatives of the
home-owners weep in the street, some embracing to ease the pain, all of them
wondering why such a powerful missile was dumped on them after the US
said its heavy bombing campaign was over.[91]

Black banners draped across the rubble mourned the deaths of family members. Yet when doubts were raised about whether Saddam had been in
the restaurant at all a Defense Department spokeswoman said she didn't
think "it matters very much. I'm not losing sleep trying to figure out if he
was in there."[92]

One might assume that these reactions were untypical. But one might
also see them as the products not only of a culture of military violence
but also of a political culture of denial and dismissal, which treats its civilian victims not even as "collateral damage" – objects and obstacles who
got in the way – but as irrelevancies. No regret, no remorse: just more
homines sacri. They simply didn't matter. These victims were people who
had been excluded from politically qualified life by Saddam, but reactions
like these showed that they were excluded from politically qualified life
by America and Britain too: ultimately, excluded from life altogether.[93]
The only Iraqi bodies that were acknowledged by the coalition were those
that could be turned to iconic account. On one side, the dead bodies of
Saddam's two sons, Uday and Qusay, were exhibited to show that the apparatus of terror in which were central parts was itself being dismembered.
The ordinary dead – thousands of them – were disavowed.[94] On another
side, the maimed body of little Ali Abbas, the beautiful 11-year-old boy
whose arms were blown off in the bombing of Baghdad, was made to stand
for – and also, horribly, to stand in the way of – countless other innocent
victims. At times, it seemed as if he was "the only tragedy of collateral
damage this war had produced." The press made Ali's story revolve
around the compassion of their readers, not the military violence that had
killed so many others and nearly destroyed his own life.[95] Those who shrug
their shoulders and think all this inevitable and, on the scale of things,
hardly worth bothering about, should reflect on an argument advanced
by Hugo Slim:

> Enemies are not just enemies. Enemies never stop being human beings. They
> are still people. Their lives are precious. They are like us. Indeed, we are the
> enemies of others. This overlap emerges from what Susan Niditch describes

as "a conflict within each of us between compassion and enmity". . . . From this sense of overlap . . . are born ideas of restraint and immunity in war that have always existed alongside more powerful and competing ideas of justifiable hatred and extreme violence. From these ideas comes the person of the civilian.[96]

For the most part, it was only when the bombing, fighting, and killing were supposed to be over that Iraq's ordinary inhabitants were recognized. Even when Baghdad was deemed to have fallen to American troops on April 9, the trauma of "liberation" was airbrushed away. Here is one young Iraqi woman, "Riverbend," describing the scene in her weblog:

For me, April 9 was a blur of faces distorted with fear, horror and tears. All over Baghdad you could hear shelling, explosions, clashes, fighter planes, the dreaded Apaches and the horrifying tanks tearing down streets and highways. Whether you loved Saddam or hated him, Baghdad tore you to pieces. Baghdad was burning. Baghdad was exploding. . . . Baghdad was falling . . . it was a nightmare beyond anyone's power to describe. Baghdad was up in smoke that day, explosions everywhere, American troops crawling all over the city, fires, looting, fighting and killing. Civilians were being evacuated from one area to another, houses were being shot at by tanks, cars were being burned by Apache helicopters. . . . Baghdad was full of death and destruction on April 9. Seeing tanks in your city, under any circumstances, is perturbing. Seeing foreign tanks in your capital is devastating.[97]

But scenes like these had no place in the liberation scenario. Ordinary Iraqis could only be allowed into the frame once they had appeared in the streets with the requisite display of jubilation. As journalist Mark Steel put it, "Iraqis only count if they're dancing in the street."[98] Suddenly Baghdad was no longer a collection of targets – a city of objects – and a new series of graphics and interactives appeared showing "Baghdad neighborhoods." These, it turned out, were not the exclusive preserve of tyrants and terrorists but of millions of ordinary men, women, and children. The *New York Times* provided summary profiles of Saddam City ("a sprawling densely populated slum that is home to as many as two million Shi'ites"), Kadhimiya ("an old middle-class Shi'ite neighborhood"), Karada ("a residential district of two and three-storey buildings"), and Mansour, Mamoun and Yarmuk ("newer and more upscale neighborhoods of less densely spaced one-storey houses and walled gardens"). *Time* presented a new map too, "Inside Baghdad," which described "a modern, sprawling urban center surrounded by dense, diverse neighborhoods" like Saddam City ("a sprawling, dense urban slum of one- and two-storey concrete buildings that house millions of poor Shi'ite Muslims," many of whom "come from rural areas and continue to raise their livestock near their small apartments)," Amiryah ("a wealthy, upscale district, home to doctors, professionals and government apparatchiks" where "houses tend to be newer and more spacious"), and Khalimiya (Kadhimiya; "a middle class Shi'ite neighborhood, where residents dress more traditionally and mosques and religious iconography are prevalent"). The juxtaposition of two small maps on the margin showed that Baghdad was about the same size as Columbus, Ohio, but with a pre-war population roughly seven times as large (figure 8.3). The *Los Angeles Times* made similar comparisons on its map. The distance from Baghdad's airport to the center of the city, for example, was "roughly the distance from downtown LA to Pasadena." For a brief moment, at least, Baghdad was a city almost like any other: no longer opaque, alien, hollowed out but *peopled*.[99]

On May 1, when he announced the end of major combat operations in Iraq, Bush told his American audience that "When Iraqi civilians looked into the faces of our servicemen and women, they saw strength and kindness and good will." No doubt many of them were men and women who displayed all these qualities. But how could the Iraqi people not also have seen in their faces a regime that had bombed and starved their families and friends for 12 years? An army that had fought its way into their cities with terror at its head and death in its wake? An occupying force that demanded complete compliance with its will? "We are the oldest civilization, but we are presented to the world as terrorists," a primary school teacher in Baghdad told one human rights worker. "Only people who fight with small guns are called terrorists. Bush, who bombs us with cluster bombs and strangles us with the embargo, is a 'civilized man.'" You might quibble over the details, but you can hardly miss her point. "Somehow when the bombs start dropping or you hear machine-guns at the end of your street," Salam Pax wrote in his weblog, "you don't think about your imminent 'liberation' any more."[100]

The Cutting-Room War

If it is hard to write about the war in Iraq, it is no less difficult to write about the occupation. Several weeks before Bush declared major combat

Figure 8.3 "Inside Baghdad" (*Time*, April 14, 2003)

operations over, columnist Adrian Hamilton had already despaired at what he called "the obscenity of bickering over death and torture." "The shaken inhabitants of Baghdad are being called on to stream out on the streets to prove the pro-war lobby right, to show that this was a war of liberation," he wrote, "while anti-war commentators have hung on to every sign of continued resistance as proof that war is a disaster." Hamilton captured the dialectics of the war with precision:

> For every mother mourning the loss of a relative who disappeared under Saddam's tyranny there is now one frantically searching and praying that her son was not one of those killed by the might of Western armour fighting a poorly equipped, badly trained army. We can say what we like about what this proves or doesn't. But then we can afford to. It's not our country and we're not caught in the firing line.[101]

And so I try to proceed with caution. The war on Iraq was, as I have said, no film. But seeing it in those terms – for a moment – helps to explain why the occupation of Iraq turned so rapidly into such a nightmare. "The buildup to this war was so exhausting, the coverage of the dash to Baghdad so telegenic and the climax of the toppling of Saddam's statue so dramatic," Friedman suggested, "that everyone who went through it seems to prefer that the story end just there."[102] This isn't just a smart-ass remark. When Bush announced the end of major combat operations in Iraq, he did so in front of a huge banner proclaiming "Mission accomplished." Washington's script required the war to end not only in triumph but also in acclamation. Its very title – Operation Iraqi Freedom – proclaimed American victory as Iraqi liberation. Anything else was to become a series of out-takes, what Rumsfeld glibly called the "untidiness" left on the cutting-room floor.

When Bush surrounded himself with the trappings of Hollywood to declare victory in "the Battle of Iraq," he projected America as superpower and superstar. This aestheticization of politics (and violence) played well with many in his domestic audience. Its space of constructed visibility had two blind spots, however, that worked to undermine the very scenario it sought to promote. First, it clearly suggested that the Superhero who had prevailed in the war would prevail afterwards. And yet in Iraq public order virtually collapsed, public services continued to be degraded and disrupted, and reconstruction faltered. As temperatures soared in the intense summer, one Iraqi, furious at the continuing shortages of electricity and water, turned

Bush's vainglorious rhetoric against him: "They are superpowers, they can do anything they want." He spoke for many others who denounced what they saw as American indifference as much as impotence. "They brought thousands of tanks to kill us," one Baghdad shopkeeper complained. "Why can't they bring in generators or people to fix the power plants? If they wanted to, they could." The dissonance between the powers to which Bush's rhetoric laid claim and the powers exercised by his forces on the ground was considerable. The anger, frustration, and disappointment of ordinary Iraqis spilled over into the streets and exposed the looking-glass fantasy of many of the pronouncements made by the Coalition Provisional Authority from inside the vast Republican Palace once occupied by Saddam.[103] Secondly, Washington's scenario envisaged Iraq as an empty screen on which America could project its own image (with the aid of proxies returned from exile in the United States). "We dominate the scene," announced the US civilian administrator, L. Paul Bremer, "and we will impose our will on this country."[104] And yet Iraqis are not extras in a silent movie – mute victims of Saddam, sanctions, and smart bombs – but educated people with their own ideas, capabilities, and agencies. They also know the long, bitter history of Anglo-American entanglement in Iraq (rather better than their American and British screenwriters), and they are perfectly capable of distinguishing between liberation and occupation. "Don't expect me to buy little American flags to welcome the new colonists," Salam Pax wrote, recalling the British occupation from the First World War. "This is really just a bad remake of an even worse movie." As Mary Riddell tartly observed, "it was always implausible that a nation of fierce anti-colonialists would follow the Pentagon productions script."[105] I want to consider each of these blind spots in turn, and show how the spaces they limned became superimposed in wars of resistance (the plural is deliberate) that the main parties to the coalition were unable and unwilling to acknowledge: ordinary, everyday acts of defiance and, eventually, a complex and increasingly vicious guerrilla war against the occupation.

When the arrival of American troops was not greeted with unbridled joy, Friedman was nonplussed: "We've gone from expecting applause to being relieved that there is no overt hostility." His explanation? The Iraqi people were "in a pre-political, primordial state of nature. For the moment, Saddam has been replaced by Hobbes, not Bush."[106] Few observers equaled Friedman's condescension, but many others thought the surge of looting that followed the collapse of the Iraqi regime was the understandable result of sheer material deprivation:

> With so many Iraqis living on the edge of starvation, it is hardly surprising
> that they took the one chance they had over the past week to loot anything
> they could get their hands on. Over the past 12 years in Baghdad you would
> see men standing all day in open-air markets trying to sell a few cracked
> earthenware plates or some old clothes. They were the true victims of UN
> sanctions while Saddam Hussein could pay for gold fittings to the bathroom
> in his presidential palace. . . . Economic sanctions really did devastate Iraqi
> society . . . [and] it is [this] terrible poverty which has given such an edge to
> the fury of the mobs of looters which have raged through Iraqi cities in recent
> weeks.[107]

I am quite sure this is right. But no matter how wretched the situation of
the people there are clearly defined legal responsibilities for public order
and safety placed on an occupying power that cannot be set aside. Indeed,
the worse the condition of the civilian population, one might expect the
greater the onus on the occupying power to come to their aid. When this
does not happen and the system of responsibilities is suspended then
sovereign power has produced another space of the exception. In his
(general) discussion of these matters, Giorgio Agamben suggested that the
two situations envisaged by Friedman, far from being polar opposites, are
intimately connected. "The state of nature and the state of exception are
nothing but two sides of a single topological process," he argued, "in which
what was presupposed as external (the state of nature) now reappears, as
in a Möbius strip or a Leyden jar, in the inside (as state of exception)."[108]
The two sides cannot be held apart by claiming that troops who have fought
a war are unable to secure the peace – that "they had orders to kill people,
but not to protect them"[109] – because the laws of belligerent occupation
are clearly established and, for that matter, clearly understood.

Perhaps it was for that very reason that the coalition prevaricated. In
the run-up to the war, the Pentagon consistently told relief organizations
that US troops would be "liberators" not occupiers, so that those laws
would not apply. Like his masters in Washington, General Tommy Franks
repeatedly insisted that the war in Iraq was "about liberation not occupation," and in mid-April his deputy operations director at CENTCOM
declared that the United States did not consider itself an occupying power
but a "liberating force." One week later, UN General Secretary Kofi
Annan, noting that the United States and Britain had gone to war without the authorization of the Security Council, called on the coalition to
respect international law as the occupying power. The US envoy to the

UN Human Rights Commission was visibly angry on both counts. He insisted that the war was legal, but he was equally adamant that it had not been established that the coalition was an occupying power.[110] In fact, however, under the terms of the Hague Convention of 1907 and the Fourth Geneva Convention (1949), the laws of belligerent occupation come into effect "as soon as territory is 'occupied' by adversary forces, that is, when the government of the occupied territory is no longer capable of exercising its authority and the attacker is in a position to impose its control over that area." Occupation is a matter of fact – not of intention or declaration – and the United States army's own manual acknowledges "the primacy of *fact* as the test of whether or not occupation exists." In direct contradiction to claims made by the Bush administration, "the entire country need not be conquered before an occupation comes into effect as a matter of law, and a state of occupation need not formally be proclaimed. . . . That some resistance continues does not preclude the existence of occupation provided the occupying force is capable of governing the territory with some degree of stability."[111]

Under the Hague and Geneva Conventions, occupying powers are responsible for restoring public order and preventing looting. "When an occupying power takes over another country's territory, it automatically becomes responsible for the protection of its civilians, their property and institutions," Fisk reported in April. "But the British and Americans have simply discarded this notion." Hence Rumsfeld's stunningly dismissive response to widespread looting: "Freedom's untidy. Stuff happens. Free people are free to make mistakes and commit crimes and do bad things."[112] This freedom extended to his own troops. There were credible reports of American soldiers urging the looters on, and of others themselves involved in pillage and theft.[113] When the International Crisis Group visited Baghdad in June its investigators were disturbed to find "a city [still] in distress, chaos and ferment." They described the protracted failure to establish civil order as "a reckless abdication of the occupying powers' obligation to protect the population." Even if the Bush administration sought to ignore the provisions of international law, the US army's own *Field Manual* is unequivocal. In the aftermath of war, it reads, the army "shall take all the measures in [its] power to restore, and ensure, as far as possible, public order and safety."[114]

And yet in post-war Iraq American troops had other priorities. Some examples.

After the capitulation of the northern city of Mosul – scene of some of the most frantic looting and destruction yesterday – a reported 2,000 American troops were deployed to secure the northern oilfields, bringing all of Iraq's oil reserves, the second largest in the world, under American and British protection. But American commanders in the field said they did not have the manpower, or the orders from above, to control the scenes on the streets of Baghdad and other cities.[115]

In what journalist James Meek called the "scurrying, burning, breaking madness of Baghdad," looters sacked almost every government ministry. But there were two exceptions, which were ringed by hundreds of American troops. These were the Ministry of the Interior and the Ministry of Oil.[116] American soldiers were detailed to chip away at a large mural on the floor of the al-Rashid hotel's lobby showing former President George H. W. Bush and the legend "BUSH IS CRIMINAL." But apparently "none could be spared to protect the treasures in the National Museum while they were being looted up the road at the same time."[117] Examples like these can be multiplied many times over, and they lead to a deeply disturbing conclusion. If parts of Iraq were reduced to a "state of nature" – "a society of either predators or prey," as Ed Vulliamy put it[118] – this cannot be attributed to the "pre-political" (read "primitive," "savage") instincts of the people of Iraq. On the contrary, most of them were clearly distressed at what they witnessed. Here is Salam Pax writing from Baghdad on April 10: "To see your city destroyed before your own eyes is not a pain that can be described or put to words. It turns you sour or was that bitter, it makes something snap in you and you lose whatever hope you had. Undone by your own hands." But then he adds: "What I am sure of is that this could have been stopped at a snap of an American finger."[119] The comment is immensely significant. The degradation of Iraq's towns and cities – the reduction of its civil society – was not an eternal "state of nature" at all: it was *produced* as the space of the exception. In Friedman's shorthand, "Bush" *begat* "Hobbes."

When reporter Euan Ferguson wrote that "Baghdad has turned into Afghanistan faster than Afghanistan," he was referring to its descent into a particular kind of lawlessness: looting, robbery, gunfights, and violent attacks on the civilian population.[120] But there was another kind of lawlessness, and other signs of the space of the exception familiar from the war in Afghanistan soon appeared. By August more than 5,000 Iraqis were held in American custody, but only 500 of them were deemed to be prisoners of war (and therefore protected by the Geneva Conventions). The others were denied legal advice or the right to contact their families. Most of them were held at Camp Cropper, a makeshift canvas prison edged with razor wire, hastily constructed by American troops at Baghdad International Airport. The regime there recalled those at Bagram and Guantánamo Bay. Inmates described the prison as being "fit only for animals." They alleged that the detainees were subjected to beatings, sleep deprivation, and hooding, and that they were punished by being made to kneel or lie on the ground, face down and hands tied, in temperatures of 50 degrees or more. "What they're doing is completely illegal," one Red Cross official confided to a reporter, "and they know it."[121] As in Afghanistan, the overwhelming thrust of continuing offensive operations was directed against America's political opponents and its military or paramilitary enemies – looters and criminals were low in the order of priorities – and coalition actions were bent on establishing order rather than the rule of law. Instead of being indivisible, the one a foundation for the other, the former consistently overrode the latter.

Responsibility for the provision of essential services to the civilian population is no less clearly established by international law. The Geneva Convention requires the occupying power to ensure "to the fullest extent of the means available to it" that the population receives adequate food, water and medical treatment; that power supplies, water and sewage systems are restored and safeguarded; and that proper public health and hygiene measures are in place.[122] The United States military is not unfamiliar with these obligations either. Its *Doctrine for Joint Urban Operations* recognizes the vital importance of "consequence management." "Because urban areas contain the potential for significant noncombatant suffering and physical destruction, urban operations can involve complex and potentially critical legal questions," it warns, and commanders in the field must be made aware of the importance of "information operations, populace and resources control, health service and logistic support, civil-military operations, and foreign humanitarian assistance."[123]

And yet in post-war Iraq there was a considerable gap between rhetoric and reality. Dualities are a desperate fact of life in colonial societies – Fanon spoke of "a world cut in two" – but, in a country where the occupiers constantly deny the press of their occupation, those divisions have a way of becoming unusually sharp-edged.[124] At the end of April, for example, the US army claimed that 60 percent of Baghdad's water and power supplies were already back in operation and that full service would be restored within a week or two. But most Baghdad residents were living in a different city:

> They reported prolonged blackouts, with power returned sporadically and not necessarily at convenient times (for example, in the middle of the night) and insufficient to keep food refrigerated, houses cooled and tempers under control. . . . Breakdowns in one part of the infrastructure can lead to disruptions or even collapse of other parts, with the impact rippling through a society already weakened by more than twelve years of debilitating international sanctions. The lengthy power shortage has affected water and sewage pumping stations, the refrigeration of medicines, the operation of laboratories (involved, for example, in testing for water-borne diseases), and even the production of oil, itself necessary to fuel the power plants. Piped water has been reaching Baghdad homes most of the time (though pressure is low in many areas) but only 37 percent of water pumped from rivers is being treated, increasing the risk of diarrhoea, cholera and typhoid. . . . The rivers themselves are the repositories of tons of raw sewage, untreated as long as treatment stations remain idle due to lack of electricity and essential repairs.[125]

By August, more than three months after Bush declared his victory, the situation was still acute. Baghdad is built on a floodplain and the terrain is flat, so water and sewage have to be pumped throughout the city. While most of the main pumping stations had been repaired by then, none of the sewage-treatment plants were working and so sewage was still being pumped straight into the river. Some sewers had collapsed completely – either through bomb damage or by tanks being driven over them – and when the pressure in the pipe built up, sewage rose to the surface through the drains. "Many of the capital's streets are flooded with untreated sewage water," according to the UN Office for the Coordination of Humanitarian Affairs. "In the city's famous Jamilah Market, boys wearing sandals pull carts through several inches of polluted water, which laps beneath food stalls at the side of the street." Diseases linked to contaminated water had already doubled – diarrhea, dysentery, cholera, and typhoid – and children were particularly vulnerable.[126] Rajiv Chandrasekaran reported that the persistent blackouts – 16 hours or more at a time – had "transformed a city that was once regarded as the most advanced in the Arab world to a place of pre-industrial privation."[127] Just as attempts had been made to shift the burden of responsibility for the war's civilian casualties onto the Iraqis themselves, so these infrastructural problems were now blamed on Saddam and on post-war sabotage carried out by Saddam loyalists. "When you have 35 years of economic and political mismanagement," Bremer airily announced, "you can't fix those problems in three weeks or three months."[128] Perhaps Iraqis did assume that things could be fixed too quickly; but they had little difficulty in tracing the problems back to American action or inaction. Iraq's power stations never recovered much more than half the operating capacity they had before the first Gulf War. They were degraded by the US-led sanctions regime for more than a decade; spare parts were in short supply and maintenance was pared back. Before the second war four-hour blackouts had been part of daily life in Baghdad, and they were much longer in other towns and cities because the government shielded the capital by diverting energy supplies from other parts of the country. The new war greatly exacerbated the gravity of the situation, when the US-led assault damaged many pylons and transmission lines. After the war, other facilities were wrecked by the looting that US troops failed to check: power stations were sacked and more transmission lines torn down and stripped of their copper covering. Iraqis knew very well that electricity was the key to their infrastructure, but they simply did not believe that the Americans understood its elemental importance for the rehabilitation of their everyday lives. Salam Pax reported that the most frequent question on people's lips was: "They did the destroying, why can't they repair them?"[129] His own question was even more astute. "I keep wondering what happened to the months of 'preparation' for a post-Saddam Iraq," he wrote in his weblog. "Why is every single issue treated like they have never thought it would come up?"[130]

Paul Krugman's answer was simple and symmetric. Just as the Bush administration's determination to see what it wanted to see led to "a gross exaggeration of the threat Iraq posed before the war," so the same selective vision led to "a severe underestimation of the problems of post-war occupation." This shortcoming was compounded by a tussle between the State Department and the Department of Defense. The State Department had been drafting strategies for a post-war Iraq since April 2002, and its officials had repeatedly warned that reconstruction would present major challenges. But when Bush granted authority over reconstruction to the Pentagon, the Defense Department and its Office of Special Plans "all but ignored State and its working groups." Attention to post-war planning was at best "haphazard and incomplete" precisely because the script drawn up by Rumsfeld and Wolfowitz called for liberation not occupation.[131]

Whatever the reason, however, the anger of most Iraqis was aroused by far more than the failure of the American and British forces to maintain public order and to restore electricity and water supplies. These were sharp provocations, to be sure, but most Iraqis were profoundly angered – abused and humiliated – by the very presence of an occupying army. Historian Avi Shlaim, who was born in Baghdad, reminded British readers that in Iraq's collective memory Britain and the United States were "anything but benign." "The inglorious history of Western involvement in Iraq goes a long way to explaining why the Iraqi people are not playing their part in our script for the liberation of their country."[132] Comparisons were increasingly made with other colonial occupations. Some commentators looked to the colonial past. Stanley Kurtz proposed British India as a model for the Anglo-American undertaking, which was exactly what Britain's own colonial administration in Iraq had attempted with such spectacularly unsuccessful results.[133] Others had a surer grasp of the dangers. Paul Kennedy saw Britain's moment in the Middle East as providing not an exemplary but a cautionary lesson. When he called the roll, his point was unmissable: "Clive in India, Kitchener in the Sudan . . . Garner in Iraq." True to form, when former Lieutenant General Jay Garner arrived to take up his post as America's first civilian administrator of occupied Iraq, he lost no time in declaring how difficult it was "to take people out of darkness and lead them into light," in perfect mimicry of the colonial mandate of the early twentieth century. "To think we had imagined such abuses gone forever," wrote an exasperated Ignacio Ramonet, "civilising people seen as incapable of running their lives in the difficult conditions of the modern world."[134]

Others looked to the colonial present in Afghanistan and Palestine for equally salutary lessons. Here is Seumas Milne writing on April 10:

> On the streets of Baghdad yesterday, it was Kabul, November 2001, all over again. Then, enthusiasts for the war on terror were in triumphalist mood. . . . Seventeen months later, such confidence looks grimly ironic. For most Afghans, "liberation" has meant the return of rival warlords, harsh repression, rampant lawlessness, widespread torture and Taliban-style policing of women. Meanwhile, guerrilla attacks are mounting on US troops. . . .
>
> Afghanistan is not of course Iraq, though it is a salutary lesson to those who believe the overthrow of recalcitrant regimes is the way to defeat anti-western terrorism. It would nevertheless be a mistake to confuse the current mood in Iraqi cities with enthusiasm for the foreign occupation now being imposed. Even Israel's invading troops were feted by south Lebanese Shi'ites in 1982 – only to be driven out by the Shi'ite Hizbullah resistance 18 years later.[135]

These were prophetic observations. Two weeks later Phil Reeves reported that many Iraqis already saw the occupation as "the Palestinisation of Iraq," and responded by throwing stones at troops, a highly symbolic gesture in the Middle East where it is widely seen "as a heroic form of resistance to an illegal occupying force." And, as he subsequently emphasized, "having watched daily TV installments of the fate of Palestinians in the West Bank and Gaza, [Iraqis] recoil with particularly strong distaste at the concept of occupation." Later he witnessed the funeral of a man shot by American troops in Baghdad, where the mourners were overcome with grief and anger. It was, he wrote, a scene "commonplace in Gaza or the West Bank after a 36-year occupation in which thousands have been shot dead by the Israeli army." But, he added, "we were in Baghdad only a month after the Americans had routed one of the most repressive and corrupt regimes of the modern age."[136]

As the occupation wore on, the excessive use of force by coalition troops against the civilian population increased rather than diminished. The US army's own Manual FH3–06.11 instructs troops that "armed force is the last resort" and that civilians must be treated "with respect and dignity," but in many cases these injunctions were honored in the breach (or breech). "When in doubt," one trio of journalists observed, "GIs, often young, exhausted and overstressed in the searing heat, have a tendency to shoot first and ask questions afterwards." The heavy burden placed on these front-line soldiers – many of them young reservists – should not to be minimized. Many of them were clearly traumatized by what they had experienced; their nervousness is understandable, and the sacrifice of their lives is tragic. They were not there by choice, and their actions were scripted and under-written by their political masters, who had assured them they would be greeted as liberators. No wonder they were shocked. It is an axiom of the movies projected by Bush and his associates that life is cheap, and on numerous occasions Iraqi civilians were dispatched without a flicker. The specter of *homo sacer* haunted Iraq as it did Afghanistan and Palestine. American troops repeatedly fired with deadly effect on unarmed demonstrators who were calling for an end to the occupation; civilians were seriously injured or killed when troops opened fire indiscriminately and without warning during raids on houses and markets; countless others were abused, beaten, and even killed at military checkpoints.[137] Excuses were offered as explanations; apologies were rare, investigations perfunctory where they were conducted at all. These are all landmarks of occupation with which Arabs are agonizingly familiar. "Just like the Israeli occupation of the West Bank and Gaza," Fisk remarked, "the killing of civilians is never the fault of the occupiers."[138] A common excuse was that actions by American troops were misunderstood. So, for example, Iraqis often complained that troops on the roofs of buildings were using their binoculars and night-glasses to peer down into domestic courtyards where women were sitting or working; this caused grave offense because Islam has strict codes governing which men may and may not see Muslim women unveiled. When this provoked demonstrations and demands that the troops withdraw from residential districts, the military replied that the Iraqis had "misread" the situation. The actions of the troops were entirely innocent: the men were merely engaged in routine surveillance of the neighborhood. But this assumes that the requirement to "read" properly – to understand different cultural traditions – applies only to Iraqis. And, as in the occupied territories of Palestine, the vast disparity in power between occupier and occupied compromises any mutual understanding that might be inscribed through a hermeneutic circle.

The public space that opened up was filled in the first instance not by the coalition or by its civil administration but by the mosques. The United States and Britain "have ripped a big hole in Iraq," Freedland explained, and Shi'a Islam "is stepping through it." This was premature; the Shi'ites are in the majority but they do not speak with a single voice, and it was not long before factional and generational schisms surfaced.[139] Sunni Muslims were by no means passive either. Even so, in the immediate aftermath of the war the mosques addressed both the restoration of public order and public services and also the demand for self-determination. In many cases, their actions were decisive. In Baghdad's Saddam City – renamed Sadr City in honor of Grand Ayatollah Mohammed Sadiq al-Sadr of Najaf who had been assassinated on Saddam's orders in 1999 – clerics called for the looting to stop and for people who had stolen property to return it; if it was not claimed, it was to be handed to the Hawza, the Shi'a seminary in Najaf where leading clerics teach. Young volunteers from the mosques set up armed checkpoints and patrolled the perimeters of the district's four hospitals to protect them against looting, and they also guarded Ministry of Health warehouses in al-Hurriya that supplied all the hospitals in Baghdad. The mosques also provided food, shelter, and money for the poor. "One cleric organized a team to drive two tankers to clear out water mains overflowing with sewage," Anthony Shadid reported. "Another drove an ambulance through the city's deserted streets at night, blaring appeals on its loudspeaker for municipal workers to return to work." Clerics organized teams to restore electricity to the hospitals, paid the doctors, and shipped in more medical supplies from Najaf. They produced newspapers, and made plans for radio and television stations. By May green and black flags were fluttering over almost every other building in Sadr City. The scene was repeated in other districts in Baghdad and in cities further south like Basra, Karbala, and Najaf. "Sadr City may be the very model of the new Iraq that America is making," wrote Peter Beaumont.[140]

These actions had tremendous political and ideological significance too. At overflowing Friday prayer services in April Iraqis heard calls for opposition to the occupation and support for the establishment of an Islamic state and the promulgation of Islamic law. In Baghdad, Nasiriyeh, and other towns, people spilled out on to the streets, calling for national unity and shouting slogans denouncing both Saddam and the continued occupation.[141] "[The] clerics stand at the center of the most decisive moment for Shi'ite Muslims in Iraq's modern history," Shadid argued. "It is a revival from both the streets and the seminaries that will most likely shape the destiny of a postwar Iraq. In the streets, the end of Hussein's rule has unleashed a sweeping and boisterous celebration of faith, from Baghdad to Basra, as Shi'ites embrace traditions repressed for decades."[142] Among the most significant of those traditions was the pilgrimage to Karbala. Thousands of Muslims from all over southern Iraq converged on the holy city to mourn the death of Imman Hussein, grandson of the Prophet Mohammed, in a display that resonated with political as well as religious significance. Saddam had banned the pilgrimage since 1977 – it was an unambiguous affirmation of the purity of Shi'a over Sunni Islam – but its resumption celebrated more than the end of his rule and the revival of Shi'a fortunes. "Now the Iraqi masses are taking to civic engagement and have begun to articulate political demands that reject occupation," one reporter observed. "Both Shi'a and Sunni religious leaders have emerged as voices for unity and as legitimising authorities for political action." At the close of the Karbala festival, the deputy leader of the Supreme Council for the Islamic Revolution in Iraq denounced the occupation and demanded that administration be turned over to "a national and independent government." Chants and banners reiterated the same theme: "No to Saddam, No to America, Yes to Islam." And some demonstrators already threatened a *jihad* against the occupiers.[143]

It has been argued that the production of a sustained emergency – the breakdown of public order and public services – was used by the coalition to justify its extraordinary actions and emergency powers and, indeed, its very presence in Iraq. What it could not do, however, was license the United States and Britain to embark on a program of wholesale reconstruction. In April the coalition held several meetings to establish an interim Iraqi administration (which was postponed in May). Many Iraqis viewed these gatherings with suspicion, regarding the former exiles invited to take part as carpetbaggers, mountebanks, and pawns of the Bush administration. "Looking at the names of some of the more dubious characters," Cockburn observed, "it may be that the real looting of Iraq is still to come." Exiles from the US-backed Iraqi Reconstitution and Development Council were also appointed as advisers to key Baghdad ministries. "It is an enormously valuable asset to have people who share our values," US Deputy Secretary of Defense Paul Wolfowitz explained, people "who also understand what we're about as a country."[144] It could not have been put more plainly: what mattered was what the United States was "about." In part, the objective was to lay the foundations for a secular state. But there were other, less public, meetings to establish what one trio of journalists called "Iraq Inc." Decisions were taken to privatize Iraq's state industries and to award major contracts to American (mainly American) and British companies. There was a brief spat between the principals (correct spelling) about the share of the spoils, which Mark Steel memorably likened to "a pair of undertakers burning down a house, then squabbling over who gets the job of making the coffins." As Naomi Klein objected,

> In the absence of any kind of democratic process, what is being planned is not reparations, reconstruction or rehabilitation. It is robbery: mass theft disguised as charity; privatisation without representation. A people, starved and sickened by sanctions, then pulverised by war, is going to emerge from this trauma to find that their country has been sold out from under them.[145]

In fact, all these actions were illegal, like many others that were undertaken unilaterally by the Office of Reconstruction and Humanitarian Aid. For the laws of belligerent occupation not only set out the duties of occupying powers; they also establish clear *limits* to their intervention. These cut through both planks of the coalition's platform. They prohibit any attempts at "wide-ranging reforms of governmental and administrative structures" and also the "imposition of major structural economic reforms." For these very reasons, Britain's Attorney-General had warned the government in March that a United Nations Security Council resolution would be required to authorize post-war reconstruction.[146]

The United States and Britain finally moved to regularize their actions through UN Security Council Resolution 1483, which was adopted on May 22, 2003. It gave the United States and Britain what the *New York Times* called "an international mandate" to administer post-war Iraq. The resolution opened by reaffirming "the sovereignty and territorial integrity of Iraq" and stressing "the right of the Iraqi people freely to determine their own political future and control their own resources." This was largely gestural. The central provisions of the resolution not only recognized the United States and Britain as occupying powers but also constituted them as a "unified command" ("the Authority"). The Secretary-General was requested to appoint a special representative for Iraq, whose main tasks were to coordinate humanitarian and reconstruction assistance by United Nations agencies and between those agencies and non-governmental agencies, and to work with the Authority and the people of Iraq to establish institutions for representative governance. The special representative was also required to "report regularly to the Council on his activities under this resolution." No such requirement was placed on the Authority. Iraq was required to fulfill its pre-existing disarmament obligations, but here too responsibility was vested with the United States and Britain alone. There was no provision for independent monitoring and verification of Iraq's WMD, or their absence, and the Council was merely to "revisit" the mandates of UNMOVIC and the IAEA. The receipts from the sale of Iraq's oil were to be deposited in a Development Fund for Iraq, held by the Central Bank of Iraq and audited by independent public accountants appointed by an International Advisory and Monitoring Board (whose members were to include representatives of the Secretary-General, the World Bank, the International Monetary Fund, and the Arab Fund for Social and Economic Development). But its funds were to be disbursed entirely "at the direction of the Authority" in order "to meet the humanitarian needs of the Iraqi people, for the economic reconstruction and repair of Iraq's infrastructure, for the continued disarmament of Iraq, and for the costs of Iraqi civilian administration, and for other purposes benefiting the people of Iraq." Finally, sanctions were to be lifted, and the oil-for-food program – on which 60 percent of the Iraqi population depended – was to be phased out within six months.[147]

Tariq Ali argued that most of the Arab world had seen Operation Iraqi Freedom as "a grisly charade, a cover for an old-fashioned European-style colonial occupation, constructed like its predecessors on the most rickety of foundations – innumerable falsehoods, cupidity and imperial fantasies." In his view, the adoption of Resolution 1483 – which gave a central role neither to the United Nations nor to the Iraqi people – confirmed that inter-pretation: it "approved [Iraq's] re-colonization by the United States and its bloodshot British adjutant."[148] Like all colonial projects, those most directly affected were not asked for their approval: power was vested unequivocally in the United States and Britain. But they needed their prox-ies. After a protracted process of negotiation, the coalition announced the formation (not election) of the Iraqi Governing Council. This did little to silence critics who thought the coalition was presiding over a colonial occu-pation. The composition of the 25-member Council duplicated the colonial strategy of institutionalizing sectarian divides within Iraq. The Council was given the power to draw up a draft constitution, to direct policy, and to nominate and dismiss ministers: but all its proposals were subject to veto by the coalition. The independence and integrity of the Council was an open question too. It was dominated by the same Iraqi exiles favored by the United States, some of whom had less than shining reputations, and its deliberations were closed and far from transparent. Salam Pax reported that Iraqis had difficulty even gaining admission to its press conferences, where, he daydreamed, a third channel of simultaneous translation would carry the truth: "We have no power, we have to get it approved by the Americans, we are puppets and the strings are too tight." The image of occupation mediated by marionettes became a commonplace among ordinary Iraqis: it was, wrote Riverbend, "the most elaborate puppet show Iraq has ever seen."[149] Everyone knew that day-to-day authority remained with the coalition, and, much as the majority of Iraqis rejoiced at the fall of Saddam's brutal regime, they were increasingly antagonized by the ignor-ance and arrogance of their occupiers. Many of them became resigned to the petty humiliations of occupation – the questions and permissions, the searches and encroachments – but for growing numbers of Iraqis resignation turned to resentment ("They have no respect for us") and, eventually, to resistance.

Resistance to the occupation multiplied and intensified throughout the summer. It was many-stranded: spontaneous and organized, non-violent and militarized. In Baghdad there were daily, often deadly, attacks against troops patrolling the streets, their assailants appearing from nowhere and disappearing into the crowd. "Every day the Americans hand out street maps of the Iraqi capital on which dangerous neighborhoods are marked in black," two journalists reported. "So far, the danger zones have not become smaller." Rocket-propelled grenades and mortars were used to ambush American convoys and to attack checkpoints in the so-called "Sunni triangle" north and west of Baghdad. The governorates of Anbar and Diyala, which had benefited from Saddam's patronage in the past, were major flash-points. In June and July thousands of American troops, backed by tanks, helicopter gunships, and aircraft, undertook an aggressive series of raids against "Ba'ath party loyalists, paramilitary groups and other subversive elements" in the region. They uncovered what they claimed was a terrorist training camp, and seized large caches of arms. But the massive deployment of firepower, the indiscriminate use of force, and the heavy-handed searches (often in the middle of the night) antagonized local people and heightened opposition to the occupation among ordinary Iraqis. "Before I was afraid of Saddam," one elderly farmer said. "Now I am afraid of the Americans." And, in a gesture redolent of other colonial counter-insurgency operations, all those killed by American troops – over 300 – were described by the military as "Iraqi fighters"; no civilian casualties were acknowledged. Other Iraqis saw the situation differently. "Saddam's tyrannical regime is being rapidly replaced by the tyranny of the occupation forces," one Iraqi exile wrote, "who are killing Iraqi civilians and unleashing Vietnam-style 'search and destroy' raids on Iraqi people's homes." In his eyes, "the invasion of Iraq has developed into a colonial war." The new commander of CENTCOM, General John Abizaid preferred to call it a "low-intensity conflict," but he admitted "it's war however you describe it." Meanwhile, demonstrations against the occupation had spread across the Shi'a south, with thousands in Basra (Iraq's second largest city), Najaf, and other places demanding the right to self-government and self-determination. At the end of June, in what was described as "the first serious confrontation in the south," six British soldiers were killed in two bloody ambushes near Amara. Popular resentment was widespread. In the largest anti-American demonstration, tens of thousands of Shi'a gathered in Najaf to demand the withdrawal of the occupying forces: "Down with the invaders" they chanted. The British fared little better. "The British occupiers are treating us the same way they treated us during colonial times in 1917," one Basra politician complained, electing to deal with tribal leaders rather than political parties because they refused to recognize the legitimacy of the Shi'a opposition. By July even the tribal leaders were losing patience. "We met them with roses," said one, "but when we can no longer bear our frustration, the rose in their hands will become the dagger in their breasts."[150]

In August the coalition was still trying to talk down the crisis, and to insist on the "dual realities" of what one journalist called "chaos and calm."

Yet even this was an admission that Iraq was now divided "between those willing to *put up with* the American occupation" – his words, my emphasis – "and those determined to fight it." And the balance between the two seemed to be shifting. While most Iraqis remained reluctant to seek political confrontation with the coalition, still less to risk armed conflict, resistance to the occupation escalated throughout the month. There were major riots in Basra, where British troops in riot gear struggled to regain control of the city, and although the coalition downplayed their significance – "a storm in a teacup," according to British authorities – reporters found that local people were seething with anger at the occupation and its chronic failings.[151] The protests in Basra seem to have been spontaneous, but elsewhere opposition of a radically different order was making its appearance. A car bomb exploded at the Jordanian embassy in Baghdad, killing 17 people and wounding scores more; another bomb tore a hole in a large water main in the capital, flooding streets and cutting off supplies to thousands of people; and in the north the pipeline from Kirkuk to Ceyhan was sabotaged, setting off fierce fires that blazed out of control and suspending the crucial export of oil to Turkey.[152] Then the United Nations mission to Baghdad came under terrorist attack. The old Canal hotel had been used as a base by UN weapons inspectors and sanctions monitors before the war – it became known as "the Sanctions Building" – and it remained a soft target after the UN mission moved in. Its local secretariat had refused high-level security in order to distance the mission from the fortified compounds of the occupying power. On August 19 a massive truck bomb exploded outside, devastating the building and a nearby hospital. At least 23 people were killed, including the UN special representative in Iraq, Sergio Vieira de Mello, and more than 100 injured, many of them seriously. Most Iraqis were appalled by the mass murder of civilians from many different countries, and there was considerable speculation about the identities and motives of those responsible for the atrocity. Although there were several reasons why the United Nations could have been the object of such an attack (UN-mandated sanctions and UN Security Council Resolution 1483 to name but two), the real target seemed to be the occupation itself. For the attack was a hideous reversal of the coalition's own strategy of "shock and awe." What one journalist described as "the horrifying spectacle of a major building in the capital blown apart" was designed not only to demonstrate the strength of the opposition but also to isolate the coalition through intimidation. Baghdad was already a city under siege, but the blast heightened the sense of impotence and vulnerability. The primary objective was to deter others from coming to the assistance of the coalition and hence to increase the burden of the occupation upon the United States.[153]

Three weeks earlier Bremer had downplayed the significance of the deteriorating security situation and, consistent with his brief to privatize Iraq, declared that his first priority was to restore the confidence of foreign investors. "The most important questions will not be [those] relating to security," he insisted, "but to the conditions under which foreign investment will be invited in."[154] But the summer whirlwind of violence – above all, the attack on the UN mission – had a dramatic chilling effect. Investments were put on hold, and foreign companies and international humanitarian agencies withdrew personnel. The Bush administration made no secret of its desire to involve troops and resources from other countries, but other governments were now markedly reluctant to commit themselves to a US-led occupation. Yet Washington refused to cede its political or military authority over Iraq, and dismissed out of hand arguments for a multinational peacekeeping force and a reconstruction process authorized by and accountable to the UN. With this impasse, it seemed not only that "a sophisticated campaign to destabilize the occupation was spreading," as Justin Huggler concluded, but that it was also succeeding.[155]

The numbers were already alarming. The White House had assured Americans that the war would pay for itself (and then some). In March Wolfowitz had told a Senate committee that Iraq "can really finance its own reconstruction, and relatively soon." But by July even the most conservative estimate of the direct military cost of occupation (Rumsfeld's) put it at $1 billion a week, which represented a significant contribution to the ballooning federal deficit. And this took no account of the costs of reconstruction.[156] The human cost to coalition forces was no less disturbing. By the time Bush declared the end of major combat operations in Iraq on May 1, 131 American and 8 British troops had been killed in action; but between May 1 and August 24, another 64 American and 10 British troops had been killed by hostile action. Public scrutiny of the rising toll of dead and wounded was discouraged; the media were not allowed to photograph the return of the coffins of US servicemen and women, and seriously injured troops were flown into Andrews air force base in the dead of night.[157]

Faced with this concatenation of increasingly violent events, the Bush administration claimed that two main groups were responsible. First, there were members of the Republican Guard, the Fedayeen Saddam militia and other diehard Saddam loyalists: the "dead-enders," Rumsfeld called them.

A taped message from the fugitive Saddam claimed that "*jihad* cells and brigades have been formed" and praised "our great *mujaheddin*" for inflicting hardship on "the infidel invaders." There were also reports that Saddam's intelligence agency had drawn up plans to subvert the occupation through sabotage, attacking oil pipelines and other crucial installations. There can be little doubt that remnants of the regime – including some drawn from the ranks of the Iraqi army that Bremer had so summarily dissolved – were responsible for some of the attacks. But, as Graham Usher argued, "to claim that the former Iraqi dictator is the ghost behind all of the resistance is to deny a reality the occupation – every bit as much as his collapsed regime has created. . . . The resistance strikes resonate among a people outraged by an administration that appears unable to find solutions to the most basic problems." Bracketing, for a moment, the terrible bomb attacks in Baghdad, many of the strikes appeared to command a considerable measure of popular support, and Iraqis killed in the guerrilla war north and west of Baghdad were often celebrated in their home towns and villages as martyrs. Saddam's attempt to appropriate Islam for his own purposes neither diminishes nor devalues the intimacy of the connections between politics and religion. One imam insisted that it was simply wrong to attribute the attacks on occupying forces to renegades. "They are coming from ordinary people and the Islamic resistance," he explained, "because the Americans haven't fulfilled their promises." Every morning in Baghdad cleaning crews were sent out to paint over graffiti that had appeared on walls during the night, and the slogans seemed to confirm this view of the diversity of the resistance: Not only "No Iraq without Saddam" but also "No dignity under the Americans" and "We demand from our imams a call to *jihad*."[158] It bears repeating that those broken promises were not fundamentally about power lines and water pipes. "The Americans said they were coming to liberate the country, not occupy it," a prominent human rights activist, Walid al-Hilli, reminded reporters. "Now they are occupying Iraq and refusing to allow Iraqis to form their own government." This was the heart of the matter, and it was for this reason that it was so flatly denied. As Jonathan Steele remarked, "it is easier to claim that the resistance comes from 'remnants of the past' than recognize that it is fuelled by grievances about the present and doubts about the future."[159]

Secondly – and crucially for the White House – there were the "foreign fighters" who, Rumsfeld had warned the Iraqi people in an early message, were "seeking to hijack your country for their own purposes." This was

Figure 8.4 "Foreign fighters" (Steve Bell, *Guardian*, July 2, 2003)

a stupefyingly rich remark even then, but it became a common refrain. As the guerrilla war intensified, a senior Defense Department official claimed that "there are clearly more foreign fighters in the country than we ever knew, and they're popping up all over" (figure 8.4). When Wolfowitz returned from a brief tour of Iraq he demanded that "all foreigners should stop interfering in the internal affairs of Iraq." As Simon Schama once remarked, "A slippery thing is this colonial geography!" Americans in Iraq presumably do not count as "foreign" because they are universal soldiers fighting for a transcendent Good. One hardly knows what to say when faced with rhetorical claims like these, which have America swallow Iraq whole until it becomes "America's Iraq."[160] But the response of most Iraqis to that predatory possessive should have been predictable, and so too should the reaction from the Islamic world at large. "In the same way as the Russian invasion of Afghanistan stirred an earlier generation of young Muslims determined to fight the infidel," it was argued, "the American presence in Iraq is prompting a rising tide of Muslim militants to slip into the country to fight the foreign occupier." But there was a critical, incendiary difference between the two. Unlike Afghanistan, Iraq is part of the heartland of Islam. Najaf and Karbala are among the holiest cities of Islam after Mecca and Medina; Basra and Kufah were founded by the early Umayyad caliphate; and Baghdad was the capital of the Abbasid caliphate for 500 years. It should not have been surprising that Iraq's occupation by the United States would turn it into a new field of *jihad* for political Islam. Maureen Dowd recalled that before the war Bush "made it sound as if Islamic fighters on a *jihad* against America were slouching towards Baghdad." At the time, she had dismissed this as an overwrought Gothic fantasy. But now, she argued, "the Bush team has created the very monster that it conjured up to alarm Americans into backing a war on Iraq." This is Afghanistan aggrandized and the performative with a vengeance. As Raban put it, "our dangerous new world is one in which seeming rhetorical embellishments are fast morphing into statements of literal fact."[161]

It was not long before the specter of al-Qaeda stalked the battlefield. Ayman al-Zawahiri, a close adviser of Osama bin Laden, had already called for al-Qaeda "to move the battlefront to the heart of the Islamic world," and the American occupation of Iraq made that possibility come vividly alive. The leader of Ansar al-Islam, a small Kurdish Islamicist group hostile to Saddam Hussein and linked to al-Qaeda, obligingly declared that "there is no difference between this occupation and the Soviet occupation of Afghanistan," and Washington described the group as "the backbone of the underground network."[162] There was little hard evidence to support such a claim, but the Bush administration understood its rhetorical power. "Iraq is now the central battle in the war on terrorism," Wolfowitz announced, and after the attack on the UN mission in Baghdad, for which some officials held Ansar al-Islam responsible, Bush lost little time in repeating his familiar mantra. The terrorists were "enemies of the civilized world," and the Iraqi people faced a choice: "The terrorists want to return to the days of torture chambers and mass graves. The Iraqis who want peace and freedom must reject them and fight terror."[163]

I fully accept that the attack on the UN in Baghdad was terrorism – as despicable as it was deadly – but the Bush administration, taking a leaf from the book of Ariel Sharon and many of his predecessors, unscrupulously used this outrage to tar any resistance to its "liberation" of Iraq as terrorism. The red flag, according to Bush, was "every sign of progress in Iraq." Leaving on one side the president's Panglossian view of post-war Iraq, such a claim worked, yet again, to place the United States on the side of the angels. Any opposition to its mission was not only mistaken but also malevolent. To Fisk, "any mysterious 'terrorists' will do, if this covers up a painful reality: that our occupation has spawned a real home-grown Iraqi guerrilla army capable of humbling the greatest power on Earth."[164] This was probably an overstatement too. Various armed groups emerged from among the Shi'a and Sunni communities, including the Army of al-Mahdi, the Army of Right, the Army of Mohammed, and the White Flags, but these hardly constituted a unified resistance.[165] Still, Fisk was surely right about the camouflage. The generic invocation of "terrorism" was an attempt to rehabilitate one of Bush's central arguments for the war, to obscure the reality of occupation and to try to rescue the American mission in Iraq by reflagging it as another front in the continuing "war on terror." What Washington refused to countenance was that the two groups which they blamed for the political violence in Iraq – Saddam loyalists and foreign fighters – were paralleled by two other groups to which most ordinary Iraqis remained equally and increasingly opposed: Bush's loyalists and his foreign fighters.

The violence did not wane with the heat of the summer. In August there had been an average of 12 attacks a day on American forces, and this rose to 15 in early September. By the beginning of October there were more than 25 a day, and at the end of that month 33 a day. Large areas of Baghdad were declared "hostile," and the guerrilla war expanded beyond the Sunni heartland into the north and south of the country. Between the beginning of May and the beginning of December nearly 40 percent of attacks on coalition targets were outside the "Sunni Triangle."[166] More resistance groups were formed; most informed estimates reckoned there were at least a dozen in operation by the end of the summer, but some suggested that there were as many as 40. Some groups consisted of cells loosely linked in a chain of command; others coordinated their attacks and collaborated with one another; still others operated more or less in-dependently. There was a constant background of hit-and-run attacks on coalition forces using small arms, but the sophistication of major attacks increased as some groups started to use improvised explosive devices and rocket-propelled grenades while others carried out more suicide car and truck bombings. As the attacks accelerated, several analysts repeated that that an insurgency had been planned by the Iraqi regime before the war. This was probably true, but by no means all of the guerrilla groups were the spawn of the Iraqi security services, and neither were they all Ba'athist. While the guerrillas certainly included militants from the deposed regime, there were many other groups involved: criminal gangs were contracted to carry out some of the attacks, as the coalition alleged, but the majority seem to have been carried out by Islamist and nationalist partisans, who were joined or supported by increasing numbers of ordinary Iraqis who were antagonized by the occupation.[167] It is difficult to generalize about the organization of so many different groups, but there were considerable tensions between the former military officers and Fedayeen militia on one side and the *mujaheddin* and nationalists on the other. The fluidity of the situation was complicated still further by the range of targets involved. Attacks on US (and British) military forces continued, and the number of coalition troops killed or wounded soared (figure 8.5). But there were also attacks on others, especially civilians, which is where armed resistance slides into terrorism. In general, these other attacks fulfilled two strategic objectives.

First, the intensifying attacks combined with the escalating reactions they provoked from coalition forces to cut the fragile and fraying threads connecting the occupiers to the occupied. Repeated acts of sabotage and attacks on coalition contractors continued to disrupt the reconstruction process. Far from a Baghdad skyline bristling with cranes, two journalists reported that "there are no visible signs of reconstruction [in the capital] at all," and Iraq's infrastructure remained in a worse state than it had been under Saddam. Interruptions in electricity and water supplies continued. "You really can't appreciate light until you look down upon a blackened city and your eyes are drawn to the pinpoints of brightness provided by generators," Riverbend wrote in her weblog. "It looks like the heavens have fallen and the stars are wandering the streets of Baghdad lost and alone." Less poetically, she described the ordinariness and oppressiveness of everyday life under occupation: struggling with gas cylinders whenever the electricity was cut, and desperately filling pots, buckets, and bottles whenever the water came back on. Equally prosaically, the price of gasoline soared and drivers waited in line all day to fill their tanks. "Of all things," one weary manager of a gas station remarked, "we never thought we'd be without gasoline in Iraq."[168]

Public order remained precarious, and Iraqis continued to be assailed by the chronic incidence of murders, kidnappings, robberies, rapes, and assaults, and by a series of spectacular ruptures as terrorist violence was directed against the civilian population. At the end of August a massive car bomb exploded outside the Imam Ali mosque in Najaf, killing more than 100 Shi'a Muslims including the most influential cleric allied with

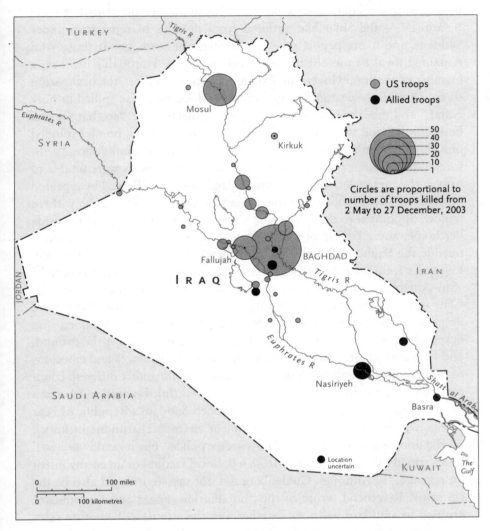

Figure 8.5 Coalition casualties, May 2–December 27, 2003 (after Richard Furno, *Washington Post*)

the coalition, the Ayatollah Mohammed Baqir al-Hakim. The devastation was dreadful: "The brick facades of shops were sheared away. Cars were flipped and hurled onto the sidewalk. Burned, mangled and dismembered bodies littered the streets, trampled as others ran in confusion and panic for safety." The three-day funeral obsequies moved between Karbala,

Baghdad, and Najaf, and while there were chants of "Death to the Ba'athists" – the Shi'a had suffered from decades of repression under Saddam, and many people pointed the finger of suspicion at those who remained loyal to the old regime – the murdered Ayatollah's brother, a member of the Iraqi Governing Council, proclaimed that "the occupation force is primarily responsible for the pure blood that was spilled in holy Najaf" and demanded that the occupying powers leave "so that we can build Iraq as God wants us to."[169] The next month a truck bomb exploded outside the Baghdad headquarters of the reconstituted Iraqi Police, "reinforcing the popular perception that the occupying powers were unable to protect themselves let alone the public," and this was followed by repeated attacks on other police stations. In early October one of only three women appointed to the Governing Council died after being shot outside her home, and a couple of weeks later another huge car bomb exploded outside the Baghdad hotel, used by members of the Governing Council, killing six Iraqi security guards and injuring more than 35 other people.[170]

In America's Iraq, all these attacks were so many signs of success. "The more progress we make on the ground," Bush repeated, "the more desperate these killers become." One could be forgiven for thinking that desperation was a two-way street. Journalists who were on the ground, and who had a more intimate knowledge of the experiences and emotions of ordinary Iraqis than the desk-warriors, saw an altogether different country. "Iraq under the US-led occupation is a fearful, lawless and broken place," Suzanne Goldenberg wrote in October. Saddam's Republic of Fear had gone, "but its replacement is a violent chaos." The midnight knock on the door was no longer Saddam's secret police "but it could very well be an armed robber, an enforcer from a political faction, or an enemy intent on revenge."[171] Although Goldenberg did not say so, it could also be the US army. Riverbend wrote of the "humiliation, anger and resentment" aroused by standard weapons searches, but she also described other raids that were much more degrading: "Families marched outside, hands behind their backs and bags on their heads; fathers and sons pushed on the ground, a booted foot on their head or back." In other cases, it was even worse: tanks crashing through walls in the dead of night, sledgehammers breaking down doors, prisoners pushed and shoved outside, duct tape slapped over their eyes and plastic cuffs snapped on their wrists; houses ransacked, torn upside-down by soldiers bellowing abuse and leaving with their frightened prisoners to the blare of rock music echoing through the streets.[172] If the objective was to make an impression on the Iraqi population, it succeeded. Was this the "liberation" they had been promised?

A second series of terrorist attacks faced outwards rather than inwards. It was guided by what Mark Danner identified as the "methodical intention to sever, one by one, with patience, care, and precision, the fragile lines that still tie the occupation authority to the rest of the world." Two months after the attack on the Jordanian embassy and the UN headquarters in Baghdad, the Turkish embassy was rocked by a suicide car bomb. At the end of the same month a rocket attack on the al-Rashid hotel, where Wolfowitz and other "internationals" were staying, was followed by a massive suicide bombing at the headquarters of the International Red Cross. On November 18 Italian paramilitary police and 13 Iraqis were killed in a suicide attack in Nasiriya. This string of attacks was directed, as Danner notes, against "countries that supported the Americans in the war (Jordan), that support the occupation with troops (Italy) or professed a willingness to do so (Turkey). They struck at the heart of an 'international community' that could, with increased involvement, help give the occupation both legitimacy (the United Nations) and material help in rebuilding the country (the Red Cross)."[173]

The Iraqi response to these widening circles of violence was complicated. The unequivocal horror that most of them had expressed at the attack on the United Nations was reaffirmed when other international organizations were targeted and whenever ordinary Iraqis were the victims. When Patrick Cockburn interviewed people on the streets of Baghdad after the attack on the Red Cross, everyone he spoke to was aghast. But "all, without exception, approved of the attacks on the al-Rashid hotel and US soldiers." When Saddam's regime fell, he said that Iraqis were more or less evenly divided between those who welcomed American liberation and those who opposed colonial occupation. Now, he concluded, "hatred of the occupation is expressed openly." As this implied, the identification between the resistance and the population at large had grown closer than the coalition acknowledged. "Coalition press officers talk of attacking 'guerrilla hideouts' and buildings being used as 'meeting places' for the rebels," Peter Beaumont noted, "suggesting a guerrilla army living in the field, separate from the population. In reality, the hideouts are people's homes, their headquarters apartments and living rooms."[174] Support for the resistance was not universal, to be sure, but it was widespread and becoming wider; and opposition to the occupation – armed or otherwise – was intensifying.

The American-led response was two-pronged. The first was political. In September, Secretary of State Colin Powell had warned that Washington would not be rushed into transferring power to an Iraqi administration; a week later Bush told the United Nations that the transition to self-government "must unfold according to the needs of the Iraqis – neither hurried nor delayed by the voices of other parties." That was still the view – "prevailing wisdom" is hardly the right phrase – when the USA and the UK returned to the United Nations Security Council in the middle of October to obtain a new mandate: they flatly refused to commit themselves to any timetable for the transfer of power.[175] In November, however, an intelligence assessment from the CIA station chief in Baghdad made no bones about it: the situation was rapidly slipping out of control. The report estimated that tens of thousands were now involved in the resistance and conceded that these were by no means all hardcore Ba'athists or foreign fighters. Bremer abruptly flew to Washington, and within days the White House announced that the transfer of power would be accelerated. What had been dismissed as imprudent and impossible less than a month earlier was suddenly imperative. Organizing committees (on which the Governing Council would have an effective veto) were to be established in each of Iraq's 18 governorates; these would select caucus members, who would in turn select representatives for a transitional national assembly in the spring. The assembly would then elect a "democratic, pluralistic" interim government by July 2004, and its assumption of power would mark the formal end of occupation; the Coalition Provisional Authority would be dissolved, and the foundations laid for the election of a new Iraqi government in a general election by the end of 2005.[176] But the proposals were immediately contested. Grand Ayatollah Ali Sistani, the most influential Shi'ite cleric in Iraq, demanded that the transitional assembly be elected by the Iraqi people – a procedure which would weaken the power of the Governing Council over the process – and many Shi'ites saw the proposals for regional caucuses overseen by "the puppets" as a ruse to prolong the occupation: "The Americans will never leave Iraq," one man told reporters. "*Jihad* is the only way to get them out." As the year turned, so tens of thousands of Shiites marched in the streets of major cities to demand full, direct, and, as Sistani repeatedly put it, "proper" elections. With the hunt for WMD proving fruitless, Bush increasingly talked as though one of the central aims of the war had been to bring democracy and freedom to the Iraqi people: they were now taking him at his word and calling for exactly that. Posters proclaimed that "Forming the provisional national assembly through an unjust method will subject the Iraqi people to a new round of oppression." The White House, the Provisional Authority, and the Governing Council temporized, arguing that there was insufficient time to organize elections. Many experts, inside and outside Iraq, disputed the claim. A more plausible reason for their reluctance was provided by the Authority's adviser on constitutional law. "If you move too fast," he told the *New York Times*, "the wrong people might get elected." It was, as Robert Scheer concluded, "colonial politics as usual."[177]

The second prong of the new American strategy was military. Determined to crack down hard on the insurgency and the civilian population that supported the guerrillas, the US army activated the lessons it had learned from the Israeli Defence Force in the occupied territories of Palestine. The level of military response was ratcheted up: firepower increased with the use of heavy tanks, artillery, and massive bombs dropped from aircraft to level suspected "guerrilla bases" in the largest air bombardment since May 1. It was the same story on the ground. The coalition had constantly disparaged remnants of the old regime, but it now had no compunction in using them to infiltrate the resistance, copying the use of Arab informers by the Israeli intelligence services. American troops turned Iraqi towns and villages into simulacra of the West Bank. Perimeters were ringed with razor wire, hung with signs reading "This fence is for your protection. Do not approach or try to cross or you will be shot," English-language identity cards were issued, and residents were forced to wait at military checkpoints to be scrutinized and searched. One man waiting in line told a reporter, "I see no difference between us and the Palestinians." Troops imposed curfews and 15-hour lockdowns. "This is absolutely humiliating," a primary school teacher said: "We are like birds in a cage." Elsewhere, in another ghastly echo of the Israeli occupation, bulldozers were brought in to uproot palm trees and groves of citrus, and the homes of suspected guerrillas were summarily demolished. "This just what Sharon would do," one furious farmer told a reporter. "What's happening in Iraq is just like Palestine." There were differences between the two, of course, but the aggression and intimidation, and the studied disregard for human rights and human dignity, scored parallels that few Iraqis missed. "With a heavy dose of fear and violence," one battalion commander declared, "and a lot of money for projects, I think we can convince these people that we are here to help them."[178] There were few signs of projects, but there was no mistaking the fear and violence. In fact, it was revealed that Israeli officers had trained assassination squads at Fort Bragg to replicate the IDF strategy of "targeted killings." Here, as elsewhere, Bush's vaunted "war on terror" had become a war *of* terror. "Terrorism versus terrorism," one officer confirmed. "We've got to scare the Iraqis into submission."[179]

On the surface, the two strategies – "Iraqification" and "Israelization" – seem to be contradictory, since one works toward a transfer of power to the Iraqi people and the other works to repress them. But the contradiction is resolved through a split screen. On one side, the principal audience for these displays of political and military power was not in Iraq at all but in the United States. By November 2003 the American presidential election was only 12 months away. The banner draped behind Bush when he gave his "victory" speech on May 1 had proclaimed "Mission accomplished"; but it was already in tatters, and the CIA intelligence assessment showed that it could soon fall around the president's head. Bush's political staff was thoroughly alarmed. But they quickly realized that if the formal occupation could be seen to have been brought to an end by the early summer, then, as Robin Wright and Thomas Ricks commented, Bush would be able to hand over responsibility "for both a deteriorating security situation and a stalled political process" and enter the final phase of the campaign unburdened by the baggage he had left in Iraq (unless, I suppose, he was asked if he had packed it himself). On the other side, however, the occupation would continue in all but name, and the impress of American political, economic, and military might would still be felt in Iraq. Whatever its formal status, the occupation would not end in any substantial sense. Indeed, the IDF strategy of violent repression in Palestine is predicated on a long-term occupation – containing the Intifada, not removing the grounds for its continuation – and the Pentagon made no secret of its expectation that tens of thousands of troops would remain in Iraq at the "invitation" of the new government. No doubt it also anticipated the permanent military bases that would need to be established on Iraqi soil. American political and economic influence would scarcely diminish either. Not only would the United States continue to control the billions of dollars authorized by Congress for reconstruction, but the coalition had already authorized the privatization of 200 Iraqi companies and, through Order 39 of September 19 (which "promotes and safeguards the general welfare and interests of the Iraqi people by promoting foreign investment through the protection of the rights of foreign investors in Iraq"), guaranteed foreign corporations unlimited access to the country's most profitable banks and industries (except the oil and gas industry, which was fast becoming a liability rather than an asset) and permitted them to repatriate their profits without restriction. As *The Economist* said, it was a "capitalist dream." For most Iraqis, it was a nightmare. "Iraq is being sold," wrote Riverbend, and "people are outraged"; but not, it seems, surprised. "After all, the puppets have been bought," she said, "why not buy the stage?" Ahmad Chalabi airily dismissed such concerns: "The culture of the Iraqis has been a culture of fear that foreigners would take advantage of the country." Just so. It was clear that the occupying powers had imposed fundamental policies determining the future of ordinary Iraqis, and Klein was surely right to conclude that if a sovereign government came to power tomorrow – or in the summer of 2004 – Iraq would still be occupied "by laws written in the interest of another country and by foreign corporations controlling its essential services." "Even after a military occupation," Riverbend observed, "we'll be under an economic occupation for years to come."[180]

As that last clause shows, most Iraqis have little difficulty in seeing the split screen, which means that the capture of Saddam Hussein – however it plays in the United States – is unlikely to make much difference to the resistance. As I have repeatedly emphasized, the insurgency is not uniquely defined by Saddam loyalists and those working for the return of Ba'athism, and it seems self-evident that the disheveled, dirty old man who was finally hauled from his spider-hole in the middle of December was no longer directing anything. In Iraq there were mixed emotions at his capture. Disbelief yielded to anger in Sunni neighborhoods in Baghdad and around Saddam's hometown; there were large pro-Saddam demonstrations in Mosul and Tikrit, and pro-Saddam riots in Falluja and Ramadi. But there was also widespread rejoicing throughout the Shi'a and Kurdish areas, and pro-American rallies in Baghdad.[181] Yet this division conceals as much as it reveals. For many Iraqis not only suffered under Saddam's rule: they also blamed him for bringing about the occupation of their country. Just days after Saddam's arrest, Edward Wong reported that "the joyous bursts of gunfire that echoed through parts of Iraq" at the news of his capture were "already a distant memory." He was writing from the Shi'ite village of Mahawil, 80 kilometers south of Baghdad, which is the site of one of the largest mass graves in Iraq. After the Shi'a uprising in March and April 1991 as many as 15,000 bodies were buried there, and many (perhaps most) local families had lost members to Saddam's execution squads. And yet Wong reported that "many people are left wondering how they will push on with their daily lives in a country controlled by a foreign power and filled with political and economic uncertainty."

"One would expect the people of Mahawil to be clamoring for account-ability from the imprisoned Mr Hussein," he concluded. "So they are, but they are also clamoring even louder for accountability from the American occupiers."[182]

It seems certain that the ongoing occupation – formal or informal – will continue to perplex, affront, and alienate vast sections of Iraqi society, and it seems very likely that more people will join the resistance. There are also good reasons to suppose that this will now take on an even more pro-nounced religious and nationalist temper. The influential young leader of the Sadr movement, Muqtada al-Sadr, has already demanded that Order 39 be repealed "or we will act." His support among Shi'ites in east Baghdad, Basra, Karbala, Kufa, Najaf, and Samarra is considerable, and he claims that his "Army of al-Mahdi" has enlisted 10,000 young men. He insists that his is a "non-violent" movement, but the provocations of occupation seem unlikely to diminish, and it seems only too probable that paramilitary violence will increase.[183] It may also be aggravated by sectarian conflict. There have been reports that the Sunni "Clear Victory Movement" plans to establish a militia in response (and as a challenge) to the "Army of al-Mahdi," and there have been repeated clashes between Kurds and Sunni Arabs in Kirkuk and Mosul. But I doubt that these anta-gonisms will supplant opposition to the occupation. Indeed, Robert Fisk reports that "more and more Iraqis were saying before Saddam's capture that the one reason they would not join the resistance was the fear that – if the Americans withdrew – Saddam would return to power. Now that fear has been taken away. So the nightmare is over – and the nightmare is about to begin."[184]

None of this should be surprising. For the imaginative geographies of colonial power have reasserted themselves: the divisions between "us" and "them," "occupier" and "occupied." During the summer and autumn of 2003 they had become ever more visible in the new geography of occu-pied Baghdad. The occupiers established themselves within a vast complex of buildings on the west bank of the Tigris that was once the preserve of Saddam and his apparatus of power and repression. His vast Republican Palace has become the headquarters of the Coalition Provisional Author-ity – in its way, another Republican Palace. The whole area, studded with parks, lakes, and fountains, intersected by wide, tree-lined avenues, is pro-tected by a triple perimeter: an inner series of barriers and concertina wire, and an outer blast wall of reinforced concrete topped with razor wire, rein-forced by sandbagged bunkers and concrete dragon's teeth, ringed by troops and tanks. Beyond the point of entry to this so-called "Green Zone," across the 14th of July Bridge, is the rest of Baghdad – "the Red Zone" – and Iraq, and the advice to Americans and the internationals working with them is unequivocal: "Do not travel there unless you have urgent business." Inside "the Bubble" is another world. "It's like I never left America," said one American interpreter. In this Baghdad – America's Baghdad – "they serve peanut butter, lobster and ice-cream. The cell phones have a 914 [White Plains, New York] area code. The television sets show Monday Night Football. The people speak English."[185] This is the classical geometry of colonial occupation, of course. But the precariousness of its partitions was revealed when Bush made his extraordinary visit to American troops on Thanksgiving Day. This was not the triumphant entry to the capital that he must have anticipated six months earlier. The flight was made under conditions of the utmost secrecy. Air Force One had to make a corkscrew approach to Baghdad International Airport, with its windows blacked out and landing lights off for fear of a rocket attack. Bush was on the ground for a little over two hours; he never left the heavily fortified airport compound and met no ordinary Iraqis. "Why didn't he walk the streets of the country he helped 'liberate?'" asked Riverbend. The answer, as she knew only too well, was that Bush's target audience was in the United States not Iraq, and that he never visited Iraq: he visited "America's Iraq." He had time to do little more than pose with a turkey before cutting and running.[186]

9 Gravity's Rainbows

A screaming comes across the sky. It has happened before but there is nothing to compare it to now.

Thomas Pynchon, *Gravity's Rainbow*

Connective Dissonance

THE world does not exist in order to provide illustrations of our theories, and I am determined not to erase the particularities of the wars in Afghanistan, Palestine, and Iraq. But it seems clear that in these interlinked situations the imaginative geographies that were given such terrifying force by the events of September 11 were connected to performances of space that have been (and continue to be) deployed in other circumstances. In the shadow of the attacks on the World Trade Center and the Pentagon, three strategic moves were made by the increasingly interdigitated administrations in Washington and Tel Aviv. These can be identified as: locating, opposing, and casting out.

"Locating" mobilized a largely technical register, in which opponents were reduced to objects in a purely visual field – coordinates on a grid, letters on a map – that produced an abstraction of other people as "the other." American bombs and missiles rained down on K-A-B-U-L, not on the eviscerated city of Kabul; Israeli troops turned their guns on Palestinian "targets" not on Palestinian men, women, and children; American firepower destroyed Baghdad buildings and degraded the Iraqi military machine but never killed Iraqis.

"Opposing" mobilized a largely cultural register, in which antagonism was reduced to a conflict between a unitary Civilization and multiple barbarisms. This was no clash of civilizations because that was war in a minor key; the war on terror was war in a major key. America, with its proxies and allies, was called to take up arms against the gathering forces of darkness: of Evil incarnate. Osama bin Laden, and Saddam Hussein became Doppelgängers, inversions of the face of Goodness reflected in the White House mirror, with fateful consequences for the people of Afghanistan and Iraq, while fundamentalists on both the Christian and the Zionist right saw the dispossession of the Palestinians as fulfilling God's ultimate purpose. All were barbarians to be summarily dispatched.

"Casting out" mobilized a largely political-juridical register, in which not only armed opponents – al-Qaeda terrorists, Taliban troops, Palestinian fighters, Iraqi soldiers – but also civilians and refugees were reduced to the status of *homines sacri*. Their lives did not matter. The sovereign powers of the American, British, and Israeli states disavowed or suspended the law so that men, women, and children were made outcasts, placed beyond the pale and beyond the privileges and protections of the Modern. The deaths of American, British, and Israeli citizens mattered, unless of course they were killed opposing or witnessing the wars in Afghanistan, Palestine, or Iraq. But in this grisly colonial calculus the deaths of Afghans, Palestinians, and Iraqis were rendered not only uncountable but also unaccountable.

A series of economic priorities and practices moved through each of these registers, but in the preceding chapters I have been most concerned with their physical and corporeal consequences. Each of them shows how performances of space articulated through imaginative geographies can fold difference into distance, simultaneously conjuring up and holding at bay the strange, the unnatural, the monstrous. "Given their monstrosity," Zygmunt Bauman wrote, "one cannot but thank God for making them what they are – the *far away* locals, and pray that they stay that way." The language of the monstrous – the throwback, the half-human, the degenerate – was repeatedly used to characterize America's opponents in Afghanistan and Iraq, and Israel's opponents in Palestine. But distance is never an absolute, fixed and frozen, and within the colonial present, like the colonial past, the power to transform distance – like the power to represent others *as* other – is typically arrogated by metropolitan cultures. Bauman distinguished between "residents of the first world" – "tourists," he called them – who he said live pre-eminently in time, who can span every distance with effortless ease, and who move because they want to, and "residents of the second world" – "vagabonds" – who live pre-eminently in space, "heavy, resilient, untouchable," and who travel surreptitiously and often illegally because they have no other bearable choice.[1]

This is, of course, a cartoonish distinction, and in any case the tourists depend on the vagabonds in all sorts of ways, not least on their cheap labor as sweatshop workers or undocumented migrants. But if this is a caricature, it's a recognizable one. For part of the shock of September 11 was surely its abrupt *reversal* of metropolitan privilege. On that bright morning, distance was spectacularly compressed and liquid modernity turned into fire. The horror, said Bauman, "brought the untouchable within touch, the invisible within sight, the distant within the neighbourhood."[2] Listen to these words from American novelist Don DeLillo written soon after the attacks on the World Trade Center and the Pentagon:

> Our world, parts of our world, have crumbled into theirs, which means we are living in a place of danger and rage. . . . The terrorists of September 11 want to bring back the past. . . . The future has yielded, for now, to medieval experience, to the old slow furies of cutthroat religion. . . . Now a small group of men have literally altered our skyline. We have fallen back in time and space. . . . There is a sense of compression, plans made hurriedly, time forced and distorted.[3]

Time and space crumbled, collapsed, compressed: not by us but by "them"; not on our terms but on "theirs."

"They" were not Bauman's vagabonds – those responsible for the attacks on the World Trade Center and the Pentagon were hardly the wretched of the earth – but they did come from a world away. It was a world made strange long before transnational terrorism erupted in the heart of metropolitan America. For John Urry, September 11 was a dramatic rupture in which the world's "safe zones" and "wild zones" – "civilization" and "barbarism"? – "collided in the sky above New York." But he also saw it as an event that brought into view a vast subterranean movement whose time-space compressions preceded the attacks and extended beyond them.

> The flows from the wild zones of people, risks, substances, images, Kalashnikovs . . . increasingly slip under, over and through the safe gates, suddenly and chaotically eliminating the invisibilities that had kept the zones

apart. Through money laundering, the drug trade, urban crime, asylum-seeking, arms trading, people smuggling, slave trading and urban terrorism, the spaces of the wild and the safe are chaotically juxtaposed, time and space is being "curved" into new complex configurations.[4]

It is through these "curvatures" – torsions of time and space – that colonialism is made over, reinscribed, and rehabilitated in our own present. "Terror has collapsed distance," wrote Michael Ignatieff after September 11, "and with this collapse has come a sharpened American focus on bringing order to the frontier zones." Later he staked the same claim in these terms:

> America has now felt the tremor of dread that the ancient world must have known when Rome was first sacked. Then and now an imperial people has awakened to the menace of the barbarians. Just beyond the zone of stable democratic states, which took the World Trade Center and the Pentagon as its headquarters, there are the border zones where, thanks to modern technology, they are able to inflict devastating damage on centres of power far away. Retribution has been visited on the barbarians, and more will follow. . . . Terror has collapsed distance, and with this collapse has come a sharpened focus in imperial capitals on the necessity of bringing order to the barbarian zones.[5]

As these comments imply, those orderings were often encased in calls for a new imperialism and a new colonialism. Ignatieff described the American project as "empire lite" – "hegemony without colonies, a global sphere of influence without the burden of direct administration and the risks of daily policing" (he was writing before the war on Iraq) – but he was by no means critical of its basic mission.[6] Other commentators were still more forthright in their demands for a much heavier impress of American power. Kipling's burden had passed from Great Britain to the United States, which had made itself responsible "not just for waging a war against terrorism and rogue states," so historian Niall Ferguson argued, "but also for spreading the benefits of capitalism and democracy overseas." But the Achilles heel of American Empire was that "it dare not speak its name" – not, I think, a recognition of the homoerotics of empire – for "it is an empire in denial." Ferguson thought this state of affairs not only preposterous – "How can you not be an empire and maintain 750 military bases in three-quarters of the countries on earth?" – but also dangerous. The United States had advertised its politico-military adventures as short-term and sold itself a "cut-price colonization": a sort of McOccupation. In Ferguson's contrary view, the United States had to accept the long haul ("Why would you collaborate with an occupying power that says it is about to leave?") and also the heavy burden (by cutting what he called its "bloated domestic programs"). In short, while the global reach of the United States was immensely important it had to reconstitute itself not as a fleeting imperial power but as a durable one.[7] For still other commentators, "fleeting" and "durable" were complementary not contradictory strategies. America needed a new Ariel, capable of putting an instant girdle around the earth in the name of what Eliot Cohen, a key member of the Project for a New American Century, called "World War Four." The Bush administration disavowed the term, but since September 11 hundreds of thousands of American troops have been deployed from overseas bases in Germany, Japan, and South Korea to new posts around the globe: east Africa (and soon west Africa), central Asia, and south-east Asia. There are also plans for hundreds of floating "lily pads" or "virtual bases" for covert or "stealth" operations, like those under way in the tri-border zone between Brazil, Paraguay, and Argentina. "Everything is going to move everywhere," said one Pentagon official. "There is not going to be a place in the world where it's going to be the same as it used to be."[8]

What is missing from all these characterizations, apart from a moral compass, is any recognition that the power to collapse distance is also the power to expand distance. The unidirectional logic of what David Harvey calls time-space compression requires distance to contract under the spasmodic compulsions of global capitalism to reduce circulation time. This has its own uneven, inconstant geography, and it jumps and short-circuits across economic, political, military, and cultural registers. But images of "the global village" and "the shrinking world" have become so powerful and pervasive that, as Cindi Katz observes, they have obscured the ways in which distance can also *expand*.[9] This happens not only within a relative space punctuated by the differential geographies of time-space compression – Katz's (sharp) point – *but also through the proliferating partitions of colonial modernity*. Palestinians know this every time they try to make an ordinary journey that once took them an hour and now takes a day (or more), if it can be made at all; there are no longer any ordinary journeys in the occupied territories. As the modern by-pass roads compress time and space for Israel's illegal settlers, so the dislocated minor roads and dirt tracks, the chokepoints and checkpoints, expand time and space for the Palestinians.

Torsions like these work through two contradictory logics. Michael Hardt and Antonio Negri offer a first approximation in their account of the formation of the constellation of power that they call "Empire":

> Imperialism is a machine of global striation, channelling, coding and territorializing the flows of capital, blocking certain flows and facilitating others. The [capitalist] world market, in contrast, requires a smooth space of uncoded and deterritorialized flows.[10]

If global capitalism is aggressively *de-territorializing*, moving ever outwards in a process of ceaseless expansion and furiously tearing down barriers to capital accumulation, then colonial modernity is intrinsically *territorializing*, forever installing partitions between "us" and "them."

I describe this as a first approximation because Hardt and Negri go on to suggest that "Empire" is busily resolving this contradiction by dissolving the distinction between "outside" and "inside." "There is no more Outside," they write. "The modern dialectic of inside and outside has been replaced by a play of degrees and intensities, of hybridities and artificiality." Similarly, Bauman believes that "September 11 made it clear that *Il n'y a pas du "dehors"* [There is no outside] any more."[11]

The same argument reappears in Robert Cooper's reflections on international politics. He argues that the distinction between "inside" and "outside," "internal" and "external," has been dissolved within the European Union, and a Kantian bargain struck so that government is now based on "transparency, openness, interdependence and mutual vulnerability." Its postmodern states still have to come to diplomatic terms with modern states like India, Pakistan, and China, but they also have to confront a new and "pre-modern" geopolitical zone. Cooper explains that this ragged penumbra is composed of former European colonies in which the (post)colonial state has failed and from where non-state actors – including organized crime and international terrorism – now pose a significant threat to the geopolitical order. "How should we deal with the pre-modern chaos?" he asks.

> The most logical way to deal with chaos and the one most employed in the past is colonisation. But colonisation is unacceptable to postmodern states (and, as it happens, to some modern states too). It is precisely because of the death of imperialism that we are seeing the emergence of the pre-modern world. Empire and imperialism are words that have become terms of abuse

in the postmodern world. Today, there are no colonial powers willing to take on the job, though the opportunities, perhaps even the need, for colonisation is as great as it ever was in the nineteenth century. . . . All the conditions for imperialism are there. . . . The weak still need the strong and the strong still need an orderly world. A world in which the efficient and well-governed export stability and liberty. . . . What is needed then is a new kind of imperialism, one acceptable to a world of human rights and cosmo-politan values. We can already discern its outline: an imperialism which, like all imperialisms, aims to bring order and organisation but which rests today on the voluntary principle.

Cooper identifies this principle with the "voluntary imperialism" (a phrase that is right up there with "military intelligence") of the multilateral mech-anisms of the global economy – including the International Monetary Fund and the World Bank – and with what he called "the imperialism of neigh-bours." "It is not just soldiers that come from the international commun-ity," he explains, "it is police, judges, prison officers, central bankers and others." I have no idea what Cooper's own neighbors are like, but if they are forever interfering in his life and imposing their own "voluntary" dis-ciplines, then I'm surprised he has not moved. But then perhaps, like so many others in the mundane rather than metaphorical world he inhab-its, he is unable to do so. In a later essay he claims that ours is a post-imperial world in which "all the empires are now gone" and with them "the wish to conquer and to rule in other lands." But he adds, this is also a "borderless world" in which the distinctions between the external and internal dissolve at critical junctures, where "large-scale crime may come to resemble small-scale war," and where the two come explosively together in terrorism.[12]

Palestinian writer Elias Sanbar is understandably more skeptical about this post-imperial world, and his argument has a radically different ring. Yet he reaches a similar conclusion. Cooper hesitates over the place of the United States in his geographical imaginary – the rupture between America and "old Europe" over the war in Iraq makes his reluctance all the more revealing – but Sanbar makes no bones about saying that "global-ization is in the process of transforming everywhere into a domestic American space." In consequence, he claims that:

[T]he notions of interior and exterior, of domestic and foreign policy, will be called upon to disappear in favour of Washington's supremacy, which is gradually becoming the enthroned capital of the world. . . . It is not a question of a new occupation of foreign territories but of an integration – an annexation, I should say – of all humanity within the borders of the United States.[13]

This is the *ideology* of American Empire, to be sure, of the New American Century in which America is cast not only as the global superpower but also as the universal (Hollywood) actor. But unless one understands "humanity" in Sanbar's last sentence in the always conditional sense produced by the excision – the ex-ception – of *homo sacer*, it is not the *practice* of American Empire. For over 200 years, as Veena Das cogently reminded us, "the distinction between an 'inside' in which values of democracy and freedom were propagated and an 'outside' which was not ready for such values and hence had to be subjugated by violence in order to be reformed has marked the rhetoric and practice of colonialism and its deep connections with Western democracies."[14] Das had good reason to say this in the aftermath of September 11, and the subsequent unfolding of "the war on terror" in Afghanistan and its violent extensions into Palestine and Iraq (and beyond) have demonstrated not the slackening but the tightening of this colonial spacing.

For colonialism's promise of modernity has always been deferred – always skewed by the boundary between "us" and "them" – and although that partition is routinely crossed, even transgressed, the dismal fact is that no colonial anxiety, no colonial guilt has ever erased it altogether. If this is still the primary meridian of imaginative geography, however, it is no simple geometry. It is, as I have repeatedly insisted, a *topology* that also marks the threshold, the space of the exception, whose seams are folded, stretched, and torn into new, ever more wrenching constellations. Borders are not only lines on maps but spacings dispersed across multiple sites – embassies, airports, detention centers – that radically contort conventional mappings of territory. Even hybrid "borderlands" bear the scar tissue of those boundaries. Through these twists and turns the divide may be annulled in some registers (in these ways, you may be modern: like "us") while it is simultaneously reaffirmed in others (in these ways you will never be modern: always irredeemably "other").

Our "six degrees of separation" mean that the modern world is marked by spacings of connection, which are worked by transnational capital circuits and commodity chains, by global flows of information and images, and by geopolitical alignments and military dispositions. These have their own uneven geographies – they do not produce a single, smooth surface

– and they are made intelligible through their own imaginative geographies. But the modern world is also marked by spacings of disjuncture between the same and the other that are installed through the same or parallel economic, cultural, and political networks but articulated by countervailing imaginative geographies that give them different force and sanction. Imaginative geographies are thus doubled spaces of articulation. Their inconstant topologies are mappings of *connective dissonance* in which connections are elaborated in some registers even as they are disavowed in others.

These are all "gravity's rainbows." In his novel of (almost) that name, Thomas Pynchon described the arc of the V-2 rockets launched against Britain from occupied Europe in the dying days of the Second World War as a "screaming coming across the sky." Several writers have used the same image to describe the events of September 11. Hijacked aircraft crashing into the Twin Towers, cruise missiles and "daisy-cutters" raining down on Afghanistan: so many "screamings across the sky" whose terrifying arcs at once marked and made viscerally physical connections.[15] But they also made disconnections, marked by an unwillingness to see an altogether more solid geometry and to hear an altogether different sound: the misshapen bodies of the dead and the screamings of the injured as they lay among the rubble. Imaginative geographies are like gravity's rainbows. They map the twists and turns of engagement and estrangement.

The Colonial Present and Cultures of Travel

Mappings of engagement and estrangement articulate contemporary cultures of travel. Bauman's tourists probably know this without being told; at least those accustomed to move from one exotic site/sight to another, gazing upon the other but always able to withdraw to the security of the familiar, know this. As the young British protagonist in Will Rhode's *Paperback Raita* puts it, "Half the attraction of coming to India is the ability to leave it." Tourists move in the folds between compression and expansion, and cultures of travel are some of the most commonplace means through which colonialism is abroad in our own present. If, as Urry once remarked, it is now the case that in the first world "people are much of the time tourists, whether they like it or not," it is also the case that they – we – are implicated in the performance of the colonial present.[16] Ironically one of the immediate consequences of September 11 was to contract the space of American tourism as flights were cancelled and aircraft flew half-empty. Two weeks later Bush told enthusiastic airline employees at Chicago's O'Hare airport that "one of the great goals of this war is to tell the traveling public: Get on board."[17] This must count as one of the most bizarre reasons for waging war in human history, and yet it also speaks a powerful truth. Modern metropolitan cultures privilege their own mobility.

"Privilege" has to be understood literally; there are other cultures of travel within which movement is a burden, an imposition, even a tragedy.[18] What, then, of Bauman's vagabonds? Three weeks after September 11 the metropolis reasserted its customary powers and privileges as military action was launched against Afghanistan, and thousands of refugees were displaced by these time-space compressions. Many of them were trapped at borders – not only at Afghanistan's borders but at other borders around the world. Here is Gary Younge on their experience almost in Britain:

[S]hould those whom we seek to protect [by our international military actions] arrive on our shores, all apparent concern evaporates in a haze of xenophobic bellicosity. Whatever compassion may have been expressed previously is confiscated at the border. As soon as they touch foot on British soil they go from being a cause to be championed to a problem to be dealt with. We may flout international law abroad, but God forbid any one should breach immigration law here. . . . We love them so we bomb them; we loathe them so we deport them.[19]

Thousands of displaced people, refugees, and asylum-seekers found that, in the very eye of these wrenching time-space compressions, time and space had dramatically expanded for them. Then in April 2003 the British government began the forcible repatriation of Afghan refugees. According to the Home Office, "the deportation was aimed partly at testing the situation in Afghanistan." The refugees were the creatures of a cruel experiment: "We need to ensure that the process is sustainable and that there is adequate infrastructure and security on the ground to receive them." There are, of course, other – less violent – ways of investigating conditions on the ground than sending desperate human beings back to the danger zone. In fact, there is credible, compelling evidence that Afghanistan is not safe, and the British government continues to advise its own citizens against travelling there.[20] But refugees are allowed few rights. "The globe shrinks for those who own it," Homi Bhabha once remarked, but "for the displaced or the dispossessed, the migrant or refugee, no distance is more awesome than the few feet across borders or frontiers."[21] The figure of the refugee – as both wanderer and prisoner – throws into crisis what Agamben calls "the originary fiction of sovereignty" because it calls into question the connective imperative that makes *nativity* the foundation of *nationality* and hence of the sovereign space of the *nation-state*. The refugee is, figuratively and physically, a border figure who, if not excluded or confined, threatens to perforate the territorial integrity of the state.[22]

It should, then, come as no surprise to find close parallels between the extra-territoriality of Camp X-Ray at Guantánamo Bay, where the United States detains hundreds of "unlawful combatants" captured during its military operations in Afghanistan, and Woomera Detention Centre in the Australian outback, where hundreds of asylum-seekers were detained in "a place that is, and yet is not, Australia." "Razor wire and metal fencing mark out the camp as a space of exception," Suvendri Perera writes. "Five layers of wire protect the threshold between Australia and its other, not-Australia." Australia's Pacific Solution works to the same end: asylum-seekers who are intercepted by Australian forces are transferred to camps on the tiny island nation of Nauru, on Manus Island in Papua New Guinea, or on Australia's Christmas Island.[23] Or again, in early 2003 the British government drew up plans to deport asylum-seekers to "Regional Processing Areas" in the zone of origin or to "Transit Processing Centres" on the borders of the European Union, institutionalizing yet another space of the exception.[24] We need to remind ourselves that camps like these have their origins in the European colonial wars of the late nineteenth century. In such conditions, now as then, the "external" and the "internal" are articulated not to erase the "outside" but to produce it *as the serial spacing of the exception*, for ever inscribing exclusion through inclusion.

Pandora's Spaces

As these zones of indistinction multiply around the world, so it becomes clear that "third spaces" or "paradoxical spaces" are not always and everywhere the emancipatory formations that some writers have taken them to be.[25] Before September 11 Agamben had warned that "the camp is the space that opens up when the state of the exception starts to become the rule." After September 11 he worried that the "war on terror" would be invoked so routinely that the exception would indeed become the rule, that the law would be forever suspending itself.[26] His fears were well founded.

Less than a year later the American director of Human Rights Watch reported that "the US government has failed to uphold the very values that President Bush declared were under attack on September 11." The Bush administration attempted to curtail democratic freedoms in at least three arenas: by circumventing federal and international law; by suppressing public information; and by discriminating against visible minorities. Even the conservative Cato Institute objected to the proliferation of "secretive subpoenas, secretive arrests, secretive trials, and secretive deportations."[27] Much of this was authorized by the USA PATRIOT Act – "Uniting and Strengthening America by Providing Appropriate Tools Required to Intercept and Obstruct Terrorism" – which was passed less than two months after September 11 to allow law enforcement and intelligence agencies unprecedented powers of surveillance and investigation.[28]

This series of exceptions was perfectly consistent with the imaginative geographies of civilization and barbarism that were mobilized by the White House to wage its war on terror. Paul Passavant and Jodi Dean describe "a constant and mutual production of the civilized and the savage *throughout* the social circuitry." The homeland had to be defended not only against the enemy without but also against the enemy within.[29] On September 11, 2002, for example, the US Immigration and Naturalization Service introduced a new registration system for designated "non-immigrant aliens." Visitors from specified countries were not only to be interviewed but also photographed and fingerprinted at the port of entry, and later required to report to an INS office to provide additional documentation and information. Compliance with this National Security Entry and Exit Registration System was made retroactive for all visitors 16 years of age and older already resident in the United States who came from Afghanistan, Algeria, Bahrain, Bangladesh, Egypt, Eritrea, Indonesia, Iraq, Jordan, Kuwait, Lebanon, Libya, Morocco, North Korea, Oman, Pakistan, Qatar, Saudi Arabia, Somalia, Syria, Sudan, Tunisia, the United Arab Emirates, and Yemen. The only country on the call-in list with no substantial Muslim population is North Korea.[30]

This is a strategy familiar from the Cold War, whose geography of containment was double-headed:

> The first conception speaks to a threat outside of the social body, a threat that therefore has to be excluded, or isolated in quarantine, and kept at bay from the domestic body. The second meaning of containment, which speaks to the domestic contents of the social body, concerns a threat internal to

the host which must then be neutralized by being fully absorbed and thereby neutralized.[31]

Although the Bush administration abandoned containment for pre-emption, its national security strategy was also given an interior as well as an exterior focus: "Profiling and pre-emption work together to define the human targets of the 'war on terror.'"[32] This is more than the reha-bilitation of the Cold War and its paranoid silencing of difference and dis-sent, however, because the permanent state of emergency institutionalized through these imaginative geographies of the alien "other" also reactivates the dispositions of a colonial imaginary. Its spacings are mirror images of the "wild zones" of the colonial imagination. "The national security state," Susan Buck-Morss points out, "is called into existence with the sovereign pronouncement of a 'state of emergency' and generates a wild zone of power, barbaric and violent, operating without democratic over-sight, in order to combat an 'enemy' that threatens the existence not merely and not mainly of its citizens, but of its sovereignty."[33]

The process of surveillance and screening, profiling and purification, has not been confined to the United States. When Kanishka Jasuriya warned against the creeping internationalization of the state of exception – already in train before September 11 – he drew special attention to the application of strategies of risk management and profiling to "target populations" around the world.[34] Throughout the non-Islamic world Arabs and Muslims have been made desperately vulnerable by these identifications. In Israel their status has been made ever more precarious as one-fifth of Israel's own population has increasingly been excluded from politically qualified life; Israeli Arabs have been demonized not only as a fifth column but as a "cancerous growth," and in the occupied territories – for which Israel takes no civil responsibility – Sharon's chief of staff has chillingly promised the Palestinians "chemotherapy" as his armed forces set about excluding them from bare life too.[35]

Immigrants, refugees, and asylum-seekers have been the victims of paranoia and hysteria in Europe too. At the beginning of *The Clash of Civilizations* Samuel Huntington cites a passage from novelist Michael Dibdin's *Dead Lagoon* that speaks directly to these issues: "There can be no true friends without true enemies. Unless we hate what we are not, we cannot love what we are." Huntington described this as "an unfortunate truth," as though it were somehow inscribed in the nature of things. But in the novel these sentences come from a speech given by Ferdinando Del

Maschio – hardly the hero of the story – to drive home the cause of self-determination for Venice and the need to preserve and purify its Venetian culture. At the end of the novel Del Maschio rounds on Dibdin's detective, Aurelio Zen, and tells him:

> Sooner or later you're going to have to choose. . . . The new Europe will be no place for rootless drifters and cosmopolitans with no sense of belonging. It will be full of frontiers, both physical and ideological, and they will be rigorously patrolled. You will have to be able to produce your papers or suffer the consequences.[36]

Dibdin is clearly saying that this *is* a choice and not, as Huntington seems to think, an irrefutable given, so that the construction of an archipelago of inclusion and exclusion cannot be attributed solely to the threat posed by external or internal "others." In constructing multiple others *as* "other," and in assenting to these constructions and impositions, we not only do this to others: *we do it to ourselves*. We all become the subjects *and the objects* of the "securitization" of civil society. This is as ugly as it sounds – it means taking the "civil" *out* of "society" – and as its partitions proliferate internally and externally, inscribed through and legitimized by the so-called "war on terror," so colonialism is surreptitiously repatriated and rehabilitated and the camp is confirmed as the *nomos* of a continuing colonial modernity.[37] The choice that is offered, as Henry Giroux and Paul Street have argued, is the false choice between being safe and being free: "War is individualized as every citizen becomes a potential terrorist who has to prove that he or she is not a menace to society. Under the rubric of the new permanent war against the never-ending specter of terrorist apocalypse, which feeds off government-induced media panics, war provides the moral imperative to collapse the boundaries between innocent and guilty, between suspect and non-suspect, between peaceful political dissent and pathological, extremist alienation."[38] We are all – actually or potentially – *homines sacri*.

In his essay on the concept of history, Walter Benjamin wrote that "the tradition of the oppressed teaches us that the 'state of emergency' in which we live is not the exception but the rule. We must attain to a conception of history that is in keeping with this insight."[39] Benjamin was writing in 1940, but his commentary on the rise of fascism has a resonance in our own times that is as deep as it is disturbing. His call for a critical reflection on the concept of history is immensely important, but we also need a conception of geography that is in keeping with this same insight. If we can understand the multiple ways in which difference is folded into distance, and the complex figurations through which time and space are threaded into these tense constellations, we might perhaps see that what Ignatieff once called "distant strangers" are not so distant after all – and not so strange either.[40] For this possibility to be realized – for us to cease turning on the treadmill of the colonial present – it will be necessary to explore other spatializations and other topologies, and to turn our imaginative geographies into geographical imaginations that can enlarge and enhance our sense of the world and enable us to situate ourselves within it with care, concern, and humility.[41] This is not a call for an empty relativism; there will still be disagreements, conflicts, and even enemies. But in order to conduct ourselves properly, decently, we need to set ourselves against the unbridled arrogance that assumes that "We" have the monopoly of Truth and that the world is necessarily ordered by – and around – Us. If we can do this, then we might see that the most enduring memorial to the thousands who were murdered in the catastrophic destruction of the World Trade Center and parts of the Pentagon on September 11 – and to the thousands more who have been killed in Afghanistan, Israel, Palestine, and Iraq – would be the destruction of the architectures of enmity that produced and have been sustained by those dreadful events.

Notes

Chapter 1: The Colonial Present

1   Jorge Luis Borges, "John Wilkins' analytical language," in his *Selected Non-Fictions* (New York: Viking, 1999), pp. 229–32: 231. The essay was first published in Spanish in 1942.

2   Michel Foucault, *The Order of Things: An Archaeology of the Human Sciences* (London: Tavistock, 1970), p. xv; 1st pub. in French as *Les Mots et les choses* (Paris: Gallimard, 1966).

3   Foucault, *Order of Things*, p. xix; emphasis added. I have taken "tableau of queerness" from Edward Said, *Orientalism* (London: Penguin, 1995; 1st pub. 1978), p. 103.

4   It should be said that Foucault's later writings and lectures were by no means indifferent to colonial power. For example:

> At the end of the sixteenth century we have, if not the first, at least an early example of political structures of the West. It should never be forgotten that while colonization, with its techniques of political and juridical weapons, obviously transported European models to other continents, it also had a considerable boomerang effect on the mechanisms of power in the West, and on the apparatuses, institutions and techniques of power. A whole series of colonial models was brought back to the West, and the result was that the West could practice something resembling colonization . . . on itself.

Michael Foucault, *"Society Must Be Defended": Lectures at the Collège de France 1975–1976* (New York: Picador, 2003), p. 103. But Foucault never developed these ideas in any systematic fashion, a point that Said has consistently sharpened: see Derek Gregory, "Imaginative geographies," *Progress in Human Geography* 19 (1995), pp. 447–85.

5   For another example, see Roland Barthes's brief account of his visit to Japan in *Empire of the Signs* (New York: Hill & Wang, 1982; 1st pub. in French, 1970); but see Joanne Sharp, "Writing travel/traveling writing: Roland Barthes detours the Orient," *Environment and Planning D: Society & Space* 20 (2002), pp. 155–66.

6   Zhang Longxi, *Mighty Opposites: From Dichotomies to Differences in the Comparative Study of China* (Stanford, CA: Stanford University Press, 1998), pp. 21–2. Foucault does of course concede that his description of China as a "privileged site of space" belongs to "our dreamworld"; but he does not pursue those spectral footprints. In Borges's original essay, in contrast, the "Chinese encyclopaedia" was not summoned up to represent a system of thought alien to European culture, since its (imaginary) "absurdities" were used to parallel the (real) "ambiguities, redundancies and deficiencies" in the attempt made by the English cleric John Wilkins to develop a universal language in his *Essay Towards a Real Character and a Philosophy of Language* (1688). I have placed "Latin America" in scare-quotes to draw attention to its colonial implications. The term was originally proposed in the 1850s and carries within it the traces of French, Portuguese, and Spanish occupations: indigenous cultures and languages were, of course, not derived from Latin. Borges is perfectly well aware of this; for a discussion of the hybrid spaces between magical realism and the critique of colonialism, and of the vexed politics to which they give rise, see Stephen Slemon, "Magic realism as postcolonial discourse," *Canadian Literature* 116 (1998), pp. 9–24.

7   The concept of transculturation was developed by the Cuban ethnographer Fernando Ortiz, who juxtaposed the term to "acculturation." Whereas acculturation implies the adjustment of a subordinate culture to the impositions and exactions of a dominant culture, transculturation implies a dynamic relation of combination and contradiction. For a critical discussion of the genealogy of the concept, see John Beverley, *Subalternity and Representation: Arguments in Cultural Theory* (Durham, NC: Duke University Press, 1999), pp. 43–7, and for its deployment see Mary Louise Pratt, *Imperial Eyes: Travel Writing and Transculturation* (London: Routledge, 1992).

8   Said, *Orientalism*; Fernando Coronil, "Beyond Occidentalism: toward non-imperial geohistorical categories," *Cultural Anthropology* 11 (1996), pp. 51–87. Said thought it unlikely that anyone would imagine "a field symmetrical to [Orientalism] called Occidentalism" because the imaginative geographies produced by other cultures are not bound in to a system of power-knowledge comparable to the tensile strength and span of European and American colonialism and imperialism. In his view (and mine) it would be wrong to

suppose that reversing the terms equalizes them, and it is this fundamental *asymmetry* that Coronil seeks to redeem through his (contrary) reading of "Occidentalism."

9   Niall Ferguson, *Empire: How Britain Made the Modern World* (London: Allen Lane, Penguin Press, 2003), p. xxi. Recognizing other sensibilities, the American edition has a different subtitle: *Empire: The Rise and Demise of the British World Order and the Lessons for Global Power* (New York: Basic Books, 2003).

10 Enrique Dussel, "Eurocentrism and modernity," *Boundary 2* 20/3 (1993), pp. 65–76; see also his *The Invention of the Americas: Eclipse of "the Other" and the Myth of Modernity* (New York: Continuum, 1995).

11 Joseph Conrad, "Geography and some explorers," in his *Last Essays*, ed. Richard Curle (London: Dent, 1926), pp. 1–31.

12 Felix Driver, *Geography Militant: Cultures of Exploration and Empire* (Oxford: Blackwell, 2001), pp. 200–1, 216.

13 Nicholas Thomas, *Colonialism's Culture: Anthropology, Travel and Government* (Cambridge: Polity, 1994), p. 10. Thomas is signaling another departure from Foucault, whose genealogies of the modern worked to defamiliarize the taken-for-grantedness of the present by accentuating its specificity and contingency – how *different* it is from the past – whereas the subversive power of postcolonial critique derives from its power to trace continuities and parallels: how *similar* the present is to the past. Both strategies are of critical importance. If, as I will claim in a moment, we need to recover the coexistence and collision of multiple temporalities, then Foucault's "history of the present" is indispensable for its disruption of the unilinear and progressive trajectory of continuist histories. But postcolonialism's critique is invaluable for its disruption of the no less unilinear and progressive trajectory of episodic histories that dispatch the past to the archive rather than the repertoire.

14 Akhil Gupta, *Postcolonial Development: Agriculture in the Making of Modern India* (Durham, NC: Duke University Press, 1998), p. 17.

15 Andreas Huyssen, "Present pasts: media, politics, amnesia," in Arjun Appadurai (ed.), *Globalization* (Durham NC: Duke University Press, 2001), pp. 57–77; see also his *Twilight Memories: Marking Time in a Culture of Amnesia* (London and New York: Routledge, 1995).

16 Edward Said, *Culture and Imperialism* (New York: Knopf, 1993), p. 57.

17 Thomas, *Colonialism's Culture*, p. 2.

18 Robert Young, *Postcolonialism: An Historical Introduction* (Oxford: Blackwell, 2001); see also his *Postcolonialism: A Very Short Introduction* (Oxford: Oxford University Press, 2003). Young's emphasis on the three continents is in marked contrast to most other accounts of postcolonialism that

focus instead on the foundational significance of three academic figures: Edward Said, Homi Bhabha, and Gayatri Chakravorty Spivak. This is not to disparage their work – which would be absurd – but to recover the political-economic filiations of postcolonialism. See Bart Moore-Gilbert, *Postcolonial Theory: Contexts, Practices, Politics* (London: Verso, 1997).

19 Ali Behdad, *Belated Travelers: Orientalism in the Age of Colonial Dissolution* (Durham, NC: Duke University Press, 1996), pp. 6–8.

20 Terry Eagleton, *Crazy John and the Bishop and Other Essays* (Notre Dame: University of Notre Dame Press, 1999).

21 Wlad Godzich, *On the Emergence of Prose* (Minneapolis: University of Minnesota Press, 1978), p. 162.

22 Seumas Milne, "An imperial nightmare," *Guardian*, November 8, 2001; Maria Misra, "Heart of smugness," *Guardian*, July 23, 2002.

23 Renato Rosaldo, "Imperialist nostalgia," in his *Culture and Truth* (London: Routledge, 1993), pp. 68–87; Paul Smith, "Visiting the Banana Republic," in Andrew Ross (ed.), *Universal Abandon? The Politics of Postmodernism* (Minneapolis: University of Minnesota Press, 1992), pp. 128–48; Derek Gregory, "Colonial nostalgia and cultures of travel: spaces of constructed visibility in Egypt," in Nezar AlSayyad (ed.), *Consuming Tradition, Manufacturing Heritage: Global Norms and Urban Forms in the Age of Tourism* (New York: Routledge, 2001), pp. 111–51; Graham Huggan, *Postcolonial Exotic: Marketing the Margins* (London: Routledge, 2001).

24 David Cannadine, *Ornamentalism: How the British saw their Empire* (London: Allen Lane, The Penguin Press, 2001).

25 Pierre Nora, "Between memory and history: *les lieux de mémoire*," *Representations* 26 (1989), pp. 7–25; id., "From *lieux de mémoire* to realms of memory," in Pierre Nora and Lawrence Kritzman (eds), *Realms of Memory: Rethinking the French Past*, vol. 1: *Conflicts and Divisions* (New York: Columbia University Press), pp. xv–xxiv; Jean Starobinski, 'The idea of nostalgia,' *Diogenes* 54 (1966), pp. 81–103; Huyssen, "Present pasts," p. 65.

26 Said, *Culture and Imperialism*, p. 51.

27 Fredric Jameson, "The end of temporality," *Critical Inquiry* 29 (2003), pp. 695–718: 700–1. This from the man who famously could not find his way around the Bonaventure Hotel in Los Angeles! See my *Geographical Imaginations* (Oxford: Blackwell, 1994), pp. 152–7, 278–81.

28 Donna Haraway, "Situated knowledges: the science question in feminism and the privilege of partial perspective," in *Simians, Cyborgs and Women: The Reinvention of Nature* (London: Routledge, 1992), pp. 183–201; John Rajchman, "Foucault's art of seeing," in his *Philosophical Events: Essays of the 80s* (New York: Columbia University Press, 1991), pp. 68–102.

29 Giles Foden, *Zanzibar* (London: Faber & Faber, 2002), pp. 335–6.

Chapter 2: Architectures of Enmity

1 Edward Said, *Orientalism* (London: Penguin, 1978), p. 54; see also Derek Gregory, "Imaginative geographies," *Progress in Human Geography* 19 (1995), pp. 447–85.

2 Giles Foden, *Zanzibar* (London: Faber & Faber, 2002), p. 241. Foden's novel is of direct interest to my argument, and not only because it centers on the bombing of the US embassies in Nairobi and Dar es Salaam in 1998 (as I noted in ch. 1); it is also relevant because it troubles the divide between "fact" and "fiction."

3 James Clifford, *The Predicament of Culture: Twentieth-Century Ethnography, Literature and Art* (Cambridge, MA: Harvard University Press, 1988), p. 6.

4 Said, *Orientalism*, pp. 63, 71.

5 Nidhal, cited in Nuha al-Radi, *Baghdad Diaries: A Woman's Chronicle of War and Exile* (New York: Vintage, 2003), p. 151.

6 Alexander Moore, "Postcolonial 'textual space': towards an approach," *SOAS Literary Review* 3 (2001), pp. 1–23; Edward Soja, *Postmodern Geographies: The Reassertion of Space in Critical Social Theory* (London: Verso, 1989), p. 7. Soja was trading on Henri Lefebvre, *The Production of Space* (Oxford: Blackwell, 1991). For space as performance, see Gillian Rose, "Performing space," in Doreen Massey, John Allen, and Phillip Sarre (eds), *Human Geography Today* (Cambridge: Polity, 1999), pp. 247–59.

7 Judith Butler, *Bodies that Matter* (London and New York: Routledge, 1993), p. 241; cf. Homi Bhabha, *The Location of Culture* (London: Routledge, 1994), p. 219.

8 Ken Booth and Tim Dunne, "Worlds in collision," in Booth and Dunne (eds), *Worlds in Collision: Terror and the Future of Global Order* (London: Palgrave, 2002), pp. 1–23: 1.

9 On "overlapping territories, intertwined histories," see Edward Said, *Culture and Imperialism* (New York: Alfred Knopf, 1993), pp. 1–61. The reference to a horizon of danger derives from Walter Benjamin's sixth thesis on the concept of history. "To articulate the past historically," he wrote, "means to seize hold of a memory as it flashes up at a moment of danger."

10 Michael J. Shapiro, *Violent Cartographies: Mapping Cultures of War* (Minneapolis: University of Minnesota Press, 1997), p. xi.

11 James der Derian, "The war of networks," *Theory and Event* 5/4 (2002), at <http://muse.uq.edu.au/journals/theory_and_event/v005/5.4derderian.html>; see also his "9/11: before, after and in between," in Craig Calhoun, Paul Price, and Ashley Timmer (eds), *Understanding September 11* (New York: The New Press, 2002), pp. 176–90: 185.

12 "When you hear the thought expressed that now the US knows what it is to suffer," Robert Fisk explained, "it's not intended to suggest that the US deserved such horrors; merely a faint hope that Americans will now understand how much others have suffered in the Middle East over the years": "One year on: a view from the Middle East," *Independent*, September 11, 2002.

13 Michael Binyon, "How the Islamic world learned to hate the US," *Times*, September 13, 2001; President George W. Bush, "Address to a Joint Session of Congress and the American People," at <http://www.whitehouse.gov/news/releases/2001/09>, September 20, 2001. See also Ziauddin Sardar and Meryl Wyn Davies, *Why Do People Hate America?* (Cambridge: Icon Books, 2002).

14 Susan Buck-Morss, "A global public sphere?," in her *Thinking Past Terror: Islamism and Critical Theory on the Left* (London: Verso, 2003), pp. 21–35: 24; Joseba Zulaika, "The self-fulfilling prophecies of counter-terrorism," *Radical History Review* 85 (2003), pp. 191–9; Roxanne Euben, "Killing (for), politics: *jihad*, martyrdom and political action," *Political Theory* 30 (2002), pp. 4–35; cf. Seumas Milne, "They can't see why they are hated," *Guardian*, September 13, 2001.

15 John Wideman, "Whose war? The color of terrorism," *Harper's Magazine* (March 2002), pp. 33–8: 36–7. In much the same way, Susan Sontag writes that "the other, even when not an enemy, is regarded only as someone to be seen, not someone (like us) who also sees": *Regarding the Pain of Others* (New York: Farrar, Straus & Giroux, 2003), p. 72.

16 Fareed Zakaria, "The politics of rage: Why do they hate us?," *Newsweek*, October 15, 2001.

17 Cf. Edward Said, *Covering Islam* (New York: Vintage, 1997), p. 8: Within contemporary Orientalism, Said wrote, " 'Islam' seems to engulf all aspects of the diverse Muslim world, reducing all to a special malevolent and unthinking essence." This cultural essentialism also works to depoliticize opposition to the actions of successive US governments by ruling out any discussion of "the things that Muslim opponents of the US actually care about": Michael Mann, *Incoherent Empire* (London: Verso, 2003), p. 169.

18 Mahmood Mamdani, "Good Muslim, bad Muslim – an African perspective," SSRC/After September 11 at <http://www.ssrc.org/sept11/essays>; reprinted (with revisions) as "Good Muslim, bad Muslim: a political perspective on culture and terrorism," in Eric Hershberg and Kevin Moore (eds), *Critical Views of September 11: Analyses from Around the World* (New York: The New Press, 2002), pp. 44–60. See also *Islamophobia: A Challenge for us All* (London: Runnymede Trust, 1997) which distinguishes between "closed" views that treat Islam as (for example) monolithic, static, and irredeemably other, and "open" views that treat Islam as diverse, dynamic, and intrinsically interdependent with the other "religions of the Book," Christianity and Judaism.

These criteria do not exempt Islam from disagreement or criticism, but they do identify the wellsprings of what the authors see as a "phobic dread" of Islam.

19 Fareed Zakaria, "Our way," *New Yorker*, October 14–21, 2002, p. 81. Several months later, in the shadow of an impending US attack on Iraq, Zakaria acknowledged that the Bush administration had provoked "a deep and widening resentment of American foreign policy" around the world. But he still clung to the myth of American universalism, however tarnished it had become: "In principle, American power is not simply good for America," he affirmed, "it is good for the world." America's "special role" is based "not simply on its great strength," Zakaria continued, "*but on a global faith that this power is legitimate*" (my emphasis). The title of his essay mocks his own hubris: "The arrogant empire," *Newsweek*, March 24, 2003, pp. 30, 33.

20 Veena Das, "Violence and translation," SSRC/After September 11 at <http://www.ssrc.org/sept11/essays>; also in *Anthropological Quarterly* 75 (2002), pp. 105–12: 108.

21 Perry Anderson, "Internationalism: a breviary," *New Left Review* 14 (March–April 2002), pp. 5–25: "The American ideology of a republic simultaneously exceptional and universal: unique in the good fortune of its institutions and endowments, and exemplary in the power of its radiation and attraction" has reached a climax today when "in the absence of any alternative or countervailing power, American hegemony has for the first time been able to impose its self-description as the global norm."

22 Arundhati Roy, "The algebra of infinite justice," *Guardian*, September 29, 2001; reprinted in her *Power Politics* (Cambridge, MA: South End Press, 2001), pp. 105–24. I should also add that to ask these questions is not to be "anti-American," an outrageous charge that not only signals a failure of critical intelligence but also betrays the victims of the terrorist attacks. See Simon Schama, "The dead and the guilty," *Guardian*, September 11, 2002; Arundhati Roy, "Not again," *Guardian*, September 27, 2002.

23 I am thinking most particularly of the response to Susan Sontag's brief comment suggesting that America might be hated not for what it *is* but what it *does*: "Where is the acknowledgement that this was not a 'cowardly' attack on 'civilization' or 'liberty' or 'humanity' or 'the free world' but an attack on the world's self-proclaimed superpower, undertaken as a consequence of specific American alliances and actions?" ("First reaction," *New Yorker*, September 24, 2001). See Judith Butler, "Explanation and exoneration, or What we can hear," *Theory and Event* 5 (2002), at <http://muse/uq.edu.au/journals/theory_and_event/v005/5.4butler.html>; Joan Didion, "Fixed opinions, or the hinge of history," *New York Review of Books*, January 16, 2003.

24 Al-Radi, *Baghdad Diaries*, p. 21 (January 29, 1991); cf. Chris Toensing, " 'The harm done to innocents,' " *Boston Globe*, September 16, 2001; republished

as "Muslims ask: Why do they hate us?" at <http://www.alternet.org>, September 25, 2001.

25 Edward Said, "The clash of definitions," in his *Reflections on Exile and Other Essays* (Cambridge, MA: Harvard University Press, 2000), pp. 569–90: 577.

26 Mike Davis, "The flames of New York," *New Left Review* 12 (2001), pp. 34–50.

27 The distinction derives from art historian Alois Riegl, for whom optical visuality depended on a separation between the viewing subject and the object whereas haptic visuality pulled the viewer in to the surface of the object and thus privileged the material presence of the image. Riegl believed that one of the signs of the passage to modernity was the haptic yielding to the optical; for Walter Benjamin, however, the converse was the case. See Laura Marks, *The Skin of the Film: Intercultural Cinema, Embodiment and the Senses* (Durham, NC: Duke University Press, 2000), pp. 162–4 and *passim*. For a reading of the images of September 11 which is at odds with my own in its emphasis on "de-realization," see David Campbell, "Imaging the real, struggling for meaning," *InfoInterventions*, at <http://www.watsoninstitute.org/infopeace/911>, October 6, 2001.

28 Samantha Power, "Genocide and America," *New York Review of Books*, March 14, 2002; see also her *"A Problem from Hell": America and the Age of Genocide* (New York: Basic Books, 2002), and Mahmood Mamdani, *When Victims Become Killers: Colonialism, Nativism and the Genocide in Rwanda* (Princeton, NJ: Princeton University Press, 2001).

29 Barbara Kingsolver, "A pure, high note of anguish," *Los Angeles Times*, September 23, 2001. As Booth and Dunne, "Worlds in collision," p. 6, put it, "The point is not about forgetting September 11, but [about] remembering what the world is like every day." Kingsolver's reference to Hiroshima and Nagasaki is particularly instructive, because "Ground Zero" was originally used to describe the sites of the atomic bombs dropped by the US air force on those two Japanese cities. But the comparison that was repeatedly made after the attacks on New York City and Washington was between September 11 and the Japanese attack on Pearl Harbor, which effectively reversed the arrows of enmity and the target of terror. Amy Kaplan argues that to describe the crater left when the twin towers of the World Trade Center collapsed as "Ground Zero" was thus to rely on a historical analogy that could not be acknowledged, "because to do so would be to trouble the very binary oppositions and exceptionalist narratives erected on that ground," between "before" and "after," "us" and "them." And yet, as she shows, it is still possible to "hear [in 'Ground Zero'] the echoes of earlier forms of terror perpetuated by the United States, which locates Americans within world history rather than as an exception to it." If September 11 was not an "out-of-geography" event (above, p. 19), neither was it an "out-of-history" event.

See Amy Kaplan, "Homeland insecurities: reflections on language and space," *Radical History Review* 85 (2003), pp. 82–93: 84. In a parallel essay Gene Ray notes that President Harry Truman's announcement of the bombing of Hiroshima began by reminding Americans of Pearl Harbor. The infamy of the Japanese attack was used to justify the US attack on Hiroshima: "Since by their brutality the Japanese had forfeited their humanity, avenging American victims could do as they liked" in this scenario, because the enemy – "combatants and non-combatants alike" – had been placed outside the bounds of reason and law. See Gene Ray, "Ground Zero: Hiroshima haunts 9/11," *Alternative Press Review* 8/1 (2003), pp. 58–63. After September 11 the same argument was used to construct people in Afghanistan – combatants and non-combatants alike – as *homines sacri*: see below, pp. 62–72.

30 Stephen Holmes, "Looking away," *London Review of Books*, November 14, 2002; Gilbert Achcar, *The Clash of Barbarisms: September 11 and the Making of the New World Disorder*, trans. Peter Drucker (New York: Monthly Review Press, 2002), pp. 22–3.

Chapter 3: "The Land where Red Tulips Grew"

1 Edward Said, *Culture and Imperialism* (New York: Knopf, 1993), p. 138. Said also draws a compelling analogy between the Great Game and the novel itself:

> To be able to see all India from the vantage of controlled observation: this is one great satisfaction. Another is to have at one's fingertips a character who can sportingly cross lines and invade territories, a little Friend of all the World – Kim O'Hara himself. It is as if by holding Kim at the center of the novel (just as Creighton the spymaster holds the boy in the Great Game) Kipling can have and enjoy India in a way that even imperialism never dreamed of. (p. 155)

The conjunction that Said makes here between visuality and the performance of space is of considerable importance for my argument.

2 Karl Meyer and Shareen Blair Brysac, *Tournament of Shadows: The Great Game and the Race for Empire in Central Asia* (Washington: Counterpoint, 1999).

3 William Maley, *The Afghanistan Wars* (London: Palgrave, 2002), pp. 8–11.

4 Nick Cullahas, "Damming Afghanistan: modernization in a buffer state," *Journal of American History* 89 (2002), pp. 512–37.

5 Maley, *Afghanistan Wars*, pp. 15–17, 22–3, 25–33; Ahmed Rashid, Taliban: *Militant Islam, Oil and Fundamentalism in Central Asia* (New Haven: Yale

University Press, 2000), p. 13; Dilip Hiro, *War Without End: The Rise of Islamist Terrorism and Global Response* (London: Routledge, 2002), pp. 197–207.

6   Roxanne Euben, "Killing (for), politics: *jihad*, martyrdom and political action," *Political Theory* 30 (2002), pp. 4–35; John Esposito, *Unholy War: Terror in the Name of Islam* (Oxford: Oxford University Press, 2002), pp. 26–70; Bernard Lewis, *The Crisis of Islam: Holy War and Unholy Terror* (New York: Modern Library, 2003), pp. 30–3.

7   Rashid, Taliban, pp. 32–3; Valentine Moghadam, "Patriarchy, the Taliban and the politics of public space in Afghanistan," *Women's Studies International Forum* 25 (2002), pp. 19–31.

8   As Chomsky grimly observes, it is one thing to support resistance to invasion, but quite another to have deliberately incited invasion in the first place: see Noam Chomsky, *9–11* (New York: Seven Stories Press, 2001), p. 40. See also Hiro, *War Without End*, pp. 209–25; Andrew Hartman, " 'The red template': US policy in Soviet-occupied Afghanistan," *Third World Quarterly* 23 (2002), pp. 467–89; Tariq Ali, "Afghanistan: between hammer and anvil," in his *The Clash of Fundamentalisms: Crusades, Jihads and Modernity* (London: Verso, 2002), pp. 203–16.

9   Human Rights Watch, "Crisis of impunity: the role of Pakistan, Russia and Iran in fueling the civil war," at <http://www.hrw.org>, July 2001; Patricia Gossman, "Afghanistan in the balance," *Middle East Report* 221 (Winter 2001); John Cooley, *Unholy Wars: Afghanistan, America and International Terrorism* (London: Pluto, 2002), pp. 4–10; Gilles Kepel, *Jihad: The Trail of Political Islam* (Cambridge, MA: Harvard University Press, 2002), pp. 137–40; Timothy Mitchell, "McJihad: Islam in the US global order," *Social Text* 73/2 (2002), pp. 1–18; Jason Burke, Al-Qaeda: *Casting a Shadow of Terror* (London: I. B. Tauris, 2003), pp. 57–8.

10 For an account that seeks to minimize US involvement – I think unconvincingly – and places much of the responsibility on Pakistan, see Michael Rubin, "Who is responsible for the Taliban?", *Middle East Review of International Affairs* 6/1 (March 2002); cf. John Prados, "Notes on the CIA's secret war in Afghanistan," *Journal of American History* 89 (2002), pp. 466–71. The guerrilla campaign was also financed through a forced expansion of the heroin trade in territory taken by the *mujaheddin* – the Helmand proved to be a highly productive area of poppy cultivation – and the borderlands between Pakistan and Afghanistan soon became the world's major source of heroin. Weapons were trucked into the mountains from Karachi and the lorries loaded with heroin for the return journey.

11 Rohan Gunaratna, *Inside al Qaeda: Global Networks of Terror* (London: Hurst, 2002), p. 3; Burke, Al-Qaeda, p. 8; Kepel, *Jihad*, pp. 145–6, 315.

12 Hartman, "Red template," p. 483. The analogy with US involvement in Vietnam – which, as I noted above, was exactly what the Carter administration

had in mind – was forcefully criticized by Arthur Bonner, *Among the Afghans* (Durham, NC: Duke University Press, 1987). His objections were cogent but his conclusion – "Moscow has no intention of abandoning Afghanistan" (p. 241) – was overtaken by events in both Afghanistan and the Soviet Union.

13 Suzanne Schmeidl, "(Human) security dilemmas: long-term implications of the Afghan refugee crisis," *Third World Quarterly* 23 (2002), pp. 7–29.

14 *Women in Afghanistan: A Human Rights Catastrophe* (London: Amnesty International, 1995); Michael Griffin, "A gruesome record," *Guardian*, November 16, 2001; Larry Goodison, *Afghanistan's Endless War: State Failure, Regional Politics and the Rise of the* Taliban (Seattle, WA: University of Washington Press, 2001); Human Rights Watch, "Crisis of impunity," p. 15; Hiro, *War Without End*, pp. 233–4; Maley, *Afghanistan Wars*, pp. 194, 201–4.

15 Kepel, *Jihad*, p. 315.

16 Dilip Hiro, "The cost of an Afghan 'victory,'" *The Nation*, February 15, 1999; id., *War Without End*, pp. 160–3.

17 Omayma Abdel-Latif, "Playing on Western fears," *Al-Ahram*, September 19–25, 2002; Burke, Al-Qaeda. Burke is right to emphasize how radical this vision is. In traditional Islam, as Stephen Schwartz explains, armed *jihad* "is a rational system of combat fought according to strict rules." It cannot be declared by "local figures, political agitators or bandit-like chiefs" and neither can it be fought "against women, children, the aged, the infirm and non-combatants in general." See Stephen Schwartz, "*Jihad*: the true belief," at <http://www.opendemocracy.net>, August 13, 2003; for a detailed exploration of the radicalized connections between *jihad*, political violence, and martyrdom, see Malise Ruthven, *A Fury for God: The Islamist Attack on America* (London: Granta Books, 2002).

18 Mary Anne Weaver, "The real bin Laden," *New Yorker*, January 24, 2000; Jason Burke, "The making of bin Laden," *Observer*, October 28, 2001.

19 Rashid, Taliban, pp. 87–94; Burke, Al-Qaeda, pp. 86–9, 110; see also Khaled Abou El Fadl, "Islam and the theology of power," *Middle East Report* 221 (2001).

20 Rashid, Taliban, pp. 50–1, 105–16, appendix I; see also Maggie O'Kane, "Afghanistan's relentless war on women," *Guardian*, December 17, 1997.

21 Gossman, "Afghanistan in the balance"; Human Rights Watch, "Crisis of impunity," pp. 23, 31–3; Burke, Al-Qaeda, pp. 113–16.

22 Rashid, Taliban, p. 124; Christopher Kremmer, *The Carpet Wars* (Sydney: Flamingo, 2002), p. 123; Barnett Rubin, "The political economy of war and peace in Afghanistan," *World Development* 28 (2000), pp. 1789–1803. See also Cooley, *Unholy Wars*, pp. 118–29; Michael Griffin, *Reaping the Whirlwind: The* Taliban *Movement in Afghanistan* (London: Pluto, 2001); Pankaj Mishra, "The Afghan tragedy," *New York Review of Books*, January

17, 2002; Neamatollah Nojumi, *The Rise of the* Taliban *in Afghanistan: Mass Mobilization, Civil War and the Future of Afghanistan* (New York: Palgrave, 2002); Olivier Roy, *From Holy War to Civil War* (Princeton: Princeton University Press, 1995).

23   Kepel, *Jihad*, pp. 223, 231.

24   Burke, Al-Qaeda, pp. 108, 156–7, 164.

25   Gunaratna, *Inside al Qaeda*, pp. 42–7.

26   Burke, Al-Qaeda, p. 167.

27   Jonathan Belke, "Year later, US attack on factory still hurts Sudan," *Boston Globe*, August 22, 1999; Chomsky, *9-11*, pp. 48–51; Burke, Al-Qaeda, p. 167; see also Hiro, *War Without End*, pp. 267–99. After the attacks on the two US embassies, Saudi Arabia withdrew its official support from the Taliban, but Saudi money continued to reach the Taliban through private contributions: Human Rights Watch, "Crisis of impunity," pp. 31–3.

28   United Nations Security Council Resolutions 1214 (December 1998) and 1267 (October 1999). It was much easier to impose financial sanctions on the Taliban than to cut off the flows of capital on which the polymorphous al-Qaeda relied: bin Laden and his associates were extraordinarily successful in mobilizing formal and informal transnational financial networks, including charities and legitimate companies: see John Willman, "Trail of terrorist dollars that spans the world," *Financial Times*, November 29, 2001; Gunaratna, *Inside al Qaeda*, pp. 60–9.

29   United Nations Security Council Resolution 1333 (December 2000). These demands were to be repeated by President George W. Bush after September 11, backed by the immediate threat of military action.

30   Max Boot, "The case for American Empire," *Weekly Standard*, October 15, 2001; Philip Hensher, "Let's be honest: we need to impose our imperial rule on Afghanistan," *Independent*, October 17, 2001. These were not isolated idiocies: see, for example, Paul Johnson, "The answer to terrorism? Colonialism," *Wall Street Journal*, October 9, 2001, who proposed reviving the old colonial Mandate system under which Britain had taken control of Palestine after the First World War.

31   Mahmood Mamdani, "Good Muslim, bad Muslim: a political perspective on culture and terrorism," in Eric Hershberg and Kevin Moore (eds), *Critical Views of September 11: Analyses from Around the World* (New York: The New Press, 2002), pp. 44–60: 56.

32   Charles Hirschkind and Saba Mahmood, "Feminism, the Taliban and the politics of counter-insurgency," *Anthropological Quarterly* 75 (2002), pp. 339–54: 347.

33   Rashid, Taliban, pp. 145–6, 163–79. On December 31, 2001 Bush appointed Zalmay Khalilzad as his Special Envoy to Afghanistan. He had acted as a consultant for Unocal during its negotiations with the Taliban, but it would

be wrong to reduce these various coalitions to the political economy of energy. Russia wanted to curb Taliban support for Islamic insurgents in Chechnya, for example. After the Soviet invasion of Chechnya in December 1994 Chechen nationalists increasingly drew inspiration from the Afghan struggle and, after 1999, they began to describe their own fight for independence as a *jihad*.

34　Suchandana Chatterjee, "Empire, kingdoms and mobile frontiers in central Asia," in Ranabir Samaddar (ed.), *Space, Territory and the State* (Hyderabad: Orient Longman, 2001), pp. 43–62: 45.

35　Jasbir K. Puar and Amit S. Rai, "Monster, terrorist, fag: the war on terrorism and the production of docile patriots," *Social Text* 72 (2002), pp. 117–48.

36 ᵼAnthony Barnett, "Too soon to look back," at <http://www.opendemocracy. net>, September 4, 2002.

Chapter 4: "Civilization" and "Barbarism"

1　President Clinton's National Security Adviser had arranged for the incoming Bush administration to be briefed in early January 2001 on the threat posed by international terrorism in general and al-Qaeda in particular, and Richard Clarke, chair of the inter-agency Counter-Terrorism Security Group, had out-lined a series of proposals for "rolling back" al-Qaeda that foreshadowed much of what the Bush administration implemented *after* September 11. See Michael Elliott, "Could 9/11 have been prevented?," *Time*, August 12, 2002. For a detailed account of the Clinton's counter-terrorism strategy, and the central place it accorded to al-Qaeda, see Daniel Benjamin and Steven Simon, *The Age of Sacred Terror* (New York: Random House, 2002); both authors served as staff members of Clinton's National Security Council until 1998.

2　Paul Gilroy, "The American Jihad," at <http://www.opendemocracy.net>, September 18, 2001; Robin Blackburn, "The imperial presidency and national messianism," chapter 2 of his *Terror and Empire* (November 2001), at <http://www.counterpunch.org>. See also Rahul Mahajan, *The New Crusade: America's War on Terrorism* (New York: Monthly Review Press, 2001) for confirmation of the specter of capitalism that haunted this version of the Protestant ethic. But there were other messianisms at work. From the bizarre right, one contributing editor to the *National Review* proposed that "We should invade their countries, kill their leaders and convert them to Christianity": Ann Coulter, "This is war," at <http://www.nationalreview.com/coulter/ coulterprint091301.html>, September 13, 2001. And evangelist Jerry Falwell joined host Pat Robertson on the Christian Broadcasting Network to hail September 11 as divine retribution against feminists and abortion rights supporters, gays and lesbians: "God will not be mocked." See John Harris, "God gave US 'what we deserve' Falwell says," *Washington Post*, September 14, 2001.

3 "President's State of the Union Address" at <http://www.whitehouse.gov/news/releases/2002/01>, January 29, 2002. On May 6, 2002 Under-Secretary of State John Bolton extended the axis to include Cuba, Libya, and Syria. All six states – with Sudan – had been designated "sponsors of terrorism" by the US State Department since 1993, but Afghanistan had never been included on that list. The State Department's "overview of state-sponsored terrorism" had none the less drawn attention to the Taliban, "which controlled most Afghan territory, permitted the operation of training and indoctrination facilities for non-Afghans and provided logistics support to members of various terrorist organizations," and had also identified bin Laden as "one of the most significant sponsors of Sunni Islam terrorist groups" who had "played a significant role in financing, recruiting, transporting and training Arab nationals who volunteered to fight in Afghanistan." There was no mention of the role played by the United States in financing, supplying and aiding the *mujaheddin*'s struggle (above, pp. 35–6). See <http://www.state.gove/www/global/terrorists/1997Report/sponsored.html> and <http://www.state.gov/s/ct/rls/pgtrpt/2000>.

4 David Campbell, *Writing Security: United States Foreign Policy and the Politics of Identity* (Minneapolis: University of Minnesota Press, 1992), p. 195; id., "Time is broken: the return of the past in the response to September 11," *Theory and Event* 5 (2001), at <http://muse/uq.edu.au/journals/theory_and_event/v005/5.4campbell.html>. Bush's recollections are recorded in Frances Fitzgerald, "George Bush and the world," *New York Times Review of Books*, September 26, 2002.

5 Giovanna Borradori, *Philosophy in a Time of Terror: Dialogues with Jürgen Habermas and Jacques Derrida* (Chicago: University of Chicago Press, 2003), p. 92.

6 Rowan Williams, "End of war," *South Atlantic Quarterly* 101 (2002), pp. 267–78. The author is the archbishop of Canterbury.

7 Stephen Bronner, "Us and Them: the State of the Union and the Axis of Evil," *Logos* 1/2 (2002), pp. 42–50. On Schmitt's political theology, see Heinrich Meier, *The Lesson of Carl Schmitt* (Chicago: University of Chicago Press, 1998); Gopal Balakrishnan, *The Enemy: An Intellectual Portrait of Carl Schmitt* (London: Verso, 2000). There seems to me a more compelling affinity between the Republican pursuit of power and Schmitt than that proposed by commentators who point instead to the figure of Leo Strauss. Strauss's assertion of "the natural right of the stronger," his belief in the use of the West's immense military power to put "tyrannies" to flight and allow "reason" and "civilization" to flourish, his insistence on the immutability of moral values:

all these things are (plainly) of considerable weight. But so too is political theology – about which Strauss was at best ambivalent – and here Schmitt is of central importance. Cf. Shadia Drury, *Leo Strauss and the American Right* (London: Palgrave, 1997); Alain Frachon, Daniel Vernet, "Le Stratège et le philosophe," *Le Monde*, April 15, 2003; James Atlas, "A classicist's legacy: New Empire Builders," *New York Times*, May 4, 2003; Jeff Heer, "The philosopher," *Boston Globe*, May 11, 2003.

8   Cf. George Monbiot, "America is a religion," *Guardian*, July 29, 2003; Jim Wallis, "Dangerous religion: George W. Bush's theology of empire," *Sojourners Magazine* 32/5 (2003), pp. 20–6.

9   Salman Rushdie, "Fighting the forces of invisibility," *Washington Post*, October 2, 2001.

10   Simon Dalby, "Calling 911: Geopolitics, security and America's new war," *Geopolitics* 8/2 (2003), pp. 61–86: 74; cf. Cynthia Weber, *Simulating Sovereignty* (Cambridge: Cambridge University Press, 1995).

11   Carl Conetta, "Dislocating Alcyoneus: how to combat al-Qaeda and the new terrorism," Commonwealth Institute Project on Defense Alternatives, Cambridge, MA, Briefing Memorandum 23, June 17, 2002 at <http://www.comw.org/pda/0206dislocate.html>; Mark Duffield, "War as a network enterprise: the new security terrain and its implications," *Cultural Values* 6 (2002), pp. 153–65; id., "Network society, network-centric warfare and the state of emergency," *Theory, Culture and Society* 19 (2002), pp. 71–9; Paul Smith, "Transnational terrorism and the al-Qaeda model: confronting new realities," *Parameters* (Summer 2002), pp. 33–46; Paul Rogers, "The prospects for al-Qaida," at <http://www.opendemocracy.net>, January 15, 2003.

12   As Amy Kaplan shows, however, the new Office of Homeland Security that was established in the wake of September 11 marks a site that is distinctly uncanny, *unheimlich*, literally "unhomely." "Although homeland security may strive to cordon off the nation as a domestic space from external threats, it is actually about breaking down the boundaries between inside and outside, about seeing the homeland in a state of constant emergency from threats within and without": "Homeland insecurities: reflections on language and space," *Radical History Review* 85 (2003), pp. 82–93; see also chapter 9 below. For a vivid discussion of the ways in which the attacks on the World Trade Center were constructed as at once local, national, *and* international events, see Neil Smith, "Scales of terror and the resort to geography: September 11, October 7," *Environment & Planning D: Society & Space* 19 (2001), pp. 631–7.

13   Charles Krauthammer, "To war, not to court," *Washington Post*, September 12, 2001.

14   Terry Jones, "OK George, make with the friendly bombs," *Observer*, February 17, 2002.

15 Borradori, *Philosophy in a Time of Terror*, p. 101. I amplify the significance of technoscience (and technoculture) below.

16 William Pfaff, "The war on terror turns into a war on Afghanistan," *International Herald Tribune*, November 3, 2001.

17 Frédéric Mégret, " 'War?' Legal semantics and the move to violence," *European Journal of International Law* 13 (2002), pp. 361–400. The alternatives included treating terrorism as a crime – and pursuing the guilty through the intelligence, police, and criminal justice systems – and examining the material roots – the enabling conditions – of terrorism. Both are forensic strategies with local, national, and international dimensions, but neither of them is equivalent to the generalized violence of "war."

18 "Letter to President Clinton on Iraq," January 26, 1998; "Rebuilding America's defenses: strategy, forces and resources for a new century" (A Report of the Project for the New American Century, September 2000), pp. 14, 51. Both documents may be accessed at <http://www.newamericancentury.org>. The signatories to the Clinton letter included Francis Fukuyama, Robert Kagan, William Kristol, Richard Perle – and Zalmay Khalilzad, whom Bush appointed as his Special Envoy first to Afghanistan (see p. 274 n. 33 above) and then to "Free Iraq."

19 Neil Smith, *American Empire: Roosevelt's Geographer and the Prelude to Globalization* (Berkeley: University of California Press, 2003).

20 President George W. Bush, "Address to a Joint Session of Congress and the American People," September 20, 2001, at <http://www.whitehouse.gov/news/releases/2001/09>; "Presidential Address to the Nation," October 7, 2001, at <http://www.whitehouse.gov/news/releases/2001/10>. For a chronology of the war, see Dilip Hiro, *War Without End: The Rise of Islamist Terrorism and Global Response* (London: Routledge, 2002), pp. 335–72, 383–6.

21 Patrick Bishop, "The planes came at nine . . . at 2 a.m. I buried my son," *Daily Telegraph*, October 15, 2001; Duncan Campbell, "US buys up all satellite war images," *Guardian*, October 17, 2001; "The satellite wars" at <http://www.spacetoday.org/Satellites.html>. I have borrowed "spaces of constructed visibility" from John Rajchman, "Foucault's art of seeing," in his *Philosophical Events: Essays of the '80s* (New York: Columbia University Press, 1991), pp. 68–102. After two months the Pentagon allowed the contract to lapse, and Ikonos-2 images were finally released to the public in mid-February 2002. In November 2003 NIMA became the National Geospatial-Intelligence Agency. It was explained that, after September 11, NIMA had "accelerated the convergence of various analytic tradecrafts," including cartography, geospatial analysis, imagery analysis, and regional analysis, into "a new discipline" of geospatial intelligence that would "provide customers [with] a more complete visualization of geographically reference areas" from "specialized three-dimensional city graphics to animated 'fly-throughs' ": Media release OCRP 03–15, November 24, 2003.

22 Robert McCrum, "A war without witnesses," *Observer*, October 28, 2001 (also citing Maggie O'Kane); Robert Hickey, "Access denied: the Pentagon's war reporting rules are the toughest ever," *Columbia Journalism Review* (January/February 2002), at <http://www.cjr.org/year/02/1/hickey/asp>. For an illuminating discussion of previous attempts to construct another "war without witnesses" – and O'Kane's persistent attempts to subvert such masculinist framings – see Gearóid Ó'Tuathail, "An anti-geopolitical eye: Maggie O'Kane in Bosnia, 1992–93," *Gender, Place and Culture* 3 (1996), pp. 171–85.

23 Here I depart from Slavoj Žižek, *Welcome to the Desert of the Real! Five Essays on September 11 and Related Dates* (London: Verso, 2002), p. 13:

> It is surprising how little of the actual carnage [at the World Trade Center] we see: no dismembered bodies, no blood, no desperate faces of dying people . . . in clear contrast to reporting on Third World catastrophes where the point is to produce a scoop of gruesome detail. . . . Is this not yet further proof of how, even in this tragic moment, the distance which separates Us from Them, from their reality, is maintained: the real horror happens *there*, not here?

While it is true that we saw "little of the actual carnage" at the World Trade Center – for a variety of reasons – the juxtaposition of the detailed recovery at "Ground Zero" with the detached assault on Afghanistan precisely reverses Žižek's claim: the "real horror" emphatically happened "here" not *there*. That said, in some part following Paul Virilio, Žižek does subsequently describe the development of an "invisible war," "a virtual war fought behind computer screens, a war experienced by its [American] participants as a video game" (p. 37), which sharpens the point I seek to make here. Cf. Mark Durden's observation that "the relentless and repeated video and still images of the exploding World Trade Center towers, the succession of portraits and stories about those who died, the pictures of Ground Zero, have been followed by a generally controlled and limited photographic coverage of the war in Afghanistan": "Revulsion and pathos: covering the war in Afghanistan," *Afterimage* 29/5 (March/April 2002).

24 Norman Solomon, "Media war and the rigors of self-censorship," *Situation Analysis* 1 (2002), pp. 40–7.

25 Michael Macedonia, "Games soldiers play," *IEE Spectrum Online*, at <http://www.spectrum.ieee.org>, March 7, 2002; Zygmunt Bauman, "Wars of the globalization era," *European Journal of Social Theory* 4 (2001), pp. 11–28: 27.

26 Mark Bowden, "The Kabul-ki dance," *Atlantic Monthly* (November 2002), pp. 66–87.

27　Allen Feldman, "Ground Zero Point One: on the cinematics of history," *Social Analysis* 46 (2002). See also Jennifer Hyndman, "Beyond either/or: a feminist analysis of September 11," *ACME: An International E-Journal for Critical Geographies* 2 (2003), pp. 1–13, who offers a passionate critique of the disembodied vision of this high-level geopolitics and its "god's-eye cartographies of peopleless places" (p. 7).

28　Slavoj Žižek, "Are we in a war? Do we have an enemy?", *London Review of Books* 24/10, 23 May 2002; id., *Welcome to the Desert of the Real!*, p. 110. Žižek argued that, during the post-Cold War search for schematizations of the Enemy, the modern geopolitical imaginary slid "from narco-cartel bosses to the succession of warlords of so-called 'rogue states' (Saddam, Noriega, Aidid, Milosevic) without stabilizing itself on one central image; only with September 11 did this imagination regain its power by constructing the image of Osama bin Laden, the Islamic fundamentalist *par excellence*, and al-Qaeda, his 'invisible' network" (p. 110).

29　Samuel Huntington, *The Clash of Civilizations and the Remaking of World Order* (New York: Simon & Schuster, 1996). A sketch of the argument was first presented in Samuel Huntington, "The clash of civilizations?," *Foreign Affairs* 72/2 (1993). The title was derived from Bernard Lewis, "The roots of Muslim rage," *Atlantic Monthly* 26 (1990): "This is no less than a clash of civilizations – the perhaps irrational but surely historic reactions of an ancient rival against our Judeo-Christian heritage, our secular present, and the world-wide expansion of both."

30　Here Huntington invoked Gilles Kepel, *Revenge of God: The Resurgence of Islam, Christianity and Judaism in the Modern World* (University Park, PA: Pennsylvania State University Press, 1994). Since then, however, Kepel, *Jihad*, p. 375, has argued that Islamicism rose to prominence in the 1970s, peaked in the 1980s, but span out of control after the Soviet withdrawal from Afghanistan. In his view, the attacks on New York City and Washington were not signs of its continued strength but, on the contrary, "a desperate symbol of the isolation, fragmentation and decline of the Islamicist movement." See also his "The trail of political Islam" at <http://www.opendemocracy.net>, July 3, 2002.

31　Huntington, *The Clash of Civilizations*, pp. 21, 42, 45–7, 95–6, 209–11, 217, 255–6.

32　Edward Said, "The clash of definitions," in his *Reflections on Exile and Other Essays* (Cambridge, MA: Harvard University Press, 2000), p. 583; see also "The uses of culture," in his *The End of the Peace Process: Oslo and After* (New York: Vintage, 2001), pp. 139–43, where he describes Huntington's construction (I think correctly) as a "fundamentalism" (p. 142). Cf. Ahdaf Soueif, "Nile blues," *Guardian*, November 6, 2001. Writing from Cairo, she reported that "Nobody even bothers to discuss the 'clash of civilizations' theory except to marvel that the West wastes any time on it at all. Can't they see, people ask, how much of their culture we've adopted?" For a radically different criticism of Lewis, Huntington, and their purchase on the events of September 11, see Jeffrey Sachs, "Islam's geopolitics as a morality tale," *Financial Times*, October 29, 2001. Sachs insists that "the role of culture" has been "vastly overrated." According to him – and other so-called "new economists" –

> The difficulties in Islamic societies have more to do with geopolitics and geography than with any unbridgeable differences with the west … Islam was both made and undone in part by its geography. The Christian–Islamic divide is also an ecological divide, between the temperate zone of Christian Europe and the encroaching aridity (desert and steppes) of the Middle East, Islamic north Africa and central Asia.

In Sachs's view, "geography" reduces to location and climate, so that the problems of the Islamic world are blamed on what economist Ricardo Hausmann calls "bad latitude": see his "Prisoners of geography," *Foreign Policy* 122 (2001), pp. 44–53. The solution Sachs offers is a scientific-technological one – the familiar nostrum of mainstream development projects – that treats nature as obdurately "there" (especially "there") and which fails to recognize the performative force of political and cultural constructions of "nature." For a brilliant discussion, see Timothy Mitchell, "The object of development," in his *Rule of Experts: Egypt, Techno-Politics, Modernity* (Berkeley, CA: University of California Press, 2002), pp. 209–43; see also Derek Gregory, "(Post)colonialism and the production of nature," in Noel Castree and Bruce Braun (eds), *Social Nature: Theory, Practice and Politics* (Oxford: Blackwell, 2001), pp. 84–111.

33 "The world holds its breath," *New Internationalist* 340 (November 2001).
34 Paul Gilroy, "Raise your eyes," at <http://www.opendemocracy.net>, September 11, 2002. If their diversity is to be valued as a civic asset, however, this should not be at the expense of recognizing the deep discriminations that only too often turn such cultural distinctions into vivid scars on the body politic. Some commentators have pressed this further and cautioned against romanticizing the innocent victims of September 11 as "ordinary Americans." They emphasize that most were executives, brokers, traders, and dealers – which is presumably why the symbolic capital of the World Trade Center determined its selection as a target – and while "we do not mourn any more or less for the rich then the poor" they argue that the representation of the victims as "ordinary Americans" may also work to efface class discriminations. See Kathy Laster and Heinz Steinert, "Unspeakable September 11: taboos and cliches," at <http://www.eurozine.com/netmagazine>, March 5, 2002.

35 Edward Said, *Covering Islam* (New York: Vintage, 1997; 1st pub. 1981), p. lvi; Michael Shapiro, "Samuel Huntington's moral geography," *Theory & Event* 2/4 (1999), pp. 1–11.

36 Michael Steinberger, "A head-on collision of alien cultures?", *New York Times*, October 20, 2001; Samuel Huntington, "The age of Muslim wars," *Newsweek*, December 17, 2001 [January 2002 special issue].

37 Cf. Mark Salter, *Barbarians and Civilization* (London: Pluto, 2002). Gilbert Achcar, *The Clash of Barbarisms: September 11 and the Making of the New World Disorder*, trans. Peter Drucker (New York: Monthly Review Press, 2002), pp. 62–3 makes the mutation symmetrical: "Each civilization produces its own specific form of barbarism."

38 John Keegan, "In this war of civilizations, the West will prevail," *Daily Telegraph*, October 8, 2001.

39 Bauman, "Wars," p. 15.

40 Fareed Zakaria, "The politics of rage: why do they hate us?," *Newsweek*, October 15, 2001. Cf. Bernard Lewis, *What Went Wrong? Western Impact and Middle Eastern Response* (New York: Oxford University Press, 2002), p. 159: "If the peoples of the Middle East continue on their present path, the suicide bomber may become a metaphor for the whole region . . ." For a critical review of Lewis, see Edward Said, "Impossible histories," *Harper's Magazine* (July 2002), pp. 69–74. It is distressing to see Lewis's analysis repeated by Anthony Pagden in the epilogue to his *Peoples and Empires* (New York: Modern Library, 2003), pp. 171–80.

41 John Agnew, "Not the wretched of the earth: Osama bin Laden and the 'clash of civilizations' ": forum on September 11, 2001 events, *Arab World Geographer* 4/2 (2001).

42 Tariq Ali, *The Clash of Fundamentalisms: Crusades, Jihads and Modernity* (London: Verso, 2002); Michael Thompson, "Beyond good and evil," *Logos* 1/1 (2002), pp. 28–34: 33.

43 Giorgio Agamben, *Homo Sacer: Sovereign Power and Bare Life*, trans. Daniel Heller-Roaxen (Stanford, CA: Stanford University Press, 1998; 1st pub. 1995); Carl Schmitt, *Political Theology: Four Chapters on the Concept of Sovereignty* (Cambridge, MA: MIT Press, 1985; 1st pub. 1934), p. 5. The originality of Agamben's contribution turns, in part, on the way in which he brings Schmitt's claim to bear on Foucault's genealogy of modern power and biopolitics and, in doing so, takes his distance from Schmitt's own repellent politics and at the same time offers a series of objections to Foucault's theses. For Agamben, in contradistinction to Foucault, biopolitics is not opposed to sovereign power, neither is it a distinctively modern modality of power. For a lucid introduction to Agamben, see Jenny Edkins, "Sovereign power, zones of indistinction and the camp," *Alternatives* 25 (2000), pp. 3–25. As she notes, the figure of *homo sacer* is more than nominally male, but many of those

placed in this position (in Afghanistan and elsewhere) are women. For a critical engagement with Agamben, see Peter Fitzpatrick, "Bare sovereignty: *Homo Sacer* and the insistence of law," *Theory and Event* 5 (2001).

44 Agamben, *Homo Sacer*, pp. 18–19, 25, 37, 82–3; Andrew Norris, "The exemplary exception," *Radical Philosophy* 119 (2003), pp. 6–16: 10. Whereas Foucault showed how spaces of disciplinary power work to produce a subject, Agamben seeks to show how spaces of the exception work to *efface* a subject: cf. Michel Foucault, *Discipline and Punish: The Birth of the Prison* (New York: Vintage, 1995).

45 Agamben, *Homo Sacer*, p. 84; Andrew Norris, "Giorgio Agamben and the politics of the living dead," *Diacritics* 30/4 (2000), pp. 38–58: 41.

46 Couze Venn, "World Dis/Order," *Theory, Culture and Society* 19 (2002), pp. 121–36: 128; Agamben, *Homo Sacer*, pp. 84–5.

47 Luke Harding, "Allies direct the death rites of trapped Taliban fighters," *Guardian*, November 27, 2001; id., "Dead lie crushed or shot, in the dust, in ditches, amid the willows," *Guardian*, November 29, 2001; Nicholas Watt, Richard Norton-Taylor and Luke Harding, "Allies justify mass killings," *Guardian*, November 29, 2001.

48 Luke Harding, "Afghan massacre haunts the Pentagon," *Guardian*, September 14, 2002; George Monbiot, "One rule for them," *Guardian*, March 25, 2003. See also Jamie Doran's remarkable independent film, *Afghan Massacre: Convoy of Death*. "The details of what happened there are wreathed in that greatest of clichés – the fog of war – and the British and American militaries may well want to keep it that way": Jonathan Freedland, "Playing the Great Game," *Guardian*, November 28, 2001.

49 John Keegan, "Death may be only way out for 'Arabs,'" *Daily Telegraph*, November 23, 2001.

50 Žižek, "Are we in a war?"; id., *Welcome to the Desert of the Real!*, p. 93; for Amnesty International's objections, see <http://web.amnesty.org/ai.nsf>. For a defense of the administration's actions, see Anthony Dworkin's interview with Charles Allen, "Law and the campaign against terrorism: the view from the Pentagon," Crimes of War project at <http://www.crimesofwar.org>, December 16, 2002. Allen insisted that "US law appropriately limits access to the courts by enemy combatants detained outside of the United States during hostilities to challenge their detention" and reaffirmed that the scope of their rights is necessarily determined "by the Executive and the military, not by the courts." For a more detailed (and nuanced) argument about *international* law and "unlawful combatants," see Joseph Lelyveld, "In Guantánamo," *New York Review of Books*, November 7, 2002. For lucid expositions of the necessity of upholding and strengthening – rather than suspending – international law and its framework of rights in the wake of September 11, see David Held, "Violence, law and justice in a global age,"

SSRC/After September 11 at <http://www.ssrc.org/sept11/essays>, reprinted in Craig Calhoun, Paul Price, and Ashley Timmer (eds), *Understanding September 11* (New York: The New Press, 2002), pp. 92–105; Daniele Archibugi and Iris Marion Young, "Envisioning a global rule of law," at <http://www.eurozine.com/netmagazine>, June 14, 2002. It is as well to remember that international legal arenas are available to judge horrific crimes. International criminal tribunals have been established to prosecute war crimes and crimes against humanity in both the former Yugoslavia and Rwanda. And on April 11, 2002 the Rome Treaty received a sufficient number of ratifications for the International Criminal Court to be established; on May 6, 2002 the US announced that it would remove its signature from the treaty: <http://www.usaforicc.org>. Noam Chomsky, *9–11* (New York: Seven Stories Press, 2001), p. 66, sharpens what I take to be the essential point: "The fundamental principles of international law should apply to ourselves, not only to those we dislike".

51 Nicholas Mirzoeff, "The empire of the camps," *Situation Analysis* 1 (2002), pp. 20–5; Julian Borger, "In a sniper's sight: life in Camp X-Ray," *Guardian*, January 25, 2002; Paul de la Garza, "72 hours at Camp X-Ray," *St Petersburg Times*, February 20, 2002. The US leased its base at Guantánamo Bay from Cuba in 1903; the lease can only be terminated with the agreement of both parties. Camp X-Ray was closed at the end of April 2002 and the detainees transferred to smaller, walled cells at Camp Delta constructed from shipping containers placed end to end, 48 cells in each block. These and other camps on the base were originally used to house Haitian refugees between 1991 and 1995.

52 As these four men were released, 30 new detainees arrived, bringing the total held at Guantánamo to 625. See David Rohde, "Low-risk prisoners freed from high-security hell," *Guardian*, October 30, 2002. For Achcar, *Clash of Barbarisms*, p. 64, these dehumanizations recalled the most abject form of *homo sacer*, that of the *Muselmann* ("the Muslim") in the concentration camp: see p. 133 below. It was later revealed that the detainees included three teenagers who were between the ages of 13 and 15 when they were captured. Amnesty International strenuously objected: "That the US sees nothing wrong with holding children at Guantánamo and interrogating them is a shocking indicator of how cavalier the Bush administration has become": BBC News, April 23, 2003. The Convention on the Rights of the Child (1989) requires detained juveniles to be provided with legal assistance and a court's prompt decision on their detention. The United States is providing neither: Ted Conover, "In the Land of Guantánamo," *New York Times*, June 29, 2003.

53 Conover, "Land of Guantánamo."

54 Dana Priest and Barton Gellman, " 'Stress and duress' tactics used on terrorism suspects held in secret overseas facilities," *Washington Post*, December 26,

2002; Suzanne Goldenberg, "CIA accused of torture at Bagram base," *Guardian*, December 27, 2002; Paul Harris and Burhan Wazir, "Briton tells of ordeal in Bush's torture jail," *Observer*, December 29, 2002; Duncan Campbell, "Afghan prisoners beaten to death at US military interrogation base," *Guardian*, March 3, 2003; Virginie Ladisch, "Stress and duress: drawing the line between interrogation and torture," Crimes of War Project, April 24, 2003. Amnesty International is now allowed to visit any prison in Afghanistan except one: Bagram. See Paul Vallely, "The invisible," *Independent*, June 26, 2003.

55 Agamben, *Homo Sacer*, pp. 1–8. Agamben argues that it is only as the bearers of "bare life" that refugees can be "made into the object of aid and protection" (p. 133).

56 Felicity Lawrence, "A war without witnesses," *Guardian*, October 11, 2001.

57 "Presidential Address," October 7, 2001.

58 Žižek, *Welcome to the Desert of the Real!*, p. 94. See also George Monbiot, "Folly of aid and bombs," *Guardian*, October 9, 2001. Even this was too much for conservative columnist Charles Krauthammer, who argued that the attack on Afghanistan ought to be purely "a war of revenge and deterrence." Afghanistan should only matter to America, he insisted, "because of what was done to Americans, not Afghans." See his "Bread and bombs," *Washington Post*, October 12, 2001.

59 Suzanne Schmeidl, "(Human) security dilemmas: long-term implications of the Afghan refugee crisis," *Third World Quarterly* 23 (2002), pp. 7–29. It should also be noted that relief agencies regard air-drops as a strategy of last resort, not least because they are much less effective in reaching target populations: Margaret Emery and Hiram Ruiz, "Descent into disaster? Afghan refugees," *Middle East Report* 221 (Winter 2001).

60 Niall Ferguson, "Welcome to the new imperialism," *Guardian*, October 31, 2001; id., "2011," *New York Times*, December 2, 2001.

61 Marc Herold, "Above the law and below morality: data on 11 weeks of US cluster-bombing of Afghanistan," at <http://www.cursor.org/stories/abovethelaw.htm>, February 1, 2002.

62 Homi Bhabha, *The Location of Culture* (London: Routledge, 1994), pp. 99–100; cf. Derrida, quoted above in this chapter (see text at n. 15).

63 Julian Strauss, "The horror that drives Afghans to flee the Taliban regime," *Daily Telegraph*, October 1, 2001; Hiram Ruiz, "Solutions not imminent for Afghan displaced and refugees," *Middle East Report*, Press Information Notice 78, December 4, 2001; Schmeidl, "(Human) security dilemmas."

64 John Lee Anderson, *The Lion's Grave: Dispatches from Afghanistan* (London: Atlantic Books, 2002), pp. 116, 195; Human Rights Watch, "Paying for the Taliban's crimes: abuses against ethnic Pashtuns in northern Afghanistan," April 2002 at <http://hrw.org/reports/2002/afghan2/>. See also Ahmed Rashid, "Afghanistan imperilled," *Nation*, October 14, 2002.

65 Carl Conetta, "A critical appraisal of Operation Enduring Freedom and the Afghanistan war," Project on Defence Alternatives, Research Monograph 6 (January 2002); Marc Herold, "A dossier on civilian victims of United States' aerial bombing of Afghanistan," at <http://www.cursor.org>; id., "US bombing and Afghan civilian deaths: the official neglect of 'unworthy bodies'," *International Journal of Urban and Regional Research* 26 (2002), pp. 626–34; Seumas Milne, "The innocent dead in a coward's war," *Guardian*, December 20, 2001; Ian Traynor, "Afghans are still dying as air strikes go on," *Guardian*, February 12, 2002; Jonathan Steele, "Forgotten victims," *Guardian*, May 20, 2002. These figures are inevitably estimates, and Bowden, "Kabul-ki dance," dismisses them as "inflated" and prefers studies using "fewer data" (*sic*). In his contrary view, "the astonishing precision of modern American weaponry deflates [the] sense of outrage." Part of that "deflation" has been the result of decisions by US media organizations to minimize the reporting of civilian casualties: see "Fairness and accuracy in reporting" at <http://www.fair.org/activism/fox-civilian-casualties.html>, November 18, 2001. In fact, the ratio of civilian to military casualties increased significantly between the Gulf War and Afghanistan: see Scott Peterson, "Smarter bombs still kill civilians," *Christian Science Monitor*, October 22, 2002.

66 Noam Chomsky, "The world after September 11 (2001)," in his *Pirates and Emperors, Old and New* (London: Pluto, 2002), pp. 144–59: 150.

67 Gilroy, "Raise your eyes"; Arundhati Roy, "The algebra of infinite justice," *Guardian*, September 29, 2001; reprinted in her *Power Politics* (Cambridge, MA: South End Press, 2001), pp. 105–24. Cf. Žižek, *Welcome to the Desert of the Real!*, pp. 51–2, who also objects to "the moralizing mathematics of guilt and horror" and insists that "the terrifying death of each individual is absolute and incomparable." Some of the victims are given names – and faces – in a report prepared by Global Exchange on the basis of fieldwork carried out in Afghanistan in January and February 2002: see "Afghan Portraits of Grief: The Civilian/Innocent Victims of US Bombing in Afghanistan," at <http://www.globalexchange.org/september11/apogreport.pdf>, September 2002. The title deliberately mirrored the *New York Times*'s year-long series on the victims of September 11; Global Exchange praised that series for portraying the faces and voices of those murdered, thereby communicating "the preciousness of each individual," but compared this to the way in which Afghan victims were rarely seen in the US media where they were often categorized – and camouflaged – as "collateral damage."

68 Paul Gilroy, " 'Where ignorant armies clash by night': homogeneous community and the planetary aspect," *International Journal of Cultural Studies* 6 (30 (2003), pp. 261–76: 263.

69 Robert Fisk, "Collateral damage," *Independent*, August 6, 2002.

70 Dan Plesch, "Failure of the 82nd Airborne," *Guardian*, December 19, 2002; for another example, see Ian Traynor and Julian Borger, "Storm over Afghan civilian victims," *Guardian*, February 12, 2002.

71 Richard Norton-Taylor, "Afghanistan littered with 14,000 unexploded bomblets, says UN," *Guardian*, March 23, 2002; Robert Fisk, "Explosives that US knew would kill innocents continue to take their toll," *Independent*, August 10, 2002; Human Rights Watch, "Fatally flawed: cluster bombs and their use by the United States in Afghanistan," <http://hrw.org/reports/2002/afghan2/>, December 2002.

72 Polly Toynbee, "Was it worth it?," *Guardian*, November 13, 2002.

73 Derek Brown, "Promises, promises," *Guardian*, May 21, 2003.

74 Jason Burke "Afghan anarchy hinders aid," *Observer*, September 1, 2002; see also his "Chaos lurks in an abandoned land," *Observer*, September 8, 2002.

75 Michael Ignatieff, "Nation-building lite," *New York Times Magazine*, July 28, 2002; see also his *Empire Lite: Nation-Building in Afghanistan, Kosovo and Bosnia* (Toronto: Penguin, 2003). US foreign aid – which includes military aid – amounts to just 0.1 percent of GNP: the lowest proportion among all the advanced economies. In grim confirmation of these priorities, the White House budget proposals for 2003 included no request for humanitarian and reconstruction aid for Afghanistan; Congress agreed to add $300 million (*sic*) on its own initiative. This did not include the $300 million (*sic*) allocated for reconstructing the US embassy in Kabul. In July 2003 the White House announced that it would propose a further $1 billion aid package for Afghanistan "to fund projects that can be completed within a year to have maximum impact on the lives of the Afghan people before scheduled elections in October 2004." To put these allocations in perspective, the World Bank estimates that the reconstruction of Afghanistan will require $10 billion, while US Senator Joseph Biden argues (like Hamid Karzai) that the total is closer to $20 billion. See Peter Oborne, "On the roads of ruin," *Observer*, May 25, 2003; Vernon Loeb and Glenn Kessler, "US to seek new Afghan aid package of $1 billion," *Washington Post*, July 27, 2003. For a discussion of the financial and logistical difficulties besetting reconstruction, see Peter Marsden, "Afghanistan: the reconstruction process," *International Affairs* 79 (2003), pp. 91–105. Marsden emphasizes shortfalls in international aid, the priority accorded to UN agencies and NGOs in its disbursement (so that the interim government is often sidelined), and the emphasis on humanitarian relief rather than conventional reconstruction. These are all sharp points – many of the contracts and much of the investment flow to overseas companies – but they are more than technical issues and Marsden says little about the political and paramilitary barriers I identify below.

76 Robert Fisk, "Americans begin to suffer grim and bloody backlash," *Independent*, August 14, 2002.

77 Robert Fisk, "For the forgotten Afghans, the UN offers a fresh hell," *Independent*, August 7, 2002.

78 Marc Kaufman, "On Afghan border, war drags on," *Washington Post*, January 25, 2003; Tim McGirk, "The other war," *Time*, February 3, 2003; Anthony Davis, "Afghan security deteriorates as Taliban regroup," *Jane's Intelligence Review*, April 23, 2003; Carlotta Gall, "In Pakistan border towns, Taliban has a resurgence," *New York Times*, May 6, 2003; Daniel Bergner, "Where the enemy is everywhere and nowhere," *New York Times*, July 20, 2003.

79 Kathy Gannon, "Taliban reviving structure in Afghanistan," *Newsday* at <http:/www. newsday.com>, April 7, 2003; see also Phil Reeves, "Afghan clerics call for new holy war," *Independent*, April 1, 2003; Paul Krugman, "Conquest and neglect," *New York Times*, April 11, 2003.

80 Barry Bearak, "Unreconstructed," *New York Times*, June 1, 2003; Sarah Chayes, "Afghanistan's future, lost in the shuffle," *New York Times*, July 1, 2003.

81 Robert Evans, " 'Climate of fear' rules Afghanistan," *Reuters*, April 22, 2003; Carlotta Gall, "In Afghanistan, violence stalls renewal effort," *New York Times*, April 26, 2003.

82 Baheer Safi, "The Empire's witch hunt," at <http://www.zmag.org>, June 26, 2003.

Chapter 5: Barbed Boundaries

1 On travel writing, see Lester Vogel, *To See a Promised Land: Americans and the Holy Land in the Nineteenth Century* (University Park, PA: Pennsylvania State University Press, 1993); Hilton Obenzinger, *American Palestine* (Princeton, NJ: Princeton University Press, 1999). On the visual arts see John Davis, *The Landscape of Belief: Encountering the Holy Land in Nineteenth-Century American Art and Culture* (Princeton, NJ: Princeton University Press, 1996); Kathleen Stuart Howe, *Revealing the Holy Land: The Photographic Exploration of Palestine* (Berkeley, CA: University of California Press, 1997). See also Yehoshua ben-Arieh, *The Rediscovery of the Holy Land in the Nineteenth Century* (Detroit: Wayne State University Press, 1979). For contemporary resonances, see W. J. T. Mitchell, "Holy Landscapes: Israel, Palestine and the American wilderness," *Critical Inquiry* 26 (2000), pp. 193–223.

2 Michael Brown, *The Israeli–American Connection: Its Roots in the Yishuv* (Detroit, MI: Wayne State University Press, 1996); Joseph Glass, *From New Zion to Old Zion: American Jewish Immigration and Settlement in Palestine 1917–1935* (Detroit, MI: Wayne State University Press, 2002).

3   Perry Anderson, "Scurrying towards Bethlehem," *New Left Review* 10
    (2001), pp. 5–30: 15; see also Naseer Aruri, *Dishonest Broker: The US Role
    in Israel and Palestine* (Cambridge, MA: South End Press, 2003).

4   Douglas Little, *American Orientalism: The United States and the Middle East
    since 1945* (Chapel Hill, NC: University of North Carolina Press, 2002),
    pp. 101, 279, 309; M. Shahid Alam, "The 'special relationship' comes home:
    Israelization of the United States," *Counterpunch*, April 5, 2003. It was also
    in the wake of the "Six Day War" that what Norman Finkelstein calls the
    "sacralization" of the Holocaust assumed its contemporary significance:
    see his *The Holocaust Industry: Reflections on the Exploitation of Jewish
    Suffering* (London: Verso, 2000).

5   Melani McAlister, *Epic Encounters: Culture, Media and US Interests in
    the Middle East, 1945–2000* (Berkeley, CA: University of California Press,
    2001), pp. 158, 197–9; see also her "A cultural history of the war without
    end," *Journal of American History* 89 (2002), pp. 439–55. The gendering
    and sexualization of American geopolitics runs as a leitmotiv throughout the
    period. See, for example, Avi Shlaim, *War and Peace in the Middle East: A
    Concise History* (New York: Penguin, 1995), p. 45: "The military prowess
    Israel demonstrated in the Six-Day War helped transform the unequal
    US–Israel relationship into a strategic partnership. Israel's ability to use force
    in such a crushing and decisive manner provided a sharp contrast to the im-
    potence of American forces in Vietnam. Having such a virile proxy in the
    Middle East enticed Nixon and Kissinger to assume military risks polar to
    Soviet caution." The construction of America and Israel in these masculinist
    terms intersects with an established tradition of Orientalism that renders "the
    Orient" as elaborately feminized and sexualized.

6   McAlister, *Epic Encounters*, p. 200. The conjunction between "Islam" and
    "terrorism" registers a significant departure from nineteenth- and earlier
    twentieth-century Orientalisms.

7   Matt Brules, "US aid: the lifeblood of occupation," *Left Turn* (March/April
    2002); Frida Berrigan and William Hartnung, "US arms transfers and secur-
    ity assistance to Israel," at <http://www.foreignpolicy-infocus.org>, May 8,
    2002; Shirl McArthur, "Congress watch," *Washington Report on Middle East
    Affairs* (January/February 2001). Israel's GNP is higher than that of Egypt,
    Lebanon, Syria, Jordan, the West Bank, and Gaza *combined*.

8   Cf. Arnon Golan, "European imperialism and the development of modern
    Palestine: was Zionism a form of colonialism?" *Space and Polity* 5 (2001),
    pp. 127–43, who treats Zionism as a national liberation movement and seeks
    to disentangle it from European colonialism.

9   This paragraph relies on Gabriel Piterburg, "Erasures," *New Left Review*
    10 (2001), pp. 31–46: 32. An English translation of Theodor Herzl, *Der*

Judenstaat, is available online at <http://www.us-israel.org/jsource/Zionism/herzl2.html>.

10 Foundation for Middle East Peace, "Israeli settlements in the occupied territories: a guide," at <http://www.fmep.org/report/2002>, March 2002.

11 The Mandate system was codified in Article 22 of the Constitution of the League of Nations in 1919; the text for the Mandate for Palestine is available at <http://electronicintifada.net>/referencelibrary and through the Avalon Project at <http://www.yale.edu/lawweb/avalon>. The paternalism of the Mandate was not lost on the Palestinians. "The British cheated us," one village elder told journalist Jonathan Dimbleby 60 years later. "They promised us freedom and instead we had the Mandate . . . [which] said that we, the people of Palestine, were not mature enough to govern ourselves": Jonathan Dimbleby, *The Palestinians* (London: Quartet, 1979), pp. 28–9.

12 The (summary) report of the Commission is available at <http://domino.un.org/UNISPL.NSF>. On such pathological metaphors, see also Sander Gilman, "Mark Twain and hysteria in the Holy Land," in his *Picturing Health and Illness: Images of Identity and Difference* (Baltimore: Johns Hopkins University Press, 1995), pp. 3–114.

13 Martin Gilbert, *Israel: A History* (New York: William Morrow, 1998), p. 84, citing Maurice Pearlman, *Collective Adventure: An Informal Account of the Collective Settlements of Palestine* (London: Heinemann, 1938).

14 Nur Masalha, *Expulsion of the Palestinians: The Concept of "Transfer" in Zionist Political Thought 1882–1948* (Washington, DC: Institute for Palestine Studies, 1992), p. 59; Tom Segev, *One Palestine, Complete: Jews and Arabs under the British Mandate* (London: Abacus, 2001), pp. 402–8. The Commission estimated that only 1,250 Jews lived in the area that would be allocated to the Arab state.

15 Benny Morris, *Righteous Victims: A History of the Zionist–Arab Conflict 1881–2001* (New York: Vintage, 2001), pp. 138–9; Avi Shlaim, *The Iron Wall: Israel and the Arab World* (New York: Norton, 2001), pp. 25–7.

16 Little, *American Orientalism*, pp. 80–5; the text of the resolution together with the Plan for Partition with Economic Union is available through the Avalon Project at <http://www.yale.edu/lawweb/avalon>.

17 Begin's own memoir insisted that the actions in which he and his henchmen were involved cannot properly be called terrorism. "The historical and linguistic origins of the political term 'terror' prove it cannot be applied to a revolutionary war of liberation": Menachem Begin, *The Revolt* (New York: Dell, 1977), pp. 100–1. Whatever one makes of these exculpatory claims, how can they not be extended to Palestinian resistance to military occupation? See Joel Beinin, "Is terrorism a useful term in understanding the Middle East and the Palestinian–Israeli conflict?," *Radical History Review* 85 (2003), pp. 12–33.

18 The Haganah (Hebrew: "Defense") had been formed in 1920; it was originally a loose confederation of local militias, but after 1929 it became much larger and more coordinated, and between 1936 and 1945 dramatically enhanced both its military capability and its organizational structure. In the middle of 1948 the Haganah was reconstituted as the Israel Defense Forces (IDF) although the "defensive" appellation hardly describes the aggressive actions of the IDF in the occupied territories.

19 These Green Lines were not recognized as international borders (so-called "Blue Lines"); the border with Egypt turned blue in 1979, the border with Jordan in 1994; but Green Lines continue to mark Israel's military occupation of Gaza and the West Bank.

20 Samih Farson with Christina Zacharia, *Palestine and the Palestinians* (Boulder, CO: Westview Press, 1997), p. 14; Mahmoud Darwish, "Not to begin at the end," *Al Ahram*, May 10–16, 2001; see also Elias Sanbar, "Out of place, out of time," *Mediterranean Historical Review* 16 (2001), pp. 87–94; Ahmad Sa'adi, "Catastrophe, memory and identity: *al-Nakbah* as a component of Palestinian identity," *Israel Studies* 7/2 (2002), pp. 175–98.

21 Joseph Massad, "The 'post-colonial' colony: time, space and bodies in Palestine/Israel," in Fawzia Afzal-Khan and Kalpana Seshadri-Crooks, *The Pre-occupation of Postcolonial Studies* (Durham, NC: Duke University Press, 2000), pp. 311–46. For detailed discussions, see Benny Morris, *The Birth of the Palestinian Refugee Problem 1947–1949* (Cambridge: Cambridge University Press, 1988); Ilan Pappe, *Britain and the Arab–Israeli Conflict 1948–1951* (New York: Macmillan, 1988); Avi Shlaim, *Collusion Across the Jordan: King Abdullah, the Zionist Movement and the Partition of Palestine* (Oxford: Clarendon Press, 1988). For a critical appraisal, see Norman Finkelstein, "Myths, old and new," *Journal of Palestine Studies* 21 (1991), pp. 66–89.

22 Alexandre Kedar, "The legal transformation of ethnic geography: Israeli law and the Palestinian landholder," *New York University Journal of International Law and Politics* 33 (2000–1), pp. 923–1000: 999. See also Ghazi-Walid Falah, "Dynamics and patterns of the shrinking of Arab lands in Palestine," *Political Geography* 22 (2003), pp. 179–209, who notes that Israel refers to the process as "land redemption" whereas the Palestinians refer to the same process as *nahb* (robbery) or *salb* (plunder). For a discussion of the subsequent dispossession of the Bedouin in the Negev – in which the Israeli legal system mobilized a profoundly colonial conception of space – see Ronen Shamir, "Suspended in space: Bedouins under the law of Israel," *Law and Society Review* 30 (1996), pp. 231–57.

23 Edward Said, "An ideology of difference," *Critical inquiry* 12 (1985), pp. 38–58; Ghazi Falah, "The 1948 Israeli–Palestinian war and its aftermath: the transformation and de-signification of Palestine's cultural landscape," *Annals*

of the Association of American Geographers 86 (1996), pp. 256–85. See also Ibrahim Abu-Lughod, Roger Heacock, and Khaled Nashef (eds), *The Landscape of Palestine: Equivocal Poetry* (Birzeit, Palestine: Birzeit University Publications, 1999); Meron Benvenisti, *Sacred Landscape: The Buried History of the Holy Land since 1948*, trans. Maxine Kaufman-Lacusta (Berkeley, CA: University of California Press, 2000); Nadia Abu El-Haj, *Facts on the Ground: Archaeological Practice and Territorial Self-Fashioning in Israeli Society* (Chicago: University of Chicago Press, 2001), pp. 91–8; Oren Yiftachel, "Territory as the kernel of the nation: space, time and nationalism in Israel/Palestine," *Geopolitics* 7 (2002), pp. 215–48.

24 Elia Zureik, "Constructing Palestine through surveillance practices," *British Journal of Middle Eastern Studies* 28 (2001), pp. 205–27; Piterburg, "Erasures."

25 Barbara McKean Parmenter, *Giving Voice to Stones: Place and Identity in Palestinian Literature* (Austin, TX: University of Texas Press, 1994). Poetry has a particular force, which is why I draw on it in my own narrative; it is not only that it is invested with much more emotional depth than conventional academic prose, though that is important, but, as Palestinian poet Mourid Barghouti explains, it also involves "stepping out of the orchestra to play solo with the single instrument of language. That is why the poetic imagination becomes an act of resistance par excellence. It is a declaration of mutiny on board of this world's ship whose course we are never allowed to direct." Through its improvisations and experimentations, we cease turning forever on the treadmill of the colonial present. See Mourid Barghouti, "War butlers and their language," at <http://www.autodafe.org/autodaf_03/art_07.htm>, November 2002.

26 Shlaim, *The Iron Wall*, p. 260; John McHugo, "Resolution 242: a legal reappraisal of the right-wing Israeli interpretation of the withdrawal phrase with reference to the conflict between Israel and the Palestinians," *International and Comparative Law Quarterly* 51 (2002), pp. 851–82.

27 This was the opinion of the legal adviser of the US Department of State, presented to the Carter administration and to Congress in April 1978: see "Israeli settlements in the occupied territories," p. 2. The Reagan administration ignored this finding, but the applicability of Article 49 to the occupied territories was reaffirmed by successive UN Security Council Resolutions 338 (October 22, 1973), 446 (March 22, 1979), 452 (July 10, 1979) and 465 (March 1, 1980), and by a conference of the High Contracting Parties to the Fourth Geneva Convention on December 5, 2001, which the US and Israel refused to attend. See <http://www.un.org.Docs.scres>; Foundation for Middle East Peace, *Report on Israeli Settlement in the Occupied Territories*, 12/1 (January–February 2002), p. 11.

28 Morris, *Righteous Victims*, p. 341.

29 "Israeli settlements in the occupied territories," p. 1; Shlaim, *Iron Wall*, pp. 256–8.

30 Ian Lustick, "In search of hegemony: nationalism and religion in the Middle East," *Hagar* 3/2 (2002) at <http://www.bgu.ac.il/hagar/articles>; id., "Hegemony and the riddle of nationalism: the dialectics of nationalism and religion in the Middle East," *Logos* 1/3 (2002), pp. 18–44.

31 This explains why, ten years later, only two states opposed United Nations General Assembly Resolution 42/159 that condemned international terrorism. They were Israel and the United States, acting in lonely concert to contest the right – also upheld in the resolution – of peoples under "foreign occupation or other forms of colonial domination" to struggle for "self-determination, freedom and independence."

32 In a side-letter to the Camp David Accords of 1978 between Israel and Egypt, Begin specified that he understood "Palestinians" and "Palestinian people" to mean merely "the Arabs of Eretz Israel": see Anton La Guardia, *War Without End: Israelis, Palestinians and the Struggle for a Promised Land* (New York: St Martin's Press, 2002), p. 156.

33 Gilbert, *Israel*, pp. 470–1, 480; Morris, *Righteous Victims*, pp. 456, 461–75, 487–8; "Israeli settlements in the occupied territories," p. 1.

34 Shlaim, *Iron Wall*, pp. 352–5, 364–91.

35 For a discussion of these incentives – and the difficulties of establishing their financial cost – see Gershom Gorenberg, "At what price?," *Mother Jones* 28/4 (2003), pp. 43–9. "No one knows how much Israel spends on settlements," he writes: "not the settlers themselves, nor even government ministers or members of the Knesset."

36 Michael Ben-Yair, "The Six Day War's Seventh Day," in Roane Carey and Jonathan Shainin (eds), *The Other Israel: Voices of Refusal and Dissent* (New York: New Press, 2002), pp. 13–15: 13. The author was Israel's Attorney-General under Yitzhak Rabin from 1993 to 1996. As Amos Elon notes, "it is a pity than Ben-Yair did not publicly voice such views in a legal brief while he was still Attorney-General": "No exit," *New York Review of Books*, May 23, 2002. For a similar argument, see R. Reuveny, "Fundamentalist colonialism: the geopolitics of Israeli–Palestinian conflict," *Political Geography* 22 (2003), pp. 347–80. Both Ben-Yair and Reuveny – like many other critics – date Israeli colonialism from 1967, but this at best minimizes the colonial violence and dispossession of *al-Nakba* in 1948–9.

37 Edward Said, *The Politics of Dispossession: The Struggle for Palestinian Self-Determination, 1969–1994* (New York: Pantheon), p. xxvii; Joel Beinin and Lisa Hajjar, "Palestine, Israel and the Arab–Israeli conflict," Middle East Research and Information Project (2001), at <http://www.merip.org/palestine-israel_primer>; Geoffrey Aronson, *Israel, Palestinians and the Intifada: Creating Facts on the West Bank* (New York: Routledge, 1990); Morris,

Righteous Victims, pp. 561–610. It was during the Intifada that Hamas was established by the devout Muslim Brothers, in opposition to both Israel and the secular nationalism of the PLO. See John Esposito, *Unholy War: Terror in the Name of Islam* (Oxford: Oxford University Press, 2002), pp. 94–102; Gilles Kepel, *Jihad: The Trail of political Islam* (Cambridge, MA: Harvard University Press, 2022), pp. 150–8, 323–4; Anthony Shadid, *Legacy of the Prophet: Despots, Democrats and the New Politics of Islam* (Boulder, CO: Westview Press, 2002), pp. 118–33.

38 F. Robert Hunter, *The Palestinian Uprising: A War by Other Means* (Berkeley: University of California Press, 1993).

39 Shlaim, *Iron Wall*, pp. 487–92, 509–16; Said, *Politics of Dispossession*, p. xxxvi; Allegra Pacheco, "Flouting convention: the Oslo agreements," in Roane Carey (ed.), *The New Intifada: Resisting Israel's Apartheid* (London: Verso, 2001), pp. 181–206: 188. Pacheco emphasizes that rights under the Geneva Convention *cannot* lawfully be conceded by anyone, so that even the PLO could not agree to set aside its provisions.

40 Burhan Dajani, "The September 1993 Israeli–PLO documents: a textual analysis," *Journal of Palestine Studies* 23 (1994), pp. 5–23; Said, *Politics of Dispossession*, pp. xxxiv, xxxix; id., *End of the Peace Process*, pp. 341–5.

41 Marwan Bishara, *Palestine/Israel: Peace or Apartheid* (London: Zed, 2001).

42 Glenn Robinson, "The peace of the powerful," in Carey (ed.), *New Intifada*, pp. 111–23; Said, *End of the Peace Process*, p. 16.

43 Salah Hassan, "Terminus nation-state: Palestine and the critique of nationalism," *New Formations* 45 (2002), pp. 54–71; id., "Undertaking partition: Palestine and postcolonial studies," *Journal x* (2001), pp. 19–45; Said, *End of the Peace Process*, p. 31.

44 Shlaim, *Iron Wall*, pp. 564–88, 604–5; Geoffrey Aronson, "Eating away at Palestine," *Le Monde Diplomatique*, November 1998.

45 Pacheco, "Flouting convention"; "Israeli settlements in the occupied territories," pp. 4, 8; B'Tselem, the Israeli Information Center for Human Rights in the Occupied Territories, "Land Grab: Israel's Settlement Policy in the West Bank," May 2002, at <http://www.btselem.org>. "Imagine the effect on the peace process in Northern Ireland if the British government continued moving thousands of Protestants from Scotland into Ulster and settling them, at government expense, on land confiscated from Irish Catholics": Amos Elon, "Israelis and Palestinians: what went wrong?," *New York Review of Books*, December 19, 2002. The comparison is made all the more pointed by the aspiration of Sir Ronald Storrs, the first British military governor of Jerusalem, who had anticipated the establishment of what he called " 'a little loyal Jewish Ulster' in a sea of potentially hostile Arabism": see his *Orientations* (London: Nicholson & Watson, 1937), p. 405.

46 Palestinian Society for the Protection of Human Rights and the Environment, *By-Pass Road Construction in the West Bank: The End of the Dream of Palestinian Sovereignty*, February 28, 1996; Samira Shah, *The By-Pass Road Network in the West Bank: An Analysis of the Effects of the Network on the Palestinian Territories* (Ramallah, Palestine: al-Haq, 1997); Camille Mansour, "Israel's colonial impasse," *Journal of Palestine Studies* 30 (2001), pp. 83–7. On the surreal "fragmentation of Palestinian life in time and space," see Janet McMahon, "For security reasons? The surreal reality of post-Oslo Palestine," *Washington Report on Middle East Affairs* (September 1998), at <http://www.washington-report.org>. For a moving reconstruction of the impact of these fractures on the day-to-day lives of Palestinians seeking to make the most mundane of journeys, see "What if you were Palestinian for a day?" *Palestine Report* at <http://www.palestinereport.org/sect/jer.htm>.

47 Edward Dimendberg, "The will to motorization: cinema, highways and modernity," *October* 73 (1995), pp. 91–137: 99, 108.

48 *Israel Yearbook and Almanac* 52 (Jerusalem: IBRT, 1988), p. 288.

49 Sara Roy, "The Palestinian economy after Oslo," *Current History* 97 (1998), pp. 19–25; id., "De-development resisted: Palestinian economy and society since Oslo," *Journal of Palestine Studies* 28 (1999), pp. 64–82; id., "Decline and disfigurement: the Palestinian economy after Oslo," in Carey (ed.), *The New Intifada*, pp. 91–109; Jeff Halper, "Why Israel won't make peace," Israeli Committee against House Demolitions, at <http://www.icahd.org>, December 20, 2001; Farson and Zacharia, *Palestine and the Palestinians*, p. 273; Shlaim, *Iron Wall*, p. 530.

50 Ilan Pappe, "Fear, victimhood, self and other," *MIT Electronic Journal of Middle East Studies* 1 (2001), pp. 4–14: 8; see also Yiftachel, "Territory," pp. 239–40.

51 The details of the negotiations are contentious because no formal, written record was kept: see Robert Malley, "Fictions about the failure at Camp David," *New York Times*, July 8, 2001; Tanya Reinhart, "The Camp David fraud," *Yediot Ahronot*, July 13, 2001; Deborah Sontag, "The quest for Middle East peace: how and why it failed," *New York Times*, July 26, 2001; Robert Malley and Hussein Agha, "Camp David: the tragedy of errors" *New York Review of Books*, August 9, 2001; "Camp David and after: an exchange" (1: Benny Morris, "An interview with Ehud Barak") (2: Hussein Agha and Robert Malley, "A reply to Ehud Barak"), *New York Review of Books*, June 13, 2002; "Camp David and after – continued" (1: Benny Morris and Ehud Barak, "Response"); (2: Hussein Agha and Robert Malley, "Response"), *New York Review of Books*, June 27, 2002; Tanya Reinhart, *Israel/Palestine* (New York: Seven Stories Press, 2002), pp. 21–60.

52 Amnon Kapeliouk, "Camp David dialogues," *Le Monde Diplomatique*, September 2000 (my emphasis).
53 Morris, "Interview with Ehud Barak."
54 Kathleen Christison, "The full story of Resolution 242: how the US sold out the Palestinians," *Counterpunch*, June 28/30, 2002 at <http://www.counterpunch.org>; see also her *Perceptions of Palestine* (Berkeley, CA: University of California Press, 2000), pp. 278–9, 297–8.
55 The proportions are controversial because Israel and the Palestinian Authority calculated them on different territorial bases. Barak and Clinton claimed the final – "generous" – Israeli offer was 94 percent, but this was calculated on a base that included parts of the Dead Sea and excluded East Jerusalem and the "no man's land" around Latrun. The exclusion of East Jerusalem was deliberate: Barak did not offer East Jerusalem as the Palestinian capital but the outlying village of Abu-Dis, which was to be renamed Al-Quds (the Arabic name for Jerusalem): Reinhart, *Israel/Palestine*, pp. 34–41. The Israeli Committee against House Demolitions put Barak's offer at 88–89 percent of the West Bank, but the Foundation for Middle East Peace calculated that Israel proposed to relinquish control over only 78–81 percent of the West Bank excluding East Jerusalem: see Jeff Halper, "Why the Palestinians refused Barak's 'generous' offer," *Cornerstone* 21 (Spring 2001); "How generous is generous?," in *Crossroads of Conflict, Foundation for Middle East Peace Special Report, Winter 2000*; Nigel Parry, "Misrepresentation of Barak's offer," at <http://electronicintifada.net>, March 20, 2002. Remember, too, that these are all percentages of percentages. According to Gush Shalom, Barak's plan "left the Palestinians able only to tortuously navigate through 17.6 percent of their historic homeland": <http://www.gush-shalom.org/media/barak>_end.swf.
56 Eyal Weizman, "The politics of verticality," at <http://www.opendemocracy.net>, April 2002; see also Rafi Segal and Eyal Weizman (eds), *A Civilian Occupation: The Politics of Israeli Architecture* (London: Verso, 2003). Weizman's phrase gives a redoubled force to the Zionist vision of an *aliyah* (ascent) to the Land of Israel. Falah, "Dynamics and patterns," describes this contorted geography in the vocabulary of "enclaves" and "exclaves," but I don't find this helpful: partly because it does not connect with sufficient directness to the specifically *colonial* project of Israeli settlement, and partly because it retains the geometric logic of Euclidean space whereas – as Weizman shows, and as I seek to develop below – the torsions of time and space require a *topological* rendering of the terrain. The complexity of representation is part of Weizman's point and it has demonstrable performative consequences. "Complexity was always a propaganda technique of Israel," he explains. "Whenever you speak to an Israeli politician and you say, 'Well, why don't you retreat?' they say, 'Oh, it's far too complex.' So the territorial

aspect of the conflict has become very much the domain of experts, and that was what Israel wanted": Esther Addley, "Lines in the sand," *Guardian*, July 25, 2002.

57 Jeff Halper, "The 94 percent solution," *Middle East Report* 216 (Fall 2000); id., "The key to peace: dismantling the matrix of control," the Israeli Committee against House Demolitions at <http://www.icahd.org/eng/articles>, and in Carey and Shainin (eds), *Other Israel*, pp. 20–40; Weizman, "Politics of verticality."

58 Ze'ev Shiff, cited in Jerome Slater, "What went wrong? The collapse of the Israeli–Palestinian peace process," *Political Science Quarterly* 116 (2001), pp. 177–99.

59 Sharon was vilified by Palestinians for his role in willfully allowing Phalangist militias to massacre more than 3,500 Palestinian refugees in camps at Sabra and Shatila in west Beirut in September 1982. Robert Fisk describes this horrifying episode as "the worst single act of terrorism in modern Middle East history": Robert Fisk, "This is a place of filth and blood that will forever be associated with Ariel Sharon," in Carey (ed.), *The New Intifada*, pp. 293–6; id., *Pity the Nation: The Abduction of Lebanon* (New York: The Nation Books, 2002); see also Morris, *Righteous Victims*, pp. 542–9; international campaign for justice for the victims of Sabra and Shatila, at <http://www.indictsharon.net>; Leila Shahid, "The Sabra and Shatila massacres: eyewitness reports," *Journal of Palestine Studies* 32 (2002), pp. 36–58. On September 28, 2000, accompanied by hundreds of Israeli troops and riot police, Sharon asserted his right to visit the Temple Mount (Har Habayit), a place sacred to Jews because it marks the site where Abraham offered Isaac as a sacrifice to God and where Solomon built the First Temple to house the Ark of the Covenant. The same site is known to Muslims as the Noble Sanctuary (al-Haram al-Sharif) and is sacred to them because it is the place from which the Prophet Mohammed is said to have ascended to heaven on his Night Journey. It is marked by two mosques, the Dome of the Rock and the al-Aqsa mosque. On the politics of representation invested in this riven architecture, see Daniel Bertrand Monk, *An Aesthetic Occupation: The Immediacy of Architecture and the Palestine Conflict* (Durham, NC: Duke University Press, 2002). Sharon absurdly described his foray as "a visit of peace" whereas *its* politics of representation – offensive in a calculatedly double sense – were quite otherwise. See also Reinhart, *Israel/Palestine*, pp. 88–98.

60 Mourin Rabbni, "Rocks and rockets: Oslo's inevitable conclusion," *Journal of Palestine Studies* 30/3 (2001), pp. 68–81.

61 Adi Ophir, "A time of occupation," in Carey and Shainin (eds), *The Other Israel*, pp. 51–66: 61; Tanya Reinhart, "Israel: the generals' grand design," at <http://www.opendemocracy.net>, April 18, 2002; see also Reinhart, *Israel/Palestine*, pp. 95–6.

62 Uri Avnery, "The day Barak's bubble burst," *Palestine Monitor*, September 15, 2001; Reinhart, *Israel/Palestine*, pp. 209–21. The Taba negotiations are summarized in a report prepared by the European Union's Special Representative to the Middle East, following consultations with the Israeli and Palestinian sides, and available as "EU description of the outcome of permanent status talks at Taba," *Ha'aretz*, February 15, 2002.

63 I am indebted to John Agnew for these observations.

64 Rema Hammami and Salim Tamari, "The second uprising: end or new beginning?," *Journal of Palestine Studies* 30/1 (2001), pp. 5–24.

65 Ghassan Hage, " 'Comes a time we are all enthusiasm': understanding Palestinian suicide bombers in times of exighophobia," *Public Culture* 15 (2003), pp. 65–89; cf. Bruce Hoffman, "The logic of suicide terrorism," *Atlantic Monthly* 29/5 (June 2003), pp. 40–7. For reviews of arguments over violent and non-violent resistance, and suicide bombings in particular, see Lori Allen, "Palestinians debate 'polite' resistance to occupation," *Middle East Report* 225 (Winter 2002) and Avishai Margalit, "The suicide bombers," *New York Review of Books*, January 16, 2003. Here I also rely on Amnesty International, "Without distinction: attacks on civilians by Palestinian armed groups," July 11, 2002 at <http://www.amnesty.org/ai.nsf/recent/MDE020032002!Open>; Human Rights Watch, "Erased in a moment: suicide bombings attacks against Israeli civilians," October 2002, at <http://www.hrw.org/reports/2002/isrl-pa>.

66 Mahmoud Darwish, "But then nothing, nothing justifies terrorism," *al Ayyam*, September 17, 2001.

Chapter 6: Defiled Cities

1 Suzanne Goldenberg, "Israeli tanks invade two West Bank towns," *Guardian*, September 13, 2001; Philip Jacobson, "Sharon is urged to crush Arafat 'once and for all,' " *Daily Telegraph*, September 16, 2001.

2 Flore de Préneuf, "Israel's pivotal role," at <http://www.salon.com>, September 17, 2001.

3 Edward Said, "Collective passion," *Al-Ahram*, September 20–6, 2001; see also his "A people in need of leadership," *New Left Review* 11 (September–October 2001), pp. 27–33.

4 Ewen MacAskill and Virginia Quirke, "US forces Middle East ceasefire," *Guardian*, September 19, 2001; see also Camille Mansour, "The impact of 11 September on the Israeli–Palestinian conflict," *Journal of Palestine Studies* 31 (2002), pp. 5–18; Anton La Guardia, *War Without End: Israelis, Palestinians and the Struggle for a Promised Land* (New York: St Martin's Press, 2002), pp. 332–41.

5 The comparison had its roots in an older one, in which right-wing Israeli politicians frequently represented Arafat as a new Hitler: see La Guardia, *War Without End*, p. 156. Sharon had made similar remarks before. "Palestinian terror got tremendous support and encouragement [from] the United States," he told the *Wall Street Journal* in 1989, when he compared Israel's predicament to "what happened in Czechoslovakia at the end of the 1930s." Netanyahu took up the same theme just before the Oslo accords were signed in 1993, when he cautioned against "appeasement" and compared the Arab states to Nazi Germany, the Palestinians to the Sudeten Germans, and Israel to Czechoslovakia: Benjamin Netanyahu, *A Place Among the Nations: Israel and the World* (New York: Bantam Books, 1993). The revival of the comparison after September 11 was applauded by some neo-conservative commentators who urged Bush to "think about the meaning of Munich": Seth Lipsky, "Munich's moral," *Wall Street Journal*, October 10, 2001.

6 Julian Borger, "US backs state for Palestine," *Guardian*, October 3, 2001; Suzanne Goldenberg and Julian Borger, "Furious Bush hits back at Sharon," *Guardian*, October 6, 2001; Jane Perlez and Katharine Seelye, "A nation challenged," *New York Times*, October 6, 2001.

7 Jennifer Steinhauer, "A nation challenged: the donations," *New York Times*, October 12, 2001. Mahmoud Darwish sharpened the same point as Alwaleed bin Talal. He passionately condemned the attacks on New York City and Washington, but also insisted that "the great American values of freedom, democracy and human rights" had been withdrawn from the occupied territories, where Israel "remains free from answering to international law while the US provides it with what it needs of rationalizations and justifications for practices which border on 'state terrorism.'" See his "But then nothing, nothing justifies terrorism," *Al Ayyam*, September 17, 2001.

8 Thomas Friedman, "It's freedom, stupid," *New York Times*, October 9, 2001.

9 Tanya Reinhart, *Israel/Palestine* (New York: Seven Stories Press, 2002), p. 105; Suzanne Goldenberg, "Sharon on collision course with America," *Guardian*, October 12, 2001; id., "Sharon defies US demand to retreat," *Guardian*, October 24, 2001.

10 Rema Hammami, "Intifada in the aftermath," *Middle East Report* Press Information Notice 74, 2001.

11 Reinhart, *Israel/Palestine*, pp. 139–41.

12 Suzanne Goldenberg, "Carnage as suicide bombs hit Jerusalem," *Guardian*, December 2, 2001; id., "After 13 hours of carnage, 26 lie dead and ceasefire hopes buried," *Guardian*, December 3, 2001; Roland Watson, "Bush hands tied as Sharon joins war on terror," *Times*, December 4, 2001; Seumas Milne, "Targeting Arafat is not the answer," *Guardian*, December 6, 2001; Gary Younge, "Lots of wars on terror," *Guardian*, December 10, 2001.

13 William Safire, "Israel or Arafat," *New York Times*, December 3, 2001; Simon Tisdall, "Bush's backing for Israeli retaliation puts role as broker into question," *Guardian*, December 4, 2001; Suzanne Goldenberg, "They ran for their lives through a field of death," *Guardian*, December 5, 2001; id., "Reprisals risk collapse of Arafat's rule," *Guardian*, December 6, 2001.

14 Edgar Lefkovitz, "Giuliani steals show as New York delegation visits Jerusalem," *Jerusalem Post*, December 10, 2001; Judy Siegel, "Giuliani, Bloomberg, Pataki visit the wounded," *Jerusalem Post*, December 10, 2001; Ewan MacAskill and Suzanne Goldenberg, "US loses patience with Arafat," *Guardian*, December 10, 2001. I have taken Giuliani's remarks from an agency report: "Rousing reception for Giuliani in Jerusalem," *Ha'aretz*, December 10, 2001. This was not his first visit; New York City and Jerusalem had signed a mutual cooperation agreement in 1993, which Giuliani reaffirmed on taking office in 1995, and in 1996 he made a "solidarity visit" to Jerusalem which he described as "the unified and undivided capital of the state of Israel": a claim which was, of course, bitterly contested by the Palestinians.

15 Anton La Guardia, "Bush says Arafat is backing terrorism," *Daily Telegraph*, January 26, 2002; Delinda Hanley, "US moves from condemnation to tacit approval of Sharon's war on Palestinians," *Washington Report on Middle East Affairs* 21/2 (March 2002).

16 Graham Usher and Brian Whitaker, "Israelis seize town in terror hunt," *Guardian*, January 22, 2002; Greg Myre, "Israel strikes after rocket attack," *Guardian*, February 17, 2002; Suzanne Goldenberg, "Assault on refugee camps," *Guardian*, March 1, 2002; id., "Israelis launch massive attack," *Guardian*, March 13, 2002.

17 Reinhart, *Israel/Palestine*, p. 148; Suzanne Goldenberg, "Israel turns its fire on Arafat," *Guardian*, March 30, 2002; Charles Krauthammer, "Banish Arafat now," *Washington Post*, April 5, 2002.

18 Raja Shehadeh, *When the Bulbul Stopped Singing: A Diary of Ramallah Under Siege* (London: Profile Books, 2003), pp. 57, 85; Rema Hammami, "Interregnum: Palestine after Operation Defensive Shield," *Middle East Report* 223 (Summer 2002).

19 Uri Avnery, "The real aim of Operation Defensive Shield," *Arab News*, May 17, 2002.

20 Amnesty International, "The heavy price of Israeli incursions," at <http://web.amnesty.org/library/index/ENGMDE150422002>, April 2002).

21 Peter Beaumont, "Israeli tanks take war into Manger Square," *Guardian*, April 3, 2002.

22 Peter Beaumont, "Pull back, Bush orders Sharon," *Observer*, April 7, 2002; Sarah Left, "Sharon defies calls to end offensive," *Guardian*, April 8, 2002.

23 Reinhart, *Israel/Palestine*, pp. 161–5; Tsadok Yeheskeli, "Demolishing Jenin: riding a 60-ton bulldozer," *Yediot Aharonot*, May 31, 2002; trans. at <http://www.gush-shalom.org/english, June 2002>.

24 Suzanne Goldenberg, "The lunar landscape that was the Jenin refugee camp," *Guardian*, April 16, 2002; Janine di Giovanni, "Inside the camp of death," *Times*, April 16, 2002; Amira Hass, "What kind of war is this?," *Ha'aretz*, April 20, 2002; Chris McGreal and Brian Whitaker, "Israel accused over Jenin assault," *Guardian*, May 23, 2002.

25 Yitzhak Laor, "After Jenin," *London Review of Books*, May 9, 2002. Human Rights Watch estimated that at least 52 Palestinians had been killed during the incursions; 22 of them were civilians, many of whom were killed willfully and unlawfully. "Palestinians were used as human shields and the IDF employed indiscriminate and excessive force": Human Rights Watch, "Jenin: IDF military operations," at <http://hrw.org/reports/2002/israel3/>, May 2002; see also Amnesty International, "Heavy price" and "Shielded from scrutiny – IDF violations in Jenin and Nablus," the latter at <http://web.amnesty.org/library/index/ENGMDE151432002>, November 2002. There are plausible reasons for treating these casualty figures as minima: see Reinhart, *Israel/Palestine*, pp. 152–70. Her doubts have been reinforced by an analysis of satellite imagery – see "Jenin, Palestine 32° 27'39'N 35° 17'20'E" at <http://www.globalsecurity.org/military/world/palestine/jenin_imagery.htm> – and by eyewitness reports: Ida Audeh, "Narratives of siege: eyewitness testimonies from Jenin, Bethlehem and Nablus," *Journal of Palestine Studies* 31/4 (2002), pp. 13–34; Ramzy Baroud (ed.), *Searching Jenin: Eyewitness Accounts of the Israeli Invasion* (Seattle, WA: Cune Press, 2003).

26 Reinhart, *Israel/Palestine*, pp. 157–8; cf. Arundhati Roy, "The algebra of infinite justice," in her *Power Politics* (Cambridge, MA: South End Press, 2001), pp. 105–24.

27 Camille Mansour, "Israel's colonial impasse," *Journal of Palestine Studies* 30 (2001), pp. 83–7: 86–7.

28 Stephen Graham, "Lessons in urbicide," *New Left Review* 19 (2003), pp. 63–77: 71–4.

29 Eyal Weizman, "The politics of verticality," at <http://www.opendemocracy.net>, April 2002; see also "Border security systems" at <http://www.eurosatory.mod.gov.il/border.htm>.

30 Akiva Eldar, "How to cease from a cease-fire," *Ha'aretz*, July 25, 2002; Suzanne Goldenberg, "Israelis row over bombing blame," *Guardian*, July 25, 2002; Graham Usher, "Sharon accused of shattering ceasefire," *Guardian*, July 27, 2002; Levy-Barzilai Vered, "The high and mighty," *Ha'aretz*, August 22, 2002; Aryeh Dayan, " 'One day in five, the IDF attempts assassination,' " *Ha'aretz*, May 21, 2003. On the legal issues surrounding the attack, see Ariel Meyerstein, "Case-study: the Israeli strike against Hamas leader Salah Shehadeh," Crimes of War Project, at <http:www.crimesofwar.org/onnews/news-shehadeh.html>, September 19, 2002.

31 Hanan Elmasu, "Where the streets had a name," at <http://electronicIntifada.net/v2>, January 24, 2003.

32 Yigal Shochat, "Red line, Green line, Black flag," in Roane Carey and Jonathan Shainin (eds), *The Other Israel: Voices of Refusal and Dissent* (New York: New Press, 2002), pp. 126–30: 127–8. The author finished his military career as Surgeon-General of the Israeli air force.

33 Scott Anderson, "An impossible occupation," *New York Times*, May 12, 2002.

34 Meron Benvenisti, "The checkpoints of arrogance," *Ha'aretz*, March 7, 2002; Jessica Azulay, "Breeding points of terror," at <http://www.zmag.org>, July 5, 2002.

35 See "Courage to refuse" at <http://www.seruv.org.il>, and "Refuser Solidarity Network" at <http://www.refusersolidarity.net>.

36 Joanne Mariner, "Refusing to fight in Israel," *Counterpunch*, December 26, 2002; Oren Yiftah'el, "On refusal and geography," at <http://www.seruv.org.il/MoreArticles.English/OrenyifEng_geo.htm>; Susan Sontag, "The power of principle," *Guardian*, April 26, 2003 (my emphasis). It should be noted that, unlike the imaginative geographies that choreographed US military operations in Afghanistan, Israel mobilized the technocultural sphere not only to territorialize its "others" – to fix them within a carceral archipelago of "areas" and "zones" – but also, ultimately, to *deterritorialize* them.

37 Samuel Huntington, *The Clash of Civilizations and the Remaking of World Order* (New York: Simon & Schuster, 1996), pp. 256, 264; Robert Wistrich, "It is a clash of civilizations," *Jerusalem Post*, October 19, 2001; Thomas L. Friedman, "The hard truth," *New York Times*, April 3, 2002.

38 Barak's epithets are reported in Jerome Slater, "What went wrong? The collapse of the Israeli-Palestinian peace process," *Political Science Quarterly* 116 (2001), pp. 177–99: 180. After Foucault we know how *un*reasonable – how truly terrifying – modern Reason can be.

39 Lena Jayyusi, "Letters from the Palestinian ghetto, March 8–13, 2002," *Critical Arts* 16 (2002), pp. 47–52: 52. This text is also available at <http://www.autodafe.org/correspondence/cor_art_12.htm>. Jayyusi is director of the Oral History Program and Shami Palestinian Diaspora and Refugee Center.

40 Shehadeh, *Bulbul*, p. 95; diary entry dated April 12, 2002.

41 Giorgio Agamben, *Homo Sacer: Sovereign Power and Bare Life*, trans. Daniel Heller-Roaxen (Stanford, CA: Stanford University Press, 1998; 1st pub. 1995).

42 Tanya Reinhart, "Gaza and the West Bank: Israel's present and future penal colonies," at <http://www.opendemocracy.net>, July 10, 2002; id., *Israel/Palestine*, pp. 18–19. See also Safwat Al Kahlout, "Trapped in misery," *Palestine Report*, May 29, 2002: "Gazans often call the Gaza Strip their 'giant prison',," in which entry and exit is closely controlled and movement between its security zones is determined by "Israeli troops manning the checkpoints very much like prison guards."

43 David Rudge, "Official launch of security fence planned," *Jerusalem Post*, June 15, 2002; John Kifner, "Israel begins West Bank fence project," *New York Times*, June 16, 2002; Ilan Pappe, "The fence at the heart of Palestine," *Al-Ahram*, July 11–17, 2002; B'Tselem, the Israeli Center for Human Rights in the Occupied Territories, "Separation barrier," at <http://www. btselem.org>, September 2002; Sune Segal, "The Berlin Wall," *Palestine Monitor*, October 14, 2002; Isabelle Humphries, "Building a wall, sealing the occupation," *Middle East Report* Press Information Notice 107, September 29, 2002; Palestinian Society for the Protection of Human Rights and the Environment, *Israel's Apartheid Wall: We Are Here and They Are There*, at <http://www.lawsociety.org>, November 2002; Matthew Brubacher, "Israel: walled in, but never secure," *Le Monde Diplomatique*, November 2002; Jonathan Cook, "Sharon's real fence plan," *Electronic Intifada*, March 28, 2003; Uri Avnery, "The evil wall," at <http://www. electronicintifada.net>, May 6, 2003; Meron Rappaport, "A wall in the heart," *Yedioth Ahronoth*, May 31, 2003; Special Report on the West Bank security barrier, UNRWA, at <http://www.electronicintifada.net>, July 15, 2003; Geoffrey Aronson, "Sharon government's separation plan defines Palestine's provisional borders," *Report on Israeli Settlements in the Occupied Territories* (Foundation for Middle East Peace) 14/4 (July–August 2003). See also Eyal Weizman, "Sharon's wall: the geometry of occupation," September 2003, at <http://www.openDemocracy.net>.

44 Agamben, *Homo sacer*, p. 20.

45 This phrase is taken directly from paragraph 6 of the petition to the Supreme Court of Israel on behalf of the eight reserve soldiers, at <http://www. refusersolidarity.net/images/resources/zonsheine_petition.pdf>.

46 Agamben, *Homo sacer*, p. 19.

47 Juan Goytisolo, "From Netanya to Ramallah," at <http://www. autodafe.org> (my emphases).

48 For maps of curfew, during which movement is banned and Palestinian civilians are confined to their residences, see <http//www.reliefweb.int/ hic-opt/curf1.htm>. Since the start of the Al-Aqsa Intifada the "safe passage" between Gaza and the West Bank has been closed, and "absolute closure" – which prohibits all Palestinian travel between communities in "Area A" – has been imposed with increasing severity. The tightening of these restrictions has brought the Palestinian economy to the brink of destruction: see World Bank, "Fifteen months – Intifada, closures and Palestinian economic crisis," at <http://lnweb18.worldbank.org/mna/mena.nsf/Countries/West+Bank/67FB14AF 1F54168785256B85003C5F07?OpenDocument>, March 2002; UN General Assembly, "Economic and social repercussions of the Israeli occupation on the living conditions of the Palestinian people," May 2002 at <http:// www.reliefweb.int>; Salem Ajluni, "The Palestinian economy and the second

Intifada," Journal of Palestine Studies 32/3 (2003), pp. 64–73. By the end of 2001 the World Bank estimated that 40–50 percent of the Palestinian population had fallen below the poverty line, and by the end of 2002 this figure had soared to 60 percent. This is deliberate, punitive impoverishment of the mass of the population.

49 Hammami, "Interregnum"; Foundation for Middle East Peace, *Report on Israeli Settlement in the Occupied Territories*, 12/3 (May/June 2002), pp. 3–4. The remark radicalizes a common slogan of both right and left. The political platform of the extreme right Moledet ("Homeland" party) advocated the forcible transfer of Palestinians from the West Bank and Gaza – "We are here, they are there" – while in 1999 the Labour Party promised "Peace through partition: we are here, they are there." See Robert Blecher, "Living on the edge: the threat of 'transfer' in Israel and Palestine," *Middle East Report* 225 (Winter 2002). In March 2003 Israel introduced the same tactics in Gaza. "Israel for the first time has begun doing here what it has done since last summer in the West Bank: taking back territory ceded to Palestinian control under the Oslo accords": James Bennet, "Israelis step up Gaza intervention," *New York Times*, March 8, 2003.

50 Iris Jean-Klein, "Nationalism and resistance: the two faces of everyday activism in Palestine during the Intifada," *Cultural Anthropology* 16 (2001), pp. 83–126.

51 Mourid Barghouti, *I Saw Ramallah*, trans. Ahdaf Soueif (New York: Anchor, 2003; 1st pub. 1997), p. 26.

52 Adi Ophir, "A time of occupation," in Carey and Shainin (eds), *Other Israel*, pp. 51–66: 60 (my emphasis). "Since the outbreak of the al-Aqsa Intifada in October 2000, the theft of time and of any semblance of normal activity has reached undreamed of proportions": Amira Hass, "Israel's closure policy: an ineffective strategy of containment and repression," *Journal of Palestine Studies* 31/3 (2002), pp. 5–20: 10; see also id., "Indefinite siege" *Ha'aretz*, June 13, 2002.

53 Christian Salmon, "Palestine from near and far," at <http://www.autodafe.org>; see also his "Sabreen, or patience . . .": ibid.

54 B'Tselem, "Imprisonment of Illegal Combatants Law," at <http://www.btselem.org.english/Administrative_Detention/Hostageslaw.asp>, March 2002. Israel also has its own Guantánamo at "Camp 1391." This "non-place" has been erased from aerial photographs and maps; the cells have no windows, the detainees are blindfolded when they arrive, and they have no idea where they are. They are allowed neither legal advice nor visitors (including visitations by the International Red Cross), and they are subjected to brutal interrogation. See Aviv Lavie, "Inside Israel's secret prison," *Ha'aretz*, August 20, 2003.

55 Amnesty International, "Israel and the occupied territories: state assassination and other unlawful killings," at <http://www.amnesty.org>, February 2001;
   Palestinian Society for the Protection of Human Rights and the Environment,
   "Extra-judicial executions during the Al-Aqsa Intifada," March 2001, at <http://
   www.lawsociety.org/Reports/reports/2001/extrajud.html>; Chris Toensing
   and Ian Urbina, "Israel, the US and 'targeted killings'," *Middle East Report
   Online*, February 17, 2003; Aryeh Dayan, "One day in five, the IDF attempts
   assassination," *Ha'aretz*, May 21, 2003.

56 Amira Hass, "Always a fighter, always a terrorist," *Ha'aretz*, October 9, 2002.
   "The occupied are being told it is up to them to guarantee the peace and
   security of the occupiers": id., "Are the occupied protecting the occupier?",
   in Carey and Shainin (eds), *Other Israel*, pp. 162–4: 164. In wor(l)ds
   such as this the abuse of language marks – and masks – other abuses: see
   Paul de Rooij, "Glossary of occupation," *Counterpunch*, at <http://www.
   counterpunch.org/rooij/0912.html>, September 12, 2002.

57 Slavoj Žižek, *Welcome to the Desert of the Real! Five Essays on September
   11 and Related Dates* (London: Verso, 2002), p. 93.

58 Amira Hass, "The routine calamities that destroy lives," *Ha'aretz*, February
   26, 2003.

59 Adnan Abu Audah, "Israel launches conquest wars against Palestinians," at
   <http://www.albawaba.com>, April 28, 2002.

60 Salmon, "Palestine from near and far."

61 "The territory has been mutilated," Salmon (ibid.) observes. "We know that
   geography's primary purpose is to serve the needs of war. But in Palestine
   war is designed mostly to conquer geography." Here Salmon reverses the
   central claim of Yves Lacoste, *La Géographie, ça sert, d'abord, à faire la
   guerre* (Paris: Maspero, 1976). See also Salmon, "L'Abolition du territoire,"
   Le Monde Diplomatique, May 2002, also available as "The bulldozer war"
   at <http://www.counterpunch.org>, May 20, 2002. This is neither fanciful
   nor unprecedented. In his exemplary account of another space of colonial
   terror – the Putamayo in the upper Amazon – Michael Taussig describes
   how, in the early twentieth century, agents of the Peruvian Amazon Rubber
   Company, backed by British capital and a board of directors in London,
   identified "wild Indians" as creatures of a wild, tropical Nature that they feared
   would overwhelm them. The collapse of "culture" into "nature" is a commonplace of colonial discourse, but in this case it took an astonishingly violent
   form. Unable to beat back the rainforest through their network of trading-
   posts and encampments, the company's agents and overseers instead staged
   a spectacular theater of cruelty in which the local Huitotos were brutally
   sacrificed on the altar of their own abject terror: see Michael Taussig,
   Colonialism, Shamanism and the Wild Man: A Study in Terror and Healing

(Chicago: University of Chicago Press, 1987). One hundred years later, and armed with its hideously modern technology, the IDF has found a way to assault both "nature" and "culture" in Palestine, and produce what Oona King, writing from Gaza in the summer of 2003, called "a desecrated land": "Israel can halt this now," *Guardian*, June 12, 2003. It comes as no surprise to find that Sharon is known as "The Bulldozer."

62 Meron Benvenisti, "Systematically burying ourselves," *Ha'aretz*, January 18, 2002. In an earlier essay, Benvenisti deliberately turned the tables on Zionism's usual rhetoric and described the distance between the Israeli offices of those who authorize the demolition of Palestinian houses and the Israeli security forces who carry them out on the ground as the distance "separating civilization from barbarism." Here too, it seems, "civilization" produces its own barbarism (above, p. 282 n. 37). See id., "House demolitions continue under Barak government," *Ha'aretz*, October 28, 1999.

63 Yuli Tamar, "Protection in the territories," *Ha'aretz*, March 18, 2003; Samantha Shapiro, "The unsettlers," *New York Times Magazine*, February 16, 2003. Although several orders have been issued for the evacuation of those outposts that Israel concedes are illegal, the number of outposts increased from over 60 in May 2001 to over 90 in May 2003. To imply that most of these have a legal foundation – that there are only "anomalies in the field" – is yet again to suspend international law: Ze'ev Schiff, "Spreading a big lie," *Ha'aretz*, May 9, 2003.

64 Stephen Graham, "Clean territory: urbicide in the West Bank," at <http://www.opendemocracy.net>, August 7, 2002; id., "Bulldozers and bombs: the latest Palestinian–Israeli conflict as asymmetric urbicide," *Antipode* 34 (2002), pp. 642–9; id., "Lessons in urbicide"; see also Chris Smith, "Under the guise of security: house demolition in Gaza," *Middle East Report Press Information Notice* 63, July 13, 2001. Cf. Henri Lefebvre, *Le Droit à la ville* (Paris: Anthropos, 1968).

65 Serge Schlemann, "Attacks turn Palestinian plans into bent metal and piles of dust," *New York Times*, April 11, 2002 (my emphasis); see also Amira Hass, "Destruction and degradation," *Ha'aretz*, May 6, 2002; Anat Mahar, "The war to annihilate Palestinian civil society" at <http://electronicintifada.net>, December 29, 2002.

66 Jonathan Cook, "The bulldozer's mandate," *al-Ahram*, February 6–12, 2003.

67 The quotation comes from an e-mail message Rachel Corrie sent to her parents on February 27, 2003: "Rachel's war," *Guardian*, March 18, 2003. When she was killed on March 16, she was identified as an unarmed peace activist, standing in the path of the bulldozer and clearly visible to the driver: see Nigel Parry and Arjan El-Fassad, "Israeli bulldozer driver murders American peace activist," at <http://electronicintifada.net/v.2/article1248.shtml>, March 16, 2003.

68 Laurie King-Irani, "Of broken bodies and unbreakable laws," at <http://electronicintifada.net/v2/article1259.shtml>, March 19, 2003; Justin Podur, "Murdering solidarity," *Z-Net*, May 10, 2003; Elias Sanbar, "Is the war over?" at <http://www.autodafe.org/correspondence/chroniques/elias2.htm>, June 2002.

69 Mahmoud Darwish, "We have an incurable malady: hope," at <http://www.autodafe.org/correspondence>.

70 Agamben, *Homo sacer*, pp. 184–5. Here is part of Levi's description:

> Their life is short, but their number is endless; they, the *Muselmänner*, the drowned, form the backbone of the camp, an anonymous mass, continually renewed and always identical, of non-men who march and labour in silence, the divine spark dead within them, already too empty to really suffer. One hesitates to call them living: one hesitates to call their death death, in the face of which they have no fear, as they are too tired to understand. (Primo Levi, *If This Is a Man*, trans. Stuart Woolf (pbk. edn, London: Abacus, 1987), p. 96; 1st pub. in Italian, 1947)

Levi was an Italian Jew who was imprisoned in Auschwitz in 1944. The *Muselmann* is produced through the production of "a space empty of people," Agamben explains, which is to say a biopolitical intensity "that can persist in every space and through which peoples pass into populations and populations pass into *Muselmänner*": see his *Remnants of Auschwitz: The Witness and the Archive*, trans. Daniel Heller-Roazen (New York: Zone, 1999), pp. 84–5. At the height of the Israeli siege of Palestinian towns and villages in 2002, Barghouti, *Ramallah*, p. 59, realized "how blurred the distinction has become between conditions for the living and the dead."

71 Sara Roy, "Living with the Holocaust: the journey of a child of Holocaust survivors," *Journal of Palestine Studies* 32/2 (2002), pp. 5–12. For a wonderfully lucid discussion of the distinction between criticism of the state of Israel and anti-Semitism, see Judith Butler, "No, it's not anti-Semitic," *London Review of Books*, August 21, 2003. "It is one thing to oppose Israel in its current form and practice," she writes, but "quite another to oppose 'Jews' or assume that all 'Jews' have the same view, that they are all in favour of Israel, identified with Israel or represented by Israel."

72 Graham, "Lessons in urbicide," p. 75; Blecher, "Living on the edge"; Amir Oren, "At the gates of Yassergrad," *Ha'aretz*, January 25, 2002; Ari Shavit, "Dear God, this is Effi," *Ha'aretz*, March 24, 2002; Akiva Eldar, "A Nazi by any other name," *Ha'aretz*, April 4, 2002. For an artful reversal of the Warsaw/West Bank comparison, that identifies the resistance of the Jewish population to the Wehrmacht during the Warsaw Ghetto uprising with the resistance

of the Palestinian population to the Israeli occupation, see Sherri Muzher, "From Warsaw to the West Bank," at <http://www.ramallahonline.com>, March 12, 2003.

73 Jayussi, "Letters from the ghetto," pp. 49–50. Cf. Agamben, *Homo sacer*, p. 174: "If the essence of the camp consists in the materialization of the state of exception and in the subsequent creation of a space in which bare life and the juridical rule enter into a threshold of indistinction, then we must admit that we find ourselves virtually in the presence of a camp every time such a structure is created." The gap between life in Palestinian cities (most of all in East Jerusalem) and life in the cramped alleyways and cinder-block homes of the camps has narrowed dramatically: see, for example, James Bennet, "Dim dreams and life in Nablus," *New York Times*, December 29, 2002; Amira Hass, "Breeding grounds of despair and fatigue," *Ha'aretz*, December 30, 2002.

74 Barghouti, *Ramallah*, p. 13.

75 Ibid., p. 157; id., "War butlers and their language," at <http://www.autodafe.org/autodafe_03/art_07.htm>, November 2002.

76 Id., *Ramallah*, pp. 61–2. Cf. Edward Said, *After the Last Sky: Palestinian Lives* (New York: Pantheon Books, 1986). There is no more poignant sentence in that book than this one: "I cannot reach the actual people who were photographed, except through a European photographer [Jean Mohr] who saw them for me" (p. 14). For a detailed discussion, see Derek Gregory, "Imaginative geographies," *Progress in Human Geography* 19 (1995), pp. 447–85.

77 B'Tselem, the Israeli Information Center for Human Rights in the Occupied Territories, "Fatalities in the al-Aqsa Intifada, September 29, 2000–December 28, 2002," at <http://www.btselem.org/English/Statistics/Al_Aqsa_Fatalities.asp>. Over the same period B'Tselem estimates that 171 Israeli civilians had been killed by Palestinians in the occupied territories and a further 272 within Israel; 141 members of the IDF had been killed in the occupied territories and a further 63 within Israel.

78 Achille Mbembe, "Necropolitics," *Public Culture* 15 (2003), pp. 11–40. Where Mbembe speaks of "necropolitics" Agamben, *Homo sacer*, p. 122, speaks of "thanatopolitics," but the terminus is much the same.

79 Edward Said, "Archaeology of the roadmap," *al-Ahram*, June 12–18, 2003; id., "A road map to where?," *London Review of Books*, June 19, 2003.

80 Darwish, "Incurable malady"; Graham Usher, "Facing defeat: the *Intifada* two years on," *Journal of Palestine Studies* 32/2 (2003), pp. 21–40.

81 Edward Said, "Thoughts about America," *Al-Ahram*, February 28–March 6, 2002. Noam Chomsky, *Pirates and Emperors, Old and New* (London: Pluto, 2002), similarly and symmetrically refers to the struggle over the occupied territories as the "US/Israel–Palestine conflict" (pp. 160–80).

82   P. Mitchell Prothero, "Hard-line Israeli supporters boo Wolfowitz," *Washington Times*, April 15, 2002; Steve Twomey, "Thousands rally for Israel," *Washington Post*, April 16, 2002.

83   "Congress shows support for Israel," at <http://www.cbsnews.com/stories/2002/05/02>.

84   See, for example, Anthony Shadid, *Legacy of the Prophet: Despots, Democrats and the New Politics Of Islam* (Boulder, CO: Westview Press, 2002), pp. 110–26.

85   Benjamin Netanyahu, "Terrorism: how the West can win," in id. (ed.), *Terrorism: How the West can Win* (New York: Farrar, Straus & Giroux, 1986), pp. 199–226: 204. In his "Defining terrorism," ibid., pp. 7–15, Netanyahu also attributes terrorism to "the political ambitions and designs of expansionist states," and notes that terrorists erode "the crucial distinction between combatant and non-combatant" and "often engage in assassination of a society's leaders": he does not of course recognize that these three claims apply *a fortiori* to the massacres at Sabra and Shatila refugee camps in the Lebanon and to Israel's attacks on the occupied territories.

86   Bradley Burton, "Occupation now, occupation forever," *Ha'aretz*, August 7, 2002.

87   Edward Said, "Punishment by detail," *Al-Ahram*, August 6–14, 2002.

88   Amira Hass, "Operation destroy the data," *Ha'aretz*, April 24, 2002.

89   Jonathan Freedland, "For Israelis – and Jews – fear is now international," *Guardian*, November 29, 2002; James Bennet, "Fight against terror: two conflicts or one?," *New York Times*, November 29, 2002.

90   Jason Burke, "Terror's myriad faces," *Observer*, May 18, 2003.

91   Jonathan Freedland, "Parallel universes," *Guardian*, April 17, 2002.

Chapter 7: The Tyranny of Strangers

1   Tom Sleigh, *The Chain* (Chicago: University of Chicago Press, 1996).

2   Jonathan Raban, "The greatest gulf," *Guardian*, April 19, 2003.

3   Charles Tripp, "The imperial precedent," *Le Monde Diplomatique*, January 2003; Gary Yonge, "The limits of generosity," *Guardian*, April 7, 2003.

4   Marian Kent, *Oil and Empire: British Policy and Mesopotamian Oil* (London: Macmillan, 1976).

5   *Harper's Magazine* (May 2003), p. 31.

6   Helmut Mejcher, *Imperial Quest for Oil: Iraq 1910–1928* (London: Ithaca Press, 1976), pp. 35–42.

7   Sandra Mackey, *The Reckoning: Iraq and the Legacy of Saddam Hussein* (New York: Norton, 2002), p. 107; cf. above, p. 80.

8   Toby Dodge, *Inventing Iraq: The Failure of Nation-Building and a History Denied* (New York: Columbia University Press, 2003); Charles Tripp, *A History of Iraq* (Cambridge: Cambridge University Press, 2002), p. 41.

9   Peter Sluglett, *Britain in Iraq 1914–1932* (London: Ithaca Press, 1976); David Omissi, *Air Power and Colonial Control: The Royal Air Force, 1919–1939* (Manchester: Manchester University Press, 1990); id., "Baghdad and British bombers," *Guardian*, January 19, 1991. Among the fiercest critics of Britain's repressive regime in Mesopotamia was T. E. Lawrence. Britain had claimed that the aim of its occupation was "to deliver the Arabs from the oppression of the Turkish Government," but in practice Mesopotamia was ruled by a dangerously independent colonial administration "from the empty space which divides the Foreign Office from the India Office" and which contested "every suggestion of real self-government." "How long will we permit millions of pounds, thousands of Imperial troops, and tens of thousands of Arabs to be sacrificed," he demanded, "on behalf of colonial administration which can benefit nobody but its administrators?" T. E. Lawrence, "A report on Mesopotamia," *Sunday Times*, August 22, 1920.

10   Martin Gilbert, *Winston Churchill*, vol. 4: *The Stricken Years, 1917–1922* (London: Heinemann, 1975), p. 496.

11   "The term *al-Iraq* (meaning the shore of a great river along its length, as well as the grazing land surrounding it) had been used since at least the eighth century by Arab geographers to refer to the great alluvial plain of the Tigris and Euphrates Rivers": Tripp, *History of Iraq*, p. 8.

12   Omissi, "Baghdad." The officer was Arthur "Bomber" Harris, who was later to be in charge of the firebombing of German cities carried out by RAF Bomber Command between 1942 and 1945.

13   Gertrude Bell, letter from Baghdad, July 2, 1924.

14   Peter Sluglett, "Iraq, Britain and the United States: new perspectives, old problems," at <http://www.opendemocracy.net>, June 2003. As Sluglett shows elsewhere, the (ab)use of air power in this way drew stringent criticism in both the British press and Parliament. Labour's George Lansbury denounced it as a "barbarous method of warfare against unarmed people," and even the Foreign Secretary, Lord Curzon, was not persuaded that it was appropriate: see Sluglett, *Britain in Iraq*, pp. 262–70. None the less, the use of air power as a means of asserting colonial control was institutionalized between 1923 and 1932 and, consistent with the colonial model, it was a modality of power that could neither explain nor negotiate: Dodge, *Inventing Iraq*, p. 156.

15   Sluglett, *Britain in Iraq*, pp. 103–25.

16   Mackey, *The Reckoning*, p. 116. British colonialism thus perpetuated the power of the *ancien régime* and marginalized the emergent middle class: Keith Watenpaugh, "The *Guiding Principles* and the US 'Mandate' for Iraq:

twentieth-century colonialism and America's new empire," *Logos* 2/1 (2003), pp. 26–37.

17 Freya Stark, *Beyond Euphrates: Autobiography 1928–1933* (London 1951); letter from Baghdad, January 1930.

18 John Blair, *The Control of Oil* (New York: Pantheon, 1976), pp. 31–9; Benjamin Shwadran, *The Middle East, Oil and the Great Powers* (New York: Wiley, 1973), pp. 202–7, 225–6, 237–40.

19 Freya Stark, *Baghdad Sketches* (Evanston: Northwestern University Press, 1996; 1st pub. 1938), p. 123. The Kuwait Oil Company had been established in 1934 as a joint venture between the Anglo-Persian Oil Company (which 20 years later became British Petroleum) and Gulf Oil Corporation. See Shwadran, *Middle East*, pp. 407–12.

20 Mackey, *The Reckoning*, pp. 172–185, 273–4; Tripp, *History of Iraq*, pp. 163–7. The first OPEC conference was attended by Iraq, Iran, Kuwait, Saudi Arabia, and Venezuela.

21 Fred Halliday, *Islam and the Myth of Confrontation* (London: I. B. Tauris, 2003), p. 84.

22 Dilip Hiro, *Iraq: In the Eye of the Storm* (New York: Nation Books, 2002), pp. 25–6; Hanna Batatu, *The Old Social Classes and the Revolutionary Movements of Iraq* (Princeton: Princeton University Press, 1978).

23 There were two main foci of Shi'a opposition: al-Dawah al-Islamiyah, which called for an Islamic government in an independent Iraq, and al-Mujaheddin, which sought a universal Islamic state under the religious authority of the Ayatollah Khomeini: Mackay, *The Reckoning*, pp. 247–8.

24 Lawrence Freedman and Efraim Karsh, *The Gulf Conflict 1990–1991: Diplomacy and War in the New World Order* (Princeton, NJ: Princeton University Press, 1993), pp. 19–21; Tripp, *History of Iraq*, p. 232; Mackey, *The Reckoning*, pp. 241–52.

25 Hiro, *Iraq*, pp. 28–33; id., *The Longest War: the Iran–Iraq Conflict* (London: Routledge, 1991), pp. 71–2; John Bulloch and Harvey Morris, *Saddam's War: The Origins of the Kuwait Conflict and the International Response* (London: Faber & Faber, 1991), p. 6. Freedman and Karsh, *Gulf Conflict*, persistently describe Saddam's foreign policy throughout the 1970s as moderate and pragmatic.

26 These had been suspended since the Arab–Israeli war of 1967.

27 The military aid to the Contras violated a Congressional ban. Reagan's vice-president, George H. W. Bush, became president in January 1989, and in December 1992 he pardoned all six principals in the affair who had been convicted of criminal wrongdoing.

28 This paragraph relies on Michael Dobbs, "U.S. had key role in Iraq build-up," *Washington Post*, December 30, 2002; Gabriel Kalko, *Another Century*

of War? (New York: The New Press, 2002), p. 35; Tripp, *History of Iraq*,
p. 345; Hiro, *Iraq*, p. 30; Freedman and Karsh, *Gulf Conflict*, pp. 25–8;
Research Unit for Political Economy, *Behind the Invasion of Iraq* (New York:
Monthly Review Press, 2003), pp. 30–4; David Campbell, *Politics without
Principle: Sovereignty, Ethics and the Narratives of the Gulf War* (Boulder,
CO and London: Lynne Rienner Publishers, 1993), pp. 34–42; Hiro,
Longest War; Stephen Shalom, *Imperial Alibis* (Boston: South End Press, 1993).
On the use of chemical weapons, see also Javed Ali, "Chemical weapons and
the Iran–Iraq war: a case study in noncompliance," *Nonproliferation Review*
(Spring 2001), pp. 43–58; Patrick Tyler, "Officials say US aided Iraq in war
despite use of gas," *New York Times*, August 18, 2002; Joost Hiltermann,
"The men who helped the man who gassed his own people," in Micah Sifry
and Christopher Cerf (eds), *The Iraq War Reader* (New York: Touchstone,
2003), pp. 41–4. It should be noted that the US was not alone in its Iraqi
predispositions: Britain, France, Germany, and the Soviet Union were also all
actively involved in seeking to contain Iran by enhancing Iraq's war economy.
In Britain, the Scott inquiry (1996) concluded that successive Conservative
governments – under Margaret Thatcher and John Major – had approved
arms sales to Iraq in the 1980s and 1990s, but repeatedly and deliberately
denied doing so when questioned. Ministers were even prepared to allow
HM Customs and Excise to prosecute senior executives of Matrix Churchill
for breaking export restrictions rather than allow their own complicity to be
revealed. Lines of credit were also extended to enable private companies to
supply Iraq with machine tools for the manufacture of missiles and shells,
military radios and radar equipment, and sodium cyanide and sodium sulfide
for use in chemical weapons. See Richard Norton-Taylor, *Truth is a Difficult
Concept: Inside the Scott Inquiry* (London: Fourth Estate, 1995); David Leigh,
Rob Evans, "How £1 bn was lost when Thatcher propped up Saddam,"
Guardian, February 28, 2003.

29 Mackey, *The Reckoning*, p. 252.
30 Joel Stork and Ann Lesch, "Why war?," *Middle East Report* 167 (November–
December 1990), pp. 11–18.
31 Tripp, *History of Iraq*, p. 252; Freedman and Karsh, *Gulf Conflict*, pp. 89–90,
92–3; Bulloch and Morris, *Saddam's War*, p. 139. In 1983 the Pentagon transformed the Rapid Deployment Joint Task Force that had been established
by the Carter administration into a permanent, unified command, "Central
Command," whose area of responsibility extended from the Horn of Africa
through the Middle East and the Arabian peninsula to central and south Asia.
Its creation was described as "a practical solution to the problem of projecting
US military power to the Gulf region from halfway round the world," and
its area of operations identified as "the area where US interests are most likely
to be threatened." See <http://www.centcom.mil>.

32 Joel Stork and Martha Wenger, "From rapid deployment to massive deploy-
    ment," *Middle East Report* 168 (January–February 1991), pp. 22–6: 23.

33 Paul Aarts and Michael Renner, "Oil and the Gulf War," *Middle East
    Report* 171 (1991), pp. 25–9, 47; Timothy Mitchell, "McJihad: Islam in the
    US global order," *Social Text* 73 (2002), pp. 1–18; Yahya Sadowski, "No
    war for whose oil?," *Le Monde Diplomatique*, April 3, 2003. The price of
    crude shot up from $22 to $30 a barrel overnight on news of the Iraqi inva-
    sion of Kuwait; the market only "settled" when Saudi Arabia and other Gulf
    states agreed to meet the shortfall imposed by the embargo on Iraqi and Kuwait
    crude: Bulloch and Morris, *Saddam's War*, p. 66.

34 Gilles Kepel, *Jihad: The Trail of Political Islam* (Cambridge, MA: Harvard
    University Press, 2002), p. 206; see above, p. 38. King Fahd was plainly
    sensitive to the presence of US troops on Saudi soil. It was more than a week
    after the invasion before he addressed his nation on state television, and even
    then he elected for circumlocution: "The kingdom of Saudi Arabia expressed
    its desire for the participation of sister Arab forces and other friends." See
    Bulloch and Morris, *Saddam's War*, pp. 167–8.

35 Cf. Norman Finkelstein, "A double standard in the application of inter-
    national law," in his *The Rise and Fall of Palestine* (Minneapolis: University
    of Minnesota Press, 1996), pp. 44–57.

36 Gearóid Ó'Tuathail, "The effacement of place: US foreign policy and the
    spatiality of the Gulf Crisis," *Antipode* 25 (1993), pp. 4–31. Similarly,
    David Campbell notes that Bush's imagery also reactivated "the myth of the
    frontier, in which territorial space becomes intertwined with ethical identity
    such that the fluid boundary and persistent struggles between "civilization"
    and "barbarism" is rendered in terms of geopolitical conflict": *Politics with-
    out Principle*, p. 22.

37 Freedman and Karsh, *Gulf Conflict*, pp. 167–8; transcripts of President
    Bush's speeches are available at <http://bushlibrary.tamu.edu>.

38 Jean Heller, "Public doesn't get picture with Gulf satellite photos," *St
    Petersburg Times*, January 6, 1991. Not surprisingly, the Pentagon's own
    "photographs" are still classified.

39 Campbell, *Politics without Principle*, p. 26; Philip Golub, "United States: invent-
    ing demons," *Le Monde Diplomatique*, March 3, 2003; my emphasis.
    Campbell also argues that territorial boundaries were substituted for moral
    boundaries as a way of giving "the geography of evil" shape and substance.
    State sovereignty and territorial integrity were not absolutes – the US had been
    complicit in both the Soviet invasion of Afghanistan (above, p. 35) and the
    Iraqi invasion of Iran (above, p. 154) – but instead were invoked selectively
    and strategically. "The performative constitution of a complex array of
    boundaries (both ethical and territorial) designed to secure the identity and
    purpose of the United States and its allies was one of the major effects of the

war" (p. 80). See also Phyllis Benn, " 'And they called it peace': US policy on Iraq," *Middle East Report* 215 (2000). After the formal end of the war, General Colin Powell, chairman of the Joint Chiefs of Staff, complained: "I'm running out of demons, I'm running out of villains."

40 Campbell, *Politics without Principle*, pp. 64–5; Jack Calhoun, "How Bush Backed Iraq," *Middle East Report* 176 (1992), pp. 35–7. I say "again" because, as Reagan's vice-president, Bush had intervened on several occasions during the Iran–Iraq war to secure continuing credit for Iraq from the Export-Import Bank despite the bank's own doubts about the viability of the loans.

41 Charles Krauthammer, "The crescent of crisis: global intifada," *Washington Post*, February 16, 1990; see also Joe Stork, "New enemies for a new world order: from arc of crisis to global intifada," *Middle East Report* 176 (1992), pp. 28–34.

42 James Sidaway, "What is in a Gulf? From the 'arc of crisis' to the Gulf War," in Gearóid Ó'Tuathail and Simon Dalby (eds), *Rethinking Geopolitics* (London: Routledge, 1998), pp. 224–39. On Orientalist excess see, for example, Paul William Roberts, who repeats rumors of an island in the Tigris "where a cabal of senior government and military personnel regularly staged Dionysian revels [regularly attended by Saddam], wildly extravagant parties for young boys and older men at which blind musicians were hired to be heard but not see what went on . . . [as] people were brutally murdered during acts of sadistic sex." See his *The Demonic Comedy: Some Detours in the Baghdad of Saddam Hussein* (Toronto: Stoddart, 1997), p. 75.

43 Ella Shohat and Robert Stam, *Unthinking Eurocentrism: Multiculturalism and the Media* (New York: Routledge, 1994), p. 128; see also Susan Jeffords, "Rape and the new world order," *Cultural Critique* 19 (1991), pp. 203–15.

44 Maggie O'Kane, "Bloodless words, bloody war," *Guardian*, December 16, 1995.

45 Robert Stam, "Mobilizing fictions: the Gulf War, the media and the recruitment of the spectator," *Public Culture* 4 (1992), pp. 101–26; Paul Virilio, *Desert Screen: War at the Speed of Light* (London: Continuum, 2002), p. 42. These general arguments ought not to blind us to the ways in which the meanings of the Gulf War were produced through contestation and elaboration among differently situated subjects and within multiple public spheres: see Robert Hanke, "The first casualty," *Public* 6 (1992), pp. 135–40.

46 Ó'Tuathail, "Effacement of place." What Susan Sontag calls the "breathtaking provincialism" of this conceit needs emphasis: it maps a zone whose privileged inhabitants have the power of agreeing or declining to become spectators of other people's suffering: see her "Looking at war: photography's view of devastation and death," *New Yorker*, December 9, 2002; Sontag, *Regarding the Pain of Others* (New York: Farrar, Straus & Giroux, 2003), pp. 110–11. On the hyperreality of the Gulf War, see Jean Baudrillard, *The Gulf War Did Not Take Place* (Indianapolis: Indiana University Press, 1995); these essays

were originally published in *Libération* in 1990–1. The title is not the cruel, absurdist fantasy that many critics assumed it to be – it presumably alludes to Giradoux's *La Guerre de Troie n'aurait pas lieu* – and Baudrillard's argument was an eminently serious one. His point was double-headed: the "Gulf War" was not a war but a desperately one-sided annihilation of one side by the other; its American and European audience was persuaded otherwise by the mediatization – the "electronic spatiality" – of military violence.

47 Roberts, *Demonic Comedy*, pp. 188–9, 192–3; the verse is from the Koran. Charles Krauthammer would have no truck with any of this. "Saddam's strategy is one the Palestinians have perfected over the last decade: Provoke a fight, lose the fight, pile up the bodies and invite the press": "Bombing Baghdad: no cause for guilt," *Washington Post*, February 14, 1991.

48 Patrick Sloyam, "What bodies?," in Sifry and Cerf (eds), *Iraq War Reader*, pp. 129–34. I have cited these passages because they reveal another dimension of dehumanization. It is not just Iraqi troops who are made to disappear from view; so too, rhetorically, do American troops. The killing and burying is made to appear the work of machines – tanks, Bradley fighting vehicles, and Armored Combat Earthmovers – not men. The actions themselves were carried out under the circular sign of an Orientalism that Margot Norris glosses thus: "We Westerners count our dead because we cherish human life; you Orientals hold human life cheap, therefore we may bury you uncounted in ditches": "Military censorship and the body count in the Persian Gulf War," *Cultural Critique* (1991), pp. 223–45: 240.

49 Research Unit for Political Economy, *Behind the Invasion*, p. 41.

50 In the circumstances, however, "Snake" seems a perfectly appropriate nickname.

51 These details are taken from the summaries in Freedman and Kirsh, *Gulf Conflict*, p. 403; Hiro, *Iraq*, pp. 38–9; William Arkin, Damian Durrant, and Marianne Cherni, *On Impact: Modern Warfare and the Environment: A Case Study of the Gulf War* (Washington DC: Greenpeace, 1991), pp. 107–13, available at <http://www.greenpeace.org/international_en/reports/more-reports?campaign_id=135736>. There were other horror stories, none more disturbing than those documented in Seymour Hersh, "Overwhelming force," *New Yorker*, May 22, 2000, pp. 49–82. On March 2, two days into the ceasefire, Major-General Barry McCaffrey ordered units of his 24th Infantry Division into the path of an Iraqi column that was complying with the requirements of the retreat, its tanks traveling with their cannons reversed and locked, heading toward a safe passage over the causeway at Rumailia; he ordered attack helicopters to cut the head of the column, and then set about the systematic destruction of tanks, trucks, and troops.

52 Robert Fisk, "Does Tony Blair have any idea what the flies are like that feed off the dead?," *Independent*, January 26, 2003. In an equally powerful commentary, John Pilger recalled that "nocturnal images of American bulldozers burying thousands of teenage Iraqi conscripts, many of them alive

and trying to surrender, were never shown." Suppressions like these, he argued, worked to normalize the unthinkable: John Pilger, "The unthinkable is becoming normal. Do not forget the horror," *Independent*, April 20, 2003. Cf. Sontag, "Looking at war", and ead., *Regarding the Pain of Others* (New York: Farrar, Straus & Giroux, 2003). See also Norris, "Military censorship," and id., "Only the guns have eyes," in Susan Jeffords and Lauren Rabinowitz (eds), *Seeing through the Media: The Persian Gulf War* (New Brunswick, NJ: Rutgers University Press, 1994), pp. 234–74.

53 Maggie O'Kane, "Bloodless words"; cf. Gearóid Ó'Tuathail, "An anti-geopolitical eye: Maggie O'Kane in Bosnia, 1992–93," *Gender, Place and Culture* 3 (1996), pp. 171–85. Not surprisingly, the memories still haunted her on the eve of renewed war in 2003: Maggie O'Kane, "The most pitiful sight I have ever seen," *Guardian*, February 14, 2003. Refusing these connections is also refusing to acknowledge that the "suturing of American families" on the safe return of the troops is produced through "the splintering of Iraqi families": Donna Przybylowicz and Abdul Jan Mohammed, "The economy of moral capital in the Gulf War," *Cultural Critique* 19 (1991), pp. 5–14.

54 Articles 15–17 of the Geneva Conventions for the amelioration of the condition of the wounded and sick in armed forces in the field (October 1950); see also Norris, "Military censorship," p. 242.

55 Arkin, Durrant, and Cherni, *On Impact*; Human Rights Watch, "Needless deaths in the Gulf War: civilian casualties during the air campaign and violations of the laws of war," at < http://www.org/reports/1991/gulfwar>. For an incisive critique of "Needless deaths" see Finkelstein, "A double standard," appendix 1, pp. 57–65; I have taken these objections into account in my own use of the report. For another study, see Beth Daponte, "A case study in estimating casualties from war and its aftermath: the 1991 Persian Gulf War," *PSR Quarterly* 3 (1993), pp. 57–76, which confirmed that the majority of Iraqi civilian casualties occurred after the formal end of hostilities: 3,500 during the air and ground wars, 35,000 during the post-war rebellions and 110,000 from "war-induced adverse health effects."

56 Felicity Arbuthnot, "Allies deliberately poisoned Iraq public water supply in Gulf War," *Sunday Herald*, September 17, 2000; Abu Spinoza, "War crimes, US planners and Iraq's water vulnerability," *Z Magazine*, June 3, 2003. These reports are based on the work of Professor Thomas Nagy of George Washington University.

57 "Needless deaths."

58 Faleh Abd al-Jabbar, "Why the uprisings failed," *Middle East Report* 176 (1992), pp. 2–14; Martin Walker, Simon Tisdall, Jane Rosen, David Fairhall, and Hella Pick, "Bush rejects peace 'hoax,' " *Guardian*, February 16, 1991; Editorial, "No help for the people," *Guardian*, March 8, 1991; *Overview of Human Rights Developments: Iraq and Occupied Kuwait* (Washington, DC:

Human Rights Watch, 1991); *Endless Torment: The 1991 Uprising in Iraq and its Aftermath* (Washington, DC: Human Rights Watch, 1992); Hiro, *Iraq*, pp. 40–6; Mackey, *The Reckoning*, pp. 286–98; Tripp, *History of Iraq*, pp. 256–7. In August 1992 the US and UK declared a second "no-fly zone" in the south to protect the Sh'ia.

59 Sarah Graham-Brown, *Sanctioning Saddam: The Politics of Intervention in Iraq* (London and New York: I. B. Tauris, 1999), pp. 27–9, 108–11; Thomas Ricks, "Containing Iraq: a forgotten war," *Washington Post*, October 25, 2000; Sarah Graham-Brown, "No fly-zones: rhetoric and real intentions," *Middle East Report*, February 20, 2001; John Pilger, "Britain and America's pilots are blowing the cover on so-called 'humanitarian' no-fly zones," *New Statesman*, March 19, 2001; Jon Lee Anderson, "No place to hide," *New Yorker*, November 25, 2002; Stephen Zunes, "The abuse of the no-fly zones as an excuse for war," *Foreign Policy in Focus*, December 6, 2002; Peter Clark, "The Iraqi Marshlands: a pre-war perspective," Crimes of War Project at <http://www.crimesofwar.org>, March 7, 2003.

60 This was a viciously cynical attack that was deliberately timed to coincide with – and hence delay – the vote in Congress on the impeachment of President Clinton: see Hiro, *Iraq*, pp. 120–31.

61 Edward Cody, "Under Iraqi skies, a canvas of death," *Washington Post*, June 16, 2000.

62 Tariq Ali, "An ocean of terror," in his *The Clash of Fundamentalisms: Crusades, Jihads and Modernity* (London: Verso, 2002), pp. 141–53; James Sidaway, "Iraq/Yugoslavia: banal geopolitics," *Antipode* 33 (2001), pp. 601–9; Nuha al-Radi, *Baghdad Diaries: A Woman's Chronicle of War and Exile* (New York: Vintage, 2003), p. 194.

63 Robert Fisk, "Dusty farm ditches and trenches in the tomato plantations are still killing fields," *Independent*, March 4, 1998; id., "The catastrophe Blair, Clinton and Saddam have in common," *Independent*, March 9, 1998; id., "The West's poisonous legacy," *Independent*, May 28, 1998; Andy Kershaw, "US depleted uranium yields chamber of horrors in southern Iraq," *Independent*, April 12, 2001; Norman Solomon, Reese Erlich, *Target Iraq* (New York: Context Books, 2003), pp. 57–66; Scott Taylor, "The weapons we gave Iraq," *Globe and Mail*, February 17, 2003. At the UN Human Rights Conference in August 2002 only two states voted against a motion banning the use of DU munitions: the USA and the UK.

64 This was – and remains – a noble goal, but neither the US nor the UN has acted against the state of Israel for its possession of nuclear, chemical, and biological weapons.

65 See Hiro, *Iraq*, pp. 95–136.

66 "Guide to sanctions" (Cambridge UK: Campaign Against Sanctions on Iraq) at <http://www.casi.org.uk>; see also Sarah Zaidi, "War, sanctions and humanitarian assistance: the case of Iraq 1990–1993," *Medicine and Global*

Survival 1 (1994), pp. 147–55; Sarah Graham-Brown, "Intervention, sovereignty and responsibility," *Middle East Report* 193 (1995), pp. 2–12, 32; ead., *Sanctioning Saddam*, pp. 73–8.

67 Roberts, *Demonic Comedy*, p. 215.

68 Ibid., p. 235.

69 Wadood Hamad, "Iraq, sanctions and the ongoing tragedy," *Logos* 1/2 (2002), pp. 31–41. Albright subsequently admitted that this "was a genuinely stupid thing to say": David Rieff, "Were sanctions right?", *New York Times*, July 27, 2003.

70 Alain Gresh, "Iraq's silent agony," *Le Monde Diplomatique*, July 8, 1991; Geoff Simons, *The Scourging of Iraq* (New York: Routledge, 1998); Graham-Brown, *Sanctioning Saddam*; Anthony Arnove (ed.), *Iraq Under Siege* (Cambridge, MA: South End Press, 2002); Joy Gordon, "Cool war: economic sanctions as a weapon of mass destruction," *Harper's Magazine* (November 2002); Rahul Mahajan, *Full Spectrum Dominance: US Power in Iraq and Beyond* (New York: Seven Stories Press, 2003), pp. 96–106.

71 David Cortright, "A hard look at Iraq sanctions," *The Nation*, November 19, 2001; Mohamed Ali and Iqbal Shah, "Sanctions and childhood mortality in Iraq," *The Lancet* 355 (2000), pp. 1851–7.

72 Isam al-Khafaji, "State terror and the degradation of politics in Iraq," *Middle East Report* 176 (1992), pp. 15–21; Graham-Brown, "Intervention"; "Guide to sanctions" (my emphasis). Graham-Brown quotes an aid worker who makes the same sharp point: "We break their legs and give them crutches" (p. 7).

73 Rieff, "Were sanctions right?"

74 See Denis Halliday, "The impact of UN sanctions on the people of Iraq," *Journal of Palestine Studies* 28/2 (1999), pp. 29–51; id., "Time to see the truth about ourselves and Iraq," *Guardian*, August 2, 2000. Halliday was not the last coordinator of humanitarian aid to resign for these reasons; his successor, Hans von Sponeck, resigned in February 2000.

75 Hiro, *Iraq*, pp. 89–90; Editorial, "Fantasies about Iraq," *New York Times*, October 20, 1998; Randeep Ramesh, *The War We Could Not Stop* (London: Faber & Faber, 2003), pp. 14–15.

Chapter 8: Boundless War

1 President's remarks at the United Nations General Assembly, September 12, 2002 at <http://www.whitehouse.gov/news/releases/2002/09/20020912-1html>.

2 These objectives were specifically linked to Iraqi disarmament in UN Security Council Resolution 687 (see above, p. 173).

3   See chapter 6 above.

4   In the last 30 years the United States has vetoed 34 resolutions criticizing Israel: Henry Porter, "One US rule for Israel, another for Saddam," *Guardian*, February 16, 2003.

5   Perry Anderson, "Casuistries of war and peace," *London Review of Books*, March 6, 2003. Such arguments also need to address the non-democratic constitution of the United Nations itself and the extraordinary powers granted to the permanent members of the Security Council.

6   See Dilip Hiro, *Iraq: In the Eye of the Storm* (New York: Nation Books, 2002), pp. 99–124, 249–50.

7   The stream of reports turned into a torrent and then a flood. For concise summaries, see Raymond Whitaker, "How the road to war was paved with lies," *Independent*, April 27, 2003; Spencer Ackerman and John Judis, "The first casualty," *The New Republic*, June 30, 2003. These allegations were not limited to the dossier produced by the British government in September 2002 to underwrite its case for war, and they were not answered by the 740-page Hutton Report which, as Andrew Grice noted, for all its length "failed to settle the crucial question of whether Mr Blair took Britain to war on a false prospectus." Other commentators were more forthright (and with every reason). Seamus Milne described the report as "comically tendentious" and spectacularly one-sided, and Jonathan Freedland – like many others – dismissed it as a whitewash. See Andrew Grice, "Demands grow for inquiry into the case for war, as Hutton is accused of a 'whitewash,'" *Independent*, January 29, 2004; Seumas Milne, "The shadow of Iraq," *Guardian*, January 29, 2004; Jonathan Freedland, "If it went to the West End they'd call it Whitewash," *Guardian,* January 29, 2004.

8   In the immediate aftermath of the war, there were endless reports of discoveries of WMD sites, each one then quietly denied. Paul Krugman suggested that most Americans probably believed that WMDs had been found:

> Each potential find gets blaring coverage on TV; how many people catch the later announcement – if it ever is announced – that it was a false alarm? It's a pattern of misinformation that recapitulates the way the war was sold in the first place. Each administration charge against Iraq received prominent coverage; the subsequent debunking did not. (Paul Krugman, "Matters of emphasis," *New York Times*, April 29, 2003)

See also Nicholas Kristof, "Missing In Action: Truth," *New York Times*, May 6, 2003. An elite Special Forces unit, Task Force 20 from Delta Force, staged crucial raids ahead of the coalition ground advance – before key sites could be stripped or, for that matter, looted – but found "no working nonconventional munitions, long-range missiles or missile parts, bulk stores of chemical or biological warfare agents or enrichment technology for the core of a nuclear weapon." By May, some senior US officials were conceding that it was unlikely that weapons-grade plutonium or uranium or large stockpiles of biological or chemical munitions would be found, and the 75th Exploitation Task Force – biologists, chemists, arms treaty enforcers, nuclear weapons specialists, and computer and document experts – charged with overseeing the search was being wound down; the nuclear special operations group, the Direct Support Team from the Defense Threat Reduction Agency, had already scaled back its staff by one-third.

> They expected to find what Secretary of State Colin Powell described at the UN Security Council on February 5 – hundreds of tons of biological and chemical agents, missiles and rockets to deliver the agents, and evidence of an ongoing programme to build a nuclear bomb. Scores of fruitless missions broke that confidence, many task force members said in interviews . . . They consistently found targets identified by Washington to be inaccurate, looted and burned, or both.

In October 2003 David Kay, the leader of the Iraq Survey Group, testified before congressional intelligence committees and, as Thomas Powers put it, "it is difficult to convey the completeness of Kay's failure to find just about anything Powell cited as a justification for war." To the contrary, Kay's team found new evidence that the Iraqi regime had destroyed stockpiles of biological and chemical weapons in the mid-1990s. Kay resigned in January 2004, announcing that he didn't think any stockpiles of weapons of mass destruction had existed. "What everyone was talking about [was] stockpiles produced after the end of the [1991] Gulf War," he said, "and I don't think there was a large-scale production programme in the 'nineties." See Guy Dinmore and James Harding, "Doubts grow over Iraqi 'smoking gun,'" *Financial Times*, May 2, 2003; Barton Gellman, "Frustrated, US arms teams to leave Iraq," *Washington Post*, May 11, 2003; Andrew Buncombe, "US weapons team ends its search with no discovery," *Independent*, May 12, 2003; Barton Gellman, "Covert unit hunted for Iraqi arms," *Washington Post*, June 13, 2003; Thomas Powers, "The vanishing case for war," *New York Review of Books*, December 4, 2003; Andrew Buncombe, "Saddam's WMD never existed, says chief American arms inspector," *Independent*, January 24, 2004; Walter Pincus and Dana Milbank, "Kay cites evidence of Iraq disarming," *Washington Post*, January 28, 2004.

9   Robin Cook, "Britain must not be suckered a second time by the White House," *Independent*, May 30, 2003. Neither must it be suckered by Downing Street.

10 Ackerman and Judis, "First casualty"; see also Ignacio Ramonet, "State-sponsored lies," *Le Monde Diplomatique*, July 15, 2003; John Prados, "Iraq: a necessary war?," *Bulletin of the Atomic Scientists* 59/3 (2003), pp. 26–33. These are matters of grave concern too. Paul Krugman believes that if the claim that Saddam posed an imminent threat was fraudulent, then "the selling of the war is arguably the worst scandal in American political history – worse than Watergate, worse than Iran-Contra." But he also notes that one difference between the Watergate scandal that drove President Richard Nixon from office and the present one "is that it's now almost impossible to imagine a Republican senator asking 'What did the President know and when did he know it?'" Paul Krugman, "Standard Operating Procedure," *New York Times*, June 3, 2003; "Denial and deception," *New York Times*, June 24, 2003; "Pattern of corruption," *New York Times*, July 15, 2003.

11 See, for example, Ben Russell, Andy McSmith, "The case for war is blown apart," *Independent*, May 29, 2003; Glen Rangwala, "The lies that led us to war," *Independent*, June 1, 2003; Andrew Grice, David Usborne, "The Niger connection: Tony Blair, forged documents and the case for war," *Independent*, June 5, 2003; Ben Russell, "Exposed: Blair, Iraq and the great deception," *Independent*, June 16, 2003; Glen Rangwala, Raymond Whitaker, "Twenty lies about the war," *Independent*, July 15, 2003.

12 Human Rights Watch, World Report, 2002, at <http://www.hrw.org/wr2k2>.

13 Philip Webster, "Discovery of mass graves justifies war, says Blair," *Times*, May 15, 2003; Ed Vulliamy, "Saddam's killing fields give up their gruesome secrets," *Observer*, May 25, 2003; Human Rights Watch, *The Mass Graves of al-Mahawil: The Truth Uncovered* (Washington, DC: May 2003). "Hypocrisy and immorality simply do not come on uglier terms": John Chuckman, "Of Blair, Hussein and genocide," *Counterpunch*, May 19, 2003.

14 Salam Pax, "Where is Raed?" at <http://dear_raed.blogspot.com>, December 3, 2002; he was responding to the dossier on human rights abuses in Iraq published by the British government in November 2002, "Saddam Hussein: crimes and human rights abuses" at <http://www.fco.gov.uk/Files/kfile/hrdossier.pdf>.

15 Nicholas Watt and Julian Borger, "'History will forgive us,'" *Guardian*, July 18, 2003.

16 Sarah Anderson, Phyllis Benn, and John Cavanagh, *Coalition of the Willing or Coalition of the Coerced* (Washington, DC: Institute for Policy Studies, February 26, 2003; Part II: March 24, 2003). Ken Roth, "War in Iraq: not a humanitarian intervention," in Human Rights Watch, World Report 2004 "Human rights and armed conflict," at <http://hrw.org/wr2k4/>, January 2004. Roth also noted that "the Iraq war and the effort to justify it in humanitarian terms risk giving humanitarian intervention a bad name. If that breeds

cynicism about the use of military force for humanitarian purposes, it could be devastating for people in need of future rescue."

17 Milan Rai, *War Plan Iraq* (London: Verso, 2002), pp. 127–32; *Face the Nation* transcript, CBS News.com, September 8, 2002; Mike Allen, "Bush asserts that al-Qaeda has links to Iraq's Hussein," *Washington Post*, September 26, 2002; Glenn Kessler, "US decision on Iraq has a murky past," *Washington Post*, January 12, 2003.

18 President's remarks at the UN General Assembly (my emphases).

19 The text of the resolution is available at <http://www.law.duke.edu/lib/libserv/thomas.html> and at <http://www.gpoaccess.gov/bills>; the resolution was passed by 296:133 votes in the House and by 77:23 votes in the Senate.

20 Kenneth Pollack, *The Threatening Storm: The Case for Invading Iraq* (New York: Random House, 2002), pp. x, xxi–xxii, 364, 368. The author also served as director for Gulf Affairs at the National Security Council during 1995–6 and 1999–2000.

21 Jacqueline Rose, "We are all afraid, but of what, exactly?," *Guardian*, March 20, 2003. The US Department of Homeland Security instituted a "Homeland Security Advisory System" with five "threat conditions": low (green), guarded (blue), elevated (yellow), high (orange), and severe (red). Richard Falk accused the administration of manipulating these terrorist alerts "as a way of scaring the American people into a submission that is at once abject and incoherent. The combination of the September 11 shock effect and the constant official warnings that there will be a repetition of such attacks has so far disabled Americans from mounting an effective opposition": "Resisting the global domination project," *Frontline* 20/8, April 12–25, 2003.

22 Pollack, *Threatening Storm*, pp. xxii–xxiii, 364, 419. The heart of Pollack's case was Iraq's supposed possession of WMD; for his subsequent attempt to muffle the retreat, see Steven Lukes, "The perils of expertise: Kenneth Pollack and the Iraq war," at <http://www.opendemocracy.net>, June 23, 2003.

23 Robert Byrd, "The road to coverup is the road to ruin," at <http://www.commondreams.org>, June 24, 2003; see also Daniel Benjamin and Steven Simon, "The next debate: the al-Qaeda link," *New York Times*, July 20, 2003; Peter Canellos, Brian Bender, "Questions grow over Iraq links to [al-]Qaeda," *Boston Globe*, August 3, 2003.

24 John Brady Kiesling resigned his post as Political Counsellor at the US embassy in Athens in a letter to Secretary of State Colin Powell on February 27, 2003; it was reprinted as "A letter of resignation," *New York Review of Books*, April 10, 2003.

25 Fred Kaplan, "This is not terrorism," *Guardian*, April 3, 2003; Kaplan notes that Article 37 of Protocol 1 to the Geneva Conventions (1977) forbids the

feigning of surrender or of civilian, non-combatant status by troops, but the United States has refused to ratify the Protocol; Kim Sengupta, "US says flag incident was a coincidence," *Independent*, April 11, 2003.

26 "President Bush announces combat operations in Iraq have ended," at <http://www.whitehouse.gov/news/releases/2003/05/Iraq/20030501-15.html>, May 1, 2003.

27 Robert Byrd, "Bush used military as a stage prop: a troubling speech," *Counterpunch*, May 7, 2003. Bush avoided service in Vietnam by enlisting in the National Air Guard – though he was absent from his "post" for much of the period – and Byrd also questioned the motives of "a desk-bound president who assumes the garb of a warrior for the purposes of a speech." Three months later Blue Box Toys announced its latest action figure: "Elite Force Aviator: George W. Bush – US President and Naval Aviator." It was advertised, mercifully, as a "limited edition."

28 Richard Falk, "Resisting the global domination project."

29 Greg Miller, "No proof connects Iraq to 9/11, Bush says," *Los Angeles Times*, September 18, 2003.

30 Thomas Rocks, "Briefing depicted Saudis as enemies," *Washington Post*, August 6, 2002.

31 *Strategic Energy Policy Challenges for the Twenty-First Century* (2001), sponsored by the James A. Baker III Institute for Public Policy at Rice University and the Council for Foreign Relations. The report recommended reviewing US policies toward Iraq – specifically, the implementation of "highly focused and enforced sanctions" that would target the regime's ability to maintain and acquire WMD while also attempting "to enhance the well-being of the Iraqi people" – which would help to reduce anti-Americanism in the Middle East and prepare the path for easing restrictions on the Iraqi oil industry. But the report consistently noted that Saddam himself was a major obstacle to the stability its authors sought.

32 Thomas Friedman, "Oil price formula calls for critical maths if Saddam is taken out of the equation," *Guardian*, August 6, 2002. There were other economic dividends on offer too. In 2000 Iraq had elected to denominate its oil in euros not dollars, and there was a well-grounded fear that if a sufficient number of other states followed suit the strength of the US dollar would be endangered. There was also the prospect of using unfettered control of Iraqi oil to stabilize – if not solve – the deepening fiscal crisis of the American state. Another war would certainly distract attention from the troubled American economy and the White House's embattled domestic agenda, and also perhaps relieve what Norman Mailer called "the malaise of the white American male": "The white man unburdened," *New York Review of Books*, July 17, 2003. Arguments like these run through David Harvey's critique of *The New Imperialism* (Oxford: Oxford University

Press, 2003) and what he calls the "iron laws" that frame "accumulation by dispossession."

33   James Paul, "Oil in Iraq: the heart of the crisis," Global Policy Forum at <http://www.globalpolicy.org>, December 2002; Daniel Yergin, "A crude view of the crisis in Iraq," *Washington Post*, December 8, 2002; John Tatom, "Iraqi oil is not America's objective," *Financial Times*, February 17, 2003; Lutz Kleveman, "The new 'Great Game' being played out over oil," *Independent*, March 31, 2003; Yahya Sadowski, "No war for whose oil?," *Le Monde Diplomatique*, April 3, 2003; Raad Alkadiri and Fareed Mohamedi, "World oil markets and the invasion of Iraq," *Middle East Report* 227 (203), pp. 20–31; Jeff Girth, "Oil experts see long-term risks to Iraq reserves," *New York Times*, November 30, 2003.

34   David Hare, "Don't look for a reason," *Guardian*, April 12, 2003; John Berger, "To the mountain" at <http://www.opendemocracy.net>, April 14, 2003.

35   *The National Security Strategy of the United States of America*, September 2002, pp. 1, 13–15, 29–30. For an elaboration of the administration's view, and some doubts about its practical implementation, see Walter Slocombe, "Force, pre-emption and legitimacy," *Survival* 45 (2003), pp. 117–30.

36   Richard Perle, "United they fall," *Spectator*, March 22, 2003. It is important to situate these comments within the long history of antagonism toward the United Nations when the views of the United States did not prevail. Congress became increasingly critical of the UN in the late 1970s, and the election of President Ronald Reagan in 1981 marked the beginning of overt hostility. In particular, the United States withdrew from UNESCO, refused to fund other "politicized" programs, and withheld a considerable proportion of its assessments. After 1989, President George H. W. Bush pursued a more conciliatory policy: the UN played a more important role in US foreign policy – notably during the Gulf War of 1990–1 – and US arrears to the UN fell substantially. In many ways, however, the Clinton administration reverted to the position of the Reagan administration, especially when both houses of Congress were controlled by the Republicans. See "Background and history of the UN financial crisis," at <http://www.globalpolicy.org/finance/chronol/hist.htm>.

37   For examples of the aggressive othering of what Rumsfeld dismissively called "old Europe" in general and France in particular, see Christopher Hitchens, "The rat that roared," *Wall Street Journal*, February 8, 2003; Thomas Friedman, "Vote France off the island," *New York Times*, February 9, 2003; Brendan Miniter, "The sickness of 'old Europe' is a danger to the world," *Wall Street Journal*, February 11, 2003.

38   <http://projects.sipri.org>. It should be noted that these are raw figures based on market exchange rates; there are several other ways of representing

military expenditure (including as a percentage of GDP) and the Stockholm International Peace Research Institute (SIPRI) provides a discussion of their relative merits as well as longitudinal data. Global military expenditure rose by 6 percent in 2002, and the United States accounted for nearly three-quarters of that increase. *National Security Strategy of the United States of America*, pp. 5–6, 13–15, 29.

39 *National Security Strategy of the United States of America*, pp. ii, 21.

40 Oliver Burkeman and Julian Borger, "War critics astonished as US hawk admits invasion was illegal," *Guardian*, November 20, 2003. This was not the first time that international law had stood in the way of US foreign policy, and neither was it the first time that the United States had set it on one side: see Noam Chomsky, *Hegemony or Survival: America's Quest for Global Dominance* (New York: Metropolitan Books/Henry Holt, 2003): see especially the discussions of Cuba (pp. 80–95) and of Nicaragua (pp. 96–108).

41 Anthony Dworkin (ed.), "Iraq and the 'Bush doctrine' of pre-emptive self-defence," Crimes of War Project, August 20, 2002, and Anthony Dworkin's interview with Vaughan Lowe, "Would war be lawful without another UN resolution?," Crimes of War Project, March 10, 2003, both at <http://www.crimesofwar.org>; Duncan Currie, " 'Preventive war' and international law after Iraq," at <http://www.globelaw.com/Iraq/Preventive_war_after_iraq.html_Toc41379606>, May 22, 2003.

42 I describe this as fantasmatic on strategic as well as ideological grounds. In its first annual report to Congress in December 1999, the Advisory Panel to Assess Domestic Response Capabilities for Terrorism involving Weapons of Mass Destruction (the Gilmore Commission) concluded that the prospect of a "rogue state" supplying a transnational terrorist organization with WMD was highly improbable because any such group was "unpredictable even to the point of using the weapons against its sponsor." And such states had good reason to doubt that their proxies could carry out attacks against the United States without detection, and so feared massive retaliation that would threaten their own survival: see Benjamin and Simon, "The next debate." A National Intelligence Estimate prepared for President Bush in October 2002 identified one exception: if Saddam "were facing death or capture and his government was collapsing after a military attack by the United States" he might then, in those circumstances alone, provide terrorists with WMD. If this assessment is correct, then attacking Saddam *increased* the likelihood of an alliance between the Iraqi regime and transnational terrorism: Walter Pincus, "October report said defeated Hussein would be a threat," *Washington Post*, July 21, 2003.

43 Edward Said, "The Academy of Lagado," *London Review of Books*, April 17, 2003; see also Ignacio Ramonet, "Lawless war," *Le Monde*

Diplomatique, April 2003; Simon Dalby, "Geopolitics, the Bush doctrine and war on Iraq," forum on the 2003 war on/in Iraq, *The Arab World Geographer*, May 2003.

44　Noam Chomsky, "Preventive war: the supreme crime," *Le Monde Diplomatique*, August 2003. Chomsky makes the sharp point that the doctrine of "preventive war" paralleled the justification Japan offered for attacking Pearl Harbor and was "the supreme crime that was condemned at Nuremberg."

45　Salam Pax, "Where is Raed?," February 16, 2003.

46　Most prominent were the Reverend Franklin Graham and his "Samaritan's Purse" organization and the Southern Baptist Convention. Graham gave the invocation at Bush's inauguration in 2000 and preached at the Pentagon on Good Friday 2003. He is on record as describing Islam as a "wicked" and "evil" religion, and declaring the difference between Christianity and Islam the difference between "lightness and darkness." See Jean Marbella, "Graham's appearance at Pentagon draws fire," *Baltimore Sun*, April 19, 2003; Andrew Gumbel, "Evangelical crusaders prepare to fight Islam with aid and a Bible," *Independent*, April 22, 2003; Mohamed Elmasry, "Christian evangelists in postwar Iran: who are the infidels now?," *Globe and Mail*, April 23, 2003.

47　Thomas Friedman, "Come the revolution," *New York Times*, April 2, 2003.

48　John Keegan, "Saddam was easily defeated – which is why the war goes on," *Daily Telegraph*, June 4, 2003. Salam Pax also cited Huntington on his site, but not with approval: "The West won the world not by the superiority of its ideas or values or religion but rather by its superiority in applying organized violence. Westerners often forget this fact, but non-Westerners never do." See "Where is Raed?"

49　E. A. Torriero, "Hussein dots Iraq landscape with mosques," *Chicago Tribune*, October 10, 2002; Rory McCarthy, "If God wants to take us, he will take us," *Guardian*, December 24, 2002; John Daniszewski, "As bombs fall, a song rises from the mosques," *Los Angeles Times*, April 1, 2003.

50　"Saudi Arabia rejects participation in war against Iraq," at <http://edition.cnn.com>, March 18, 2003. Although combat missions were not flown from Saudi Arabia, CENTCOM did direct the air war from its Combined Air Operations Center outside Riyadh. After the war was declared over, the United States announced that the Center would be moved to Qatar and that US troops would be withdrawn from Saudi Arabia; the Pentagon would continue to have access to bases in Saudi Arabia and was reported to be seeking access to four additional bases in Iraq to "project American influence into the heart of the unsettled region." Thomas Shanker and Eric Schmitt, "Pentagon expects long-term access to four key bases in Iraq," *New York*

Times, April 20, 2003. One of Osama bin Laden's key demands was for the withdrawal of US troops from the holy lands of Mecca and Medina, and to have announced these withdrawals before the war would have risked the appearance of capitulation. But, as Saad al-Fagih argues, many Muslims "regard US actions since the September 11 events as far more oppressive than the presence of their forces in Arabia": "The war that bin Laden is winning," *Guardian*, May 13, 2003.

51 "Sam Huntington attacks Bush on Iraq," Indo-Asian News Service, April 29, 2003.

52 Susan Sachs, "In Arab media, war shown as a 'clash of civilizations,' " *International Herald Tribune*, April 5, 2003; see also Makram Khoury-Machool, "Losing the battle for Arab hearts and minds," at <http://www.opendemocracy.net>, May 2, 2003, who notes that Arab satellite channels and online newspapers "united in conveying the message that the coalition consists of 'invaders' and in representing the Iraqi people as an aggressed Arab nation alongside the Palestinians: occupied, humiliated, and suffering under siege."

53 "Rumsfeld rejects 'cleric-led' rule," *BBC News*, April 25, 2003.

54 M. Shahid Alam, "Is this a clash of civilizations?," *Counterpunch*, February 28, 2003; Yasmin Alibhai-Brown, "Bush is right: this is not a clash of civilisations," *Independent*, April 7, 2003. But the sense of aggression – of violation – that was felt by Muslims around the world was, I think, strikingly different from that experienced by non-Muslims: see below, pp. 209–10.

55 See also Berger, "To the mountain."

56 Gary Younge, "Stay at home to avoid Saddam's fate, Rumsfeld tells Iraqis," *Guardian*, March 21, 2003; Robert Fisk, "Minute after minute the missiles came, with devastating shrieks," *Independent*, March 22, 2003; Aijaz Ahmad, "The war of occupation," *Frontline* 20/7 (2003). For a presentation of "shock and awe" by its original architects, see Harlan Ullman and James Wade, *Shock and Awe: Achieving Rapid Dominance* (Washington: National Defense University, 1996).

57 Cf. Andy Dick, "State vigilantism: American adventure politics," at <http://www.artcontext.com>, 2002; John Kampfner, "The truth about Jessica," *Guardian*, May 15, 2003; Robert Scheer, "Saving Private Lynch, Take 2," *Los Angeles Times*, May 20, 2003; Robert Fisk, "Saddam statue scene staged," *Independent*, April 11, 2003.

58 "Military Operations in Urbanized Terrain" (MOUT) can be repatriated to US cities too – a classical colonial gesture – in order to contain political demonstrations and mobilizations: see Robert Warren, "Situating the city and September 11th: military urban doctrine, 'pop-up' armies and spatial chess," *International Journal of Urban and Regional Research* 26 (2002), pp. 614–19.

59 "Classroom edition," at <http://www.cnn.com>, November 26, 2002. An exemplary contrast was provided by the *National Geographic*. Its lesson plan (for Grades 9–12) on "Daily life in the Middle East" – and specifically Iraq – invited students "to think critically about what the media delivers, why it focuses so heavily on war coverage, and how this may contribute to skewed views of Iraq and its people."

60 Michael Macedonia, "Games soldiers play," IEEE Spectrum Online, at <http://www.spectyrum.ieee.org>, March 7, 2002; the author is chief scientist and technical director of the US army Simulation Training and Instrumentation Command. See also Sandra Erwin, "Urban warfare simulation helps train company commanders," *National Defense Magazine*, February 2003, on "Full Spectrum Command," an urban war game developed for the US army by the Institute for Creative Technologies at the University of Southern California.

61 *Doctrine for Joint Urban Operations*, September 16, 2002.

62 David Corn, Mark Perry, "The battlespace for Baghdad," at <http://slate.msn.com/id/2081098>, April 3, 2003.

63 The choreographic metaphor, like all metaphors, only travels so far before it breaks down. After Operation Desert Storm in 1991, General Norman Schwarzkopf complained that analysts wrote about war "as if it's ballet, like it's choreographed ahead of time, and when the orchestra strikes up and starts playing, everyone goes out there are plays a set piece. It is choreographed, but what happens is, the orchestra starts playing and some son of a bitch climbs out of the orchestra pit with a bayonet and starts chasing you around the stage. And the choreography goes right out the window." William Arkin, "Will 'Shock and Awe' be sufficient?," *Los Angeles Times*, March 16, 2003.

64 Ann Scott Tyson, "Block to block combat," *Christian Science Monitor*, January 17, 2003.

65 James Baker, "Urban warfare: advantage US," *Seattle Times*, April 3, 2003 (emphasis added); Baker was Deputy Assistant Secretary of Defense under Reagan, and senior adviser to the Joint Chiefs of Staff under Clinton.

66 Scott Peterson, "Iraq prepares for urban defense," *Christian Science Monitor*, October 4, 2002.

67 Michelle Orecklin, "Urban warriors," *Time*, April 7, 2003; see also "Taking it to the streets," *Newsweek*, April 7, 2003.

68 Justin Huggler, "Israelis trained troops in Jenin-style urban warfare," *Independent*, March 29, 2003; Yagil Henken, "The best way into Baghdad," *New York Times*, April 3, 2003; Seth Stern, "How the US plans to take control of Baghdad," *Christian Science Monitor*, April 7, 2003.

69 Baker, "Urban warfare" (my emphasis).

70 Robert Schlesinger, "US sees tactics, technology keys to Baghdad fight," *Boston Globe*, October 14, 2002; Stan Crock and John Casey, "Storming

the streets of Baghdad," *Business Week*, October 21, 2002; Fred Kaplan, "Eyes over Baghdad," at <http://slate.msn.com/id/2081236>, April 7, 2003; "Urban combat takes street smarts," at <http://www.wired.com/news/business>, April 9, 2003; Orecklin, "Urban warriors." These images of network-centric warfare culminated in the ultimate fantasy of the United States eventually achieving "total battlespace knowledge" through "myriads of miniaturised robot sensors and tiny flying videocams whose information would be fused together in a single panoptic picture shared by ordinary grunts in their fighting vehicles as well as by four-star generals in their Qatar or Florida command posts": Mike Davis, "Shock and awe," *Socialist Review* 272 (March 2003); see also Stephen Graham, "Vertical geopolitics: Baghdad and after," *Antipode* 36 (2004), pp. 12–23.

71 Ahmad, "War of occupation."

72 Human Rights Watch concluded that pre-planned targeting of government, intelligence, and security facilities was largely successful in minimizing civilian casualties; but it also noted that neither the US nor the UK "does an adequate job of investigating and analyzing why civilian casualties do occur." Its own report drew particular attention to the repeated and reckless use of cluster bombs in residential neighborhoods (almost 13,000 were used by coalition forces) and to the so-called "decapitation strikes" against leadership targets that had unacceptable margins of error. The last were often carried out using "precision weapons," but these are by no means error-free and Carl Conetta points out that such "improved capabilities in precision attacks [were] used to pursue more ambitious objectives rather than to achieve lower numbers of civilian dead." See Human Rights Watch, "Off target: the conduct of the war and civilian casualties in Iraq," at <http://www.hrw.org/reports/2003/usa1203/>, December 2003; Suzanne Goldenberg, "Up to 15,000 killed in invasion, claims think tank," *Guardian*, October 29, 2003.

73 David Zucchino, "The Thunder Run," *Los Angeles Times*, December 7, 2003.

74 Rajiv Chandrasekaran and Molly Moore, "Urban combat frustrates army," *Washington Post*, 8 July 2003.

75 <http://ww.usatoday.com/news/world/iraq/baghdadsatmap/flash.htm>; <http://www.washingtonpost.com/wp-srv/inatl/longter/fogofwar/dbasetargets.htm>.

76 Michiko Kakutani, "Shock, awe and razzmatazz in the sequel," *New York Times*, March 25, 2003; James der Derian, "Who's embedding whom? InfoInterventions at <http://www.watsoninstitute.org/infopeace/911>, March 26, 2003.

77 This was subsequently confirmed by a firefight between US troops and Iraqi guerrillas in Samarra at the end of November. The US claimed to have killed 54 insurgents, and when these figures were challenged by reporters and eyewitnesses a military spokesman insisted that: "Every commander is responsible for doing battle damage assessment. *Part of that includes*

counting the dead and wounded on both sides." Phil Reeves, "Iraqis deny US accounts of fierce fight with guerrillas," *Independent*, December 2, 2003 (my emphasis).

78 John Broder, "Iraqi army toll a mystery because no count is kept," *International Herald Tribune*, April 2, 2003; Jeffrey Kluger, "Counting the casualties: how many Iraqis have died?" <http://www.time.com>, April 13, 2003; Ferry Bidermann, "What happened to Iraq's army?" at <http://www.salon.com>, April 22, 2003; Jonathan Steele, "Body counts," *Guardian*, May 28, 2003.

79 Julian Barnes, "This was not worth a child's finger," *Guardian*, April 11, 2003. On the formal networks through which families of British casualties were notified, see Randeep Ramesh (ed.), *The War We Could Not Stop* (London: Faber & Faber, 2003), pp. 194–5; for an indication of the cruelly haphazard way in which Iraqi families heard similar news, see Maggie O'Kane, "Bloodless words, bloody war," *Guardian*, December 16, 1995 (and above, p. 167).

80 Bradley Graham, Dan Morgan, "US has no plans to count civilian casualties," *Washington Post*, April 15, 2003. The gesture of Powell's last clause, a weasel attempt at absolution, was repeated time and time again as the American and British governments sought to attribute Iraqi civilian casualties to Iraqi military actions. As Derrick Jackson remarked, the very people that the US claimed to be liberating were not worth counting: "US stays blind to Iraqi casualties," *Boston Globe*, November 14, 2003.

81 "The embedding of the majority of foreign journalists with the fast-moving military machine meant that meticulous on-the-ground reports were relatively rare," two analysts noted, and the subsequent refusal by occupying forces to allow independent NGOs and aid agencies to carry out their own operations with any degree of freedom "means that an accurate and comprehensive picture of the cost of the war in human lives has hardly begun to emerge." See John Sloboda and Hamit Dardagan, "The holes in the map: mapping civilian casualties in the conflict in Iraq," at <http://www.iraqbodycount.net>, April 28, 2003.

82 Laura King, "Baghdad's death toll assessed," *Los Angeles Times*, May 18, 2003. The survey covered all the large hospitals as well as most of the smaller specialty facilities in the city center, and scrutinized both official records and original handwritten records. These covered the five weeks beginning March 20, 2003, and included deaths directly caused by the American bombardment and ground battle, "plus deaths from unexploded ordnance and those as a result of injuries suffered earlier in the fighting." The survey did not include "dozens of deaths that doctors indirectly attributed to the conflict. Those cases include pregnant women who died of complications while giving birth at home because they could not get to a hospital and

chronically ill people, such as cardiac or dialysis patients, who were unable to obtain needed care while the fighting raged." For other (partial) estimates, see Matthew Schofield, Nancy Youssef, and Juan Tamayo, "Civilian deaths in Baghdad total at least 1,101," *Philadelphia Inquirer*, May 4, 2003; Peter Ford, "Surveys pointing to high civilian death toll in Iraq," *Christian Science Monitor*, May 22, 2003; Niko Price, "AP tallies 3,240 civilian deaths in Iraq," *Associated Press*, June 10, 2003.

83   <http://www.iraqbodycount.net>. The start date is necessarily arbitrary because the United States and Britain escalated their air attacks on Iraq well before the "formal" start of the war on March 19; the end date is indeterminate because coalition forces continued to kill Iraqi civilians after Bush declared the end of "major combat operations" on May 1 and because coalition cluster bombs that failed to detonate on impact continue to kill Iraqi civilians: see Human Rights Watch, "Hearts and minds: post-war civilian deaths in Baghdad caused by US forces," at <http://www.org/reports/2003/iraq1003>, October 2003; Paul Wiseman, "Cluster bombs kill in Iraq even after looting ends," at <http://www.usatoday.com/news/world/iraq/soo3-12-10-cluster-bomb-cover_x.htm>, December 10, 2003. For reviews of Iraq Body Count and other estimates of civilian casualties, see Melissa Murphy and Carl Conetta, "Civilian casualties in the 2003 Iraq war: a compendium of accounts and reports," Project on Defense Alternatives at <http://www.comw.org/pda/0305iraqcasualtydata.html>, May 21, 2003; John Sloboda and Hamit Dardagan, "Counting the human cost: a survey of projects counting civilians killed by the war in Iraq," at <http://www.iraqbodycount.net>, June 12, 2003. This last report concluded that all of these projects, independent of one another, "provide converging evidence that current estimates putting the number of civilians killed at significantly above 5,000 are well founded." On civilian casualties, see "Adding indifference to injury," <http://www.iraqbodycount.net>, August 7, 2003. Dr Mohammed al-Obaidi, a principal of the Iraqi Freedom Party, has argued that even these figures severely underestimate the number of civilian deaths: reporters were unable to reach many of the sites where they occurred, as Sloboda and Dardagan acknowledge, and many Iraqis were understandably reluctant to talk to outsiders. He claims that an intensive survey carried out by hundreds of his party members throughout Iraq (with the exception of the Kurdish-controlled areas in the north) has revealed a total of 37,137 civilian deaths in the 14 central and southern governorates (6,734 in Basra and 6,103 in Baghdad alone). See "Memo on the margin: civilian war deaths in Iraq," at <http://www.wanninski.com>, August 21, 2003. A later report by the Project on Defense Alternatives estimated that 11,000–15,000 Iraqis were killed between March 19 and May 1, 2003, of whom 3,200–4,300 were non-combatants: see Carl Conetta, "The wages of war: Iraqi combatant

and noncombatant fatalities in the 2003 conflict," Project on Defense Alternatives, Monograph 8, October 2003.

84 Salam Pax, "Where is Raed?," March 23, 2003.

85 Faisal Bodi, "Al-Jazeera tells the truth about the war," *Guardian*, March 28, 2003; Ramesh, *The War We Could Not Stop*, p. 89. On images of the war in the Arabic media, see also Oliver Burkeman, Ian Black, Matt Wells, Sean Smith, and Brian Whitaker, "Television agendas shape images of war," *Guardian*, March 27, 2003; Jonathan Steele, "It feels like 1967 all over again," *Guardian*, April 9, 2003; Michael Massing, "The unseen war," *New York Review of Books*, May 29, 2003. On the targeting of al-Jazeera and other journalists, see Jason Deane, "Al-Jazeera's Basra hotel bombed," *Guardian*, April 2, 2003; Robert Fisk, "Is there some element in the US military that wants to take out journalists?," *Independent*, April 5, 2003; Chris Tryhorn, "Military accused of targeting non-embedded journalists," *Guardian*, April 8, 2003; Galal Nassar, "The collapse," *al-Ahram*, April 17–23, 2003; Philip Knightley, "Turning the tanks on the reporters," *Observer*, June 15, 2003. Ironically, al-Jazeera's operations in Iraq had been shut down twice before for unfavorable reporting; those orders were issued by Saddam Hussein.

86 I elaborate this in *Dancing on the Pyramids* (Minneapolis: University of Minnesota Press, forthcoming).

87 Jonathan Raban, "The greatest gulf," *Guardian*, April 19, 2003 (my emphases); Lawrence Rosen, *The Culture of Islam: Changing Aspects of Contemporary Muslim Life* (Chicago: University of Chicago Press, 2002). Cf. Akbar Ahmed, *Islam Today* (London: I. B. Tauris, 2002), p. 8: "The concept of the *ummah*, community or brotherhood, may be intangible and even amorphous but it is powerful. It allows ideas to be carried across national borders and can generate powerful emotions. It is the notion of the *ummah* that triggers a response when Muslims see or hear scenes of other Muslims being denied their rights or being brutally suppressed when voicing them." I should add that Raban's purpose is not to deny the significance of local allegiances – far from it – but to unsettle the "national" partitions of colonial cartography. See his "Here we go again," *Guardian*, December 11, 2002.

88 Suzanne Goldenberg, " 'A picture of killing inflicted on a sprawling city – and it grew more unbearable by the minute,' " *Guardian*, April 9, 2003.

89 Robert Fisk, "This is the reality of war. We bomb. They suffer," *Independent*, March 23, 2003; Cahal Milmo and Andrew Buncombe, "Surgeons using headache pills instead of anaesthetic," *Independent*, April 9, 2003.

90 These details are from Robert Fisk, "In Baghdad, blood and bandages for the innocent," *Independent*, March 30, 2003; Cahal Milmo, "Proved: deaths in Iraqi marketplace were caused by American missile," *Independent*, April 2, 2003; Jason Deane, "Fisk 'has not been duped by Saddam'," *Guardian*,

April 4, 2003; Marc Herold, "The evil, the grotesque and US official lies" *Frontline* 20/9, April 26–May 3, 2003; Derrick Jackson, "US clouds Iraqi civilian deaths," *Boston Globe*, June 13, 2003. I base my sense of Mr Hoon's humanitarian instincts on his own claim that mothers of Iraqi children killed by cluster bombs might well one day thank British forces for their actions: Paul Waugh and Ben Russell, "Hoon is cruel for claims on cluster bombs," *Independent*, April 5, 2003.

91 Paul McGeough, "A gaping hole full of tough questions," *The Age*, April 9, 2003.

92 Robert Fisk, "The dogs were yelping. They knew bombs were on the way," *Independent*, April 9, 2003; Barnes, "This was not worth a child's finger"; Thanassis Cambanis, "Strike at Hussein left neighborhood shattered, angry," *Boston Globe*, April 13, 2003; David Blair, "Smart bombs aimed at Saddam killed families," *Telegraph*, April 21, 2003. Dropping such bombs on a crowded residential neighborhood is a grim and exorbitant repeat of the IDF's assassination of Saleh Shehadeh in July 2002 by bombing a crowded residential neighborhood in Gaza (above, p. 118): see Robert Fisk, "What Israel does to Palestine, we are doing to Iraq," *Independent*, July 12, 2003.

93 For other instances, see, for example, Mark Franchetti, "US Marines turn fire on civilians at the bridge of death," *Times*, March 30, 2003; Ed Vulliamy, "Iraq: the human toll," *Observer*, July 6, 2003. These reports describe not only the needless, heedless killing of Iraqi civilians but also the brutal way in which the injured and bereaved were treated.

94 Robert Fisk, "What Iraqis will think about the photos of Uday and Qusay," *Independent*, July 25, 2003; "What are Iraqis to make of this theatre of the macabre?", *Independent*, July 26, 2003.

95 Paul William Roberts, "Beyond Baghdad: lost in the cradle of civilization," *Harper's Magazine* (July 2003), pp. 68–73. Roberts also recorded how one editor, leafing through press photographs of the boy in his hospital bed, racked with pain and fear, demanded of his photographer: "Don't you have any of him smiling?" Cf. Esther Addley, "Ali's story," *Guardian*, August 1, 2003.

96 Hugo Slim, "Why protect civilians? Innocence, immunity and enmity in war," *International Affairs* 79 (2003), pp. 481–501: 485.

97 Riverbend, "Baghdad is burning" at <http://riverbendblog.blospot.com>, August 26, 2003; she is commenting on the decision of the Iraqi Governing Council to establish April 9 as a national holiday.

98 Mark Steel, "Iraqis only count if they're dancing in the street," *Independent*, April 17, 2003.

99 <http://www.time.com/time/covers/1101030414/map/> The comparisons were not beside the point; if only they had been made before the bombing started. But there were moments in which those parallels were drawn. In

an unguarded comment one of the military instructors preparing American troops for urban combat in a mock city at Fort Polk conceded that "Baghdad would be incredibly hard, sort of like attacking Los Angeles." Troops had also trained for urban combat in American cities: Dayton, Ohio, for example, found itself "playing the role of Baghdad" in September 2002, when abandoned buildings and empty shopping centers were used as "stand-ins" for Iraqi cities. See Tyson, "Block to block combat"; Howard Wilkinson, "Marines train in Dayton for urban combat," *Cincinnati Inquirer*, September 17, 2002.

100 Caoimhe Butterly, "Al-Thawra [Sadr City]," at <http://electronicIraq.net/news>, May 6, 2003; Salam Pax, "Where is Raed?", May 7, 2003.

101 Adrian Hamilton, "The obscenity of bickering over death and torture," *Independent,* April 11, 2003.

102 Thomas Friedman, "Bored with Baghdad – already," *New York Times*, May 18, 2003. As he noted, however, it was not only the American public that quickly tired: "The Iraqis are an exhausted people."

103 Patrick Cockburn, "Powerless Iraqis rail against ignorant, air-conditioned US occupation forces," *Independent*, June 22, 2003; Rajiv Chandrasekaran, "Blackouts return, deepening Iraq's dark days," *Washington Post*, July 3, 2003; Robyn Dixon, "Basra could boil over again," *Los Angeles Times*, August 12, 2003.

104 Andrew Murray, "Hostages of the empire," *Guardian*, July 1, 2003. L. Paul Bremer III was appointed as Presidential Envoy to Iraq on May 6, 2003; he arrived in Baghdad on May 11 to replace the former director of the Office of Reconstruction and Humanitarian Assistance (ORHA), Lieutenant General Jay Garner, as Civilian Administrator. Like Garner, he reports directly to the US Secretary of Defense. Bremer had previously served as US ambassador to the Netherlands and as President Reagan's Ambassador at Large for Counter-Terrorism in the 1980s; he retains the title of ambassador. ORHA was folded into the Coalition Provisional Authority on June 1, 2003.

105 Salam Pax, "Where is Raed?," October 12, 2002; Mary Riddell, "The testimony of the dead," *Observer*, March 30, 2003.

106 Thomas Friedman, "Hold your applause," *New York Times*, April 9, 2003.

107 Patrick Cockburn, "Poverty and despair behind Iraq's ethnic violence," *Independent*, April 14, 2003. Although I accept Cockburn's account of the motivations of most of the looters, there were also reports of criminal gangs whose plunder was more selective and more systematic.

108 Giorgio Agamben, *Homo Sacer: Sovereign Power and Bare Life*, trans. Daniel Heller-Roaxen (Stanford, CA: Stanford University Press, 1998), p. 37.

109 Arundhati Roy, "Instant-Mix Imperial Democracy (buy one, get one free)," lecture in New York, May 13, 2003; at <http://www.commondreams.org>, May 18, 2003.

110 James Fallows, "Blind into Baghdad," *Atlantic Monthly* 293(1) (2004), pp. 52–74: 63; Katherine Butler and Donald Macintyre, "General Franks strides into his Iraqi palace," *Independent*, April 17, 2003; Jonathan Fowler, "US bridles as Annan calls it 'occupying power,'" *Toronto Star*, April 24, 2003; see also Khaled Dawoud, "Indefinitely at war," *al-Ahram*, April 26, 2003. A post-war assessment by the US army's 3rd Infantry Division (Mechanized) subsequently admitted that the political decision to call US troops "liberators" not "occupying forces" left officers uncertain about their legal authority to halt looting or impose curfews: John Lumpkin and Dafina Linzer, "US officials were reluctant to call troops occupiers," *Associated Press*, November 27, 2003.

111 These arguments are taken from "Military occupation of Iraq: I: Application of I[nternational] H[umanitarian] L[aw] and the maintenance of law and order," International Humanitarian Law Research Initiative, at <http://www.ihlresearch.org/iraq>, April 14, 2003; Michael Schmitt, "The law of belligerent occupation," Crimes of War Project, at <http://www.crimesofwar.org>, April 15, 2003; Jordan Paust, "The US as occupying power over portions of Iraq and relevant responsibilities under the laws of war," ASIL Insights, American Society of International Law, at <http://www.asil.org/>/insights/insigh102.htm>, April 2003.

112 Robert Fisk, "Who is to blame for the collapse in morality that followed 'liberation?,'" *Independent*, April 12, 2003; Brian Whitaker, "Free to do bad things," *Guardian*, April 12, 2003.

113 Daniel McGrory, "UN and army at odds as troops encourage looting," *Times*, April 5, 2003; Tom Squitieri, "US troops, journalists investigated for looting," *USA Today*, April 23, 2003; Oliver Burkeman, "Four US soldiers 'held for $1m theft,'" *Guardian*, April 24, 2003; Jonathan Duffy, "US troops 'encouraged' Iraqi looters," BBC News at <http://news.bbc.co.uk/2/hi/middle_east/3003393.stm>, May 6, 2003.

114 *Baghdad: A Race Against the Clock* (International Crisis Group, June 11, 2003), pp. 1, 5.

115 Andrew Buncombe and John Lichfield, "A city in flames. A nation in chaos," *Independent*, April 12, 2003. Field commanders do not need "orders from above" to restore public order; they are required to do so under international law.

116 James Meek, "Sunni or Shi'a, fault line runs between haves and have nots," *Guardian*, April 11, 2003; Robert Fisk, "Americans defend two untouchable ministries from the hordes of looters," *Independent*, April 14, 2003.

117 Alexander Chancellor, "Barbarians at the gates," *Guardian*, April 26, 2003; Paul Martin, Ed Vulliamy, and Gaby Hinsliff, "US army was told to protect looted museum," *Observer*, April 20, 2003. The looting of the museum was one of the most controversial post-war episodes. First reports indicated wholesale ransacking of the building, and there were suggestions that this

had been undertaken by criminal gangs fulfilling contracts placed in advance of the war by wealthy American and European collectors; it was subsequently reported that many of the treasures had been stored in secret vaults or removed in advance of the final assault on Baghdad for safe keeping. But 3,000 to 10,000 objects remained unaccounted for. See Hamza Hendawi, "Treasure of Nimrud found in Iraqi vault," *Washington Post*, June 7, 2003; Eleanor Robson, "Iraq's museums: what really happened," *Guardian*, June 18, 2003.

118 Ed Vulliamy, "Gun gangs rule streets as US loses control," *Observer*, May 25, 2003.

119 Salam Pax, "Where is Raed?," April 10, 2003.

120 Euan Ferguson, "A latte – and a rifle to go," *Observer*, June 8, 2003. By August the situation had deteriorated even further, and the attacks on civilians were not only carried out by Iraqis. "Life is far more violent in Baghdad now than it was three months ago," announced a surgeon at the city's Institute of Forensic Medicine. "Many of the bodies have US bullets in them. . . . The others are finished off by robbers. It is nothing for them to kill now." Harry De Quetteville, "Silent witnesses reveal the growing lawlessness of Baghdad," *Daily Telegraph*, August 18, 2003; see also Sarmad Ali, "From a coroner's point of view, Baghdad is as deadly as ever," *Iraq Today* at <http://www.iraq-today.com>, August 25, 2003.

121 Robert Fisk, "The ugly truth of America's Camp Cropper," *Independent*, July 22, 2003; Rod Norland, "Rough justice," *Newsweek*, August 18, 2003.

122 "Military occupation of Iraq: II: International assistance in occupied territory," International Humanitarian Law Research Initiative, at <http://www.ihlresearch.org/iraq>, April 22, 2003.

123 *Doctrine for Joint Urban Operations*, pp. x–xi.

124 Frantz Fanon, *The Wretched of the Earth* (London: Penguin, 1979), pp. 29–30; cf. Thomas Ricks and Anthony Shadid, "A tale of two Baghdads," *Washington Post*, June 2, 2003.

125 *Baghdad: A Race Against the Clock*, p. 4 and n.

126 "Water: a source of life and death," UN Office for the Coordination of Humanitarian Affairs, at <http://www.irinnews.org>, August 13, 2003.

127 Chandrasekaran, "Blackouts return."

128 Rajiv Chandrasekaran, "Troubles temper triumphs in Iraq," *Washington Post*, August 18, 2003.

129 Salam Pax, "Where is Raed?," May 9, 2003.

130 Ibid.; "Iraq: running short of power and patience," UN Office for the Coordination of Humanitarian Affairs, at <http://www.irinnews.org>, August 20, 2003; Kim Sengupta, "They did the destroying. So why can't they get everything working again?," *Independent*, April 19, 2003; Phil Reeves, "Liberation one month on: chaos on the streets, cholera in the city and killings in broad daylight," *Independent*, May 9, 2003; Jo Dillon, "Occupiers are failing desperate city," *Independent*, June 1, 2003.

131 Paul Krugman, "Who's accountable?," *New York Times*, June 10, 2003; Michael Duffy and Massimo Calabresi, "Clash of the administration Titans," *Time*, April 14, 2003; Peter Slevin and Dana Priest, "Wolfowitz concedes Iraq errors," *Washington Post*, July 24, 2003. See also Robert Dreyfuss, "More missing intelligence," *The Nation*, July 7, 2003:

> An even bigger intelligence scandal is waiting in the wings: the fact that members of the Administration failed to produce an intelligence evaluation of what Iraq might look like after the fall of Saddam Hussein. Instead, they ignored fears expressed by analysts at the Central Intelligence Agency, the Defense Intelligence Agency, and the State Department who predicted that postwar Iraq would be chaotic, violent and ungovernable, and that Iraqis would greet the occupying armies with firearms not flowers.

Accordingly, Dreyfuss proposed a barbed reversal of the Watergate question: "What didn't the President know and when didn't he know it?" Four months later, when the situation had deteriorated still further, David Rieff, "Blueprint for a mess," *New York Review of Books*, November 2, 2003, reached exactly the same conclusion:

> It is simply not true that no one could have predicted the chaos that ensued after the fall of Saddam Hussein. In fact, many officials in the United States, both military and civilian, as well as many Iraqi exiles, predicted quite accurately the perilous state of things that exists in Iraq today. . . . What went wrong was not that no one could know or no one spoke out. What went wrong is that the voices of Iraq experts, of the State Department almost in its entirety and, indeed, of important segments of the uniformed military were ignored.

132 Avi Shlaim, " 'Liberation' is not freedom," *Observer*, March 30, 2003; for similar comments from other diaspora Iraqi intellectuals, see Burhan al-Chalabi, "You should have known we'd fight," *Guardian*, March 25, 2003; Haifa Zangana, "The message coming from our families in Baghdad," *Guardian*, April 3, 2003. See also Robert Fisk, "For the people on the streets, this is not liberation but a new colonial oppression," *Independent*, April 17, 2003.

133 Stanley Kurtz, "Democratic imperialism," *Policy Review* 118 (April 2003); cf. Toby Dodge, *Inventing Iraq: The Failure of Nation Building and a History Denied* (New York: Columbia University Press, 2003).

134 Paul Kennedy, "The perils of empire," *Washington Post*, April 20, 2003; Alan Freeman, "US outlines its timetable for new Iraqi government," *Globe and Mail*, April 25, 2003; Ignacio Ramonet, "Transition to an

empire," *Le Monde Diplomatique*, May 2003. See also Anatol Lieven, "Missionaries and marines: Bush, Blair and democratisation," at <http://www.opendemocracy.net>, September 18, 2002; id., "A trap of their own making," *London Review of Books*, May 8, 2003.

135 Seumas Milne, "Iraqis have paid the blood price for a fraudulent war," *Guardian*, April 10, 2003.

136 Phil Reeves, "Iraqis emulate Palestinians by stoning troops," *Independent*, April 27, 2003; id., "The war is over (except for Iraq)," *Independent*, May 1, 2003; id., "On the streets of Baghdad, there are no heroes or villains, only victims," *Independent*, May 24, 2003. See also Ali Abunimah and Hussein Ibish, "War in Iraq and Israeli occupation: a devastating resonance," *Chicago Tribune*, March 28, 2003; "From the West Bank to Baghdad," *Jane's Intelligence Digest*, April 3, 2003; Graham Usher, "Here and there," *al-Ahram*, April 3–9, 2003. The parallels were not lost on Palestinians either, but they also feared – with good reason – that Israel would once again take advantage of the new front opened up in Bush's "war on terrorism" to intensify its assault on the occupied territories. See Justin Huggler, "As the world focuses on Iraq, bodies pile up in Gaza," *Independent*, February 22, 2003; Amira Hass, "Horror scenarios coming true," *Ha'aretz*, March 26, 2003; Benjamin Barthe, "Palestine: the world looks away," *Le Monde Diplomatique*, April 2003.

137 In Falluja, for example, 30 miles west of Baghdad, troops from the 82nd Airborne Division opened fire on a crowd of demonstrators, killing at least 14 people and injuring more than 70 others; when the demonstrators returned the next day to condemn the shootings, troops opened fire again, killing two more people and wounding 14 others. See Sarah Left, "US troops kill 13 [*sic*] Iraqi protesters," *Guardian*, April 29, 2003; Ian Fisher, "US troops fire on Iraqi protesters, leaving 15 dead," *New York Times*, April 29, 2003; Jonathan Freedland, "The gaping hole in Iraq," *Guardian*, April 30, 2003; Jonathan Steele, "To the US troops it was self-defence. To the Iraqis it was murder," *Guardian*, April 30, 2003; Ian Fisher, "US troops fire on Iraqi protesters again, killing 2," *New York Times*, April 30, 2003; Elizabeth Neuffer, "US, Iraqis at odds on protesters' deaths," *Boston Globe*, April 30, 2003; Phil Reeves, "Iraqi rage grows after Fallujah massacre," *Independent*, May 4, 2003. For examples of civilians killed during raids or at roadblocks, see Bob Graham, " 'I just pulled the trigger,' " *Evening Standard*, June 20, 2003; Jamie Wilson, "Victims of trigger-happy Task Force 20," *Guardian*, July 29, 2003; Justin Huggler, "Family shot dead by panicking US troops," *Independent*, August 10, 2003; Brian Coughley, "What has happened to the US Army in Iraq?," at <http://www.counterpunch.org>, August 16, 2003; Caoimhe Butterly, "The things that keep us here," at <http://electronicIraq.net/news/printer1043.shtml>, August 18, 2003. That

CATALOG OF DOVER BOOKS

THE STORY OF THE TITANIC AS TOLD BY ITS SURVIVORS, Jack Winocour (ed.). What it was really like. Panic, despair, shocking inefficiency, and a little hero-ism. More thrilling than any fictional account. 26 illustrations. 320pp. 5⅜ x 8½.
20610-6

FAIRY AND FOLK TALES OF THE IRISH PEASANTRY, William Butler Yeats (ed.). Treasury of 64 tales from the twilight world of Celtic myth and legend: "The Soul Cages," "The Kildare Pooka," "King O'Toole and his Goose," many more. Introduction and Notes by W. B. Yeats. 352pp. 5⅜ x 8½.
26941-8

BUDDHIST MAHAYANA TEXTS, E. B. Cowell and others (eds.). Superb, accu-rate translations of basic documents in Mahayana Buddhism, highly important in his-tory of religions. The Buddha-karita of Asvaghosha, Larger Sukhavativyuha, more. 448pp. 5⅜ x 8½.
25552-2

ONE TWO THREE . . . INFINITY: Facts and Speculations of Science, George Gamow. Great physicist's fascinating, readable overview of contemporary science: number theory, relativity, fourth dimension, entropy, genes, atomic structure, much more. 128 illustrations. Index. 352pp. 5⅜ x 8½.
25664-2

EXPERIMENTATION AND MEASUREMENT, W. J. Youden. Introductory man-ual explains laws of measurement in simple terms and offers tips for achieving accu-racy and minimizing errors. Mathematics of measurement, use of instruments, exper-imenting with machines. 1994 edition. Foreword. Preface. Introduction. Epilogue. Selected Readings. Glossary. Index. Tables and figures. 128pp. 5⅜ x 8½.   40451-X

DALÍ ON MODERN ART: The Cuckolds of Antiquated Modern Art, Salvador Dalí. Influential painter skewers modern art and its practitioners. Outrageous evaluations of Picasso, Cézanne, Turner, more. 15 renderings of paintings discussed. 44 calligraphic decorations by Dalí. 96pp. 5⅜ x 8½. (Available in U.S. only.)
29220-7

ANTIQUE PLAYING CARDS: A Pictorial History, Henry René D'Allemagne. Over 900 elaborate, decorative images from rare playing cards (14th–20th centuries): Bacchus, death, dancing dogs, hunting scenes, royal coats of arms, players cheating, much more. 96pp. 9¼ x 12¼.
29265-7

MAKING FURNITURE MASTERPIECES: 30 Projects with Measured Drawings, Franklin H. Gottshall. Step-by-step instructions, illustrations for constructing hand-some, useful pieces, among them a Sheraton desk, Chippendale chair, Spanish desk, Queen Anne table and a William and Mary dressing mirror. 224pp. 8⅛ x 11¼.
29338-6

THE FOSSIL BOOK: A Record of Prehistoric Life, Patricia V. Rich et al. Profusely illustrated definitive guide covers everything from single-celled organisms and dinosaurs to birds and mammals and the interplay between climate and man. Over 1,500 illustrations. 760pp. 7½ x 10⅛.
29371-8

these incidents are all *examples* needs to be underscored. See also Olaf Ihlau, Claus Christian Malzahn, and Volkard Windfuhr, "In the triangle of terror," trans. Christopher Sultan, *Der Spiegel*, at <http://www.spiegel.de/spiegel/english>, August 25, 2003.

138 Robert Fisk, "So he thinks it's all over . . . ," *Independent*, May 5, 2003. See also Human Rights Watch, "Hearts and minds," which concluded that in the vast majority of cases the US had failed to conduct proper investigations into civilian deaths resulting from the excessive or indiscriminate use of military force.

139 Freedland, "Gaping hole"; see also Yitzhak Nakash, "The Shi'ites and the future of Iraq," *Foreign Affairs* 82/4 (2003), pp. 17–26; Faleh Jabar, "The worldly roots of religiosity in post-Saddam Iraq," *Middle East Report* 227 (2003), pp. 12–18; Juan Cole, "The United States and Shi'ite religious factions in post-Ba'athist Iraq," *Middle East Journal* 57 (2003), pp. 543–66.

140 Robert Fisk, "Saddam is airbrushed out by the city that bore his name," *Independent*, April 14, 2003; Peter Beaumont, "Revolution city," *Observer*, April 20, 2003; Suzanne Goldenberg, "Goodbye to Baghdad," *Guardian*, April 25, 2003; Donald Macintyre, "Children of Sadr City bear brunt of crisis made worse by war," *Independent*, May 2, 2003; Mohammed al-Jamaili, "Iraqis move to stem looting," at <http://electronicIraq.net/news>, May 27, 2003; Anthony Shadid, "Clerics vie with US for power," *Washington Post*, June 7, 2003. Here too there is a close parallel with occupied Palestine. In Gaza in particular the indifference of the Israeli occupying forces and the incompetence and corruption of the Palestinian Authority played major parts in the rise of Hamas, which stepped in to provide a range of economic, social, and cultural services for the poor.

141 Ewan MacAskill, "The nightmare scenario: freedom to choose rule by the ayatollahs," *Guardian*, April 16, 2003; John Kinfner and Craig Smith, "Sunnis and Shiites unite to protest US and Hussein" *New York Times*, April 18, 2003; Thomas Lippman, "Iraqi Muslims protest against foreign troops," *Washington Post*, April 18, 2003; Jonathan Steele, "Protesters pour from the mosques to reclaim the streets for Islam," *Guardian*, April 19, 2003; Donald Macintyre and Phil Reeves, "Shias in Iraq told to reject all Western customs," *Independent*, May 3, 2003.

142 Anthony Shadid, "Shiite clerics face a time of opportunity and risks," *Washington Post*, April 20, 2003.

143 Jonathan Steele, "Shi'as in first public pilgrimage since 1989," *Guardian*, April 21, 2003; id., "Religion and politics resurface as the new voices of Iraqi freedom," *Guardian*, April 22, 2003; Craig Smith, "Elated Shiites, on Pilgrimage, want US out," *New York Times*, April 22, 2003; Kamil Mahdi, "The real significance of Karbala," *Guardian*, April 23, 2003; Anthony Shadid, "Iraqi Shiites grow uneasy over US occupation," *Washington Post*, April

24, 2003; Kim Sengupta, "Pilgrims threaten jihad against American forces," *Independent*, April 24, 2003.

144 Patrick Cockburn, "Real looting," *Independent*, April 28, 2003; Douglas Jehl, "US-backed exiles return to reinvent nation," *New York Times*, May 4, 2003; Patrick Tyler, "In reversal, plan for Iraq self-rule has been put off," *New York Times*, May 17, 2003.

145 Naomi Klein, "Bomb before you buy," *Guardian*, April 14, 2003; Mark Steel, "Knock it down, then build it back up again," *Independent*, April 10, 2003; David Usborne, Rupert Cornwall and Phil Reeves, "Iraq Inc.: a joint venture built on broken promises," *Independent*, May 10, 2003; see also Naomi Klein, "Downsizing in disguise," *The Nation*, June 23, 2003.

146 Clare Dyer, "Occupation of Iraq illegal, Blair told," *Guardian*, May 22, 2003; John Innes, "US and UK action in post-war Iraq may be illegal," *Scotsman*, May 22, 2003.

147 Felicity Barringer, "UN vote on Iraq ends sanctions and grants US wide authority," *New York Times*, May 23, 2003; the resolution was passed 14:0 (Syria's chair remained empty). For commentaries, see Sukumar Muralidharan, "Colonising Iraq," *Frontline* 20/32 (2003); Hasan Abu Nimah, "The Security Council that betrayed its mission," *Jordan Times*, May 28, 2003; Steve Kretzmann, Jim Vallette, "Plugging Iraq into globalization," at <http://www.counterpunch.org/kretzmann07222003.htm>, July 22, 2003; Rania Masri, "The corporate invasion of Iraq," *International Socialist Review* 30 (2003) at <http://www.isreview.org>.

148 Tariq Ali, "Re-colonizing Iraq," *New Left Review* 21 (2003), pp. 5–19: 9; id., "Business as usual," *Guardian*, May 24, 2003; see also his *Bush in Babylon: The Recolonisation of Iraq* (London: Verso, 2003), pp. 161–5.

149 Michael Howard, "Ruling Council in symbolic first step," *Guardian*, July 14, 2003; Raad Alkadiri and Chris Toensing, "The Iraqi Governing Council's sectarian hue," *Middle East Report Online* at <http://www.merip.org/mero/mero082003.html>, August 20, 2003; *Governing Iraq* (International Crisis Group, August 25, 2003), pp. 15–16. The Coalition Provisional Authority had sweeping powers to control the Iraqi press, and reporters from *Iraq Today* were refused entry to the press conference that Salam Pax eventually attended: Salam Pax, "Baghdad blogger," *Guardian*, August 13, 2003; Riverbend, "Baghdad is burning," August 26, 2003.

150 Richard Norton-Taylor and Rory McCarthy, "Resistance to occupation is growing," *Guardian*, June 13, 2003; Rory McCarthy, "US troops kill 97 Iraqis in new attacks," *Guardian*, June 14, 2003; Patrick Cockburn, "Battles rage across Saddam heartland where guerrillas resist US occupation," *Independent*, June 14, 2003; id., "Villagers enraged and baffled by American show of force," *Independent*, June 15, 2003; David Rhode, "US forces launch raids across Iraq to quell uprisings," *New York Times*, June

15, 2003; Seumas Milne, "The right to resist," *Guardian*, June 19, 2003; Ewen MacAskill and Michael Howard, "Violence spreads south as forces of the rump regime get ever bolder," *Guardian*, June 25, 2003; Patrick Cockburn, "The bloody ambush of Amara," *Independent*, June 26, 2003; Sami Ramadani, "Bring the troops home," *Guardian*, June 26, 2003; Euan MacAskill, "Surge of attacks claims US life in Shia city," *Guardian*, June 28, 2003; Jonathan Steele, "Iraqis wait for US troops to leave," *Guardian*, July 5, 2003; Patrick Tyler, "In Iraq's disorder, the Ayatollahs may save the day," *New York Times*, July 6, 2003; Karim El-Gawhary, "Daggers and roses," *al-Ahram*, July 17–23, 2003; Jonathan Steele and Michael Howard, "US confused by Iraq's quiet war," *Guardian*, July 18, 2003; Gerhard Spörl and Bernhard Zand, "The wrath of the conquered," *Der Spiegel* at <http://www.spiegel.de/spiegel/english>, July 21, 2003; David Blair, "Thousand march in anti-US demo," *Daily Telegraph*, July 21, 2003; Thomas Ricks, "US adopts aggressive attacks on Iraqi fighters," *Washington Post*, July 28, 2003; *Governing Iraq*, p. 5.

151 Jamie Wilson, "British troops battle to control mobs in Basra," *Observer*, August 10, 2003; id., "Basra 'betrayed' and pushed to the brink," *Guardian*, August 12, 2003; Justin Huggler, "British soldiers face wrath of Iraqis as hatred festers on the streets of Basra," *Independent*, August 12, 2003; Dexter Filkins, "Chaos and calm are dual Iraq realities," *New York Times*, August 24, 2003 (my emphasis); *Governing Iraq*, pp. 2–6.

152 *Baghdad: A Race Against the Clock*, pp. 16–17; John Tierney and Robert Worth, "Attacks in Iraq may be signals of new tactics," *New York Times*, August 18, 2003; Justine Huggler, "Sabotage threatens Iraq's economy," *Independent*, August 18, 2003.

153 Jamie Wilson and Julian Borger, "Iraq: the agony goes on," *Guardian*, August 20, 2003; Justin Huggler, "Massacre of the peacemakers," *Independent*, August 20, 2003; Dexter Filkins and Richard Oppel, "Huge suicide blast demolishes UN headquarters in Baghdad," *New York Times*, August 20, 2003; Pamela Constable, "Nonmilitary targets face new threat," *Washington Post*, August 20, 2003; Patrick McDonnell and Tracy Wilkinson, "Baghdad bomb had the mark of experts," *Los Angeles Times*, August 21, 2003. One of the cruelest ironies was that the blast murdered one of the UN's most articulate and courageous defenders of the Iraqis' right to sovereignty. In the last interview to be published before his death, De Mello had made it plain that the occupation had to be brought to a speedy end: "It is traumatic. It must be one of the most humiliating periods in [Iraqi] history. Who would like to see their country occupied?" See Jonathan Steele, "De Mello knew sovereignty, not security, is the issue," *Guardian*, August 21, 2003.

154 Mark MacKinnon, "How to make friends and occupy people," *Globe and Mail*, July 26, 2003. Bremer described his plans for privatization – "the switch

from value-destroying public enterprises [*sic*] to value-creating private ones" – as Operation Iraqi Prosperity. He acknowledged that sacrifices would be required, and he made it very clear who was expected to make them: L. Paul Bremer, "Operation Iraqi Prosperity," *Wall Street Journal*, June 20, 2003; see also his address to the World Economic Forum at <http://www.weforum.org>, June 23, 2003.

155 Maggie Farley and Robin Wright, "US solicits help in Iraq – to a point," *Los Angeles Times*, August 22, 2003; Susan Milligan and Stephen Glain, "Violence derails Iraq rebuilding," *Boston Globe*, August 24, 2003; Justin Huggler, "A war without end?," *Independent*, August 24, 2003; Rory McCarthy, "Even the optimists are losing heart as Iraq goes from bad to worse," *Guardian*, August 27, 2003; Julian Borger, "Aid agencies evacuate their workers," *Guardian*, August 27, 2003. Some critics were equally adamant that the UN should not become "the dustbin into which the US dumps its failed adventures": see George Monbiot, "Beware the blue-wash," *Guardian*, August 26, 2003.

156 Christopher Dickey, "$1 billion a week," *Newsweek*, July 21, 2003; Martin Sieff, "Soaring costs of 'rescuing' Iraq," *Washington Times*, July 31, 2003; Justin Huggler, "Rebuilding Iraq will cost tens of billions of dollars in next year alone, US admits," *Independent*, August 28, 2003; Paul Krugman, "An expensive war, after all," *New York Times*, August 30, 2003; for a second-by-second accounting, see <http://www.Costofwar.com>.

157 For coalition fatalities, see "Iraq coalition casualty count" at <http://lunaville.org/warcasualties/Summary.aspx>. On August 27, 2003 the *total* number of members of the US armed forces who had died in Iraq since Bush declared the end of major combat operations on May 1 – including those whose deaths were not directly attributed to hostile action – exceeded the number of those who died during the conflict itself (138); by October 30, 2003 the number of those killed by hostile action since May 1 exceeded the number killed during the war. On the wounded, see Vernon Loeb, "Number of wounded in action on the rise," *Washington Post*, September 2, 2003; David Isenberg, "US wounded in the shadows," *Asia Times*, October 2, 2003; Andrew Buncombe, "The hidden cost of Bush's war," *Independent*, November 14, 2003.

158 Ihlau, Malzahn, and Windfuhr, "Triangle of terror."

159 Michael Gordon, "Iraqi saboteurs' goal: disrupt the occupation," *New York Times*, June 28, 2003; Jason Burke, "Iraq's resistance war was planned," *Observer*, June 29, 2003; Steven Gutkin, "Arab TV airs tape said to be Saddam," *Washington Times*, July 5, 2003; Steele and Howard, "US confused"; Graham Usher, "Facing resistance," *al-Ahram*, July 10–16, 2003; Scott Johnson and Evan Thomas, "Still fighting Saddam," *Newsweek*, July 21, 2003; Jonathan Steele, "Resistance has its roots in the present

– the Iraqis opposing occupation are not remnants of the old regime," *Guardian*, July 25, 2003; MacKinnon, "How to make friends"; Tracy Wilkinson, "Iraqis celebrate 'martyrs' of the resistance movement," *Los Angeles Times*, August 24, 2003.

160 "Donald Rumsfeld's address to the Iraqi people," *Guardian*, April 30, 2003; Michael Gordon and Douglas Jehl, "Foreign fighters add to resistance in Iraq, US says," *New York Times*, June 22, 2003; Eric Schmitt, "Wolfowitz sees challenge and vindication in Iraq," *New York Times*, July 22, 2003; Simon Schama, *Landscape and Memory* (New York: Knopf, 1995), p. 375; cf. "America's Iraq," *Middle East Report* 227 (2003).

161 Maureen Dowd, "Magnet for evil," *New York Times*, August 20, 2003; Raban "Greatest gulf"; see also Hossam el-Hamalawy, "Democratic dominoes? The war in Iraq and the regional revitalization of politicized Islam," at <http://www.electronicIraq.net/news>, May 2, 2003; Jessica Stern, "How America created a terrorist haven," *New York Times*, August 20, 2003; William Pfaff, "The philosophers of chaos reap a whirlwind," *International Herald Tribune*, August 23, 2003; R. C. Longworth, "When you cut off one head, do two sprout in its place?," *Chicago Tribune*, August 24, 2003. Others much closer to the conflict said much the same. One US soldier stationed in Iraq wrote in his weblog: ". . . they told us today . . . in a battalion formation . . . early in the morning . . . standing in the dirt of our motor pool . . . that we are here . . . to fight terrorism on its home ground . . . that we are taking the war to the terrorists . . . I'm not so sure about that . . . I think we've brought the terrorists/freedom fighters/militants/loyalists/whatever to Iraq." See turningtables at <http://turningtables. blogspot.com>, August 25, 2003 (ellipses in original).

162 Neil MacFarquhar, "Rising tide of Islamic militants see Iraq as ultimate battlefield," *New York Times*, August 13, 2003; Robyn Gedye, "Iraq becomes a battleground in war on infidels," *Daily Telegraph*, August 19, 2003; Nicholas Blanford and Dan Murphy, "For Al Qaeda, Iraq may be the next battlefield," *Christian Science Monitor*, August 25, 2003.

163 Maura Reynolds and Paul Richter, "A double setback for US goals in Mideast," *Los Angeles Times*, August 20, 2003; "President condemns bombing in Baghdad, Iraq," at <http://www.whitehouse.gov/news/releases/2003/08/print/20030819-1.html>, August 19, 2003.

164 Robert Fisk, "UN attack underlines America's crumbling authority and shows it cannot guarantee the safety of anyone," *Independent*, August 20, 2003; id., "Why the US needs to blame al-Qaeda," *Independent*, August 21, 2003.

165 See, for example, Patrick Cockburn, "Marsh Arabs threaten to resist 'army of occupation,'" *Independent*, June 27, 2003; Pamela Constable, "Cleric calls for 'Islamic Army,'" *Washington Post*, July 19, 2003; Jonathan Steele, "Anti-US cleric rallies recruits for Islamic army," *Guardian*, July 31, 2003;

Paul McGeough, "Inside the resistance," *Sydney Morning Herald*, August 16, 2003.

166   Eric Schmitt and David Sanger, "Guerrillas posing more danger, says US," *New York Times*, November 14, 2003; Bryan Bender, "Guerrilla war in Iraq spreading," *Boston Globe*, November 29, 2003. The geography of attacks against coalition forces can be traced through the regular Security Reports and maps of Iraq in general and Baghdad in particular provided by the UN Iraq Security Office from May through October 2003 at <http://www.hicirag.org/services/security/reports/index.asp>.

167   Peter Beaumont, "Chaos reigns as Saddam's plan unfolds," *Observer*, August 31, 2003; Tracy Wilkinson, "Resistance in Iraq is homegrown," *Los Angeles Times*, September 2, 2003; Anthony Shadid, "They deal in danger," *Washington Post*, September 4, 2003; Douglas Jehl and David Sanger, "Iraqis' bitterness is called bigger threat than terror," *New York Times*, September 17, 2003; Mark Danner, "Iraq: the new war," *New York Review of Books*, September 25, 2003; Tariq Ali, "Resistance is the first step toward Iraqi independence," *Guardian*, November 3, 2003.

168   Justin Huggler and Seb Walker, "US corporate invasion brings no respite from war," *Independent*, September 5, 2003; Ariana Eunjung Cha, "Peril follows contractors in Iraq," *Washington Post*, November 14, 2003; Riverbend, "Baghdad is burning," September 6 and November 18, 2003; Rajiv Chandrasekaran, "Fueling anger in Iraq," *Washington Post*, December 9, 2003; Edward Wong, "Saboteurs, looters and old equipment work against efforts to restart Iraqi oilfields," *New York Times*, December 14, 2003.

169   Neil MacFarquhar, "Iraqi Shi'ites flex muscle even as they mourn," *New York Times*, September 1, 2003; Anthony Shadid and Theola Labbé, "Iraqi council members denounce American occupation," *Washington Post*, September 2, 2003.

170   John Tierney, "Truck bomb explodes outside Baghdad police headquarters," *New York Times*, September 2, 2003; Rory McCarthy, "Suicide bombing at police station kills 10 in Baghdad," *Guardian*, October 10, 2003; Alex Berenson, "Baghdad car bomb heightens security concerns," *Globe and Mail*, October 13, 2003.

171   Dieter Bednarz, "The scourges of God," *Der Spiegel* at <http://www.spiegel.de/spiegel/english>, September 1, 2003; Suzanne Goldenberg, "A land ruled by chaos," *Guardian*, October 4, 2003.

172   Riverbend, "Baghdad is burning," September 19, 2003; Nir Rosen, "Operation Decapitation," *Asia Times*, October 29, 2003.

173   Michael Howard, "US hawk escapes Baghdad rocket attack," *Guardian*, 27 October 2003; Anthony Shadid, "Holy month begins in anger and ruin," *Washington Post*, October 28, 2003; Patrick Cockburn, "Slaughter in the

rush hour," *Independent*, October 28, 2003; Mark Danner, "Delusions in Baghdad," *New York Review of Books*, December 18, 2003.

174 Cockburn, "Slaughter"; Peter Beaumont, "Guerrilla war forces US to speed handover," *Observer*, November 16, 2003.

175 Alan Freeman, "Powell refuses to rush Iraq handover," *Guardian*, September 15, 2003; Shawn McCarthy, "Bush refuses to bend on Iraq," *Globe and Mail*, September 24, 2003; Ewen MacAskill and Ian Black, "Security council backs Iraq force," *Guardian*, October 17, 2003.

176 Rory McCarthy, "Governing council put in frame as US makes no bones about how situation is unravelling," *Guardian*, November 13, 2003; Julian Borger and Rory McCarthy, " 'We could lose this situation,' " *Guardian*, November 13, 2003; Robin Wright and Thomas Ricks, "New urgency, new risks in 'Iraqification,' " *Washington Post*, November 14, 2003; Beaumont, "Guerrilla war"; David Sanger, "America's gamble: a quick exit plan for Iraq," *New York Times*, November 16, 2003.

177 Michael Georgy, "Iraq Shi'ites talk of holy war, not self rule," *Reuters*, November 20, 2003; Steven Weisman, "Iraq exit plan: new obstacles," *New York Times*, November 29, 2003; Anthony Shadid and Rajiv Chandrasekaran, "Leading cleric calls for elections in Iraq," *Washington Post*, November 30, 2003; Alissa Rubin, "US resistance to direct vote galvanizes Iraq's Shi'ite clerics," *Los Angeles Times*, December 3, 2003; Robin Wright and Rajiv Chandrasekaran, "US seeks compromise plan for political transition," *Washington Post*, December 16, 2003. Patrick Cockburn, "Iraq's Shia Muslims march to demand early elections," *Independent*, January 16, 2004; Daniel Williams, "Iraqi Shiites protest US blueprint," *Washington Post*, January 16, 2004; Juan Cole, "Informed comment," at <http://www.juancole.com>, January 16, 2004; Robert Scheer, "Give Iraqis the election they want," *Los Angeles Times*, January 20, 2004; Dilip Hiro, "One Iraqi, one vote," *New York Times*, January 27, 2004. It was not only the Shiites who dismissed the baroque plans for caucuses and assemblies; the newly formed Council for Sunnis also rejected any elections organized by the Provisional Authority and insisted that free elections could not be held under military occupation: Rory McCarthy, "US must quit Iraq before vote, say Sunnis," *Guardian*, January 26, 2004.

178 "US military starts air campaign in central Iraq," Associated Press, November 18, 2003; Phil Reeves, "Americans turn Tikrit into Iraq's own West Bank," *Independent*, November 18, 2003; Phil Reeves and Kim Sengupta, "Explosions, shortages, instability: in Iraq, it's back to the future," *Independent*, November 19, 2003; Esther Schrader and Josh Meyer, "US seeks advice from Israel on Iraq," *New York Times*, November 22, 2003; Ed Blanche, "West Bank East: Americans in Iraq make war the Israeli way,"

Daily Star, December 6, 2003; Dexter Filkins, "Tough new tactics by US tighten grip on Iraq," *New York Times*, December 7, 2003; Tony Karon, "Learning the art of occupation from Israel," *Time*, December 9, 2003.

179 Julian Borger, "Israel trains US assassination squads in Iraq," *Guardian*, December 9, 2003; Seymour Hersh, "Moving targets," *New Yorker*, December 15, 2003. One of the American officers spearheading the new strategy was Lieutenant General Jerry Boykin who had described the US military as a "Christian army" at war with Satan.

180 Richard Oppel, "US seeking foreign investment for Iraq," *New York Times*, August 28, 2003; Philip Thornton and Andre Gumbel, "America puts Iraq up for sale," *Independent*, September 22, 2003; Riverbend, "Baghdad is burning," September 24 and December 12, 2003; Bernard Zand, "Slaves of the foreigners," *Der Spiegel*, October 6, 2003; Shirley Williams, "The seeds of Iraq's future terror," *Guardian*, October 28, 2003; Naomi Klein, "Iraq is not America's to sell," *Guardian*, November 7, 2003. By the end of 2003 the scale and intensity of the resistance, together with an unemployment rate of around 60 percent, had compelled the US to delay its plans for privatization, and the Coalition Provisional Authority decided to delegate responsibility to the interim government to be selected by July 2004. But the Authority's freedom of maneuver was also compromised by continued and substantial reservations about the legitimacy of Order 39 under international law. See Rajiv Chandrasekaran, "Attacks force retreat from wide-ranging plans for Iraq," *Washington Post*, December 28, 2003; Daphne Eviatar, "Free-market Iraq? Not so fast," *New York Times*, January 10, 2003.

181 John Burns, "In the streets, a shadow lifts," *New York Times*, December 15, 2003; Rory McCarthy, " 'The devil is caught and his regime is finished,' " *Guardian*, December 15, 2003.

182 Rajiv Chandrasekaran, Thomas Ricks, and Anthony Shadid, "Belief that insurgency will fade may be misplaced," *Washington Post*, December 15, 2003; Robert Fisk, "Saddam's capture will not stop the relentless killings from insurgents," *Independent*, December 15, 2003; Edward Wong, "Joy fades as Iraqis chafe under a grim occupation," *Washington Post*, December 16, 2003. On Saddam's atrocities at Mahawil, see Human Rights Watch, "The mass graves of al-Mahawil: the truth uncovered," at <http://www.hrw.org/reports/2003/iraq0503/index.htm>, May 2003; Peter Bouckaert, "Digging up the past: Iraq's killing fields," *New York Times*, May 16, 2003.

183 Cole, "Shi'ite religious factions," pp. 564–6.

184 Robert Fisk, " 'The tyrant is now a prisoner,' " *Independent*, December 15, 2003.

185 "Green Zone" at <http://www.globalsecurity.org/military/world/iraq/baghdad-green-zone-htm>; James Rupert, "Baghdad's blocked arteries,"

Newsday, October 13, 2003; Christopher Ayad, "Iraq: the authoritarian drift of the Bremer machine," *Libération*, November 11, 2003; Ariana Eunjung Cha, "Baghdad's US Zone: a stand-in for home," *Washington Post*, December 6, 2003; Mitch Potter, "Bridging Baghdad's opposite worlds," *Toronto Star*, December 7, 2003.

186 Phil Reeves and David Usborne, "The turkey has landed," *Independent*, November 28, 2003; Michael Howard and Julian Borger, "Iraqis express cynicism at Bush's 150-minute visit," *Guardian*, November 29, 2003; Riverbend, "Baghdad is burning," November 29, 2003.

Chapter 9: Gravity's Rainbows

1 Zygmunt Bauman, *Globalization: The Human Consequences* (Cambridge: Polity, 1998), pp. 75–6, 88–92; id., *Liquid Modernity* (Cambridge: Polity, 2000), pp. 117–19.

2 Zygmunt Bauman, "Reconnaissance wars of the planetary frontierland," *Theory, Culture and Society* 19 (2002), pp. 81–90: 82; id., "Living and dying in the planetary frontierland," in his *Society Under Siege* (Cambridge: Polity, 2002), pp. 87–117.

3 Don DeLillo, "In the ruins of the future: reflections on terror and loss in the shadow of September," *Harper's Magazine* (December 2001). To describe the Islamicism that motivated the attacks on the World Trade Center and the Pentagon – both icons of the late capitalist modern – as "medieval" was a common but mistaken response: cf. John Gray, *Al-Qaeda and what it Means to be Modern* (London: Faber & Faber, 2003).

4 John Urry, "The global complexities of September 11," *Theory, Culture and Society* 19 (2002), pp. 57–69: 63–4. Urry's argument mobilizes a disconcertingly utopian image of New York City – which certainly has its "wild zones" – and in mapping "asylum-seeking" onto the same plane as transparently illegal activities he makes an objectionable contraction of his own. Unfortunately he is not alone. "We are witnessing increasing insecurity in all its forms: weapons of mass destruction and terrorism that knows no limit of scale or geography, *the impact of migration* and crime on our streets": Tony Blair, "The left should not weep if Saddam is toppled," *Guardian*, February 10, 2003 (my emphasis).

5 Michael Ignatieff, "The burden," *New York Times*, January 5, 2003; id., *Empire Lite: Nation-Building in Bosnia, Kosovo and Afghanistan* (Toronto: Penguin, 2003), pp. 3, 21.

6 Ignatieff, *Empire Lite*, p. 2; for a critical review of Ignatieff's approving argument, see David Rieff, "Taking up the American's burden," *Globe and Mail*, August 30, 2003.

7   Niall Ferguson, *Empire: How Britain Made the Modern World* (London: Allen Lane, The Penguin Press, 2003), p. 370; id., "The Empire slinks back," *New York Times*, April 27, 2003; id., "America as Empire, now and in the future," *The National Interest* 2/29 (July 2003).

8   Eliot Cohen, "This is World War IV," *Wall Street Journal*, November 20, 2001; Doug Saunders, "The fourth world war," *Globe and Mail*, September 6, 2003. For Cohen, World War III was the Cold War. The enemy in World War IV is not "terrorism," he insisted, but "militant Islam," and so the United States must do everything in its power to "overthrow the first theocratic revolutionary Muslim state" (Iran) and to finish off "America's arch-enemy in the Arab world" (Iraq). Albert Einstein once predicted that World War IV would be fought "with sticks and stones." He may yet be right; but it will also be set in motion by words – by names – that also have an extraordinary capacity to kill and to maim (cf. p. xiv).

9   David Harvey, *The Condition of Postmodernity* (Oxford: Blackwell, 1989); Cindi Katz, "On the grounds of globalization: a topography for feminist political engagement," *Signs* 26 (2001), pp. 1213–34, especially pp. 1224–5.

10 Michael Hardt and Antonio Negri, *Empire* (Cambridge, MA: Harvard University Press, 2000), pp. 332–3. I have the deepest reservations about this book from which, as Timothy Brennan perceptively notes, the "colonized of today" are evacuated. "Why," he asks, "at a moment of American imperial adventure, almost Roman in its excess, is the end of imperialism confidently announced?" He continues: "As the United States ushers a new government into Kabul, criminalizes those who quibble with its military plans, and thumbs its nose at the Geneva Conventions, *Empire*'s thesis that imperialism has ended is likely to seem absurd." And yet Brennan's critique is all the more cogent because it focuses – unwaveringly – on the *epistemological* flaws in the edifice: "The Empire's new clothes," *Critical Inquiry* 29 (2003), pp. 337–67.

11 Hardt and Negri, *Empire*, pp. 188, 194–5; Bauman, "Reconnaissance," pp. 83–4.

12 Robert Cooper, "The postmodern state," in Mark Leonard (ed.), *Re-ordering the World: The Long-Term Implications of September 11* (London: Foreign Policy Centre, 2001); id., "Order, force and law in a new era," Crimes of War Project at <http://www.crimesofwar.org/sept-mag/sept-cooper.html, September 2002>; see also Sebastian Mallaby, "The reluctant imperialist: terrorism, failed states and the case for American Empire," *Foreign Affairs* 81/2 (2002), pp. 2–7. When he wrote his essay, Cooper was a principal adviser on foreign affairs to Blair's Labour government. Robert Kagan, co-founder with William Kristol of the Project for a New American Century, was – not surprisingly – dismissive of the privilege Cooper accorded to Europe: "Europe's new Kantian order flourished only under the umbrella of American power exercised according to the rules of the old Hobbesian order." Those

"rules," whatever they might be, were inherently "unreliable," he argued – particularly, one might add, where America was concerned – which is why he insisted that "true security and the defence and promotion of a liberal order still depend on the possession and use of military might." See his "Power and weakness," *Policy Review* 113 (June–July 2002).

13 Elias Sanbar, "Is the war over?," at <http://www.autodafe.org/correspondence/chroniques/elias2.htm>, June 2002.

14 Veena Das, "Violence and translation," *Anthropological Quarterly* 75 (2002), pp. 105–12: 112 n. 3.

15 See, for example, Anustup Basu, "The state of security and warfare of demons," *Critical Quarterly* 45 (2003), pp. 11–31.

16 Will Rhode, *Paperback Raita* (London: Simon & Schuster, 2002), p. 66; cf. John Hutnyk, *The Rumour of Calcutta: Tourism, Charity and the Poverty of Representation* (London: Zed Books, 1996); Derek Gregory, "Scripting Egypt: Orientalism and cultures of travel," in James Duncan and Derek Gregory (eds), *Writes of Passage: Reading Travel Writing* (London: Routledge, 1999), pp. 114–50; John Urry, *The Tourist Gaze* (London: Sage, 2002), p. 74.

17 See <http://www.whitehouse.gov/news/releases/2001/09/20010927-1.html>.

18 Cf. James Clifford, "Travelling cultures," in Lawrence Grossberg, Cary Nelson, and Paula Treichler (eds), *Cultural Studies* (London: Routledge, 1992), pp. 96–116. Metropolitan cultures are themselves differentiated, of course, and I do not mean to minimize the ways in which class, gender, "race," age, and other positionalities compromise its privileges.

19 Gary Younge, "Under a veil of deceit," *Guardian*, August 19, 2002.

20 Jeevan Vasagar, "Afghan asylum seekers forced to return home," *Guardian*, April 29, 2003; Nigel Morris, "Protests at first enforced return of Afghans since war," *Independent*, April 29, 2003.

21 Homi Bhabha, "Double visions," *Artforum* 30/5 (1992), pp. 82–90: 88. Dispossession is also inflected by class and gender, for example: as Barbara Kruger once noted, "It's a small world, but not if you have to clean it."

22 Giorgio Agamben, "Beyond human rights," in his *Means Without End: Notes on Politics*, trans. Vincenzo Binetti and Cesare Casorino (Minneapolis: University of Minnesota Press, 1996), pp. 15–26: 21.

23 Nicholas Mirzoeff, "The empire of camps," *Situation Analysis* 1 (2002), pp. 20–5; Suvendri Perera, "What is a camp?" *Borderlands* 1 (2002) at <http://www.www.borderlandsejournal.adelaide.edu.au>; Nigel Hoffmann, "The intimate space of power," at <http://www.antimedia.net/deserstorm/intimate.shtml>; "An Architektur," "Exterritories and camps: juridical-political spaces in the 'war on terrorism,'" at <http://www.republicart.net>, February 2003; Charles Bowden, "Outback nightmare and refugee dreams," *Mother Jones* (March/April 2003), pp. 47–53, 92–3. Bauman, "Living and

dying," pp. 113–14, describes refugees – suspended "in a spatial void in which time has ground to a halt" – as the undecidable, the unthinkable, the unimaginable: the ineffable made flesh.

24 Gregor Noll, "Visions of the exceptional," at <http://www.opendemocracy. net>, June 27, 2003.

25 Edward Soja, *Thirdspace: Journeys to Los Angeles and Other Real-and-Imagined Places* (Oxford: Blackwell, 1996).

26 Giorgio Agamben, *Means Without End: Notes on Politics* (Minneapolis: University of Minnesota Press, 2000), p. 38; id., "Über Sicherheit und Terror," *Frankfurter Allgemeine Zeitung*, September 20, 2001, trans. as "Security and terror," *Theory and Event* 5/4 (2002). See also Bülent Diken and Carsten Basse Laustsen, "Zones of indistinction: security, terror and bare life," *Space and Culture* 5 (2002), pp. 290–307.

27 Human Rights Watch, "Presumption of guilt: human rights abuses of post-September-11 detainees," at <http://www.hrw.org>, August 2002; "For whom the Liberty Bell tolls," *Economist*, August 29, 2002; see also David Cole, "Enemy aliens and American freedoms," *The Nation*, September 23, 2002.

28 A draft of draconian second-round proposals, the Domestic Security Enhancement Act, was circulated in early 2003.

29 Paul Passavant and Jodi Dean, "Representation and the event," *Theory and Event* 5/4 (2002), at <http://www.muse/uq.edu.au/journals/theory_and_event/ v005/5.4passavant.html>; see also Leti Volpp, "The citizen and the terrorist," *UCLA Law Review* 49 (2002), pp. 1575–1600.

30 Louise Cainkar, "No longer invisible: Arab and Muslim exclusion after September 11," *Middle East Report* 224 (2002), pp. 22–9; id., "Targeting Muslims at Ashcroft's discretion," *Middle East Report Online*, March 14, 2003; Rachel Swarns and Christopher Drew, "Fearful, angry or confused, Muslim immigrants register," *New York Times*, April 25, 2003.

31 Andrew Ross, "Containing culture in the Cold War," in his *No Respect: Intellectuals and Popular Culture* (New York: Routledge, 1989), pp. 42–64: 46.

32 Salah Hassan, "Arabs, race and the post-September 11 national security state," *Middle East Report* 224 (2002), pp. 16–21.

33 Susan Buck-Morss, "A global public sphere?," in her *Thinking Past Terror: Islamism and Critical Theory on the Left* (London: Verso, 2003), pp. 21–38: 29.

34 Kanishka Jasuriya, "9/11 and the new 'anti-politics' of 'security,'" SSRC/After September 11 at <http://www.ssrc.org/sept11/essays>; reprinted as "September 11, security and the new post-liberal politics of fear," in Eric Hershberg and Kevin Moore (eds), *Critical Views of September 11: Analyses from Around the World* (New York: The New Press, 2002), pp. 131–47; see also his "The exception becomes the norm: law and regimes of exception in

East Asia," *Asia-Pacific Law and Policy Journal*, 2 (2001). Human Rights Watch has drawn special attention to the use of the "war on terrorism" as a cloak for repression in Australia, Belarus, China, Egypt, India, Israel, Jordan, Kyrgyzstan, Macedonia, Malaysia, Russia, Syria, the USA, Uzbekistan, and Zimbabwe: Human Rights Watch, "Opportunism in the face of tragedy: repression in the name of terrorism," at <http://www.hrw.org>, September 2002. See also Naomi Klein, "Bush's war goes global," *Globe and Mail*, August 27, 2003, in which she describes how the specter of terrorism has been turned into "a shield of impunity" – and immunity – to restrict freedoms and wage war on those who dare to dissent.

35 Oren Yiftachel, "The shrinking space of citizenship: ethnocratic politics in Israel," *Middle East Report* 223 (Summer 2002); Neve Gordon, "The enemy within," in Roane Carey and Jonathan Shainin (eds), *The Other Israel: Voices of Refusal and Dissent* (New York: New Press, 2002), pp. 99–105: 102; Jonathan Cook, "Unwelcome citizens of a racist state," *Al-Ahram*, September 26–October 2, 2002.

36 Michael Dibdin, *Dead Lagoon* (London: Faber & Faber, 1994), pp. 113–15, 312.

37 For a radically different vision of Europe, see Ash Amin, "From ethnicity to empathy: a new idea of Europe," at <http://www.opendemocracy.net>, July 24, 2003. He emphasizes *hospitality* – in a Europe and a world in which "we might all be strangers one day" – and *mutuality* – that affirms our connectedness: the stranger "works away at our certitude of the purity of self-identity." Such a project cannot afford to place (or, rather, re-place) Europe at the center of the world: see Iris Marion Young, "Europe and the global south: towards a circle of equality," <http://www.opendemocracy.net> August 20, 2003.

38 Henry Giroux and Paul Street, "Shredding the social contract," at <http://www.zmag.org>, September 4, 2003.

39 Walter Benjamin, "On the concept of history," in Howard Eiland and Michael Jennings (eds), *Walter Benjamin: Selected Writings*, vol. 4: *1938–1940* (Cambridge, MA: Harvard University Press, 2003), pp. 389–400: 392.

40 Michael Ignatieff, *The Needs of Strangers* (London: Chatto & Windus, 1984); see also Stuart Corbridge, "Marxism, modernities and moralities: development praxis and the claims of distant strangers," *Environment and Planning D: Society & Space* 11 (1993) 449–72; id., "Development ethics: distance, difference, plausibility," *Ethics, Place and Environment* 1 (1998), pp. 35–54.

41 Ash Amin, "Spatialities of globalization," *Environment and Planning* 34 (2002), pp. 385–99; Eric Sheppard, "The spaces and times of globalization: place, scale, networks and positionality," *Economic Geography* 78 (2002), pp. 307–30.

Guide to Further Reading

I've provided detailed references in the footnotes to each chapter, but here I signpost some of the texts and websites that I've found most useful. Some of these books were published after I completed my own essays, and they provide important new information or other insights into the "war on terror" in Afghanistan, Palestine, and Iraq.

The ideas that I've worked with in *The Colonial Present* come from a variety of sources. The writings of Edward Said are as indispensable as they are inspirational. Said's *Orientalism* (London: Penguin, 1978; latest edition 2003) is still the most important – and deservedly now recognized as a Penguin Classic – but it needs to be read carefully and critically. Said was not as attentive to gender or sexuality as contemporary critics would now prefer, he said little about the ways in which those who were the objects of Orientalism resisted (and sometimes reinforced) its dispositions, and his reluctance to engage with visual images – in a book studded with visual metaphors and preoccupations – is remarkable. But the book is none the less an astonishing achievement: passionate, engaged, and bristling with ideas and insights. For a lucid commentary, see Gyan Prakash, "Orientalism now," *History and Theory* 34 (1995), pp. 199–212. I've also been influenced by Giorgio Agamben, *Homo Sacer: Sovereign Power and Bare Life*, trans. Daniel Heller-Roaxen (Stanford, CA: Stanford University Press, 1995); some of his short essays in *Means Without End: Notes on Politics* (Minneapolis: University of Minnesota Press, 2000) are also extremely suggestive. For an incisive commentary on Agamben's work – and most of all the space of the exception – see Andrew Norris, "The exemplary exception," *Radical Philosophy* 119 (2003), pp. 6–16, and for an essay that connects Agamben's ideas to the historical geography of colonialism in ways that resonate with my own arguments, see Achille Mbembe, "Necropolitics," *Public Culture* 15 (2003), pp. 11–40. For a brilliantly imaginative introduction to post-colonialism – its political project and its multiple geographies – I urge you to read

Robert Young, *Postcolonialism: A Very Short Introduction* (Oxford: Oxford University Press, 2003).

The attacks on the World Trade Center and the Pentagon on September 11, 2001, together with the "war on terror" that they provoked, have produced shelves of books. For more or less direct chronology and commentary, see Dilip Hiro, *War Without End: The Rise of Islamist Terrorism and Global Response* (London: Routledge, 2003) and Douglas Kellner, *From 9/11 to Terror War: The Dangers of the Bush Legacy* (Lanham MD: Rowman & Littlefield, 2003). Noam Chomsky and Arundhati Roy provide some of the most immediate and accessible reflections. Two short books capture Chomsky's central claims: *9–11* (New York: Seven Stories Press, 2001) and *Power and Terror: Post 9–11 Talks and Interviews* (New York: Seven Stories Press, 2003). These need to be read in conjunction with his much more detailed *Pirates and Emperors, Old and New: International Terrorism in the Real World* (Cambridge, MA: South End Press, 2003) and *Hegemony or Survival: America's Quest for Global Dominance* (New York: Metropolitan Books/Henry Holt, 2003). Roy's essays will also be found in two slim volumes whose significance far exceeds their length: *Power Politics* (Cambridge, MA: South End Press, 2001) and *War Talk* (Cambridge, MA: South End Press, 2003). There are legions of edited collections that provide critical discussions of September 11 and the "war on terror." Two of the best were spun off from the Social Science Research Council website (and the SSRC should be congratulated for the speed, range, and sheer courage of its response to the attacks on the World Trade Center and the Pentagon at a time when so many critical voices were stilled): Eric Hershberg and Kevin Moore (eds), *Critical Views of September 11: Analyses from Around the World* and Craig Calhoun, Paul Price and Ashley Timmer (eds), *Understanding September 11* (New York: The New Press, 2002). Other important collections include Ken Booth and Tim Dunne (eds), *Worlds in Collision: Terror and the Future of Global Order* (London: Palgrave, 2002) and Susan Hawthorne and Bronwyn Winter (eds), *After Shock: September 11, 2001/Global Feminist Perspectives* (Vancouver: Raincoast Books, 2003). Two authors who offered pugnacious collections of their own essays were Tariq Ali, *The Clash of Fundamentalisms: Crusades, Jihads and Modernity* (London: Verso, 2002), and Slavoj Žižek, *Welcome to the Desert of the Real! Five Essays on September 11 and Related Dates* (London: Verso, 2002).

If you have read this far, you will know that I think it impossible to understand American foreign policy under President George W. Bush without a close engagement with the Project for the New American Century: its website at <http://www.newamericancentury.org> provides a window on its aspirations, but so too does the critical eye cast on its activities at <http://www.pnac.org>. For further discussions of the Republican "war on terror," I have also enjoyed (if that is the right word) both Gilbert Achcar, *The Clash of Barbarisms: September 11 and the New World Disorder* (New York: Monthly Review Press, 2002) and Rahul

Mahajan, *The New Crusade: America's War on Terrorism* (New York: Monthly Review Press, 2002). If the prospect of American Empire depresses you as much as it does me, solace of sorts is to be found in two books that emphasize (in very different ways) the brittleness of American power: Michael Mann's *Incoherent Empire* (London and New York: Verso, 2003) and Immanuel Wallerstein's *The Decline of American Power: The US in a Chaotic World* (New York: The New Press, 2003). For some sobering reflections on modern warfare, see Zygmunt Bauman's essay, "Living and dying in the planetary frontierland," in his *Society Under Siege* (Cambridge: Polity, 2002), pp. 87–117 and also Carl Boggs and Ted Raill (eds) *Masters of War* (London and New York: Routledge, 2003).

Among the many short books on the cultural politics and theology of contemporary Islam, I recommend two by Akbar Ahmed, *Islam Today: A Short Introduction to the Muslim World* (London: I. B. Tauris, 2002), and *Islam Under Siege: Living Dangerously in a Post-Honor World* (Cambridge: Polity, 2003). On the connections between politics, political violence, and Islamicism, see John Esposito, *Unholy Terror in the Name of Islam* (New York: Oxford University Press, 2002) and Gilles Kepel, *Jihad: The Trail of Political Islam* (Cambridge, MA: Harvard University Press, 2002). For a radically different – and also profoundly constructive – engagement with Islamicism, see Susan Buck-Morss, *Thinking Past Terror: Islamism and Critical Theory on the Left* (London: Verso, 2003).

A book like this is inevitably a hostage to fortune; the world turns. Among the many websites providing critical perspectives on current events and media reporting, three stand out: Alternet (at <http://www.alternet.org>), Cursor (at <http://www.cursor.org>), and the superb Information Clearing House (at <http://www.informationclearinghouse.literati.org>). All of them have daily, direct links to media reports. There is another, equally brilliant website that focuses on the war on terror in Afghanistan, Palestine and Iraq – "The war in context" – that also has media links: <http://warincontext.org>.

On the first Great Game in Afghanistan (and beyond) see Karl Meyer and Shareen Blair Brysac, *Tournament of Shadows: The Great Game and the Race for Empire in Central Asia* (Washington: Counterpoint, 2002). Among the many books on the rise of the Taliban, I recommend John Cooley, *Unholy Wars: Afghanistan, America and International Terrorism* (London: Pluto, 2002) – which puts the uncivil wars in Afghanistan in their geopolitical and economic context – and also Michael Griffin, *Reaping the Whirlwind: The Taliban Movement in Afghanistan* (London: Pluto, 2001) and Ahmed Rashid, *Taliban: Militant Islam, Oil and Fundamentalism in Central Asia* (New Haven: Yale University Press, 2000). Marc Herold's vital work on civilian casualties and the "reconstruction" of Afghanistan will be found in his column for Cursor at <http://www.cursor.org/stories/archivistan.htm>, and in his *Blown Away: Myth and Reality of Precision Bombing in Afghanistan* (Monroe, ME: Common Courage Press, 2003). For